THE
Custer Story

*The Life and Intimate Letters
of General George A. Custer
and His Wife Elizabeth*

EDITED BY

MARGUERITE MERINGTON

Illustrated

New York

THE DEVIN-ADAIR COMPANY

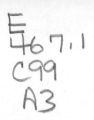

To the country
the Custers loved and
served with such devotion,
this, their book,
is dedicated.

Designed by Peter Döblin

PRINTED IN THE UNITED STATES OF AMERICA

Contents

7/75

Acknowledgments

For supplementary and corroborative material I am indebted to the following persons and institutions: The executors, trust officers, and residuary legatees of Mrs. Custer's estate, for access to papers collected by her for biographical purposes; the late Mrs. Charles Elmer (May Custer); Mr. George L. Yates (son of the Captain Yates who died with Custer); Mr. J. Bronson Case; Miss Virginia Smith; the Cincinnati *Enquirer;* the librarian and assistant librarians of West Point Military Academy; Dorsch Memorial Library, Monroe, Michigan; Mr. Karl F. Zeisler, managing editor of the Monroe (Michigan) *Evening News;* State Historical Society, Bismarck, North Dakota; Captain E. S. Luce, superintendent of the Custer Battlefield National Cemetery; Mr. Robert Yellowtail, superintendent of the Crow Agency, Montana; the Cadiz *Republican;* Mr. Stanhope Foster (for Mrs. Elmer); librarians of the New York Public Library, the Congressional Library, the Philadelphia Free Library; Colonel A. B. Welch, U. S. A.; Mr. Coley Taylor, for Custer data; to all who have given me access to data or verifying statements.

The Ohio State Papers have been drawn on for material.

I am indebted to the Bettmann Archive for the frontispiece picture of Custer.

Foreword

THIS IS THE first-hand story of General George Armstrong Custer and his wife Elizabeth Bacon Custer. The protagonists, "Autie" and "Libbie" to each other, are the narrators of their own dramatic twelve years as husband and wife.

This assembling of their intimate letters was prepared at Mrs. Custer's request. She had written and lectured copiously throughout most of the fifty-seven years she survived her husband, but there are personal things one cannot say or suffer to be said during one's lifetime, but which ought to be said. For some decades, ending only with her death in 1933, I was her nearest friend. In her last years she had laid aside the pen, and when called upon for some incidental article she would turn the matter over to me. At the fifty-year celebration of the battle of the Little Big Horn she designated me to write her semiofficial account of it.

While she still had strength to seek relief from neuritis in Florida, she occupied her time making notes of Civil War happenings for which her books had held no place. These notes could not be put into publishable form, for they betokened failing hand and waning strength, though a clear memory for things gone by.

Mrs. Custer's letters and papers were neatly docketed. The older ones, those letters to her family and husband, were written on paper so thin, with crossings on every sheet, that even while I was deciphering them with a magnifying glass, they crumbled to the touch.

Custer's letters offered no such difficulty. The official army stationery was like parchment, his handwriting legible as print. But trunks full of his outpourings to Mrs. Reed had been lost. His impassioned pleas to his sweetheart to hasten the date of their wedding she had destroyed. By the wish of Mrs. Charles Elmer, his brother Nevin's daughter May Custer (who had been adopted by the Reeds), who was his next of kin, many letters that I copied were burned. With her sanction I retained a few as specimens of his handwriting, so markedly a projection of himself.

The official documents from which I made corroborative notes I returned to May Custer Elmer, suggesting they should be lodged in an accredited repository. Whatever I retained in preparing this book —letters, portraits, a lock of Custer's red-gold hair—by agreement will be turned over to the library of Yale University.

As Mrs. Custer's apartment was closed in a hurry after her death, her loose papers, unsorted, were packed in trunks. These wandered about unhoused, apparently unwanted, until they found haven in the cellars of West Point. They will remain there until the completion of the Custer Museum on the National Cemetery that marks the tragic battlefield of the Little Big Horn in Montana.

Arduous though the work of copying old letters, many of them all but illegible, has been, it fulfils a friendship's obligation. There have been no suppressions, no evasions, no glossing over dark passages or unlovely episodes; likewise, no enhancing nor shifting of lights to obtain a flattering angle. Selection and condensing there have been, but no editing to turn fact into fiction.

In many cases, letters were undated or had no heading whatever; the day or month or season, even sometimes the year, has had to be inferred, but has in no instance been set down unless established with certainty. The same is true of the places at which the letters were written. As for the connecting and explanatory text, this is based on authentic sources.

MARGUERITE MERINGTON

New York, 1950

THE
Custer Story

1: "My Boy Custer"

GEORGE ARMSTRONG CUSTER was born December 5, 1839, at the Custer homestead in New Rumley, Ohio. He died June 25, 1876, when his detachment was overwhelmed in the battle of the Little Big Horn, Montana Territory, by a massed force of Sioux warriors. He was a few months short of thirty-seven.

The Custers were of English origin, descended from the Cusiters of the Orkney Islands. In the words of a pamphlet circulated in the family, they were "agriculturists, working for themselves, not for wage; strong, healthy, industrious, living to a great age on their own farms, law-abiding and religious."

Emmanuel Custer, George Armstrong's father, began as a blacksmith, "the best in miles around." This was in a day when the smithy was one of life's indispensables, when the cheery glow of the forge was a welcome sight to the wayfarer on horseback or to the driver of a covered wagon.

Emmanuel Custer worked tirelessly until he had saved enough to follow his ancestral calling: he bought a farm. A widower at thirty-one, he married Maria Ward Kirkpatrick, a widow. Both brought children to the union, and of it were born five more. As the children grew up, they made homes for themselves; Lydia-Ann Kirkpatrick was the last to remain in the Custer household.

Except for one member of Emmanuel's generation who was a Dunkard preacher, receiving no pay for his religious ministrations and supporting his family with his flour mills and inventions, the Custers were Methodists. George Armstrong was named for a preacher, with the hope that his vocation would thereby be arranged. But that was not his turn of mind; though he was devotional by nature and moral by training, he never was a professed adherent of any denomination.

After George Armstrong there were born, in this order, Nevin,

Thomas, Boston, and Margaret. Thomas and Boston were to fall
with him at the battle of the Little Big Horn. Nevin was physically
disqualified for military service.

Emmanuel Custer, though a farmer, was a militant character. His
very being was set to war tunes—and to the strains of contemporary
politics. Late in life, when his daughter-in-law, George Armstrong's
wife, herself brought up to believe that salvation was reserved ex-
clusively for Republicans, enquired how Emmanuel, son of a Whig,
could possibly have apostasized in favor of the Democratic party,
he explained: "As a boy I was greatly stirred by a character, a
veteran of the Revolution, also of the War of 1812, who used to
come around piping war tunes on a fife. A Democrat, he professed
himself. And then I made up my mind that if that was the side a
man could come out on, after two wars, that would be the side for
me."

"But does it not shake your party faith," persisted Elizabeth,
"that most of the clergy are Republicans?"

"Not a bit," he assured her. "But it does shake my faith in their
religion."

At the close of his life he boasted, "My first vote was cast for Andrew Jackson, my last for Grover Cleveland. Good votes, both!"

The political caucus was his life blood, yet when discussion became sharp and vindictive, he would withdraw to the little Methodist church he had helped to found and pray that whatever was
best should prevail. Then, along with those who had followed him
in, for he was a born leader, he would raise his lusty voice in some
hymn of sanguinary metaphor.

When Elizabeth wrote him during the Civil War that rumors of
George Armstrong's death were unfounded, he replied with simple
piety that, proud as he had cause to be, and grateful, yet there was
something beyond military glory: "I have every confidence in my
dear son Autie [as George Armstrong was called], surrounded as
he is by temptations . . . but, Libbie, I want you to counsel
Thomas. I want my boys to be, foremost, soldiers of the Lord."

After the political caucus, in Emmanuel's affections, was militia
drill. The land still echoed to the cannon booming to announce the

death of Napoleon, to celebrate the victories of Taylor and Scott in Mexico. And who could say whether, to keep the frontiers beyond the Rio Grande, the plowshare beaten from the sword might not have to be beaten back to sword again?

Emmanuel would proudly take little "Autie" to drill meetings, where, clad in his tiny suit of velvet with brave big buttons, the child would go through the manual of arms perfectly, even before he could utter its terminology. "A born soldier," the militiamen called the Custer boy.

A classmate of young Custer's in the New Rumley School District described Autie as he was in the hobbledehoy period: "Without advantages," says Judge R. M. Voorhees, "despite the hard work of the farm, he was a leader in sports, by nature manly, exuberant, enthusiastic, with a noble, knightly countenance."

One day an enterprising young businessman from Monroe, Michigan, was having midday dinner at the home of Emmanuel Custer in New Rumley. He eyed with approval the young Lydia-Ann Kirkpatrick. At parting, he held her hand a thought longer than formality demanded. "Will you be my girl?" he asked.

Lydia-Ann had returned his gaze at table, less overtly but just as approvingly. "Yes," she replied, "I will."

Young David Reed drove back posthaste to Monroe and bought himself new team, new buggy, and new outfit, then returned to the Custer home to claim his bride.

When the couple were but a few miles on their wedded way, Mrs. Reed felt it was her prerogative to voice a belated hesitancy as to the wisdom of so precipitate a step. David drew rein and listened in silence. When she was finished, he said, "Very well. If that's the way you feel, I'll take you straight back to your mother!"

Lydia-Ann's hesitations vanished. "You get going again," she said decisively. "And don't stop until we reach Monroe!"

She had no cause for regret. The promise of that first interchange of glances was abundantly fulfilled. Even so, Ann Reed was lonely. She missed Autie, always the object of her passionate sisterly devotion. She had helped her mother make the garments of his expectation. She had helped with his velvet military suit. The only scar he carried through life, on his forehead, even that she had caused: she had lifted him onto a skittish heifer, the heifer resented being used as a pony, and little Autie was thrown to the ground.

Monroe was famous for the excellence of its schools, and Autie had his early education there. This enabled him to be with his sister and to help out with the chores on David Reed's farm. He was sent back to New Rumley during vacations, being needed there to help with the harvesting of his father's crops. Autie was docile and willing always, and he performed speedily and well any task assigned to him. When years later Emmanuel, acknowledging a gift from his son, expressed his regret that he had not been able to do more for his advancement, Autie replied.

Custer to Emmanuel Custer:
I never wanted for anything necessary. You and Mother instilled into me principles of industry, self-reliance, honesty. You taught me the value of temperate habits, the difference between right and wrong. I look back on the days spent under the home-roof as a period of pure happiness, and I feel thankful for such noble parents.

Mrs. Custer to her son:
My loveing son—When you speak about your boyhood home in your dear letter I had to weep for joy that the recollection was sweet in your memory. Many a time I have thought there was things my children needed it caused me tears. Yet I consoled myself that I had done my best in making home comfortable. My darling boy, it was not for myself. I was not fortunate enough to have wealth to make home beautiful, always my desire. So I tried to fill the empty spaces with little acts of kindness. Even when there was a meal admired by my children it was my greatest pleasure to get it for them.

I have no doubt I have said some things to you and my other children that was not always pleasant, but I have no regrets about that. You, my son, have more than compensated your mother for all she has done for you. It is sweet to toil for those we love.

Partings were always emotional occasions for mother and son: the one realizing the hazards of a soldier's life, the other fearful; for

Mother Custer's health was frail, and at his next homecoming he might not find her there.

At Stebbins' Academy in Monroe young Custer applied himself with diligence—but only to the studies that appealed to him. On the side he zestfully devoted himself to the reading of military fiction. Mr. Stebbins' supervision was good-naturedly lax, and Autie's geography would conceal well-worn copies of Lever's *Charles O'Malley*, *Irish Dragoon* or *Jack Hinton* or *Tom Burke of Ours*.

In most of his studies he did well. Graduated, he was appointed, at the age of sixteen, principal of a school in Hopedale, Ohio. His wages were $25.00 a month, with board, at the start. In his second term he received $2.00 more a month. When he received his first month's pay, he rushed home to New Rumley, where he surprised his mother, sitting in a rocker, her day's work done. He threw the precious money into her lap. "My first earnings . . . for you!" he cried breathlessly.

Autie's ambition was to enter West Point and become an army officer. "Had I been thwarted in this," he wrote later, "my intention was to work my way through one of the great Eastern colleges, and qualify myself as a teacher, educator." While teaching, he also was studying. He had been deficient in mathematics, having had little interest in it, and he knew how essential to entrance into the military academy was a proficiency in this subject. There was a normal school nearby, and here he made up his deficiency.

Application for nomination to West Point had to be made by a representative in Congress. Emmanuel Custer was a Democrat, and an outspoken one. The representative to be approached was a Republican. Young George Armstrong took the matter into his own hands. We learn the story in the Hon. John A. Bingham's *Reminiscences:*

I had not been long in Congress when I received a letter, a real boy's letter, that captivated me. Packed among my papers I have it yet, but, written over forty years ago, I remember every word. Written in a boyish hand, but firmly, legibly, it told me that the writer—a "Democrat boy," that I might be under no misapprehension—wanted to be a soldier, wanted to go to West Point, and asked what steps he should take regarding it. Struck by its originality, its honesty, I replied at once.

Under the kindly instructions of Representative Bingham, George Armstrong made formal application, giving the required particulars: Age, about seventeen. Above medium height. Of remarkably vigorous frame and strong constitution. Testimonials as to character available. Consent of parents. To a friend he wrote: "Mother is opposed to it, but Pop and David favor it very much." Mother was won over speedily. But there was another candidate in the field with a prior claim, and a year's wait ensued. Finally in February, 1857, a letter came addressed to George A. Custer, Esq., on the stationery of the House of Representatives. It was from Representative Bingham and told him when to present himself for preliminary examinations at the Military Academy.

A few anecdotes and many letters survive from his successful course at West Point, as well as a composition on "The Red Man," somewhat in the vein of James Fenimore Cooper. Custer's second-hand information on the subject was to be amplified considerably by his own encounters with the Indians of the West.

Of deviltry, the young Custer had full measure. He and a comrade one day swam the Hudson, clothes tied to head. A banquet was being held in the James home on the opposite shore. The swimmers did not sit with the guests, but they did full justice to the delectable courses, served to them in the stable by a conniving butler.

In French class Custer was bidden to translate at sight *Léopold, duc d'Autriche, se mettit sur les plaines.* His too-free rendering began, "Leopard, duck and ostrich . . ." And in Spanish class, Squad Leader Custer started the session by asking the instructor to translate into Spanish "Class is dismissed." Complying, the instructor was taken at his word.

Custer's "darling sister Ann" was his favorite correspondent through the West Point days. His letters to her and to his parents always were full of solicitude and affection.

Custer to his sister Ann, from West Point:
I am writing from Camp Jefferson Davis, so-called for the last

Secretary of War. I would not leave this place [West Point] for any amount of money, for I would rather have a good education and no money than a fortune and be ignorant.

Concerning his parents' welfare he had this to say: "If there is one reason why I wish I were through here it is that I might be of some aid to them." But he did have a personal grievance in one instance:

Custer to his sister Ann, from West Point:
I am surprised at Pop not signing my permit to use tobacco. I said distinctly I did not want tobacco for myself, but for my room-mate who smokes, and would get me things I want. Even if I had wanted tobacco for myself they might have given me the permit. Because Tom and Bos—I do not know about Nev—who are at home where they can control them, are allowed to smoke and chew, but because I am way off here by myself, where I need a permit to use tobacco, they refuse to give me one. My room-mate uses it all the time, and I feel the same liberty about using his things that he does about mine. But nothing could induce me to use tobacco, either in smoking or chewing. I consider it a filthy, if not an unhealthy practise. I can say what few of my age can—I never chewed tobacco in my life. Tell Bos he must quit using tobacco.

"War between North and South? My dear Madam, inconceivable!" so spoke Mr. Jefferson Davis to Mrs. Gillespie, great-granddaughter of Benjamin Franklin, in 1860. "Two friendly nations, rather, living side by side. Why, see how quietly they let us go!" And indeed his valedictory to Congress, dignified and, though restrained, yet laden with grief, had been received with amazing calm. The following spring one "friendly nation" opened fire upon the other.

Custer to Ann, from West Point:
I feel confident we will be at war within less than a week. A cadet just arrived from New York says that a telegraphic despatch from Washington states that the President has called on the Governor of Pennsylvania for several troops to defend Washington immediately.

There no longer was any doubt. The country was at war. At the end of May, 1861, Custer was writing Ann Reed:

Custer to Ann, May, 1861, from West Point:
Glad you are helping the good work by sewing clothes for soldiers. We study incessantly. I and others only average about four hours' sleep in the twenty-four. I work until one at night. and get up at five. All my classmates are becoming pale and thin. We do not complain. On the contrary, everyone is anxious and willing.

Now he replies to entreaties that he ask permission to come home for a farewell visit.

Custer to Ann, from West Point:
I would not ask for a leave when all are needed. It is my duty to take whatever position they assign me. It is useless to hope the coming struggle will be bloodless or of short duration. Much blood will be spilled and thousands of lives, at the least, lost. If it is to be my lot to fall in the service of my country and my country's rights I will have no regrets.

The West Point course of training was cut short by a year. High spirits imperfectly curbed and with low marks in many subjects, Custer was at the foot of the graduating class of thirty-four. Had all the 165 entrants remained, had not the Southerners withdrawn, he might have had a somewhat better rating. In 1853 the great Phil Sheridan was also thirty-fourth in his class, but in a class of fifty-two he was further removed from the bottom. Nonetheless, Custer's ambition was fulfilled. He was a duly certified officer, a 2nd lieutenant in the United States Army.

While still within the academy precincts, awaiting assignment, he came near to facing court-martial. As officer of the day he was patrolling the grounds when toward dusk he observed a group of cadets absorbed in watching a fist fight between two of their number. Custer approached and, instead of arresting the offenders, he allowed the sportsman in him to get the better of his sense of duty. Exuberantly he shouted to the onlookers, "Stand back, boys. Let's have a fair fight!" His suggestion was well received and all was fine until two officers, senior to Custer, drew near, unnoticed. Belligerents and backers melted into the shadows, and the self-appointed referee found himself under arrest on the charge of inciting a riot. (Sheridan for a somewhat similar offence had been suspended for a year. But Sheridan had been one of the pugilists.) The country was at war now, needing every graduate of Mr. Jefferson Davis's own West Point to fight Mr. Jefferson Davis. After a short detention Custer was ordered to Washington.

The Adjutant General looked up from the paper he was about to sign. His eye had been caught by the name it bore. And the young man, standing expectant, was every inch the soldierly figure he had known was coming. Examination marks? Who cared. There were other qualities, and this was wartime. "Mr. Custer, would you care to be presented to General Scott? He may have some special service for you."

Winfield Scott, Chief of Staff of the United States Army, with a record of distinguished achievement! Would Mr. Custer care . . . ?

General Scott received him cordially, offered him a choice: a position on his own staff training recruits or riding that night—for dawn was breaking—with dispatches to General McDowell in the field. Knowing Custer, even so early in his life, who could doubt his choice?

It was not easy to find a mount in horseless Washington; but he found one before the day was old. And he gained a staunch adherent. This was Joseph Fought, a boy bugler "with splendid lungs" who had been attached to a regiment of Pennsylvania cavalry then quartered, for lack of suitable accommodations, in the Treasury Building.

Joseph Fought's account:
I do not know how I came to attach myself to him. He was a conspicuous figure from the first, attracting attention wherever he went. I remember especially seeing him walking around the stables. Then, later, in the city I was holding his horse for him.

On Pennsylvania Avenue Custer recognized an old acquaintance, a trooper formerly stationed at West Point, under whose tutelage he had taken part in cavalry exercises. This man's detachment had been summoned hurriedly to Washington when it was rumored that an attempt was expected on the life of Lincoln at his inaugural. Now serving with Griffin's battery in the field, the trooper had been sent back to Washington to fetch the "spare" horse the captain, his owner, had left there. But this horse was "Wellington," and Custer had ridden him at West Point. Surely Wellington would rather be ridden, than led, to Centreville, Custer's destination! And so it was arranged. The dispatches safely buttoned in his tunic, Custer set out on General Scott's errand that very night.

Three days after leaving West Point, 2nd Lieutenant Custer, Company G, Second Cavalry, received his baptism of fire at Bull Run.

The failure of that first encounter with the enemy under Beauregard is a sad page in history. But Custer came out of it with credit. He had demonstrated resourcefulness in a crisis, ability to bring order from confusion, all the essentials of true leadership. "I little imagined," he wrote, "when making my night ride from Washington on July 20th, that the night following would find me returning with a defeated and demoralized army."

The day lost irrevocably, Custer was among the last to leave the field, his detail in orderly march among the panic-stricken soldiers that cluttered the routes in their flight toward Washington. Some soldiers were said not to have paused until they reached New York, where in a crowded metropolis they could lose their military identity.

Fought's account:
The roads were jammed with people clamoring for news of the fight. But, though famished, exhausted, spent, Custer never let up, never slackened control. Then, when Arlington was reached and his company assigned to its camp, he snatched a few hours' sleep, beneath a tree, in a pouring rain, even while his name was being cited for bravery in the Capital.

For the sequel, we turn to the Hon. John A. Bingham, to whom Custer owed his nomination to West Point:

I had never seen him, and was so engrossed with political cares in Washington that I almost forgot him. Then the war came on, and all the senior cadets were graduated before the fifth year of the course was spent. The nation needed every one of them to drill the raw recruits rushing from the North to defend the Capital.

I heard of him after the First Battle of Bull Run. In the report of that miserable fiasco he was mentioned for bravery. A leader was needed to re-form the troops, and take them over a bridge. Like Napoleon at Lodi young Custer sprang to the front—and was a hero.

I heard of his exploit with pride, and hunted several times for my boy, but unsuccessfully. Then one day a young soldier came to my room without the formality of sending in a card.

Beautiful as Absalom with his yellow curls, he was out of breath, or had lost it from embarrassment. And he spoke with hesitation: "Mr. Bingham, I've been in my first battle. I tried hard to do my best. I felt I ought to report to you, for it's through you I got to West Point. I'm . . ."

I took his hand. "I know. You're my boy Custer!"

2: The Bacons and Pages

WHENEVER THAT eminent citizen of Monroe, Michigan, Judge Daniel Stanton Bacon, was asked how he had made the journey as a young man from his father's home in Onondaga County, New York, to what was then a western outpost, he would reply with a flourish, "Madam (or Sir), I walked!"

There was more drama than truth in what he said. His purse was slender, but not too slender to provide for transportation by stagecoach and sailboat. He literally taught his way from East to what was then the West. In 1822 the West was not the Far West, which was to be opened later and carved into states. But it was a long way from home and was real frontier country.

Daniel's people were of English stock, having been members of the Plymouth Colony. In the annals of Onondaga County his father, Dr. Leonard Bacon, is listed as a "skillful physician and prosperous farmer." With his wife, Elizabeth Clift, he was "highly esteemed and cultured, in the community." It had been his father's wish to give this extremely able son of his a liberal education, but straitened means and a too-large family prevented this. So Daniel Stanton, aged twenty-four, determined to seek his own fortune. Being of a cautious nature, he stayed well within the frontiers. Being practical, he sought a place where the admirable schooling he had received could be turned to profitable account in teaching, and where he could "make property" in honorable business enterprises. Above all, he wished to be able to take a constructive share in shaping national destinies by engaging in "politicks."

He realized all these ambitions. Never a frontiersman, he was an organizer and brought to the rudimentary young settlement ethical and educational standards which, while often narrow, were of a right direction. He became judge of probate and one of the solid rocks on which the nation's strength and greatness rest. That he and

[*14*]

his son-in-law, George Armstrong Custer, came together in a father-and-son relation no less than in a common intolerance of injustice, wrongdoing, and subserviency to self-interest is a prime factor in the Custer story.

Steam locomotion was in the experimental stage in 1822. Canals with locks, advocated by President Washington, had not been developed. Indian trails had been beaten into roads, muddy or iron hard, according to the season, deeply rutted by the wheels of covered wagons and stagecoaches. Taverns with change of horses and refreshment for man and beast were spaced some ten miles apart. On his westward journey young Daniel Stanton Bacon stopped off at Detroit to look about him.

Daniel Bacon to his parents, September 26, 1822, from Detroit:
I arrove here safe this evening. I had a tolerable passage to Buffalo —from Rochester to Lewiston. We went on the Canada side to Blackrock. At Buffalo we took passage on the "Red-jacket." We were a week getting to Cleveland, a rather unpleasant journey, having headwinds and the heaviest blow of the season on the Lake. I continued thence by land to Peru, Sandusky, thence aboard the "Prudence" here.

I found the State of Ohio verry healthy, but schoolkeeping in poor demand. I am going to Pontiack on the Raisin in pursuit of schools, and shall get into business as soon as I can, when I will write you more lengthy. I remain Your son D. S. Bacon.

Daniel Bacon to his parents, November, 1822, from Bloomfield:
Here I stepped into a schoolhouse. The teacher informed me a vacancy may be had. The Trustees consider my price, $20., a great price, more than anyone in town is getting. I said that for three months I must have $20. but for four months or more permanent I would teach for $15. to which they agreed.

This is one of the most civilized places I ever was in. There has been a verry great revival of religion this summer. Prayer-meetings are held four times a week.

My school is at present small . . . two grammar scholars—I expect more—and a number in arithmetick.

He asks that his trunk be sent out by stage or by some trusty teamster, and a pair of coarse boots befitting the muddy soil..

Spring of 1823 finds the hardworking young Bacon settled, teaching and farming in Raisinville. This was the largest of several new communities on the River Raisin, some twenty miles above the point at which it debouches into Lake Erie. It was so named from the rich vines along its shores, which excited the admiration of the French explorers. Raisinville, with Frenchtown, was originally a fur-trading post. But the Indians took their furs elsewhere and the several posts were incorporated into a city. Monroe, as it was soon to be named, solely in expectation of a presidential visit, was a slice of the territory admitted to the Union in 1837 as the state of Michigan.

Daniel Bacon to his parents, April 30, 1823, from Raisinville:
I have cleared over 10 acres on my farm, leaving 5 trees to an acre. Lumber is $12 a thousand in good pay. Quantities of building timber come down the River, looking gracefully. The bottom I have cleared was thickly coated with hazle, sure indication of good land. I have planted a small nursery of apple, peach and plumb. I pride myself on doing more work than any other man on the Raisin, but I am a fair candidate for the ague-fever.

"Under yonder tree," Judge Bacon would say, "I spent my first summer, lying on the ground, the poor man's boarding house, alternately shivering with cold and burning up with fever. Every newcomer was a victim. Decaying vegetation, undrained swamps, marshes extending from the Lake were the cause." So he would tell his daughter. To his parents he wrote: "Doctors here? Aye, and good ones, but they hew you to the verry stump, nor is there quinine enough to go round." Business appointments had to be regulated by the exactions of the "ague-fever," lest the shaking hand of a contracting party be unable to pen the signature. Undaunted, young Bacon persevered.

Daniel Bacon to his parents, from Raisinville:
Being alone, paying board, farming tools and team work, my chances of making property look small. The money you sent me, father, will pay my small debts. You regret it is not more, but be assured it is enough.

It was a sad day when he learned of his mother's passing. And he was concerned, too, for his father's bereavement.

Daniel Bacon to his father, from Monroe:
It has pleased the Divine Disposer to take from you the worthy and amiable companion of twenty-five years. We, her children should be thankful to have been so long under her influence, but your situation must be desolate. An hospitable and generous neighbor she will long be missed and mourned.

Dr. Bacon, in his "desolate situation," thought of selling out and joining his son. From this young Daniel sagaciously dissuaded him.

Daniel Bacon to his father, from Monroe:
You are quite too old a man. It would be impolitick. Where would you ever get so good a farm as that you now possess, also such a good society? But come and see for yourself.

The father followed this excellent advice, but after roughing it for a time decided that strenuous adventure was for youth and went back, reconciled to his assured, if modest, position in Onondaga County. As young Daniel prospered, he paid visits to his boyhood home. When he married, he encouraged his sisters to visit him. They had every opportunity to remain in Monroe, but all three married in Onondaga County and settled there.

The country was rapidly building up. Seventy families came in by boat from Pontiac. A community of Friends formed a thriving settlement. The black swamp was bridged, roads pushed out. Narrow strips of farmland on the river acquired by early settlers were parceled and sold. A weekly paper was supported by "patronage." Cabins gradually were replaced by frame or native-brick houses.

The French, bearing in many cases historic names, were descendants of "gentleman adventurers" or bankrupts and runaways. A few of them rose to eminence, but for the most part they kept to Old World ways. They depended on the river for sturgeon fishing and were a gentle, kindly folk. Mr. Bacon found them of scrupulous integrity in business dealings.

The Germans came later. They had solid qualities, and Mr. Bacon

liked selling land to them as an investment—for he soon was deal-
ing in real estate. The Germans would often erect their houses on
stilts and piers, allotting the ground floor to the livestock so that the
entire establishment was housed under a single roof.

Each group put up its own place of worship—except the Catho-
lics, who had found theirs waiting for them. These had been built
by the missions; the Jesuits and Recollects had a church for every
fur-trading post, however remote.

In 1835 Daniel S. Bacon, schoolteacher, was elected to the Legislative Council of the Territory and, ten years later, to the Legislature of the State of Michigan. As associate judge and as judge of
probate he acquitted himself with credit. He became director of
railroads, banks, business enterprises. Public spirited, blameless in
his personal life, he stood high in popular esteem. At forty, in his
prime, tall, well built and strong featured, neighborly without familiarity, genial with the restraints of dignity, courteous in his manner, he had unwittingly benefited from the polished ways of the
French priests with whom he had had so much pleasant intercourse.
He was a personage. And, remarkably, he was unmarried. Not rich,
but "making property," he still was single, in a region where the
first thought of every man who could put up a one-room cabin was
to find a mate to share it—either the girl waiting "back home" or
one of the many girls growing up about him. On this subject the
young Bacon had advised his parents: "I will not marry until I can
assure my wife of every comfort. I have witnessed too many hardships, too much suffering, to have a loved wife worn out by
drudgery."

But youth was behind him now, and though he was domestic and
home loving, the habit of bacherlorhood had grown upon him,
despite the efforts of widows and young maidens to change his
state. Then he met Eleanor Sophia Page, of Grand Rapids, Michigan.

Like the Bacons, the Pages were of English stock and had settled
in the East. Major Abel Page kept a tavern at the junction of West
Street and Main in Rutland, Vermont. Though the panic of 1837
only lightly touched that state, it brought about many changes and
readjustments in life. Major Page sold out his business, loaded his
family and furniture on two covered wagons, and set out for Grand

Rapids. The journey was lightened by the Erie Canal, which had been opened in 1833.

This was a fairly new and thriving settlement. Beautifully situated, endowed with fertile soil, it enabled Abel Page to found the business for which he had prepared himself, nursery gardening. He bought and cleared land. With his two sons, Abel and Aaron, he brought in from the woods blackberry, raspberry, and plum for scientific cultivation. He purchased seeds, slips, and saplings and introduced trees and shrubs new to the region. The Lombardy poplar owed its vogue to him, and the prize-winning "mammoth potato." The "love apple," later called the tomato, he cultivated for its decorative value in herbaceous borders. Its coral fruit was shunned as a rank poison. But the day came when Major Page transplanted the fruit to his vegetable patch: a schoolteacher had made a daring experiment; he bit the fruit, tasted it, found it luscious, and devoured it. He survived. He also set a new record in dietary. The "love apple" came belatedly but firmly into its own, and the Page nurseries made it one of their prime specialties.

The Pages were people of high cultural and religious standards. The daughters were educated at a Connecticut "Female Seminary," the equivalent of the later junior college. In his retirement Mr. Page was eulogistically described as "owner of a beautiful estate, of marked refinement, deeply religious—one of the founders of the Unitarian Church." Religious they must have been. Little Libbie Bacon remembered "the warmest of welcomes" when she visited her grandparents, "also prayers—Morning and Evening prayers, and prayers in between. And prayers!"

Mr. Bacon's courtship was in the stately manner. He was encouraged by the thought that his visit to Sophia Page was "well-received" by her. The formality of their relations is evident.

Sophia Page to Daniel Bacon, 1837, from Grand Rapids, Michigan:
The society of your place is justly entitled to its reputation. All must subscribe to the correctness of your remark that "Female influence when judiciously exerted gives character to any spot."

When next he writes his "dear Sophia" Daniel extols Monroe, but with qualifications:

Daniel Bacon to Sophia Page, 1837, from Monroe, Michigan:
I would not wish to give you a false impression. The navigation of
Lake Erie is open so as to admit boats from Buffalo. But for the pecu-
niary embarrassment in the East the coming season would be a prosperous one. My feelings have undergone no change since I saw you. It
is therefore unnecessary to give you further assurances of my friendship and affection.

In June he feels the time is ripe to ask Mr. and Mrs. Page to sanction his engagement to their daughter, to whom he promises "that
protection and affection due from husband to wife." Mr. Page's
reply is in the same exalted strain.

Mr. Page to Daniel Bacon, June, 1837, from Grand Rapids, Michigan:
In all our engagements we should be governed by the Golden Rule.
May He Who knows the secrets of every heart so order it that you
and our dear child may never repent the anticipated union. In regard
to property, it is desirable, but not among the first class of blessings.
I am not rich, but we shall do for our daughter all that our circumstances permit. We chearfully consent and trust her in your hands.

As the wedding day, the second Tuesday in September, 1837, ap-
proaches, the bridegroom becomes diffident.

Daniel Bacon to Sophia Page, September, 1837, from Monroe,
Michigan:
If my friends have praised me beyond my merits I pray you to make
allowances and to view me as simple *me*—a plain man without preten-
sion beyond being a good member of society.
Bear in mind that your Intended feels much solicitude for your
welfare and is truly your friend.

The honeymoon will take them to visit Mr. Bacon's people in
Onondaga County.

Daniel Bacon to Sophia Page, September, 1837, from Monroe,
Michigan:
The uncertainty of Steam Boats and unused as you are to the naviga-
tion of the Lakes would make our return by land desirable. Bear in

mind you have a friend who in all sincerity subscribes himself D. S. Bacon.

Was the word "love" considered romantic, extravagant? It does not occur in the letters that passed between Daniel Bacon and Sophia Page. In part this explains why in later years, when Daniel's daughter Elizabeth was being courted by George Custer, the elderly father was distrustful of the young man's ardently expressed passion for Elizabeth. But there is no doubt that a deep, abiding conjugal love developed between Daniel and Sophia. At Sunday services, after his wife died, Mr. Bacon would rise, leave the church which at her behest he attended regularly, and with clenched fists, sobbing aloud, would stride down the aisle and outside. Such was the respect in which he was held that no one laughed at this manifestation of a strong man's grief.

They had fifteen years of married life. Though investments often ran ahead of profits, Mr. Bacon maintained his family in simple comfort, with margin for generous hospitality and unostentatious charities. At first he did find domesticity constricting.

Mr. Bacon to his father, 1838 (?), from Monroe, Michigan:
I have been so long a boarder in a publick house, and more or less in the turmoil of business and politicks, that for some time housekeeping rendered my situation lonely.

If Mrs. Bacon's "situation" was lonely, her letters give no indication of it.

Mrs. Bacon to her sister, Mrs. Richmond, from Monroe, Michigan:
How are the children? Have they yet learned "There is a Happy Land"? Tell them Aunt Sophia will expect them to sing it to her. . . . Harriet has sent me a double shawl from New York, the most fashionable worn, she says. Also a maroon-colored merino with fluted trimmings, also a gray silk with shirred hat.

Loraine, I do wish you and Mr. Richmond and the children would make us a long visit this winter.

More snow than I have yet seen in Michigan. It makes me think of old times and sleighing parties in Vermont. I walk a mile daily for my health. Harriet sent me notices of Jenny Lind's first concert at Castle Garden in New York.

Harriet was the youngest of the Page sisters. Most attractive, having many suitors, she married not so happily later on and went East to live.

Four children were born to the Bacons. Two small girls succumbed to the infant mortality of the day. Eddy, the only son, was his father's hope and pride. Also he was the source of needless solicitude. When Mrs. Bacon took Eddy to visit her people in Grand Rapids her husband wrote her solicitously.

Mr. Bacon to his wife, from Monroe, Michigan:
Life with grandparents is apt to be unfavorable to the discipline of children. Bear in mind that Edward is wild, ungovernable. I fear his young uncles may not control him in their rambles and that he may fall from fences, trees, into the canal or Lake. I would like to be with you, if only to see Eddy's feats and performances. I hope he may meet the expectations of his relatives.

Mr. Bacon to his father, from Monroe, Michigan:
My boy is large, destined to be as tall as myself, and one of the healthiest children I ever saw. But he requires looking after, for he is mischievous, disorderly, unmanageable.

Eddy's wildness consisted in breaking from his father's hand when out walking, and running into the ever-open Catholic church to hide among its shadows. But to Mr. Bacon's apology the kindly priests would urge that the little footsteps betokened a holy inclination, and they would not hear of punishment.

But Eddy was luckless. A broken step at the back door was covered temporarily with a plank, and he fell from it, sustaining a spinal injury that kept him recumbent for a year. Then his nurse, taking the convalescent child for an airing, led him to a quarter of the town where a contagious disease had been raging and to the very house and room where services for a victim were being held. Eddy caught the disease, and soon there was another little mound in God's Acre on the hill.

All the parents' hopes were centered now on Elizabeth. "An only child—but I was not spoiled," insisted Mrs. Custer. She was a trifle wayward. She would slip out to join playmates of her own choosing and was not above fibbing about it. At first her punishment was to be shut up in a clothes closet "between Mother's gowns and Father's pants." But, finding a wicker basket there, she would creep into it and take a peaceful nap. Then she was put to bed by daylight, again to be solaced by a nap. But, roused from this by a voice in prayer, and seeing her lovely mother kneeling beside her, she professed a repentance she did not feel and promised conformity.

To insure good schooling for its girls without having to send them to Detroit or Toledo, several leading citizens, including Judge Bacon, established a seminary, a three-storey brick structure housing, at the start, eight teachers and 112 pupils. Elizabeth attended and was delighted with it, though she was not averse to skipping lessons. When she was nine, her father gave her a diary, beautifully bound and blank, except for the inscription. It was almost a year before she used it, but then the entries came thick and fast:

The 6th of next month will be my birthday. I had a present of a piano. It cost $275 and the stool $10. . . . After scool I went to the Catolic church to see the Catolics crack eggs as I was informed they would do, but was disapointed. So I retired home. . . . A disipated german living near the depot commited suicide by hanging himself near teatime. . . . Father went out with the drayman for poles for my swing. When it was put up the yard was full of boys and girls wanting to swing in it. . . . To-night the hall lamp fell and broke without any help. . . . At Fannies they had some spiritual knockings. At night I kept awake thinking about them. But they are only humbugs. . . . My Sabath scool lesson was in the 12 chapter romans I learned it at my Mother's request. She learned it at her Mother's request. My brother Edward learned it when he was living. . . . I have been preparing some underclose for my largest doll. . . . This day was commenced with knitting my stent while Mother read to me a most excelent tract entitled The Day of Trial. . . . The weather has been a goodeal like spring. The moon shone bright almost like daytime. You could see people walking especially young gentlemen and ladies. . . .

Self-denial went into the gift of the piano. For some time Mrs. Bacon had acted as her husband's bookkeeper. And money had to be earned for the little girl's musical education. Elizabeth succeeded, however, only in mastering some of the popular melodies of the day.

Life went smoothly for the Bacons' only child. There were visits to and from Grand Rapids—by sleigh in winter, by stage in other seasons. Sunday travel was barred, for that would have contravened one of the Ten Commandments.

When Elizabeth was twelve, there came a sad day.

Mr. Bacon to his sisters, August 12, 1854, from Monroe, Michigan:
My poor wife is no more. Her physicians were unacquainted with the nature of her disease. She bore her sufferings with great composure and Christian fortitude. That she did not expect to recover I gathered. . . . She had changed directions I had given my tailor. . . . She only desired to live on account of Elizabeth and myself. . . . We have had the largest sympathy. . . . No lady in Monroe was so universally regretted. . . . I do not fully realize my terrible situation. Elizabeth bears her affliction well, but the poor girl does not realize the over-devotion of her mother. I do not yet know what I shall do.

The diary holds this final entry in the first stage of Elizabeth Bacon's story:

My Mother is laid in the cold, cold ground, never to rise again until the Last Day. Oh, why did they put her in that black coffin and screw the lid down so tight? The last thing she looked at was my portrait. . . . Aunt Harriet and I start for Grand Rapids. . . . When I return I shall board at the Seminary, and Father at the Exchange Hotel and our pleasant home will be broken up.

3 : Captain Custer

CITED FOR bravery in his first engagement at Bull Run immediately following his graduation from West Point, 2nd Lieutenant George Armstrong Custer moved upward rapidly. In August of that year, 1861, the company to which he was attached was assigned temporarily to the command of Brigadier General Philip Kearny, U. S. Volunteers. Custer was at once appointed aide, then adjutant general, to Kearny. From that master of military science he learned invaluable lessons:

Of the many officers of high rank with whom I served, Kearny was the strictest disciplinarian. Making my tour of duty with him as staff officer I found him ever engaged, either in some scheme to improve his command, or to discomfit the enemy. . . . He, Kearny, was always to be found where the danger was greatest.

Custer learned from him that a success must always be followed up by a thorough routing to prevent the enemy from re-forming for renewed attack. Not only must he be defeated; the enemy must realize defeat.

That autumn the cavalry, regular and volunteer, was assembled near Washington under Brigadier General Cooke. He was succeeded by Brigadier General Stoneman, who equipped the cavalry to operate in the field with McClellan's command, the Army of the Potomac. Custer was aide to both generals.

October found him in Monroe on sick leave—and the young girls were aware of his presence. Mrs. Reed was besieged by words and letters of solicitude for the invalid. At twilight, love calls were often heard outside—some romantic ditty being tapped out rhythmically by parasol on the picket fence. Sister Ann, fearful lest her darling fall victim to these sirens—"hussies" was her name for them

—would beg him to remain within, and Autie would good-naturedly comply.

Recovered, he returned to Washington. Mrs. Reed heard from him about the gaieties there.

Custer to Mrs. Reed, 1861, from Washington:
Last night my classmate Elbert and I started out with our band, serenading, not returning till after ten o'clock. Among others we serenaded Elbert's sweetheart, but I, unblessed with a treasure (?) only regaled my friends. All the ladies invited us in. In some houses they were in bed, but all got up. Everywhere we were offered fashionable wine and liquors, but *nowhere did I touch a drop.*

There was reason for his abstemiousness. While he was in Monroe, Custer and some old schoolmates had met in a room behind a store to "swap yarns" and reminisce. Applejack was freely partaken of. With the second round George Armstrong found he was constitutionally unable to hold his liquor. To lose control over his members and faculties was to him unthinkable. He rose, muttered some excuse, and left, heedless of jeers and taunts. He staggered home and threw himself on his bed, where he slept off the evil spell. When he awakened, completely sober, he found his sister Ann on her knees beside him, praying with the frenetic fervor of a wounded heart steeped in Methodist prohibitions that her brother be "delivered from the clutches of the Demon Rum."

She did not have to exact a promise from him. Autie had made a pact with his own conscience, which he kept through life inviolate, never again to touch intoxicants. The Methodist Custers were abstainers on principle. In Kearny's army convivial drinking was expected of Autie—but for him there would be no more of it. His moral strength was invincible.

Custer to Mrs. Reed, from Washington:
To-morrow morning I go to the City [Washington] to attend Congress and witness the presentation of flags captured in our late victories, by the Adjutant-General. Washington's Farewell Address will be read, with other exercises in commemoration of his birthday.

From Washington to Fortress Monroe, thence up the Peninsula, with Richmond, Confederate capital, the objective.

Custer to Mrs. Reed, March 11, 1862, from Warwick Court House, Virginia:

Scarcely a ten minutes' interval during the day that the rebels and our men do not fire at each other. Both parties keep hidden as well as possible, but as soon as either shows itself it is fired at. At night, when it is too dark to shoot or be shot at, both come out of hiding-places, holler at each other, calling names and bragging what they intend to do. Then, when daylight appears, the party which sees the other first, fires, and that puts a stop till night comes, when the same thing is repeated. But we will soon decide the question. The great battle will probably come off before this reaches you. General McClellan is here to lead us, so we are certain of victory.

Custer to his parents, March 17, 1862, from Headquarters, Army of the Potomac, Fairfax, Virginia:

My dear Parents—We followed the retreating rebel army from Manassas. They had a strong picket posted on a hill about half a mile from us. General Stoneman sent orders to the commander of my regiment to drive the enemy's forces back to their main body. . . . I stepped forward and volunteered to drive away the enemy pickets if I were given enough men. My commander asked how many? I said, "As many as you see fit to give me. Twenty or more." He bade me take my company, about fifty. I took my position in front at a slow trot, so as not to tire horses and men. About halfway I bade the men fire their revolvers. We then took the gallop, and the bullets rattled like hail. . . . Afterwards General Stoneman sent for me to question me and seemed pleased with the manner in which I had performed my duty. I have not had my clothes off for one week.

Col. Grier was along. He and General Stoneman slept by my camp fire. About 3 the latter wakened me to send me on a scouting party. I had only been asleep an hour. He asked me how I was feeling. I told him, "Fit!" Col. Grier then said, "Oh, he can eat and sleep as much as anyone when he has the chance. But he can do without either when necessary!"

I have more confidence in General McClellan than in any man living.

I would forsake everything and follow him to the ends of the earth. I would lay down my life for him. He is here now. Every officer and private worships him. I would fight anyone who would say a word against him.

Custer to Mrs. Reed, March 26, 1862, from Alexandria, Virginia:

We are embarking on steamers and transports. . . . The greatest expedition ever fitted out is going south under the greatest and best of men, Genl. McClellan. The utmost secrecy is observed. We have been shipping troops at the rate of 20,000 a day.

We are not certain whither we are bound, but are confident this will be Richmond. We expect a battle at Norfolk on the way. We are confident of victory. With McClellan to lead us we know no such word as fail.

Genl. McClellan and staff are on the dock. He just told the commander of my regiment that all the regulars, us included, were to go with him always. He knows who to rely on.

Custer to Mrs. Reed, March 28, 1862, on board the U. S. Transport Adèle Felicia:

They [a Rebel newspaper] say I had 500 men. I had 50. They acknowledge having 300—the number I reported to Genl. Stoneman. They say they killed 40 and took 100 prisoners. The truth is, they shot 3, and took no prisoners.

Good-bye, my darling Sister. Good-bye, all of you.

Custer to Mrs. Reed, April 20, 1862, from Camp Thomas, Warwick Court House, Virginia:

Our army is encamped in front of the rebels. We are getting ready for the expected battle. Our troops are building batteries right under their fortifications. Their line of works extends about 5 miles. Our troops threw up breastworks in the night, and mounted guns about 400 yards from them. Also we have rifle-pits for our sharpshooters, about the same distance.

When we first came the rebels would fire a shell at our men, then jump on the parapets to see where it struck, then cheer and jump down. But our artillery-men and sharpshooters have taught them better manners.

We had quite a little skirmish the other day, and got pretty badly whipped. Four companies from one of our regiments were sent to take a fort. When nearly up to it a perfect shower of musketry was opened on them, and a few shells thrown. Our men were driven back with the loss of their flag and 300 of their numbers. . . .

I was in the woods with our sharpshooters. . . . Everyone got behind a tree and blazed away as hard as he could. But the rebels made their bullets fly so thick it was all we could do to look out for ourselves. It was nearly an hour before we could get up. I got awful tired of my hiding-place. Finally we were reinforced, and soon the rebels were playing our game of hide-and-seek. This was before our troops had thrown up breastworks.

The day before yesterday we buried our dead slain in the skirmish, in the clothes they wore when killed, each wrapped in his blanket. No coffin. It seemed hard, but it could not be helped. Some were quite young and boyish, and, looking at their faces, I could not but think of my own younger brother.

One, shot through the heart, had been married the day before he left Vermont. Just as his comrades were about to consign his body to the earth, I thought of his wife, and, not wishing to put my hands in his pockets, cut them open with my knife, and found knife, porte-monnaie and ring. I then cut off a lock of his hair and gave them to a friend of his from the same town who promised to send them to his wife. As he lay there I thought of that poem: "Let me kiss him for his mother . . ." and wished his mother were there to smooth his hair.

At the camp of the 7th Mich. I was welcomed by Col. Winans and other Monroe acquaintances, and partook of their rations: crackers and tea. Then in the evening started for my own camp.

Genl. Emery who commands all the cavalry has offered me an appointment as aide-de-camp. I have accepted. He has written Genl. McClellan to allow me to join him. If I get orders to that effect my pay will be increased ten dollars a month.

The expected engagement will come off any day now. It is hard to tell how many troops McClellan has here now, but I think about 130,-000.

Give my love to David, the family and friends, and write *soon*.

Custer to Mrs. Reed, May 15, 1862, from Headquarters, Smith's Division, White House, Virginia:
You have heard long since of our battle at Williamsburg on the 5th of this month, with our complete victory, the rebels driven off the field. I was glad to aid Genl. Hancock on that day, and was in the thick of

the fight from morning till dark. Genl. Hancock's brigade was charged
by two rebel brigades with bayonets. Our troops stood firm, then,
when the rebels were twenty paces, Genl. Hancock gave orders to
advance at a charge of bayonets. They did so, putting the enemy to a
complete rout, killing and capturing a large number.

A classmate of mine was captain of one of the rebel regiments, and
was taken prisoner after being badly wounded in the leg. I took care
of him, and fed him for two days, but then had to leave him when I
went on with the army, while he would be sent North. When we first
saw each other he shed tears and threw his arms about my neck, and
we talked of old times and asked each other hundreds of questions
about classmates on opposing sides of the contest. I carried his meals
to him, gave him stockings of which he stood in need, and some money.
This he did not want to take, but I forced it on him. He burst into
tears and said it was more than he could stand. He insisted on writing
in my notebook that if ever I should be taken prisoner he wanted me
treated as he had been. His last words to me were, "God bless you, old
boy!" The bystanders looked with surprise when we were talking,
and afterwards asked if the prisoner were my brother.

The Battle of Williamsburg was hard fought, far more so than Bull
Run. I captured a Captain and five men without any assistance, and a
large rebel flag. It was afterwards sent up by McClellan to the President at Washington.

This was the first Confederate flag captured by the Army of the
Potomac. Custer is mentioned in General Hancock's report of the
battle of Williamsburg:

I placed the artillery in battery on the crest of the hill, in front of
the enemy's work at short range, deployed skirmishers on the right
and left of the road, then sent the Fifth Wisconsin, preceded by skirmishers, under command of Major Larrabee, and followed by the
Sixth Maine in column assault across the dam and into the work,
Lieutenant Custer, Fifth Regular cavalry, volunteering and leading
the way on horseback.

Custer was sent up in a balloon four times to watch the enemy
and learn what he could concerning them. Quickness of observation, a memory accurate and retentive, with proficiency in map

drawing, caused Custer frequently to be selected for special missions. Often he volunteered for them, as in the Williamsburg coup. His next exploit brought him more than a citation in the dispatches. It won him promotion to captain.

In May, 1862, the great struggle was on. Which capital—Washington (which was not wholeheartedly Union) or Confederate Richmond—would be taken? McClellan had moved cautiously to Coal Harbor, about a mile from the Chickahominy, a tributary of the York River, which feeds the James. It was essential to cross this stream in order to cover the railroad which brought supplies from the coast. The railroad terminal was held by the Confederates.

Bridges broken down, the bottom slimy and shifting, was this Chickahominy fordable? Only the trial-and-error method would decide Chief Engineer General Barnard. Turning to the young staff officer detailed to accompany him on his rounds, he said, "Jump in!"

Without removing even his tunic Custer did jump in. Revolver held above his head he waded across, an easy mark for pickets had they been alert. But they were not alert. He clambered up the muddy banks opposite, slithered behind some bushes, listened with keen ears to rebel plans, mapped out the lay of the land. Then he returned as he had come, and reported. General Barnard repaired forthwith to headquarters and described the feat to McClellan. Fourteen years later the commanding general wrote of this to Custer's widow.

General McClellan to Mrs. Custer, August 6, 1876:
He was reported to me as having accomplished an act of desperate gallantry on the banks of the Chickahominy. I sent for him at once, and, after thanking him, asked what I could do for him. He seemed to attach no importance to what he had done, and desired nothing. Whereupon I asked him if he would like to come upon my staff as Captain. He gladly accepted, and remained with me until I was relieved of my command.

In June, 1862, McClellan's appointment of Custer was ratified by Secretary of War Stanton.

The stream having been proved fordable by one man afoot, the next step was to test its fordability for the two companies of cavalry and one of infantry. This expedition Captain Custer was detailed to lead, with a view to capturing the pickets and holding the north bank. Custer accordingly waded the stream, trying out its treacherous bed up and down for the best part of a mile. This was characteristic of Custer's method: the meticulously careful preparation, the sure, cautious approach, the sudden surprise attack. When biographers describe him as "dashing," they do scant justice to the solid basis for that spectacular climax. In warfare Custer was the perfect artist, building results on sound technique.

In the gray dawn the young captain rode down to the river at the head of his command. For a moment his assumption of dignity was almost cracked when he heard himself hailed with shouts and informal cries: "Hi, there, George! . . . Armstrong! . . . Autie!" In the ranks were Monroe boys, Stebbins' Academy boys who had known him as their leader in games. He rode blithely into the water, up the slippery banks on the other side, surprising and stampeding the pickets, taking prisoners, seizing the railroad terminal from the Confederates.

Custer to Mr. and Mrs. Reed, July 13, 1862, from Harrison's Landing, James River, Virginia:
Dear Brother and Sister—The rebels came nearer being successful in this engagement than in any other. All that prevented our defeat was the arrival of reinforcements—French and Mosher's Irish Brigade restored order and confidence in our wavering lines.

We are now strongly posted on the banks of the James. I was in the saddle four consecutive nights and as many days. I generally had but one meal—coffee and hard bread—breakfast.

Custer to Mr. and Mrs. Reed, August 8, 1862, from Virginia:
I received your letter of the 30th about dark, and would have answered, but my horse was in front of my tent. . . . I had returned the day before from a successful scout and was about to start on another. . . . As we were to start at two in the morning I thought it best to rejoin my regiment in the evening.

Custer to Mr. and Mrs. Reed, August, 1862, from Virginia:
Our forces . . . about 300 cavalry, 4 guns (horse artillery) under Col. Averill. Objective, White Oak Swamp, about 40 miles, to surprise

a regiment of cavalry stationed there. We arrived about 11. I was first to discover the enemy. Our cavalry prepared to charge. Away we went, whooping and yelling lustily. The rebels broke and scattered, we following as fast as our horses could go. Many surrendered when they saw chances of escape cut off. I became separated from the command, all but a bugler boy, concealed from me by bushes. I heard him calling "Captain! Captain! Two Secesh are after me!" I found him, carbine in hand warding off the rebels. I drew my revolver and dashed after one, the bugler the other. Both put spurs to their horses. My horse was faster than that of my Rebel . . . an officer by his uniform. I could have overtaken him, but turned off. I could have fired at him, but seeing a rail fence, concluded to try him at it. He cleared it handsomely. Now came my turn. My black determined not to be outdone by a rebel and cleared the fence as well as one could wish. By avoiding soft ground which, I saw, was retarding him, I got quite close. I called on him to surrender or I would shoot him. He paid no attention but pushed on. I called again. No reply. I took deliberate aim. He sat for a moment in his saddle, reeled, fell. His horse ran on, mine also. Soon his party were around me, firing right and left.

I captured another rebel who had leaped from his horse to escape in the woods. This was some distance from our main body. The Colonel, alarmed for our safety, bade the bugler sound the "Rally!"

I saw the horse of the officer I had shot, knew him by a red morocco breast strap. . . . I took possession of him, a blooded horse—It was the officer's own fault. I called on him twice to surrender.

Our party then returned to camp, some twenty miles away, in danger any moment of being attacked. . . . Two horses were killed by the rebels, but we did not lose a man. We took about thirty prisoners.

My captured horse, bright bay, is a perfect beauty. I also captured a splendid double-barreled shot-gun, the kind with which many rebels are equipped. I am sending it home to Bos [Boston Custer, Armstrong's youngest brother]. Write soon.

A new star had risen on the Southern firmament—General Robert Edward Lee. Under his leadership the railroad terminal seized by Custer for McClellan was disputed with severe loss of life on both sides. Then, by a brilliant feint, Confederate General Jackson, by threatening Washington, had weakened McClellan's army, causing General McDowell to be withdrawn from it in order to defend the capital. In June of 1862 at Malvern Hill, marked on the map by a heavy bloodstain, McClellan had succeeded in repulsing Lee. But Lee, undaunted, joined up with Jackson and in late August met up with General Pope—McClellan having been displaced—at Bull Run.

Pope's defeat brought about McClellan's reinstatement. Then he engaged Lee at Antietam, emerging victor after great carnage.

Custer to Mr. and Mrs. Reed, September (?), 1862, from Virginia:
After about two weeks in Washington we set out on the present campaign which lasted about fifteen days, during which more has been accomplished than in the same period before. . . . We have fought three battles, one the greatest ever fought on this continent. General McClellan, after quietly submitting to the dastardly attacks of his enemies, by his last campaign in Maryland has put it beyond the power of the most lying to injure him . . . enemies who from lack of patriotism, or from cowardice, or both combined, have remained at home instead of coming forward to fight for their country.

As for that newspaper man whose name McClellan says he does not remember, if I met him I would horsewhip him.

Your loving Brother Armstrong.

Youthful loyalty might have inspired this partisanship, but in later years Custer expressed in print his continued unshaken belief in McClellan's leadership: "Had he been adequately supported. . . ."

During that summer of ferocious strife there was for Custer one pleasant interlude of friendship between North and South. The incident was told after Custer's death by one of his fellow officers, who later became Colonel Woodruff:

One of Custer's West Point Classmates, known as "Gimlet" Lea—later the Revd. John W. Lea, Rector of Trinity Church, Martinsburg, W. Va.,—was wounded on May 5th [1862] at Williamsburg, and left a prisoner on our hands. And Custer was good to him, as only a gallant soldier can be, to a captive.

When our army advanced Lea was cared for by some Southern ladies. In August of that year, when our forces were being withdrawn from the James River, returning by that route Custer, then a Captain on McClellan's staff, sought out his old friend. He found Lea a prisoner

on parole from Fortress Monroe, staying with the ladies who had be-
friended him, and about to be married to a daughter of the house. They
begged Custer to act as groomsman, which he did, in his U. S. Union
blue, Lea in a new uniform of Confederate gray.

The date of the wedding was advanced to suit the visitor, to
whom the kindly McClellan had granted a leave that would include
a brief honeymoon, the army being inactive at the time.

Bride and bridesmaid, Custer wrote the Reeds, were the prettiest
girls he ever had seen, attired simply in white with wreaths of natural flowers to crown their loveliness. Cousin Maggie at the piano
warbled "For Southern Rights, Hurrah!" challengingly, while Custer, laughing, turned the leaves; nor did "Dixie" seem to disturb him.

Custer to Mr. and Mrs. Reed, September, 1862, from Virginia:
The approach of the rebel army to Williamsburg and the departure
of our army rendered a longer stay dangerous . . . *in more ways than
one.* Lea has been exchanged, and is now back again in the rebel forces,
fighting for what he *supposes* to be right!

*Custer to Mrs. Reed, September 27, 1862, from Headquarters, Army
of the Potomac, between Sharpsburg and Harper's Ferry:*
My Darling Sister—After I get back to Monroe I do not intend to
eat hard bread, salt pork, nor drink coffee without milk—fashionable
dishes in the army.
Enclosed I send you a small strip of silk which I tore from a rebel
flag at the battle of the Antietam, pronounced "An-tee-tam," an Indian
name.
Yesterday I accompanied a rebel Colonel, a Lieutenant and several
prisoners, under a flag of truce inside rebel lines. I found several who
were acquainted with my classmates and friends . . . and we had an
hour's social chat, discussing the war in a friendly way. And we exchanged cards.

McClellan's Fabian policy was displeasing to Washington—to the
very authorities who had weakened his military strength. Richmond was still untaken. Officially thanked, at the close of the year
he was relieved of his command. Idolized, no less, by officers and
men, he could have seized power and formed an independent unit

to fight the enemy. But McClellan was a soldier. He bade his ad-
herents remember that their allegiance was not to a man but to a
nation, to the Union they were fighting to preserve in its integrity.
He set a noble example.

McClellan set about drawing up a full account of his stewardship.
Later he would need the assistance of the most efficient of his staff,
which as yet was not officially disbanded; but for the present Custer was still a captain of Volunteers "awaiting orders." He went
homing to Monroe.

The Custer family would move in installments from New Rumley, Ohio, to Monroe, Michigan, and it is with this city and state
that Custer's name is most closely identified. The Reed farm was a
second home to him. And in Monroe he was to find his wife.

Grown to full manhood, Custer was well over medium height
now, lean, well built, well proportioned. His features were strong,
his nose aquiline. His eyes were deep sapphire blue, quick, alert.
Of exceptional vigor, he had been the second strongest man in his
class at West Point. Joseph Fought has written: "He was always an
arresting figure, causing enquiry about him." A fellow officer of
Custer's, Major Drew, when a young officer, had captured a magnificent sword from a Southerner, a Spanish blade of finely tempered
steel. He gave this to Custer as the only man in a group able to arch
it above his head without its snapping. Custer wore it only on dress
occasions—in the field he used a serviceable saber—but the motto
graven on it in Spanish, he adopted for his own: "Never draw me
without cause. Never sheathe me but with honor."

Custer's hair, worn long at times—and this was a hirsute age—
was red gold, curling strongly. That he is often represented with
"locks" was due to his being too busy, after his first engagement, to
seek a barber. The young dandies would cry out, "Haircut! Custer,
when are you going to get a haircut?"

"When you stop talking about it," he flung back.

Photographs of him in his later phase show him clipped with
military precision. He had outlived the New York *Herald's* lauda-
tion of "The Boy General With the Golden Locks" and was all
soldier.

At a reunion of the Army of the Cumberland a boy pushed forward to shake hands with Sheridan. He was the son of Representative Galloway of Ohio, an intimate of Lincoln. Before reaching Sheridan he paused, struck by the appearance of a staff officer standing motionless as a statue behind the great cavalry leader: "Who's that?"

"That? Why, Custer!"

"Custer? . . . He's beautiful!"

4: Libbie Bacon

"**L**IBBIE BACON has no mother! Poor motherless Libbie Bacon!" "How shamelessly I traded on this," Elizabeth confessed. "What an excuse I made of it for not doing anything I didn't want to do! And what excuses were made for me on that score!"

Mr. Bacon, after Elizabeth's consolatory stay of petting and spoiling at Grand Rapids, found the little girl "without gloom, without a murmur at her sad fate—and even happy!"

A privileged boarder at the Seminary, she had her own quarters—bedroom and parlor—with a view of both lake and town. She had her own belongings and a congenial teacher for her companion. As for lessons, she bartered her own facility in composition for solutions in arithmetic. If results were occasionally viewed with suspicion by instructors—"Well, Libbie Bacon has no mother!"

From this time the diary shows no restraint. We learn that her kind father was never far away. His gift of a basket of Bartlett pears was stolen by voracious classmates. One Sunday an interesting sermon by Mr. Ledoux was interrupted by outside cries of "Fire!" The worshipers fled, all but Principal Boyd and his maiden seminary flock, who remained seated. Suddenly the word "Seminary" was heard amid the other shouts, on which Mr. Boyd also fled, followed by his twittering girls. Young men assiduously put the fire out; it proved to be the work of a thieving housemaid whose loot-filled trunk was awaiting salvage. The diary smugly states, "She now is snugly lodged in jail."

Libbie made frequent visits to the home of Laura Noble, a classmate and her lifelong friend. Short holidays were spent with her father, and Libbie, being the child of a widowered "star boarder," never lacked motherly attentions. For long vacations she went to the aunts in Onondaga, where there were cousins and playmates.

Bronson Case, ten years her junior, was as a little brother through the years.

After five years of the seminary, Elizabeth felt ripe for change and coaxed her "kind Pa" to enter her in a school in Auburn, New York. Here she was domiciled with the principal's family in what was called "A Christian Home." This was pure travesty. The diarist learned how to brand herself "a creature of guilt, steeped in sin!" By nature healthy minded, she soon hurried back to the seminary.

Well on in adolescence, sociable, popular, attractive, Elizabeth presented a fresh problem to her father. He had promised Sophia on her deathbed that he would take her place with the child; but she was a child no longer, and Elizabeth was tired of being "farmed out"; she demanded a home of her own. Her father heard it rumored that Elizabeth was "having beaux."

"You must marry again, sir," said his friend Judge Blanchard of Tecumseh. This was not new advice, but Mr. Bacon had always felt that the very idea of it would be disloyal to a cherished memory. "I cannot decide," he wrote his sisters, adding needlessly, "I shall do nothing in haste." Possibly he would have done nothing but for Judge Blanchard. "I know the very lady for you," said the judge.

It was Rhoda, he explained, widow of Mr. Pitts, Congregational minister who had come from the East, too late, in search of health. Suitable age. Well fixed. Fine woman. Not objectionably intellectual, but intelligent, noted for sound good sense. As a housekeeper, perfect. Not a word in advance, but you shall see for yourself!

A pressing errand took Judge Bacon of Monroe to see Judge Blanchard of Tecumseh. The errand took the two gentlemen purposefully but not too hurriedly down the village street. Without slackening a step, without staring, Mr. Bacon could observe the trim exterior of a trim house, the spotless curtains, the shining panes; a neat garden, fit setting for its owner, a personable figure in starched calico, sun bonnet, and gloves who, scissors and watering pot in her hands, was encouraging and restraining her well-tended blooms.

Judge Blanchard doffed his hat in friendly salutation. Judge Bacon doffed his hat to the lady thus saluted by Judge Blanchard, and on their way they went. Next time, Judge Blanchard would crave permission to present his friend Judge Bacon of Monroe.

The old Bacon home on Monroe Street was dispossessed of tenants and refurbished. Some of the furnishings were supplied by the new wife, among them the bed; in it, Mr. Bacon humorously complained, he was forced to lie diagonally, since his predecessor had lacked some cubits of his stature. Elizabeth approved heartily of the new state of affairs but was enjoying herself too well to hurry home. In June, 1859, her father was writing her at the Sabin farm in Howlett's Hill, New York. After describing his "rheumatick difficulties" and the virtues of a new salve prescribed for them, he goes on about his domestic arrangements.

Mr. Bacon to Elizabeth, June, 1859, from Monroe, Michigan:
It is costing a good deal to repair the house, but I hope to meet the outlay without inconvenience. It is being done very handsomely and withal will be very convenient. I desire once more to be a housekeeper, as well for its luxuries as for its economies. I hope comfort and domestic happiness are in store for us all. Your mother fears your reluctance in leaving your Howlett's Hill friends will not make you as happy as she desires. She might have added that your indulgencies with those unrestrained aunts will not fully prepare you to be under a little control. Fortunately, however, she has borrowed no trouble on that account. All the ladies here feel that you and she will be sisters, getting on well together.

The "indulgencies" consisted in the carefree gatherings of kindly folk who earned their relaxations. Singing and dancing to the accompaniment of the fiddle, home-prepared refreshments, wholesome laughter, neighborliness—who could ask for better?

Mr. Bacon might chaff his wife for making him wait at the door while she ran back for an extra dab of powder on her nose, pink from hurrying, but he was proud of her fine appearance in beaded mantle as he escorted her to church. What if she did throw the windows wide with disdainful sniff for the class of visitors he encouraged? Retired from office as judge of probate, he would be sought out at his home by some woman in rusty black, a train of bedraggled children at her heels, who had come to ask his freely given advice about her poor affairs. Mr. Bacon knew his wife to be at heart charitable for all that. She would often tell him some such incident as this: "Mr. Bacon, when talking to Mr. L. this morning on his way from market, I noticed that his basket was *less* than *half filled!*" Upon this, a gift of produce from the Bacon farm would be sent to Mr. L., with a small check and expressions of neighborly good will.

With respect to Elizabeth, the second Mrs. Bacon broke all unlovely stepmother traditions. "Mother and I laugh and grow fat," the young girl wrote to Cousin Rebecca Richmond somewhat ruefully, since her waist bid fair to exceed the fashionable twenty-two-inch girth. Later, as a bride in Washington, she was to write fondly of her Monroe life.

Elizabeth to Mrs. Bacon, 1859 (?), from Washington:
How I miss my pleasant home! Those Sunday suppers with fire blazing . . . those juicy steaks, smoking muffins, all the delicacies my Mother knows so well to prepare. . . . And, oh, Mother, won't you send your child another cake? The last is finished to the least crumb and every scrap of icing. Oh, those Saturdays when, sniffing cake, I would steal into the pantry, and . . . I can see you there in your nice starched calicoes. Oh, I'm like a boarding-school girl when I get a box from home!

For remembrance of her own mother, "Libbie" had the wedding ring and a locket containing a device woven from her mother's hair in the fashion of the day.

In the family circle a shadowy presence was included. "As my former husband Mr. Pitts used to say" was so frequently on the lips of Mrs. Pitts-Bacon that father and daughter shared a twinkling sense of the late Mr. Pitts being a valued member of their group. And the calm portrait of Sophia looked down, as if in benediction.

Mrs. Bacon would not suffer her "Young Responsibility" to assume the slightest household task, so Elizabeth took up her studies again. They had been suspended a year, lest a cold cause her to "catch a consumption."

"I cannot understand how any girl can go through life without a Aim," Aunt Eliza Sabin was told. Marriage was axiomatic, the Aim an incidental to it. But Elizabeth was in no hurry. Life was too kind to her for her to desire a change. A swain had pronounced her "the prettiest girl in Monroe." In Monroe, famed for pretty girls! Her skin was of the white transparency of alabaster. Her cheeks were apple red. Her hair, luxuriant and wavy, was chestnut brown. Her features were well cut, following the pattern of Bacons and Pages both. And her eyes were the light gray-blue of Lake Erie.

The year 1861, of such overweening significance to the country at large, touched the young girl but lightly. She participated in local activities, sewing for soldiers' families and the like, but her main preoccupation was her coming graduation. A letter from Mr. Bacon at this time is in optimistic strain.

Mr. Bacon to his sisters in New York, 1861, from Monroe, Michigan:
Libbie was never so well and fleshy and full of fun and wit. She mourns past time misapplied, and fears she will not get first honors in examinations.

The house is very comfortable. We have a furnace. We live well, but not extravagantly, have company enough to keep us cheerful, and the *neatest house you ever saw.* I have no reason to complain of my family expenses which are less than for many previous years. My wife has means of her own with which she furnishes herself and things for the house. I am building a grape-arbor, and have to build a piazza at Elizabeth's request. I do all my chores, feed the cows, two pigs, make the fire in the furnace. I have a man to saw and split wood and store it.

We have hard times, and the worst is yet to come. I am as well off as my neighbors and ought not to complain. The war is not ended, but things look better. It is a formidable rebellion, and it will take time, lives, and treasure to put it down. From this city we have 1 company, 2 Lt. Cols., 3 Captains and other officers, also several privates in the field. We expect to hear a good account of them when the day of trial shall come.

Elizabeth to Aunt Eliza Sabin, spring, 1862, from Monroe, Michigan:
Only three months more and I am over school-digging forever. I wonder I have stood up under brain-work so well. June 23rd is The day.

I suppose Howlett's Hill shares the general wartime excitement. I am unpatriotic enough to feel glad that Father is too old, for he certainly

would have gone to fight for the Union. After all, dear Aunt, we all
have our battles in the march of life. Do you realize that I shall soon
bid adieu to the teens and enter on my august twenties?

Uncle Abel Page and cousins Rebecca and Mary Richmond
came for a visit that included The day. Mr. Bacon met them at the
depot with a carriage.

*Mr. Bacon to Mr. and Mrs. Richmond, June, 1862, from Monroe,
Michigan:*
You will permit me to say in all sincerity that yours are *extra* girls,
and like their mother.

I have told the girls that they may play and laugh to their hearts'
content, promenade, and walk in good weather. But must not ride
after fast horses, and no boat rides, and have as little to do with fast
young men as is consistent.

*Rebecca Richmond to Mr. and Mrs. Richmond, June, 1862, from
Monroe, Michigan:*
Though Uncle Bacon will not allow dancing in the house we have
a delightful time, singing, playing games, and promenading on the long
piazza.

Mrs. Bacon is an excellent wife, mother, housekeeper. She thinks as
much of Libbie as Libbie does of her. She is now preparing Libbie's
graduation dress.

Libbie has a splendid disposition and lovely temperament. I never
saw her superior in qualities that go to make up a noble woman. Her
parents never restrain her, but encourage her mimicries, drolleries and
schoolgirl gaieties.

*Rebecca Richmond to Mr. and Mrs. Richmond, June, 1862, from
Monroe, Michigan:*
The [commencement] exercises began at half-past ten in the morning, and lasted till nearly three. The eleven graduates wore white swiss
muslin, high in the neck, closed at the wrist. We were all proud of
Libbie. When it came to her valedictory there was scarcely a dry eye,
so many were there who had watched her through her motherless girlhood. Her father who sat on the platform was greatly affected. He is
a person of deep feeling.

Mr. Bacon to Mrs. Richmond, June, 1862, from Monroe, Michigan:
Thankful am I that I have been able to give Elizabeth an education, knowing what would have been the wishes of her mother. The presence of so many of that mother's friends brought vividly to remembrance her who is no more of earth.

Elizabeth to Mrs. Sabin, June, 1862, from Monroe, Michigan:
I had to curtesy to teachers, trustees . . . about fifty white-neck-clothed ministers, and then to the audience. My subject was very simple, and so was my style. I tried to read without airs, for I do so hate them in anybody. It is not boasting to tell my Aunt that everybody liked it. Father was greatly affected. He had an interest in founding the school, and was always anxious that I should graduate from it. The newspapers were very kind in their criticisms. That in the Detroit "Free Press" was best. I am sending you a copy.

Libbie came greatly to value her cousin Rebecca in the years ahead. In her diary she says:

Rebecca Richmond is twenty-three, a model girl who acts entirely from principle. Mary is quite a little flirt, and though a fine girl, hardly the equal of her sister.

Rebecca, well dowered and exceptionally attractive, with many suitors, never married. In her advanced years she was invalided and gave herself to good works. To her cousin Elizabeth Bacon Custer she left the interest for life on $10,000. This was a token of old-time affection; Mrs. Custer was affluent at her life's close.

Libbie Bacon was graduated now. She was pronounced by Trustee Noble "a thoroughly educated young lady" as he handed her the coveted diploma. Her main preoccupation from that time onward would be to find a husband—or, more modestly, to be found by a husband acceptable to herself and family. Home, thanks to the second Mrs. Bacon, was all that a young lady could desire. She took up painting in the interval between one security and another—she looked forward in marriage to the sheltered life. Even in wartime there were suitors aplenty in civilian occupations. A "beau" esteemed by Judge Bacon and rather favored by Libbie was "making property" in the real-estate business. (He turned out to be a "villyain.") As for military men, they were charming as admirers, but not to be taken seriously. Why, a man in uniform might be disabled, thrown back on one's hands physically, mentally—a derelict, even!

Libbie had one or two civilians in mind—hardly in her heart. But there was no hurry. Life was very pleasant. The war was far away. Young men in uniform did pass through Monroe, and ladies did give them Havelock cap covers. Judge Bacon made speeches about the Union and the Flag and subscribed to charities for the war bereft.

It was not long before the war was, by slow but impressive degrees, brought home to Libbie and her gay group. Families were in mourning, the wounded were returning. No, one must not be so foolhardy as to marry a soldier.

So passed Libbie Bacon's first and only free summer, emancipated from education in June, 1862, and being not yet bound in marriage. For such freedom she was prepared to pay tribute on Thanksgiving Day.

But at Thanksgiving, security, property, creature comforts, well being . . . all gave way when she met and loved and was loved by a young soldier, George Armstrong Custer.

5: Courtship

CUSTER MET the girl who was to become his wife at a Thanksgiving party given by Principal and Mrs. Boyd at the Seminary. They were not wholly unknown to each other by name. Miss Bacon was something of a local belle, and Custer was much in the public eye. The families had not been acquainted, even though they were near neighbors on the same street, because social life followed church affiliation. The Reeds were Methodists, the Bacons Presbyterians.

Neither Custer nor Miss Bacon had sought an introduction to the other. Their meeting was pure chance. There is a legend which, however, should be disposed of here. Too tenuous for print, it is iterated in inaccurate biographies. The legend is that "Custer married his childhood sweetheart." A little girl, the story goes, was swinging on the gate of her father's house when she noticed a schoolboy passing. To show off, for she had heard he was half brother to Mrs. David Reed farther up the street, she called after him, "Hi, you Custer boy!" Then, abashed, for she was well brought up, she turned and fled into the house.

A year after the Thanksgiving party at the Boyds', they commemorated their first meeting. It was to be their custom always to exchange letters on this anniversary whenever during their twelve years of married life they were separated.

Elizabeth to Custer, Thanksgiving, 1863, from Monroe, Michigan:
To-night is anniversary of our first meeting. Just a year ago you and your little girl bowed heads in formal introduction. I suppose it was *willed* that we should meet for when D wanted to bring us together either I was engaged or you were out of reach. So we should have gone away strangers. . . . Only I was fearfully vexed with Conway Noble over some trifle . . . and when to propitiate me he said "Shall I in-

troduce Captain Custer?" I assented merely to be rid of him . . . for I had taken refuge in "Greenland's icy mountains." And what we said I am dying to know for I remember nary a word.

It was a cardinal rule in Deportment in that day never to suffer a bashful swain to flounder conversationally. Miss Bacon had one infallible lifeline, flattering to male vanity: "And what do you *really* think of Higher Education for Women?" But that night she had no recourse to circumlocution, for the young man, though shy and reticent, seemed simple and direct.

"I believe your promotion has been very rapid?"

"I have been very fortunate."

And that was all, or nearly all.

Custer to Elizabeth:

My heart could have told her of a promotion far more rapid in her power only to bestow. How I watched her every motion, and when she left . . . in that throng of youth and beauty she had reigned supreme . . . when she left Armstrong Custer went home to dream. . . .

I was not ignorant of her father's proclivities, of the well-nigh insurmountable obstacles. . . .

Elizabeth to Custer:

Next day I was going into Miss Milligan's with a coat over my arm to have her alter it when I saw you coming down the street. . . . After I had rung her bell I turned . . . and there you were, looking at me. . . . We had only met that once. . . . But, oh, how pleased I was.

Elizabeth to Custer, August 14, 1864:

We had forbidden ourselves to speak on account of Father. . . . But from my corner in our pew I could see a mass of handsome curls in Mrs. Paulding's pew. . . . You looked *such things* at me.

In the dressing-room at the Seminary how little did I think my fate would be sealed. . . . I thought how prettily the other girls looked. Anna had on the sweetest rose-colored tarletan. I never had evening dresses of white or colored tarletan, only plain brown skirt and lace waist. . . . Yet without the least intention I captured the greatest prize of all.

Though no doubt equally vain in some things I never spent half the time adorning myself that they did. Yet I had all the attention I desired—and more than they wanted me to have, I know.

Yet had I tried to look beautifully or be'fascinating you would not have liked me—as you did.

When I think how in those few minutes you could have made up your mind about me, and how you made the only impression that went below the surface of my seemingly impressionable heart it is a miracle. And yet, I confess, I find you fascinating.

"Her father's proclivities . . . insurmountable obstacles. . . ." The field of battle was far away, but the come-and-go of war was all-pervading. Uniformed youths passed through Monroe and ladies graciously gave them Havelock cap covers wrought by their own hands. Hospitality kept open house for lads volunteering or inducted into military service.

Mr. Bacon to his sister Charity, 1862, from Monroe, Michigan:
Libbie like her Aunt Harriet has many suitors, many of the mustached, gilt-striped and Button kind, more interesting to her than to me. My wife and I have a great deal of anxiety about her, but I expect this is true of all parents of fanciful girls.

He complains also that his wife and daughter both are so fond of society that their home at times is almost like a tavern. As for the military beaux, he was often heard to exclaim to Mrs. Bacon, "Oh, Wifey, Wifey! One of those mustached, gilt-striped and Button critters will get our Libbie yet!"

Elizabeth writes Cousin Rebecca that she has "the escort of one of General McClellan's staff whenever I put my nose out of doors . . . Captain Custer." Mr. Bacon heard of this and feared it might be serious. Custer . . . a fine military record.

But how about character? Taxing his memory, he recalled, a few years before, as he was about to enter his house, seeing a tall figure weaving uncertain steps along the street. He recognized it for young Custer. Entering, he deplored the matter to his wife, who, however, thought nothing of it. Libbie had not seen it, nor would it have mattered to her, for Custer was but a name to her, and she was not unused in her own group to young men being "politely tight" on occasion. But Judge Bacon was of those who believe that to endue a youth with his country's uniform is to transform him into a Galahad.

Had Judge Bacon but known it, the youth, however wobbly his legs, was turning a resolute back on temptation for all time. And enquiry among the judge's cronies assured him that no young man in the place bore a higher reputation than young Custer. Unwittingly the lovers themselves furnished the judge with a weapon. Custer was a trifler . . . fickle.

It might have been Annette Humphrey's suggestion. To divert gossip from Libbie, Custer was urged to squire some other young lady home from singing school. At this moment, Fanny, returned from a visit, fastened a predatory eye on the personable young officer . . . Fanny, who recited too dramatically to be a "perfect lady." It was harmless: Fanny's real affections lay elsewhere, and Custer was not given to trivial sentimentalities. But it reached Mr. Bacon's ears, and he viewed it with genuine concern. Even Libbie was none too pleased with the course she herself had sanctioned.

Elizabeth to Rebecca Richmond, 1862, from Monroe, Michigan:
Fanny is finding her match in flirting with Captain Custer. I guess she don't know of his attentions elsewhere before she returned.

Laura Noble was staying in New York at this time.

Elizabeth to Laura Noble, 1862, from Monroe, Michigan:
Ma Chère Amie. . . . *I don't care for him* except as an escort. He just passed the house and I couldn't forbear making a sketch of him for you.

Opposition to a military marriage for Elizabeth came also from a kinsman, Albert Bacon, associated with the judge's business enterprises and sometimes a member of the household. Albert was engaged to a girl in Lansing, and his feeling for Libbie, therefore, may be regarded as cousinly. He had never met Custer. But the atmosphere at home was heavy with disapproval. First Custer simply was not invited to the house. Then Elizabeth was forbidden to invite him or to have anything further to do with him.

Parental control was most rigid at that time, and the growing generation was becoming somewhat resentful of it. But Elizabeth was most dutiful, and cheerfully so; she was all that a girl of good upbringing could be, even though she might have felt some inward chafing with respect to the restraints imposed by the judge, who was sixty-five then and ultraconservative. And his daughter was twenty-one and in love.

What might have become a crisis in the father-daughter relationship came when Elizabeth was in Toledo, making a return visit to Annie Cotton, who had been staying with her. A party was to be given by friends, and Elizabeth, having accepted, sent home for suitable attire. It was forwarded, but Mr. Bacon could not resist the opportunity to moralize in a letter on the unwisdom of attending parties while she was away from home. Elizabeth's reply is admirable.

Elizabeth to Mr. Bacon, 1862, from Toledo, Ohio:
My dear Father—Your letter has damped me considerably about the party. If you did not wish me to go why did you send my things? I think Mother, who wants me to enjoy myself supremely, was instrumental in having them so kindly sent.

Mr. Cotton has ordered the hack for the party. I am to call for Mary Hamilton. We are to go together.

I have heard Gough lecture on "Temperance" and was delighted. Gottschalk and Patti's concert was beyond words. I was entranced. If you knew how much you would rejoice in having the power to afford me such a privilege.

Father, I told Mother to tell you of my interview with Captain Custer. I never had a trial that made me feel so badly. I did it *all for you.* I like him very well, and it is pleasant always to have an escort to depend on. But I am sorry I have been with him so much, and you will never see me in the street with him again, and never at the house except to say Good-bye. I told him never to meet me, and he has the sense to understand. But I did not promise *never* to see him again. But I will not cause you any more trouble, be sure.

You have never been a girl, Father, and you cannot tell how hard a trial this was for me. At the depot he assisted Annie Cotton just as much as he did me.

And Monroe people will please mind their own business, and let me alone. If the whole world Oh'd and Ah'd it would not move me as does your displeasure.

Do not blame Captain Custer. He has many fine traits and Monroe will yet be proud of him.

I did not go with him from Singing School last Monday, and *seven* people asked Mrs. Paulding what was the trouble between Libbie and Captain Custer.

I wish the gossipers sunk in the sea. It would give me great pleasure to know that you place entire confidence in me—Your affectionate daughter Libbie.

Her New Year's letter to Rebecca mentions Custer only in a postcript.

Elizabeth to Rebecca Richmond, January, 1863, from Monroe, Michigan:
I had anticipated a dull Christmas, but was pleasantly disappointed. O Rebecca, lucky girl, you had an album in your stocking. In spite of all my hints I am albumless. D had four given her. Four.

New Year's Day, fewer gentlemen than usual called, so many families are in mourning. I do think it bad taste—excessive gaiety, balls and parties, when surrounded by suffering. Our neighbor city Toledo is said to be more than usually gay.

I appeared in my Christmas present, a blue merino. I stood in a corner of the room and said forty times "It is a pleasant day for calling," and heard forty gentlemen reply, "Yes, overhead. But unpleasant underfoot." There was more walking than usual. And less "cramming" or showing the effects of "cramming" through walking. He is decidedly temperate who resists imbibing at every house he calls at.

Our callers were very pleasant gentlemen, fewer dull ones than usual. Captain Custer. . . .

In April, 1863, Custer received unofficial notice that he would shortly be called into service again. The war machine could relieve commanders of their command but could not dispense with junior officers of tested ability. He set off for Washington immediately, stopping off in New York to assist McClellan in compiling his report—a voluminous one—of his conduct of the Army of the Potomac.

But before he left Monroe something occurred that taxes credibility. He struck up a warm personal friendship with Judge Bacon.

The Humphrey House served largely as a club, particularly for citizens elderly and eminent. The judge was intrigued by a young officer, center of a highly interested group plying him with war questions, which he answered with such sound sense—for he had evidently been an active participant in field operations—as to constitute him an authority.

"Bravo . . . capital," the judge applauded. "But who is he?"

His crony Levi Humphrey suppressed amusement, for he had heard from Nettie of the thwarted romance. "That? Why, Armstrong Custer!"

"I must know him. Introduce me, please!"

First-hand news from the battlefield! What an opportunity! That little flurry with Elizabeth was forgotten. Judge Bacon assimilated Custer, appropriated him, initiated a correspondence with him, wrote him when the young soldier was recalled to service.

Custer to Mr. Bacon, May 20, 1863, from 2nd Brigade, 1st Division, 5th Army Corps, Virginia:

Judge Bacon—Dear Sir—I am gratified you are still in favor of our beloved General McClellan who, when all others are tried, will be found our only hope. Although by politicians abused, dishonored, disgraced, he will yet come forth. If in command without interference from persons intending to do right, but whose plans are the ruin of the Army, every soldier will follow, for he is no blind guide.

A year ago McClellan was under the very walls of the enemy's stronghold, Richmond—had made his way through impassable roads, driving the enemy away. Every man able to hold a musket should have been sent to support him, but he was left in a most perilous position. We should have been annihilated without McClellan to lead us.

Closing I would respectfully ask for a line—a letter from you will always be an honor to me.

The order taking McClellan's staff from him was published. Custer, 1st Lieutenant, U. S. Army, was ordered to report to his own company, with General Hooker in command.

Hooker's first task was to reorganize the Army of the Potomac, sadly confused by changes of leadership. Also he unified the cavalry corps in three divisions under Pleasanton, Gregg, and Averill.

General Pleasanton at once invited Custer on his staff, but at first Custer refused, out of loyalty to McClellan. Then better counsels prevailed, and he accepted, even as McClellan would have wished him to do. He became a prime favorite with his new leader.

Custer to Mrs. Reed, May, 1863, from Virginia:
Everyone should live in a tent, during the summer months at least. There would be less sickness, more enjoyment of health. You need have no anxiety about my food, sister. I live with the General. He sends daily to Baltimore for fresh fruit and vegetables—radishes, onions and —*fine Tomatoes.* The General has a negro cook; her husband waits on table. I call her "Aunt Hannah." Em, how would you like to see your Aunt? She does not wear hoops. She does wear a colored handkerchief about her head. You see we don't go hungry when not moving or fighting.

I am sorry to hear of Mrs. Bacon's illness. Libbie is the most devoted daughter . . . has the sweetest disposition. There are not a dozen young ladies in Monroe of whom I think so highly . . . such good sense. . . .

"Em" was Emma, one of the Reed children. As for that guarded praise of Libbie, both man and maid, through pride, at this time were masking their real feelings since unable publicly to avow them.

Thenceforth Mrs. Reed was to hear less frequently, while Nettie Humphrey would get constant news from the battlefield, with the tacit understanding that the letters were intended for Elizabeth's perusal.

Custer to Annette Humphrey, May 26, 1863, from Virginia:
. . . . With a party of 75 men, cavalry, I went by steamer down the Potomac River after dark. Next day, at 11, we landed on the banks of the Yocomico. Mounting, we made a rapid dash of forty miles in five

hours, coming in sight of the Rappahannock near Urbana. We hid in the woods till next morning. With 9 men and an officer in a small canoe I started in pursuit of a small sailing-vessel. . . . After a chase of ten miles down stream we compelled our game to run their boat aground. The crew jumped overboard and reached the shore. We captured boat and passengers. They had left Richmond the previous morning and had in their possession a large sum of Confederate money. A party of six, two of them young ladies, Jewish.

With four of my men I went ashore. The river was so shallow for three hundred yards near shore we had to wade.

As we approached the nearest house, a fine country residence I observed a man, in Confederate uniform, lying on the piazza, book in hand, reading, back toward us. I thought it might be a trap. When we were within a few feet of him he saw us. I told him he was my prisoner. He said there were no other rebel soldiers in the house. He had just come home for a short visit. When I entered and told his sisters it was my painful duty to take their brother away I thought how distressed my own dear sister would have been in like case. He had been reading Shakespeare, "Hamlet," the famous soliloquy. He and I had a hearty laugh over his literary pursuits.

Then, with twenty men, in three small boats, I rowed to Urbana on the opposite shore. Here we burned two schooners and a bridge over the bay, driving the rebel pickets out of town. We returned to the north bank where we captured 12 prisoners, thirty horses, two large boxes of Confederate boots and shoes, and two barrels of whiskey *which we destroyed.*

For the lady prisoners I pressed into service a family carriage, horses and driver. We marched till two that night, to avoid pursuit and capture, then camped till morning. We reached our boats about noon on Saturday, and arrived on Sunday morning without having lost a man.

General Hooker sent for me and complimented me very highly on the success of my expedition and the manner in which I had executed his orders. He said it could not have been better done, and that he would have something more for me to do.

In June a Michigan paper extolled Custer's gallant part in the battle of Aldie:

A crucial struggle . . . the Confederates pressing northward. Governor Curtin of Pennsylvania had issued a proclamation . . . the invasion of the State. Lee was there . . . Stuart's Cavalry coming up to join him. Hooker was sending detachments to block routes likely to be attempted by the enemy. Then Kilpatrick's Brigade ran into a Confederate Brigade about to make its way through Ashby's Gap. Reserves were giving advantage to Stuart's redoubtable cavalry, while Kilpatrick's body consisted largely of raw recruits, many of the regiments seeing service for the first time. Back and forth went the tide of battle, until a wavering, the moment preceding panic, came . . . that only a master-stroke, an inspired gesture could avert. . . . Kilpatrick went forward to face the fire, so, too, Col. Douty . . . and still. . . . Suddenly a young officer of Pleasanton's staff came up at gallop. Waving his broad-brimmed hat he shouted "Three cheers for General Kilpatrick!" On which. . . .

Captain Custer has been strongly recommended to Governor Blair by Generals Burnside, Stoneman, Humphrey, Copeland, Stahl and Pleasanton. . . . General Hooker asserts that we have not a more gallant man in the field, and that wherever there is a daring expedition or hard fighting to be done he is always among the foremost.

The hat was a Confederate soft felt that Custer had picked up and appropriated, the Regulation cap never staying on his head. His skin was the thin kind that scorches and burns, needing protection from the sun.

"How fortunate that Governor Blair had nothing for you," his friend Judge Christiancy wrote Custer some years later. "Every step of your remarkable advancement has been due to your own merit, without favor . . . often in the face of opposing influences, often of political origin."

Rallying, cheering, Kilpatrick's column made a dash, swept everything before it. But Custer came near an untimely end.

Account in a Michigan paper:
Outstripping his men in pursuit of the enemy, one of them turned, fired, but missed, his revolver being knocked by a sword blow that sent the rider toppling to the ground. Another enemy trooper tore alongside, but Custer, giving his horse a sudden check, let the man go shooting by. Then face to face they fought it out, gray going down before the blue.

Now Custer found himself surrounded, cut off from his own men.

Turning his horse "Harry" toward his own lines, he made a dash for safety. But not till then was he recognized for a union man. The hat had saved him.

He paused in his flight to pick up his first assailant who suffered himself to be taken, "a willing prisoner."

This success for his cavalry brought Pleasanton promotion to major general. "Which," as Custer blithely wrote, "makes me a Captain again!"

In those tragic days at Gettysburg he is heard of importantly. That Independence Day should be so commemorated brings to mind what Custer wrote Judge Bacon, "Throughout the war I never heard slavery mentioned as an issue. The Union—it was the Union we were fighting for!"

6: Brigadier General

A T THE first opportunity George Armstrong wrote Mrs. Reed the news already made public by the press.

Custer to Mrs. Reed, July 26, 1863, from Headquarters, 3rd Division Cavalry, Amosville, Virginia:

You have heard of my good fortune . . . promotion to a Brigadier-General. I have certainly great cause to rejoice. I am the youngest General in the U. S. Army by over two years, in itself something to be proud of. My appointment dates from the 20th of June.

I have been through many dangers since I last wrote you. I was in the battle near Gettysburg, and in many cavalry fights. I had three horses shot under me; one was "Roanoke." I have had the post of honor ever since the army crossed into Virginia—that is, I have held the advance with my Division.

Just as McClellan had learned to rely on the "scope and accuracy" of information brought him by Custer, so now did General Pleasanton. Custer was distinguished for his initiative, and such leaders were needed among the younger men. When, after Aldie, Pleasanton sent in the names of men strongly recommended by him for promotion, Captain Custer's was among the foremost.

Joseph Fought gives a first-hand account of how Custer received the news. Fought, it will be recalled, was the boy bugler who at their first meeting had felt some sort of affinity between himself and the young lieutenant who was looking around the Washington stables for a horse. Fought had accompanied Custer to Centreville, riding at some distance behind to avoid attracting enemy attention. During the following year he had so managed his assignments as to be as near as possible to Custer. The latter, valuing Fought's qualities, appointed him his orderly while on Pleasanton's staff.

Joseph Fought's account:

. . . . Someone said I was wanted at Headquarters [Pleasanton's]. It was a great surprise to see him [Custer] there. He said "I am going to be right here, and I want you with me."

He was very careful of our defences. He made it a point not to depend on others in placing pickets, but saw to it himself. In consequence we were often out together at all hours of the night, and ran terrible risks.

Genl. Pleasanton, a very active officer, was always anxious to be posted about what was doing in front of him. He himself could not be in front all the time, and in that respect his Trusties were more valuable to him than his brigade commanders.

If Lt. Custer observed that it was important to make a movement or charge he would tell the commander to do it, and the commander would have to do it, would not dare question, because he knew Lt. Custer was working under Genl. Pleasanton who would confirm every one of his instructions and movements.

Lt. Custer was obliged to be always on the alert.

He was always in the fight, no matter where it was. I was in the rebel lines many times with him. They would look us over, but I would deceive them, and they would search me and say they would do something to me, but I always managed to escape them.

We were in camp at Warrington Junction when it was discovered that the Rebel Cavalry was consolidating at Beverly Ford, preparing to join Lee's forces on the other side of the Blue Ridge, and enter Pennsylvania. It was early in the morning when the fighting began, right above Rappahannock Station.

Lt. Custer and I crossed the Ford and took the inside of the field. There were two or three Rebels near the woods, but we clipped along towards them, and they fired at us, and we fired back. One kept on in the road, and the Lt. said I shot him, and I said he did. The others got back to the woods.

We rode on through the woods, and met our advance guard, Col. Davis and his command, and reported to him.

All at once we saw the Rebels coming in a body, full speed, and we met them in the narrow road. One rode straight up to Col. Davis and shot him dead.

Lt. Custer's horse and mine had never been in a fight before, and they rammed themselves into a fence and would not budge, but just stood together and neighed. Finally we got them turned. But the Rebels had discovered us. The 8th New York had broken and retreated. The Rebels and we charged together. Our regiment had rushed to the stone wall, knowing the thing to do was to hold it. Lt. Custer and I put spurs to our horses at the same moment, expecting to go down any minute. My horse took the wall, but the Lieutenant was long-legged and his horse not large, and he fell in going over, but was up again immediately. And next our regiment was picking the rebels off their horses.

We saw a Battery on the hill and found that it was Robinson's. We rode up to it, and Lt. Custer told of Col. Davis's death. It was a great shock.

We had to make a great fight for it, but we held that stone wall. [This was before Aldie. Fought's narrative continues.]

The next move was of the cavalry, Col. Merritt's regiment. Custer and I had the lead. We all got across the road and charged a force of rebels, five times our number. At one point we thought we should have to run, but we captured a good many and pushed the others back, driving them towards Brandy Station. About noon we came to a church.

The next thing learned was that they were on their way to Edward's Ferry, then on to Lebanon. Genl. Pleasanton looked the field over, and decided to keep track of them, and, if necessary, give them battle. Accordingly he made a move toward Aldie, parallel with them. At Aldie we ran into them. Custer and I went across, and got back before they were ready to fire.

We then went to Middleburg and Upperville.

At Upperville, Virginia, at the foot of the Blue Ridge, there was a reorganization of the Union forces. Custer is next heard of importantly in command of his own brigade at Gettysburg. He was twenty-three and a half and had under him thousands of men, many of whom were gray-haired veterans. There have been several accounts of the way he received his promotion; we will give it in the plain words of his devoted orderly.

Fought's account:

He started out and hunted for me. When he found me he had the paper in his hand and said, "I have been made a Brigadier-General."

"The deuce you have," I said.

"Yes," he said, and then he read it to me. I shook hands with him. Nobody knew it was going to happen. It was a great surprise.

He said, "How am I going to get something to show my rank?"

"Well," I said, "the rebels have just gone through here and have robbed and threatened everybody. But I will see what I can do."

I went through every place where they kept such things, and found scraps for uniform furnishings, but no stars. Finally, late in the night I found an old Jew and in his place he had a box of things belonging to a uniform and some stars. I bought two, then went back and found the Captain in his room at Headquarters. He was glad to have the stars—but who would sew them on? And where could we get needle and thread? I scratched around and got them, and sewed them on, one on each corner of his collar.

The next morning he was a full-fledged Brigadier-General.

All the other officers were exceedingly jealous of him. Not one of them but would have thrown a stone in his way to make him lose his prestige. He was way ahead of them as a soldier, and that made them angry.

In his new assignment as commander of the "Michigan Brigade" Custer evolved for himself the uniform, part regulation, part personal, by which for the rest of the war he would be known.

Fought's account:

He wore a velveteen jacket with five gold loops on each sleeve, and a sailor shirt with a very large collar that he got from a gunboat on the James. The shirt was dark blue, and with it he wore a conspicuous red tie—top boots, a soft hat, Confederate, that he had picked up on the field, and his hair was long and in curls almost to his shoulders.

"The Boy General," many of the newspapers took to calling him; in some instances, romantically, not derisively, "The Boy General With the Golden Locks." The men of his command copied the red tie. Fought and a few other devotees sported the flowing locks.

Fought's account:

One day when I was back in my regiment Lt. Hastings came up to me and said, "Have your hair cut. You are not with Custer now." All the boys laughed but I did not have my hair cut. A few days later he asked me if there was not a barber in the command. I made no reply.

Next day came an order for the men with the best horses to leave camp and go on the road. Soon we met a party approaching, and who should it be but the General [Custer] and his staff in charge of an expedition. The men of my party took no chances, and kept me in between fours, for fear I should leave them. Then, when we were a few miles along the road there came an order from Lt. Hastings that I should get out of there and report to Custer. I was overjoyed. He and I had a hearty laugh. . . . I told him I had saved my hair.

While Custer was on Genl. Pleasanton's staff there never was any trouble about my being with him. But when he would leave they would send after me, right or wrong. Pete Boehm and I were persistently with him on every occasion. Pete also ran away from his regiment and joined the General.

Even before the stars were sewn to his collar, Custer had begun to select his staff, as Pleasanton had instructed him to do. Custer chose the men he could depend on to be near him. Accordingly the irregularities of which Fought speaks were straightened out. Peter Boehm, who was to have his arm shattered at Winchester, went with him. So also did Fought, who had so many horses shot under him that he lost count. A waif named Johnny, who had adopted Custer with the prescience of a stray dog, helped care for his horses. Custer, no longer a staff officer messing at General Pleasanton's table, needed a cook; to answer this need came Eliza. This loyal Negress, having learned of the new dispensation by which people of her race were no longer to be regarded as chattels, left the plantation on which she had been reared to have a look at this "freedom business." She "jined up with the Ginnil" and became a figure of no minor importance in the Custer story.

A bravura act such as turning the tide of battle in favor of General Kilpatrick would have been but an empty gesture had it not rested on a sound basis. It required a special brand of leadership which knew what it was about and which could inspire *esprit de corps*. This was the task confronting the newly made brigadier. In carrying it through successfully, he displayed such imagination and initiative that military experts have credited Custer with demonstrating the validity of using cavalry as a weapon of aggression during a charge, with dismounted skirmishers in a defensive stand.

His name appears with credit in all the reports of the operations of
the summer of 1863.

Meanwhile, Custer's courtship of Miss Bacon was conducted by
correspondence with "Friend Nettie." This was Annette Humphrey, a born confidante. One suspects her, not unkindly, of enjoying her role. In her letters to "Friend Armstrong," Elizabeth appears as "she." Custer is never allowed too abundantly to hope nor
too utterly to despair. The point was to keep him in suspense but to
hold him irrevocably—which was all the poor young man himself
desired for the time being. In his absence a girl named Fanny was
not idle. Armstrong had been warned by Annette of her activities
and challenged to defend himself.

*Custer to Annette Humphrey, July 19, 1863, from Headquarters, 3rd
Division Cavalry Corps, Bloomfield, Virginia:*
Friend Nettie—I have halted my column to feed their horses and
cook their dinner. While my staff are reclining on the grass in front of
a Secesh house I am inside, at a table, penning these few lines. I have
but a few minutes, as I intend to march several miles before night and to
attack the enemy cavalry early in the morning.

I now have command of a Division of Cavalry: Kilpatrick's, he being
gone home sick.

I was rejoiced to hear from you, Nettie, but I regret that Libbie
should suppose I had violated my promise to her in regard to her ambrotype. I never showed it, nor even described it, to Fanny. How
Fanny was able to describe it I cannot tell, unless she got the information from the picture gallery. You know her quickness in guessing. Tell
Libbie that Fanny *has nothing in her power to bestow that wd. induce
me to show her that ambrotype.* I know nothing of what representa-
tions of our intimacy she has made to Libbie. It is no different from
what I told her. I would write more, but must mount on my good horse
and away.

Please call on my sister and tell her that I am well.

P. S. Direct to Brigadier-General Custer, 3rd Brigade, 3rd Div. Cav.
Corps. Army of the Potomac.

I believe more than ever in Destiny.

From one of Custer's letters to Nettie we infer she has cautioned
him against an optimistic attitude.

Custer to Annette Humphrey, summer, 1863, from camp in Virginia:
When the time comes for me to give Her up I hope it will find me
the same soldier I now try to be—capable of meeting the reverses of
life as those of war. You know me well, yet you know little of my
disposition. Do not fear for me. I may lose everything, yet there is a
strange, indescribable something in me that would enable me to shape
my course through life, cheerful, if not contented.

There are no Custer letters about the military operations which
closed the Potomac as ferry for Lee.

*Custer to Annette Humphrey, August 13, 1863, from Headquarters,
Michigan Brigade, Hartwood Church, Virginia:*
Friend Nettie—We are living in magnificent style. The inhabitants
have long been without sugar, coffee and salt, and for these they exchange butter, milk, eggs and vegetables. Ladies young and old whose
husbands are in the rebel army come flocking to Headquarters, their
little baskets of produce on the arm.

My staff are all able and efficient officers, and also refined and companionable gentlemen. Captain Greene is doing admirably. I expected
him to make a good Adjutant-General, but he succeeds beyond expectation. I tried him the other day, took him where bullets flew thick
and fast. I watched him closely. He never faltered, was as calm and collected as if sitting at his dinner.

I do not expect an advance move of the army, not until filled up with
conscripts.

Did Judge Bacon think my promotion deserved or not? Or did he
maintain a dignified silence? The Government has been in the habit of
laying on the shelf all the unfortunate Generals who have failed to do
"just so." When I was a mere Lieutenant or Captain I was safe, but now
that I have changed the bars for a star I might for some mismanagement
be displaced, so that he has every reason for wishing me to succeed.

In the advance toward Culpepper, marked by lesser engagements,
during September a piece of shell killed Custer's horse and wounded
Custer painfully, though not seriously, in the thigh. This procured
him a leave of twenty days, which with time out for travel meant
a fortnight in Monroe.

Business just then brought Judge Bacon back to Monroe from

Traverse City, putting an end to Libbie's horseback riding and boating with "Albert Bacon's brother," a fortunate coincidence of which Libbie wrote Rebecca.

Elizabeth Bacon to Rebecca Richmond, fall, 1863, from Monroe, Michigan:

He [Custer] arrived in Monroe the day before we returned from Traverse. Mother did not come with us but went to visit relatives in Clinton, so Father and I boarded two weeks at the Humphrey House. Armstrong and Nettie had been intimate friends for a long time, so of course I saw him at once, because I could not avoid him. I tried to, but I did not succeed.

Elizabeth to Rebecca Richmond, fall, 1863, from Monroe, Michigan:

He proposed to me last winter, but I refused him more than once, on account of Father's apparently unconquerable prejudice. I never *even thought of marrying him.* Indeed I did not know I loved him so until he left Monroe in the spring.

Under a tree in the Bacon garden Elizabeth and George Armstrong Custer plighted their troth "till death do part." But marriage, even a formal engagement, must wait, she stipulated, until her father's ungrudging consent could be obtained. To this stipulation Custer agreed not unhopefully, for he and the judge were in the friendliest relations. But did that fact render him more desirable as husband for Elizabeth? A brigadier general was a greater military hazard than a captain, Mr. Bacon reasoned when to his consternation he learned that their springtime attraction had ripened unchangeably to the marrying point.

When it was conveyed to Judge Bacon that Custer intended to ask him formally for his daughter's hand, he pleaded sudden business and slipped out of town to Traverse City. Then, somewhat ashamed of himself, for he was fundamentally kind and just, he returned, but only in time to see Custer off at the railroad station. There, he contrived to keep the talk entirely in his own hands.

Custer to Annette Humphrey, October, 1863:

He spoke very encouragingly of my prospects and of the bright future he pictured for me. I had no opportunity to speak of that which lay nearest to my heart. . . . I only said that I had desired to speak to him, but that, being prevented, I would write. . . . To which he replied, "Very well!"

Custer to Annette Humphrey, October 7, 1863, from Baltimore:
In every city I pass through I see something to admire, and am struck with wonder at man's art and ingenuity in improving that which Nature already has made beautiful. But my heart turns longingly to our unassuming little town on the banks of the Raisin. . . . I have thought much of my intended letter to Libbie's father, my mind alternating between hope and fear—fear that I may suffer from some unfounded prejudice. . . . I feel that her father, valuing her happiness, would not refuse were he to learn from her own lips our real relation to one another.

Custer to Annette Humphrey, October 9, 1863, from Headquarters:
I arrived last evening and was welcomed in a style both flattering and gratifying. I feel that here, surrounded by my little band of heroes, I am loved and respected. Often I think of the vast responsibility resting on me, of the many lives entrusted to my keeping, of the happiness of so many households depending on my discretion and judgment—and to think that I am just leaving my boyhood makes the responsibility appear greater. This is not due to egotism, self-conceit. I try to make no unjust pretensions. I assume nothing I know not to be true. It requires no extensive knowledge to inform me what is my duty to my country, my command. . . . "First be sure you're right, then go ahead!" I ask myself, "Is it right?" Satisfied that it is so, I let nothing swerve me from my purpose.

Who adopts public opinion as guide cannot entertain one purpose long, for what pleases one will displease another.

Why have I written you this? You did not say it was not so. Please give these flowers to Libbie . . . they were plucked in front of Headquarters near the Rapidan.

Custer to Annette Humphrey, October 12, 1863, Headquarters, 3rd Brigade, 3rd Division Cavalry Corps, Morrisville, Virginia:
I was not with my Brigade 48 hours before we were engaged with the enemy. On Saturday I met their entire cavalry, at James City, with my entire command. We were quite successful, but had to fall back,

next morning, in obedience to orders. Our entire army was falling back to the north side of the Rappahannock, the rebel cavalry trying to out-flank us. Our cavalry had to cover the movement. Yesterday we passed through the greatest cavalry battle ever witnessed on this continent. The entire force of rebel cavalry under General Stuart attacked two Divisions—Buford's and Kilpatrick's—of ours, commanded by Pleasan-ton in person.

Oh, could you but have seen some of the charges that were made! While thinking of them I cannot but exclaim "Glorious War!"

The rebels greatly outnumbered us and had us completely sur-rounded. Their strongest force was placed directly between us and the ford we intended to cross. We had either to cut our way out or surrender—which we had no intention of doing. I was first to discover our situation, and so informed General Pleasanton that something had to be done and quickly. I volunteered to take my brigade and cut an opening to the River. He assented: "Do your best!" I then formed the 1st and 5th Michigan in two columns, ordered them, "Draw sabres!" then spoke a few words to my command . . . told the band to strike up "Yankee Doodle." I told them the situation frankly, of the great responsibility resting on them, and how confident I was that they would respond nobly to the trust reposed in them.

You should have heard the cheers they sent up.

I gave the command "Forward!" And I never expect to see a prettier sight. I frequently turned in my saddle to see the glittering sabres ad-vance in the sunlight. I was riding in front, Captain Greene's sabre in my hand. Captain Judson and Lts. Colensis and Granger by my side, and close behind me my new battle-flag so soon to receive its baptism in blood. Then came my orderlies, and behind them the regiments.

After advancing a short distance I gave the word "Charge!"—and away we went, whooping and yelling like so many demons.

My cap was so small I could not wear it, and was compelled to ride without it. This was about 2 P.M. From then till after dark it was charge upon charge. Sometimes entire Divisions would charge.

For a long time success seemed uncertain, but we finally opened a way to the river and began crossing, the rebels pressing, until ten at night.

I had two horses shot under me within fifteen minutes.

Lt. Granger's horse was shot, and his bridle cut close to his wrist. You may judge how desperate our position when I tell you that General

Pleasanton drew his sword and advanced with the charging columns. After the battle, speaking to my men, he said, "Boys, I saw your flag far in advance among the rebels." My color-bearer had his horse shot.

Heavy cannonading is going on a few miles to my right. A general engagement is expected to-morrow or in a few days. Give my love to Libbie, and tell her I thought of her so often during the battle yesterday.

A day's official report concluded, Custer squared elbows and wrote Judge Bacon.

Custer to Judge Bacon, October, 1863, from Headquarters, 3rd Brigade, 3rd Division Cavalry Corps, Virginia:
. . . . I had hoped for a personal interview. . . . It is true that I have often committed errors of judgment, but as I grew older I learned the necessity of propriety. I am aware of your fear of intemperance, but surely my conduct for the past two years—during which I have not violated the solemn promise I made my sister, with God to witness, should dispel that fear. You may have thought my conduct trifling after my visits to Libbie ceased, last winter. It was to prevent gossip. . . . I left home when but sixteen, and have been surrounded with temptation, but I have always had a purpose in life.

Annette, and Libbie through Annette, must be kept informed of army doings.

Custer to Annette Humphrey, October, 1863, from Bull Run:
We are now encamped on the Bull Run battlefield, where, as 2nd Lieutenant, I heard my first battle shot . . . under a stately oak that bears many a battle scar, surrounded by graves, many washed by rain so that skulls and skeletons are visible. We have just finished supper. Captain Judson and the Brigade Surgeon are starting a game of chequers. Lt. Granger is preparing the monthly reports (Capt. Greene's duty). . . . Capt. Pennington of the Battery is writing to his wife to whom he has been married but seven months. . . . Lt. Woodruff, also of the Battery, is writing to his father. Others are discussing the probabilities of a battle to-morrow. . . . There is heavy firing to the left. . . . I suppose my letter to Judge Bacon has been received.

Custer to Annette Humphrey, October 20, 1863, from Gainesville, Virginia:

Under very distressing circumstances I turn to you and *her* for consolation. It is for others that I feel. Yesterday, October 19th, was the most disastrous this Division ever passed through. We moved at daylight to attack the enemy. I had the advance and drove the rebels three miles. Then their entire cavalry under Generals Stuart and Fitzhugh Lee made a stand and prepared to charge my advance. They had the advantage in position. As soon as I discovered their immense superiority I sent a staff officer to Genl. Kilpatrick asking for assistance, but failed to get it, altho the other brigade was 3 or 4 miles in the rear, doing nothing. I then took my battery and 4 regiments, and succeeded in turning the enemy's flank so effectively as to drive him from his position. I followed for about a mile, then placed my command in position to await the arrival of the remainder of the command. Genl. Kilpatrick soon after rode up and complimented me: "Well done, Custer. You have driven them from a very strong position!" (I was aware of that, myself). All wd have been well if Genl. K had been content to let well enough alone. My scouts had informed me of heavy columns of infantry moving around on both my flanks, evidently intending to cut me off. I informed Genl. K. of this and advised him to guard against it, but he did not believe me, and ordered me to halt until the last Brigade passed me, then to follow it, on the road to Warrenton. Scarcely had the first brigade passed when the enemy made a vigorous attack from the direction I had foreseen, bringing both infantry and artillery against me, at the same time throwing a column between the first Brigade and mine, thus cutting me off from the main body. I held my ground until the last moment. The rebel infantry had charged my battery, nearly capturing the guns. Nothing but to retreat, which I did in good order. Now comes my trouble. Genl. K. without my knowledge, had detached Major Clark and one battalion of the 5th Michigan to skirmish in the woods. Had he given the order, as he should have done, through me, we should not now have to regret the loss of the Major and his entire battalion. Aside from this my Brigade has suffered but little in loss of men. One of Genl. K's staff officers ordered my Headquarters wagons to follow the other brigade, altho I had ordered them to go to the rear. As a consequence my wagons were captured along with those of Genl. K. and those of the 1st Brigade. Among other things Captain Greene's desk with his reports and my official reports of Gettysburg and other engagements & monthly and tri-monthly reports, &c.&c. So that yesterday was not a gala day for me. My consolation is that I was not responsible, but I cannot but regret the loss of so many brave men . . . all the more painful that it was not necessary.

I presume my letter to Judge Bacon has been received.

Custer to Annette Humphrey, October, 1863, from Gainesville, Virginia:

We have occupied our present camp three days, with favorable prospect of remaining here several days to repair our losses of the past few weeks, give our horses rest and forage, and fit ourselves for service.

I have been endeavoring to decide on a very important question, my interests seeming to point in one direction, my affections in another. Friends in Michigan and in Washington propose my being transferred to the South-west, promising a far larger command than I now have— a Division of Cavalry at least, all from Michigan, also my present Brigade, with two regiments now being raised in Michigan. In leaving I should leave those with whom I have what reputation I now have, who, acquainted with my standing as a military man, would overlook some blunder, were I to make one. Not so were I to go West. There I should have to have success unmarred for a considerable time, to establish myself. One advantage, however would be that Genl. Thomas, who commands Rosencranz's Army, is Colonel of my regiment in the regular army, and would give me every opportunity to acquire distinction. He could scarcely do more for me, however, than Genl. Meade and Genl. Pleasanton are willing to do. [In the summer of 1863 General Hooker had been replaced by General Meade. When Custer speaks of his regiment in the regular army, it is to be recalled that his brigadier general's commission was in the U. S. Volunteers.]

I do not believe a father could love his son more than Genl. Pleasanton loves me. He is as solicitous about me and my safety as a mother about her only child. You should see how gladly he welcomes me on my return from each battle. His usual greeting is, "Well, boy, I am glad to see you back. I was *anxious about you.*" He often tells me that if I risk my life so much he will place me in such a command that I shall never have the opportunity.

I received a letter in to-day's mail. . . . I tore it open, thinking it might bring intelligence of Somebody. But no. It was just from some New York publisher who informs me he is writing my biography, and wants portraits for engraving, autograph, data, documents, &c. and the address of some person who can give reliable information about me. I think I shall direct him to a young lady on Monroe Street who knows considerable about me, who could also furnish a likeness carried in a small pocket-case.

I am not surprised at Fanny's telling that my likeness is in her locket. I would be surprised at nothing she chooses to do. For myself I am indifferent, but I hope she will not annoy Libbie.

In answer to Libbie's question if I remember what she said about the Sabbath, tell her that not one goes by without her words coming back to me. About half-past eleven in the morning I see her sitting at the end of their pew at the corner of the church, and again in the evening. Though hundreds of miles away and in a place where the Sabbath is generally disregarded I feel the same solemnity as if I were in the church.

I grow more anxious each day to learn how my letter to Judge Bacon has been received. I have no fears that if Libbie tells her Mother her real feelings, Mrs Bacon will consent, or, at least, offer no opposition. I cannot imagine why Albert Bacon uses his influence against me. . . . He knows nothing of me, for or against. I believe it is because of his strong attachment for Libbie.

I should not write as I do. You will think me unhappy, discontented. I am not. I am happy, happy in her love. Nothing can deprive me of that happiness, and I shall adhere to my long-established custom of looking on the bright side of things.

Judge Bacon, on his "annual-day," the date of his leaving home, always wrote to his sisters. In 1863, at the age of sixty-five, he was more than ever philosophic in his outlook and more than ever remote in imagination from the ardors of youth. He took his time answering Custer's letter, and then with all courtesy he replied that "the subject broached calls for weeks—months, even, of deliberation!"

Custer to Annette Humphrey, October 27, 1863, from Headquarters, 2nd Cavalry Regiment, Virginia:
What does he mean? [He describes Judge Bacon's impressive letter.] A straightforward, manly letter. He spoke of Libbie's mother, of her dying injunctions, of the disinterested affection of her adopted mother. . . . He spoke with pride of Libbie herself. Of myself he spoke in terms encouraging and flattering: "I believe in the sincerity of your affection,

in your energy, ability and force of character. I have always admired you, and am more than gratified at your well-earned reputation and high and exalted position. . . ." None the less, he goes no further than to promise "to speak to Libbie on a matter which she is at full liberty to communicate to you."

This was too vague for Custer. He wrote Judge Bacon, inquiring with all respect whether he and Libbie might correspond—this, without her parents' consent, they would not do. While awaiting an answer he retailed army doings to Annette.

Custer to Annette Humphrey, November 1, 1863, from Briscoe Station, Virginia:

I mentioned that Mosby had captured two of my orderlies. Yesterday, a party of my men, while scouting, came across the body of one pierced by a rifle-bullet. The rebels had emptied his pockets of everything but a miniature of his wife and child. . . . A young man of twenty-five . . . how I pity her when she learns her fate. She wrote to him two or three times a week. I know, from the similarity of our names, his being Corser, at first glance the address might be for me. Habituated as I am to scenes of death and sorrow . . . I caused him to be buried where he fell. . . . His horse, evidently killed first, lay near him.

I heard that Kilpatrick is to be made Major-General and ordered West. I am pleased because he is my senior. Had I been promoted and he not his friends in Washington and in Congress would have attempted to defeat the confirmation. If he does not go West I will.

However much I might wish to add a star to the one I wear, yet would one word of disapproval from Libbie check my aspiration. Yet I do not anticipate that she would wish me to lose that laudable ambition to which I already owe so much.

I am anxiously awaiting an answer from Judge Bacon as to whether Libbie and I may correspond. Give Libbie my love and tell her that all will soon be well.

On Sunday night in front of the fire Captain Judson exclaimed, "That's Captain Greene's voice and Jim Christiancy's laugh!" And he bade the sentry challenge them:

"Who goes there?"

"Friends."

"Advance, and give the countersign."

"Haven't got it. I want to see General Custer!"

All the staff started up to welcome back these brothers-in-arms. Captain Greene and I spread coats on the ground beside the fire, and talked till the servants were astir at five, preparing breakfast. Of course we did not mention any special person in Monroe. Oh, no. A certain Brigadier enquired about the price of corn, the crops, the weather, &c.

A party of officers are seated around the fire, with violin and guitar, singing "Then You'll Remember Me". . . . Remind Libbie she promised to sing it for me next time I am in Monroe. Next time . . . ! Today Genl. Pleasanton sent me word that I cannot leave the army this winter, for he is going away, and we cannot both be absent at the same time. Also I am to have added to my command a large number of raw and inexperienced soldiers, and "it will take all the energies of a young and ambitious Brigadier to organize and discipline them ready for the field."

You ask where I was during Kilpatrick's last fight. Well, I was in command while he was away in Washington. Notwithstanding, he received credit for the affair.

The rebels did not capture my trunk. They got my wagon with my desk, papers, &c.

What makes you think I am going to take a young lady on my staff and Who, do you think is the young lady?

I must close. I have another letter to write. . . . To a Young Lady in Monroe.

For the desired permission had been granted. Custer's letter was answered by one from Libbie, beginning, "My more than friend—at last. . . ."

7: Marriage

WHEN CUSTER received Judge Bacon's permission to correspond with his daughter Elizabeth Clift Bacon, which the young man rightly assumed to be a consent to their marriage, he sought leave to go back to Monroe to claim his bride. If, replied General Pleasanton, he would go out and capture the Confederate cavalry leader General J. E. B. Stuart, he might have as extended a furlough as he desired. But Custer knew his forces were too weak for this and had to content himself with a courtship by letter.

Meanwhile, the preoccupations of love and war did not diminish his solicitude for his own family. A letter to Mrs. Reed accedes to Maggie's attending the Union School if she desires but advises the Monroe Seminary—expenses to be charged to him. "You Methodists are too prejudiced," he writes. His advice prevailed. The entire Custer family was settled in Monroe now, so that Mother Custer might be near her daughter Mrs. Reed and might live under conditions more generally favorable. George Armstrong contributed to his people's support, for Father Custer was only moderately successful as a farmer.

Elizabeth Bacon was writing her first letter to her love.

Elizabeth Bacon to Custer, October, 1863, from Monroe, Michigan:
My more than friend—at last—Am I a little glad to write you some of the thoughts I cannot control? I have enjoyed your letters to Nettie, but am delighted to possess some of my own.

. . . . I was surprised to hear how readily Father had consented to our correspondence. You have no idea how many dark hours your little girl has passed. . . . I had no idea six weeks could go so slowly.

Didn't Father and I sit down beside the fireplace last Sunday night and talk until the fire died out about one General Custer . . . whose name I have been afraid to mention, or to hear others mention in the family circle? Father has been so kind and considerate . . . you have no idea what a great soul he has. We have become so intimate. Mon père and I usually maintain a dignified silence. I sometimes tell him some joke, and he only walks away downtown, leaving me to finish a sentence to the wall. He is so funny. Few know what a splendid old gentleman he really is.

As for my dignified and peculiar mother, she is becoming reconciled. But it is not resignation I want, but whole-hearted consent. I love her dearly and respect her opinions, but not her prejudices. And now you wonder at my objections to our speedy union?

Ah, dear man, if I am worth having am I not worth waiting for? The very thought of marriage makes me tremble. Girls have so much fun. Marriage means trouble, and, never having had any. . . .

If you tease me I will go into a convent for a year. The very thought of leaving my home, my family, is painful to me. I implore you not even to mention it for at least a year.

I can give you no idea of Mother's devotion to me. She told my friends she was marrying the daughter as well as the father. I love her so. She makes our home so pleasant.

Father teases her about her love of flattery. . . . Flattery, which she detests. She is trying to extract a compliment from his Highness about her new bonnet. He hasn't an atom of taste. He says, "Well, wife, Armstrong will suit you. He will flatter you!" I say indignantly, "He never flatters me." And he said, "That's true. He is not that kind." Oh, he is so proud of you. It delights me to think what a comfort you will be to him. How I hope you will like us all, such a contented and cheerful family.

All this in October, 1863. At Thanksgiving the two exchange anniversary letters, already quoted, recalling their first meeting at the Seminary party. Libbie's fluent pen goes on.

Elizabeth to Custer, December 27, 1863, from Monroe, Michigan:
My dearest Armstrong, I believe you would love me a little if you knew how I say, afternoons, "Half-past four—Letter *please* arrive!" I count the time till Father returns from the post. . . .

I showed Father part of your last letter—that is, I handed him one sheet. After reading and re-reading it he looked at what I held. . . . "That isn't all!" To which I replied, "It is all you can see!" So write me what you wish. Oh, I scarce know how to write a gentleman in so unconstrained a manner. Not that I am an entire novice in corresponding with gentlemen. . . . but I have always been careful to give no indication of a warm feeling. . . . I have not wished to give a false impression. To be natural is so pleasant.

You are coming, are you not: for the holidays. If so I might relent. . . . Father accuses me of trifling, says "You must not keep Armstrong waiting." But neither you nor he can know what preparations are needed for such an Event, an Event it takes at least a year to prepare for. After I am a soldier's wife I will not urge you to leave your duty oftener than I can help. But your miserable Virginia mud does not dry sufficiently for you to fight till April. Oh, what better argument can I offer than that I long to see you?

The worst about loveing a soldier is that he is as likely to die as to live . . . and how should I feel if my soldier should die before I have gratified his heart's desire?

So run Libbie Bacon's letters to her betrothed. His letters are, in the main, urgings that they marry as soon as he can obtain a leave. Custer writes her that General Pleasanton has rallied him on the number of his rivals.

Elizabeth to Custer, winter, 1863, from Monroe, Michigan:
Genl. Pleasanton has placed the number very small. There is the prominent lawyer E of Chicago who is favoring us with a visit. . . . He invited me to a concert, begs me to correspond with him, will come this way again. His beard, dyed, he does not quite step on it. Chicago is the city of my dream. . . . And Francis C. You may denounce his taste, but he likes me. He writes that he is coming to Monroe for a visit. Shall I give him your love? And John Rauch has always been "me beau." He brings me nuts and candy. Ah, if only gentlemen knew how ladies can be won! And. . . .

Do not think me immodest. Had these gentlemen put into words what it may be they desire I should not treat the matter so lightly.

The papers give an account of a battle this week. But I trust it may be deferred until next year. Father is anxiously awaiting the papers, hoping it will confirm Grant's success. Am I not selfish to wish that every triumph might belong to the Flower of the Army!

Now I am going to surprise you. I know your family by sight. I stood near them at the Lilliputian Bazaar. I think they knew me. I could have kissed your little sister, she was so considerate of her mother.

"Friend Nettie" has written "Friend Armstrong" that, now he has his Sunbeam, she assumes their correspondence will cease. Also that she has torn up his photograph. To which he replies her photograph will never be displaced from his album and that he looks forward to a continuance of their friendly correspondence.

Custer's Christmas gift to Elizabeth that year was an enlarged photograph of himself. It cost him forty-five dollars. The Bacon parents, in on the secret, furtively placed it in their daughter's room.

Elizabeth to Custer, December 23, 1863, from Monroe, Michigan:
My dear "Beloved Star"—You could not have given me anything on earth that so delighted me—except yourself. Father and mother were so excited, they thought I would never go upstairs to my room. The likeness is perfect.

Old fellow with the golden curls, save them from the barber's. When I'm old I'll have a wig made from them.

I have often said because I love so many I could never greatly love one. Foolish girl I was. If loveing with one's whole soul is insanity I am ripe for an insane asylum. Provided . . . ! [Later, Mrs. Custer did have a wig made from her husband's hair, which she wore in camp theatricals. It was destroyed in the fire at Fort Lincoln.]

Elizabeth to Custer, December 26 (?), 1863, from Monroe, Michigan:
We had quite a nice Christmas though not a merry one.

Before church Fanny called with Mr M. She has elegant new furs. I suppose a present from Mr Q who has been in town. She is crazy to find out about my present. She asked Nan "Is Libbie's diamond larger than mine?" Nan said, "Did Libbie say it was a ring?" Then she asks "Is General Custer engaged to be married?" If she could only see the picture in my room. But she would not value it as I do.

After church Net and I went to Anna's. She had exquisite presents. . . . A book, a boquet of roses—the most beautiful I have ever seen—from Toledo, a set of lovely laces. . . .

John B and Anderson W were both tight on Christmas day. They were at Nan's and she reproved them. Oh, it is shocking. Both old enough to know better and to have fixed principles. My dearest, if you are not already repaid for your abstinence my pride in you would repay you.

And yet, love, there is a stain on your character. Mother told me Father told her someone told him that Genl. Kilpatrick used an oath with every sentence he uttered, and that General Custer was not much better. I know this is exaggerated. But . . . God cure you of it.

My own faults are legion. I am susceptible to admiration. In church I saw a handsome young man looking at me, and I blushed furiously. Mother says I am the most sarcastic girl, and say the most *withering* things.

Religion is part of my life. It is hard to think of giving up my place in church. But thankful I am that I am marrying a man who, though not professing religion, is not an unbeliever.

I seldom write letters on Sunday though I confess to spending much of the day in sleeping. But I can not think it really worse to be writing you than to be dreaming about you.

There is a New Year's Eve party at the Boyds'.

Elizabeth to Custer, January 1, 1864, from Monroe, Michigan:
I was not going, but Mother said, "Oh, that won't do." I expected a forlorn time but it turned out so jolly. Autie, I made a conquest. A strange young man said, "Pardon, I did not get your name." I pulled a long face and replied "Miss Smith." How we laughed at him! . . . Next day he called, and kissed my cheek, at greeting and at parting, saying it was the New York style. It was fearfully impertinent, but under my own roof I did not wish to make it seem important.

How glad I am I have never allowed gentlemen to kiss me, though, I own, more from principle than inclination.

When I told mother she said, "Libbie, be careful. Armstrong may not approve such actions." She quite frightened me. But, dearest, you must trust me, as I trust you.

January 1st, 1864. A happy New Year, my well-beloved. I can wish for you no greater happiness than is mine this clear, frosty, sunshiny morning.

Custer to Mrs. Reed, December 22, 1863, from Defences of Washington:
My Dear Sister—I had hoped to spend the holidays with you, but my many duties prevented. I am coming home in February to be married to Libbie Bacon. . . . I know you approve my choice. She will come back with me to the Army.

Please have my shirts done up by the time I get home.

. . . . Libbie and Nettie will call on you. I wish you would go with them when they go to see Mother. Tell Pop I forgot to get his consent. Ask Em if she don't want to come and live with her Aunt Libbie. Give my love to all and Write Soon.

Annette Humphrey to Custer, January, 1864, from Monroe, Michigan:

. . . . I almost repent Libbie's decision, I shall be so lonely when she is gone. But you are worthy of her, the highest compliment I could pay you.

Libbie and I are going to see Mrs Reed. Judge Bacon is very anxious for her to do this. He and I have had a good talk about you. He is very fond of you and very proud of you, and Mrs Bacon is getting to like you more and more. You will soon see all this for yourself.

Elizabeth to Custer, January, 1864, from Monroe, Michigan:

She is lovely. Such a lady she relieved me of all embarrassment, Father has been chuckling. He told Mother in advance the exact words I would say on my return. The little ones, aren't they cunning! The youngest so bashful, almost afraid to kiss me. In that respect so like his Uncle Autie!

Mrs Reed says she doesn't get nearly as long letters as she used to.

Your father has just passed, riding your horse. I am surprised, a man of his age, riding so well. The horse is grace itself. Mr Custer told Father I was getting the best of boys for a husband, and what think you Father Bacon replied? He thought Mr Custer would like me when he knew me better. How Mother and I laughed. Your poor father would have to stop his ears if Mother started on her daughter's merits.

I called on Mrs Noble. I feared, not knowing you, she might not approve my choice. But, dearest, a lady ordinarily so cold and indifferent. . . . She said "General Custer has elements of character which will develop . . . and, dear girl, some of that development rests with you." Oh, Autie, I tremble at the responsibility. I am but a little girl—not of course, in years, but being an only child. . . . It is a solemn thought to become a wife.

Elizabeth to Rebecca Richmond, January, 1864, from Monroe, Michigan:

My dear Rebecca—You will not be more surprised than I am to know that I am going to be married in February to General Custer. I did not expect it till next winter, but Armstrong pleaded so urgently. . . . I no longer walk in the shadow, but in bright sunshine. Father says he did not really know him or he never would have let himself be influenced against him. Mother also is happy in my choice. My own happiness is unspeakable. Oh, Rebecca, it is beyond words blissful to love and to be loved.

I do not say Armstrong is without faults. But he never tastes liquor, nor frequents the gaming-table, and though not a professing Christian yet respects religion.

I am going to Detroit to have my dresses made, and my underclothes made on the machine. I am sending to New York for my silks. . . .

Elizabeth to Custer, January, 1864, from Detroit, Michigan:
Father says I ought not to keep Armstrong waiting. But, my love . . . my preparations are not elaborate, only for the bridal tour and the summer in Washington, but they will tax Mother to the utmost. It is useless to tell me what Mrs Alger wears. She is not a bride. And you are not marrying a girl *entirely* unknown in this State and elsewhere.

My silks from New York are *lovely*. But I have to send there for the trimmings.

"It's just what we might have expected," said Mother. "February. But I'm afraid you'll have to yield to him. Though I don't see how it's possible." "But, Mother," objected her Young Responsibility, "if I yield now to such teasing I shall always have to do so."

"No," she told me. "No. For I consented to hasten my own wedding because my former husband Mr Pitts insisted on it. . . . And I always had my own way afterwards, in Everything!"

I want you to wear your full-dress uniform. I have changed my mind about not wanting ostentation. If we begin by regulating our actions by the opinions of others we shall never have any of our own. I want to be married in the evening, in the church. To-night I shall go see dear Mr Boyd. How his dear eyes will open. You are willing, are you not? that he shall perform the ceremony, he has been my friend so long. True, Mr Matson performs it beautifully, I am sorry he will not make us Man and Wife. Why do people say Man and Wife as if a man were not a man until he's married? As for bridesmaids, Oh, how can I be separated from those girls?

Yes, I have ordered a riding-habit. Would you like a description of my wedding-dress? Pea-green silk, to top of gaiters. Looped with yellow military braid. Green silk veil. Corsage boquet red roses tied with yellow cord.

Looked at closely it might be thought white corded silk that can walk into church alone.

Correspondence ensued between Custer and Mr. Bacon, now his closest intimate, about his confirmation as brigadier general.

Custer to Mr. Bacon, January, 1864:

The subject has caused me no little anxiety, but now my fears are at rest. I would have written you at once when I learned of the efforts made to injure me, but did not wish to trouble Libbie. You would be surprised at the pertinacity with which certain men labor to defame me. I have paid but little attention to them, trusting to time to vindicate me. And I do not fear the result. It was reported that I was a "copperhead," a charge completely refuted. Senator Chandler has expressed himself warmly in my favor. So, too, Mr Kellogg, [so] that it is not possible for any clique to defeat me. . . .

Elizabeth adds her own reply to Mr. Bacon's:

Armstrong, your letter to Father is so beautifully written . . . he says he is sure we shall be happy. Is not Mother's letter to you *dear!* She says if ever I am unhappy I must tell them so. But that I could never do. Father wants us to be married on the anniversary of his own wedding. . . . About my name on the cards to conciliate him I shall be married as "Elizabeth." Blessings brighten as they take their flight. How I love my name Libbie BACON. Libbie B-A-C-O-N. Bacon. Libbie Bacon.

You'll be here a week from Monday. If it takes you three days to travel you'll start on Friday. Soldiers have to travel on Sunday, I suppose, tho I hope Autie doesn't. Still, if it brings you here a day sooner. . . .

The Episcopalians want to be present. As Lent starts Wednesday, Tuesday will make it right for them.

My dear, you are exceedingly kind, but I do not want a personal maid. I have been accustomed to maiding Libbie Bacon, a damsel of many wants but always well-attended. In housekeeping I shall need an "Eliza"—for I can only keep a place tidy.

I am glad you are going to take me to New York, a place I have long wished to visit. And Father is anxious for me to visit his sisters who were so good to me when I was motherless. . . .

Oh, how soon shall I bid adieu to the spot the dearest to me in the world. Father at one side of the table, writing . . . Mother asking questions. She says By Heavens she declares he wishes her in Greenland. And he says, "Wife, stop that clacking and let me write!" You will *love* them. I hope we may be so happy. But . . . I had rather live in a tent, outdoors with you than in a palace with another. There is no place I would not go to, gladly, live in, gladly, because . . . Because I love you.

Mr. Bacon to Charity, February 11, 1864, from Monroe, Michigan:
On Tuesday evening [February 9] Libbie was married. All went off remarkably well, and no mistake made. It was said to be the most splendid wedding ever seen in the State. From one to two hundred more in the church than ever before and as many unable to enter for want of room. The number at our house afterwards estimated at three hundred.

I did not act the babe as I had feared I might at parting, for I had schooled myself beforehand.

None of us slept that first night, fearing burglars, but yesterday I placed the silver in the Bank, and we went to bed at seven to make up for lost sleep.

My wife looks well. Everybody said the house and fixings were all right, and the entertainment elegant. Affectionately, Daniel.

Returned home to Belle Plaine, Grand Rapids, Rebecca Richmond wrote her sister Mary, away on a visit, a description of her visit to Monroe for the Event.

Rebecca Richmond to Mary Richmond, February, 1864, from Grand Rapids, Michigan:
Uncle Bacon met us—myself and Mrs Bacon's niece, Mrs Bagg from Detroit—at the depot with a carriage. At the house Libbie rushed out to greet us, unaffected, natural, the old schoolgirl Libbie, soon to be wife of a famous Brigadier-General. A pleasant family party, and a jolly one. But where was the General?

Well, at last he made his appearance, and from then hardly left Libbie's side, till he left with his booty.

Not one of us was prepossessed in his favor, but in no time everyone

pronounced him "a trump," a "right bower". . . . I was most agree-
ably disappointed after the reports I had heard. Mary, he isn't one bit
foppish or conceited. He does not put on airs. He is a simple, frank,
manly fellow. And he fairly idolizes Libbie. I am sure he will make her
a true, noble husband.

As for Libbie, she is the same gay, irrepressible spirit we found her
a year ago. They cannot but be happy.

Wedding, Tuesday at eight in the evening, Presbyterian church. Dr
Boyd assisted by the rector Dr Matson officiating.

Bridesmaids, Annette Humphrey, Anna Darrah, Marie Miller. They
wore white tarletan, with gauze veils, just reaching shoulders. Grooms-
men, Captain Jacob Greene, Messrs Conway Noble and John Bulkley.

The bride wore a rich white rep silk with deep points and extensive
trail, bertha of point lace. Veil floated back from a bunch of orange
blossoms fixed above the brow.

The three couples composing the suite passed by alternate aisles, and
stationed themselves on each side of the platform. Uncle Bacon and
Libbie, Mrs Bacon and General Custer passed on opposite aisles simul-
taneously, and met before the pulpit where Uncle gave Libbie to the
General, and, stepping aside with his wife, took his place with friends
who stood on the right, with uncovered heads.

It passed off to entire satisfaction. The church was crowded by six
o'clock, and there was a throng outside.

Until ten o'clock the newly-wedded pair received congratulations.
The occasion was delightful, hilarious and social.

At midnight the bridal party—four couples—took passage for Cleve-
land, arriving there at nine next morning, stopping at the Waddell
House. That afternoon a reception for General Custer was given at Mr
Charles Noble's, followed by a brilliant party.

Next morning General and Mrs Custer left for Buffalo, visiting along
New York State. A recent letter informs that arrived in New York
they are at the Metropolitan Hotel. Thence they will proceed to Washington, and Headquarters on the Rapidan.

The bridal gifts were exhibited in a room adjoining the drawing-
room, communicating with the hall, thus affording free passage. They
included: Silver Dinner Service from the 1st Vermont Cavalry, Silver
Tea Sett, 7 pieces, 7th Michigan Cavalry. Silver card-case, card re-
ceiver, syrup cup, sugar spoons, berry spoons, thimble (gold-lined),
napkin-ring.

Two white silk fans, sandal wood. Mrs Browning's Poems; "Whispers to a Bride"; "Female Poets." Knit breakfast shawl; Mosaic chess-stand of Grand Rapids Marble.

From her parents, gold watch, handsome Bible, also from Mrs Bacon white silk parasol covered with black lace.

We were kept awake that night, Tuesday, by fancied burglar alarms, but on Wednesday Uncle Bacon packed the silver and took it to the Bank, and that night we went to bed at seven.

The trousseau was rich and in fine taste. Here are some of the chief items: travelling dress, dark brown, empress cloth, white buttons; hotel sacque of the same with black buttons (a jaunty little thing); hat same shade; (blue velvet facing); waterproof with arm-holes, buttoned from head to foot; double-dress, lilac silk, faced and trimmed with plaid; Breakfast dress, light blue merino; basque, sleeves &c. scalloped and bound with black velvet; Brown silk dress; Light green silk dress with narrow stripes a shade darker, very rich, trimmed with guipure lace and bugle ornaments. Black velvet "circle" trimmed with thread lace. Riding dress dark green, brass buttons. Dress hat, lavender velvet with beautiful white feather. Opera cloak white merino, silk-lined. Silk hood with rich tassels.

Young Mrs. Custer wrote her parents of the bridal tour, and Mr. Bacon relayed descriptions to the Richmond kin.

Mr. Bacon to his Richmond nieces, February, 1864, from Monroe, Michigan:
My dear Nieces—The wedded pair went from Cleveland to Buffalo, thence to Rochester where they saw "Uncle Tom's Cabin." Then to Onandaga, to the home of my brother-in-law, husband of my sister Charity. On Sunday forenoon they went to church, but, the weather being inclement, Libbie wore her travelling suit. But it cleared off, and at afternoon church the new things were exhibited . . . very gratifying to her friends (also to her Mother when she read about it). All the fixings were examined, and from the "Oh's" and "Exquisites" in the letters I judge the friends were pleased.

Their time was divided between the Smiths and Dr. J's, and at each they were feasted on turkey and sugar-coated cake.

On Monday morning they left for Howlett's Hill, but before train time the wardrobe was displayed to friends and relatives who had not seen it. At the height of the exhibition the porter called for their baggage, and all hands fell to packing, Armstrong among the number. He got entangled in a hoop skirt, whereon Amelia called "Surrender!" . . . since there was no way of beating a retreat. They left, everyone waving handkerchiefs. Libbie took Armstrong's hat to wave; the band fell off, but fortunately was recovered.

At Camillus they were met by my brother-in-law Sabin. At his house they were called on by all lineal descendants and many others. Here I judge they had a more than gay time, for my nephew George, who is acquainted with the arts better than with business, used fiddle and bow. Mr and Mrs Sabin opening the dance.

Elizabeth to Mr. Bacon, February, 1864, from Howlett's Hill, New York:
In the evening we all danced in the kitchen [of the Sabin house], to George's music, and I had to sit right down on the floor to laugh to see Uncle Den and Aunt Eliza dance their old-fashioned way, it was too amusing to see them bounding up and down.

Mr. Bacon's letter continues:

We are expecting to hear from them in New York. This calls to mind a time I was there, when, after a journey to Brooklyn, on reaching Broadway I found the Astor House and the Park House each on the wrong side of the street, and even with the aid of a policeman, had a time to get it right.

The New York stay included a visit to West Point.

Elizabeth to Mr. Bacon, February, 1864, from West Point:
When we got out of the train we found the river frozen, and the ferry not running. I was drawn by a man, in a sled, Armstrong pushing behind.

I never dreamed there was so lovely a place in the United States. Everyone was delighted to see Autie. Even the dogs welcomed him.

In advanced years, in reminiscent vein, Mrs. Custer described this visit as sole occasion when her husband manifested jealousy:

In the train going back I was amazed to see my blithe bridegroom turned into an incarnated thundercloud. "But," I tearfully protested, "the professor who claimed the privilege of kissing the bride was a veritable Methuselah. And the cadets who showed me Lovers' Walk were like school-boys with their shy ways and nice, clean, friendly faces. . . ." Oh, I quite expected to be sent home to my parents, till I took courage to say, "Well, you left me with them, Autie!"

Some seventy years would pass before husband and wife, after a long separation, would be reunited under the protecting wing of the West Point fortress, in one grave.

The Bacons' love for Custer and their pride in him equaled that of his own family. But there was one little matter Mr. Bacon felt called on to explain to his correspondents: when not in uniform, the bridegroom lacked the spectacular appearance expected of him.

Mr. Bacon to his Richmond nieces, 1864, from Monroe, Michigan:
Bennett in his N Y "Herald" had said so much about the "Boy General with his flowing yellow curls" that at first all were disappointed in Armstrong's appearance. But acquaintance with him changed everybody's views. Everywhere, without exception, he made a *most favorable* impression.

Oh, the luxury of a quiet fireside after all the excitement. We stay indoors, and all the calls we receive are to tell us how pleasant and agreeable all things were.

The fodder holds out yet, all but the ice-cream which was used up yesterday and the platter licked clean.

We want to adopt you, Rebecca, for our girl. A house is not a house without a young lady in it. True, we cannot promise you a General. But—it might be better in some ways—we can promise you a lawyer or a minister. Mark that.

Kindest regards to all,
Uncle D S Bacon.

8: War Correspondence

MARRIAGE OPENED a new chapter in the Custer story. From ⌐pring of 1864 to spring of 1865, during the last, flaming year of the Civil War, Custer's letters to his wife form a veritable diary of the operations of his branch of Sheridan's cavalry. Elizabeth, waiting always for an opportunity to join him, wrote him details of her boardinghouse existence in the capital, relaying his news and her own to the parents in Monroe.

Her first experience as an "army lady" came in Dixie. An old Virginia farmhouse had been requisitioned as headquarters by Custer, on the left side of the Army of the Potomac.

Elizabeth to Mr. and Mrs. Bacon, spring, 1864, from Virginia:
. . . . Orderlies come at all hours of the night from different army posts with despatches for Autie. Imagine my grief when I learned on Thursday he was to start at dawn, with 300 men, to ascertain the rebel force at Ely's Ford! The wife of an Infantry General told me she would not have her Andy in the Cavalry for the world. Their work, like a woman's, is never done.

Yesterday we took dinner with Brigadier-General Webb and his wife. They live in the cutest little huts, opening one into the other, surrounded by evergreens—all the work of soldiers.

Such style as we go in! Most army officers' wives have to ride in ambulances, but my General has a carriage with silver harness that he captured last summer, and two magnificent matched horses (not captures). We have an escort of four or six soldiers riding behind.

Such style at these army dinners! Genl. Pleasanton has 6 courses. It would delight your hearts to see Armstrong refuse wine when offered him by his best friends. They honor him for it.

Genl. H, chief of Meade's staff, calling on me, told Autie that in this last raid Kilpatrick had "flummoxed." I was ready to laugh at the word, he is so elegant in his language, a perfectly charming old gentleman, and *so* polite to me. It seems that K made the raid without consulting Meade, but went first to the President, then acted against the wishes of the two commanding generals.

It is wholly false, the newspaper's old story "All quiet along the Potomac." Something is happening all the time. One day this week six rebs escaped from the Davis dominions across this river. Four got within our lines before daybreak. The others lay all day in a graveyard near our picket lines, fearing to be fired on.

We took a lovely ride to the Signal Station . . . the white tents of the Army of the Potomac stretched far as eye could see. Tho enlisted for life, in the Cavalry the men do not have nearly as nicely finished quarters as the Infantry who are in winter quarters several months with no horses to care for.

On Sunday Armstrong had one of the regimental Chaplains talk to the men and the band played hymns.

Will the dignified Judge please *not* circulate this letter over more than half the Peninsular State? And oblige his most obedient daughter Libbie Custer. I love you all so I can't specify.

In this spring of 1864 General Grant was summoned from the Western Army, commissioned lieutenant general, and placed in full command of the Union forces. In the Army of the Potomac he relieved General Pleasanton of the command of the cavalry, replacing him with General Philip H. Sheridan.

During a spell of inaction Custer was allowed to complete his honeymoon leave.

Elizabeth to Mr. and Mrs. Bacon, March 28, 1864, from Washington:
We traveled from camp to Washington by the special train put on for Genl. Grant. Autie introduced me, and I had the honor of a short conversation with the distinguished man. . . . Sandy hair and mustache; eyes greenish-blue. Short, and, Mother, not "tasty" but very ordinary-looking. No show-off but quite unassuming, talked all the time and was funny. Told the gentlemen that small army men invariably ride horses 17 hands high.

I was the only lady, and he was so considerate he went out on to the platform to smoke his cigar, fearing it might be disagreeable to me, till Autie begged him to return. He smoked 5 on the journey.

Father, you have a modest son. Instead of speaking with **men** who could do so much for him Autie sat by me and only spoke when necessary.

The train made the quickest time ever known on the road: 57 miles in 1 hour and 52 minutes, the last 7 miles in 10 minutes. It was quite dangerous, because last summer the rebels had torn up the tracks. It swayed like a boat. Still, I thought, if the country could afford to lose so valuable a man as Grant it could afford to lose us.

Just before starting a tipsy major came aboard to shake hands with Grant who remembered him, tho not having seen him—he had been in Mexico—since they were West Point cadets together in '43.

Tho disappointed in Grant's looks I like him.

Autie took me to Baltimore. The streets are all paved, and so neat, and many of the houses really elegant, almost like those on Fifth Avenue, New York, with their brown-stone fronts.

We saw the great comedian Clarke, and I laughed till I cried, and I thought Autie would have a fit, he nearly fell off his seat laughing. In one scene Clarke is the lackey playing the lord in his master's clothes, and when he calls on a young lady the lord's pantaloons are so tight he cannot sit down without pain and has to keep his legs stretched out and not bend his knees. It was simply killing.

Washington begins to seem homelike, I have made so many friends. But at the House I was anything but impressed, such a want of order, of dignity. A wrangling set. But the Chamber is elegant, and that of the Senate more so.

I can't tell you what a place Autie has here in public opinion. I thought that a Brigadier would not be anything, but I find that mine is someone to be envied. It astonishes me to see the attention with which he is treated everywhere. One day at the House he was invited to go on the floor, and the members came flocking round to be presented. I wish I could tell you all the things they said that he is too modest to repeat. One said, "So you are the youngest General in the army. Well, I wish there were more like you." And, when some old fogy objected to his confirmation on account of his youth, the rest said, "Pity there aren't more like him!" You got his telegram about his confirmation? How glad I am he at last is really a Boy Gen—I mean, a Brigadier!

The President knew all about him when Autie was presented to him, and talked to him about his graduation.

None of the other generals receive half the attention, and their arrivals are scarcely noticed in the papers. I am so amazed at his reputation I cannot but write you about it. I wonder his head is not turned.

Tho not disposed to put on airs I find it very agreeable to be the wife of a man so generally known and respected.

Senator W was very polite to us and invited me to dance if I go to the "hop." They are held every Thursday night at the National. Senator Ch. also has invited me. I have to laugh when I think of these old men being my beaux.

Mother, I have to have a new dress if I am going to the hop. Cara B. gave me a blue tarletan—I shall give her something of equal value in return—and I am having it made.

I look like a Dutch milkmaid with my red cheeks beside these city girls.

Genl. Sickles is here. He does not use his cork leg but goes on crutches. He is very agreeable, especially to the ladies.

Their married correspondence begins when Custer returns to duty, leaving his wife in Washington.

Elizabeth to Custer, April, 1864, from Washington:

My own darling Boy—Yesterday after you went I watched you admiringly as you rode along, then went up to my room to cry.

This morning I have been in the garden, playing with the kitten, smelling the rosebuds, touching the sensitive plant to see it wither, then hearing Miss X complain of the Northerners she has for boarders, and Mr Stires expatiate on the cost of making his new suit. . . .

Her letter crosses one from him.

Custer to Elizabeth, April 16, 1864, from Virginia:

I remained at Genl. Sheridan's Headquarters last night and to-day until nearly 4 o'clock, and have been at Genl. Kilpatrick's ever since. He has invited all the officers to meet him to bid adieu before his departure for the West. Genl. Wilson takes his place.

Everything is arranged satisfactorily now; I take my Brigade and join the 1st Division Cavalry Corps under Genl. Torbert, an old and intimate friend of mine, and a very worthy gentleman. I am to retain Major Drew upon my staff. Major-General Sheridan impresses me very favorably. I will probably move with my brigade to or near Culpepper in a few days.

Everyone, all the orderlies enquire about you, seem interested in your happiness. Ever and devotedly your Autie.

Custer could ill have spared Major Drew who, during Custer's stay in Washington, had written him from camp.

Major Drew to Custer, April, 1864, from Virginia:
General—I am sorry to inform you I am to be relieved from your staff. I tried to get Genl. Kilpatrick to await your return, but he would not do this. Consequently I am compelled to leave you, which grieves me very much. After working so hard to get the Brigade in shape, and then have someone else step in and reap the benefit of my work is pretty hard.

But, General, I always felt in this way I could not do too much for you and your Brigade. The Brigade is doing well, and all they need is horses and arms to equip them.

Elizabeth to Mr. and Mrs. Bacon, April, 1864, from Washington:
I will not attempt to tell you how lonely I am. It was a far worse trial than I anticipated to part from my husband. And yet I am prouder far to be his wife than I would be to be Mrs Lincoln or a queen.

On Wednesday evening I heard George Thompson at the Capitol. He did well, but of course I am no Abolitionist. The President was present, the gloomiest, most painfully careworn looking man I ever saw. We have sat in a box opposite him at the theatre several times, and reports of his careworn face are not at all exaggerated.

Let me assure you the report you have heard of Genl. Pleasanton is false. Autie messed with him for a long time. It is true he takes wine at dinner, but never to excess. His clear eye and his manner should give the lie to such an accusation. In this Sodom and Gomorrah everybody drinks. Mr Ch. came to take me to the hop last week, and—he wasn't drunk *that night.*

Do you know Autie was on that car that was so nearly captured by Mosby? They made their dash too soon, as the cars were about an hour behind time. Autie never told me a word about it, but Mr Ferry, agent for the Gettysburg cemetery, told me.

Please send my box of watercolors; I brought my palette. And, Mother, do send a few pencil lines to your lonely child.

Everything seems to indicate an early raid. Burnside's army passed through recently, several colored regiments among them. They have gone to Alexandria to prevent Lee from making a raid. Col. Gray says my letter written to Autie last night may not go out for days.

I will try not to think of this new trouble, but will tell you of the

President's levee. Representative and Mrs Kellogg took me. We went about ten o'clock. It was the last one, and the most frightful jam I ever was in. The way was lined with carriages waiting their turn. Finally we landed on the porch. Soldiers with sabres drawn stood at the door.

The crowd was so dense I could not move my arms, but was fairly pushed in, a sabre over my head.

From the cloakroom through a hall we went into a room papered and furnished in crimson, then into the Holy of Holies, the Blue Room. Near the door stood the President with one of his secretaries. Mr Kellogg is quite a friend of his. (It was he who took Autie to pay his respects to Mr Lincoln.) He—the President—shook hands with me, as with everyone, and I felt quite satisfied and was passing on, but it seems I was to be honored by his Highness. At mention of my name he took my hand again very cordially and said, "So this is the young woman whose husband goes into a charge with a whoop and a shout. Well, I'm told he won't do so any more."

I replied I hoped he would. "Oh," said the prince of jokers, "then you want to be a widow, I see." He laughed and I did likewise. Was I not honored? I am quite a Lincoln girl now.

Afterward, meeting one of his Secretaries, I bade him tell Mr Lincoln he would have gained a vote, if soldiers' wives were allowed one.

Mrs Lincoln stood near the President. She is as her pictures represent her, short, squatty, and plain. She wore white moire antique with black lace bertha and white ribbon quillings.

From the Blue we went to the East Room which is magnificent.

I met so many nice people. Mr Kellogg introduced me to Speaker Colfax who said "I have been wishing to be presented to this lady, but am disappointed she is a Mrs!" I think he is quite the nicest gentleman in Washington—but without regret. I am too proud of being Autie's wife.

Mr Bingham called on me to-day. He is now Judge-Advocate. A charming man. He still regards Autie as his protégé.

Father, as an illustration of what you and Autie have cautioned me about holding my tongue on army and political matters—I heard lately that Genl. Pleasanton was removed, not on account of feeling between him and Genl. Meade, but because his two sisters, maiden ladies living here, have talked so badly about the President and the Sec'y of War, and it was supposed these were his views they were repeating.

And, Father dear, don't tell, but Mr Ch. is an old goosey idiot. Now his wife is away he is drunk *all* the time. And O, so silly.

Good-night. Your loving child Libbie.

April, 1864, is wearing on. Custer writes almost daily to his wife.

Custer to Elizabeth, April 23, 1864, from Virginia:
We had a splendid review to-day. Genl. Sheridan reviewed the entire Division. My Brigade never looked better. I was more than proud of it. We compared very favorably with the other Brigades. I wished my little girl might have been present to enjoy the sight. I have appointed another Aide on my staff. Lt. Stranahan of the 1st Vermont. Captain Greene is very blue because he has received no letter from Nettie for three nights.

When I think of the sacrifices you have made for me, the troubles and trials you have endured to make me happy, the debt of gratitude you have placed me under, my heart almost fails me to think I have only the devotion of my life to offer you in return.

I read your description of the President's levee with much gratification. You certainly were honored by his Highness—as you should be. You know how proud I am of my darling.

The vast array of talented and influential personages you met might make me fearful you would regret your choice, but for your comment on the remark of Speaker Colfax that you prefer being the adored wife of your Autie.

Loving so fine a being truly and devotedly as I do, it seems impossible that I ever should or could be very wicked. Neither tongue nor pen can express the intensity of my love.

We have such a pleasant camp for headquarters. The regiments are pleasantly and healthily located.

Tell Col. Gray that Genl. Sheridan said that his (Col. Gray's) regiment marched best of all in the command.

Mr Stires goes to Washington to-morrow. By him I send you $100. for safe-keeping. If you need it of course it is for you to spend. I suppose in a few days Major Rochester will give you $142. I intend to make my little wife my treasurer, and when I have a sum for which I have no immediate use I will send it to you to keep for me. I want you to use any or all, if you need it, only practice economy and avoid extravagance. I do not wish to deny you anything needful for your comfort or happiness. Only bear in mind that we are just entering on life's journey with all its cares, and, I hope, in a short time its *responsibilities*. We have only ourselves to rely on, and we cannot exercise too much care to avoid prodigality. There now, have I lectured my darling sufficiently on so dry a subject?

I am so glad you attended the Hop, and am so much obliged to Mr Chandler for inviting you. You did perfectly right in accepting; it is just what I urged you to do. Do not heed the idle opinions of those whose time is occupied with other people's business. As for Mr H and persons of his style, do not heed them. I am sorry Cara permits so much attention from him. I knew him at West Point, have known him since. He has always been shunned for his lack of principle. I believe him to be devoid of honor, and would not allow a sister of mine to receive attentions from him.

Brigade inspection lasted two hours this morning. At four this afternoon I had Divine service at Headquarters. There were three chaplains present and a large congregation from the regiments. The Chaplain of the 5th made a beautiful prayer, invoking the divine blessing on your boy, spoke of the responsibility resting on me and prayed that I might be guided by grace from above and become, not only a powerful instrument in suppressing the rebellion, but a shining leader in the Christian army.

Genl. Sheridan who has reviewed the entire Cavalry Corps and Genl. Torbert say that I have the finest and best brigade of Cavalry in the entire army. I am laboring to make it still better.

Oh, little one, you should see your boy—for boy he truly is now. He has shaven off his mustache and imperial. And what a change! The staff all laughed heartily and say it changes me far more than cutting my hair did. One of them said you would not know me. But I think I would find ways to make myself known. Jim says I look precisely as I did before I went to West Point. I send you the mustache.

Jim and I went to-day, accompanied by four orderlies, to Cedar Mountain. We saw numerous camps of rebels, one brigade of them drilling, while at other points working parties were throwing up fortifications.

The view from the mountain is lovely. We found beautiful wild flowers, some fragrantly scented. How I wished for you there to enjoy it.

This evening I received the *Free Press*. In the editorial it speaks of me in the most flattering manner. I send you the slip, but do not show it to any person except to Cara. Others might think it vanity to do so. It is certainly very kind of the *Press* to speak so well of your Boy General.

Captain Greene in the next tent is playing on his flute "Then You'll

Remember Me". . . . Now he has changed to " 'Tis Better to Laugh than to Cry."

Elizabeth to Mr. and Mrs. Bacon, May 1, 1864, from Washington:
My dearest Father and Mother—When your box came I was disappointed not to find a letter in it, but when cutting the cake your note fell out. Mother, you never forget your lonesome child. And, oh, that cake—it took me right back home. At times I am so homesick. But I do not regret the exchange.

Oh, such a surprise. Genls. Sheridan and Torbert wanted something done in Washington, and gave Autie 48 hours here in which to accomplish it. I was talking to a lady who was calling on me about Autie when the door burst open. He rushed upstairs so fast the people thought the house was on fire. The lady left immediately.

Oh Mother, the day before he came Autie in a letter sent me his mustache. He does look so funny, so young—a beardless boy. And he don't know how to act without it, his mouth seems so strange to him. With his smooth skin it seemed like kissing a girl.

The silence in the papers shows that a great battle is expected. Nobody knows what Grant is going to do. Long trains of army wagons rumble over the pavement. On an average three regiments of Potomac veterans back from furlough and some new ones pass through, a day. Mrs Wooster and I hang from my windows watching them, as, just a block from here, they turn to cross the bridge—"into the jaws of death" it seems. The bands—they have fine ones—always play.

A story was told at table of one of Mosby's gang—it might have been himself—meeting a girl near the city and giving her a lock of his hair to give Lincoln with his compliments, and he would take dinner with him within ten days.

Mother dear, I do enjoy going to church. A life of gaiety could be mine, but I do not desire it. I hope Father remembers Autie and I in his daily prayers.

I did not write you half enough about Eliza when I was in camp. She is a jewel of a servant, and the soldiers—one day someone said "The Rebels are reaching toward us!" At which a soldier said "Don't you see old Curly lying there? As long as he aint scared I aint!" Old Curly was Autie, asleep under a tree. Eliza told him, "Why, Gin'ral, the men think you can do as much as the Almighty!"

I have just trimmed my spring hat, gray neapolitan with cuir-colored ribbons on the inside. It is *very* sober. I dare not wear colors in the street, even blue, for with so many *persons of a certain class* in the city *ladies* have to dress with studied plainness.

Custer to Elizabeth, May 1, 1864, from Camp Libbie, Virginia:
I suppose my little one has been to church to-day. Among the traits of her character I first learned to love was her religious earnestness. I have always felt an utter contempt for those who, under the cloak of piety, conceal base designs. The infidel has a stronger claim on my respect than he who professes insincerely. It may seem strange to you, dear girl, that I, a non-professing (tho not an unbeliever) Christian, should so ardently desire you to remain so. I have never prayed as others do. Yet, on the eve of every battle in which I have been engaged, I have never omitted to pray inwardly, devoutly. Never have I failed to commend myself to God's keeping, asking Him to forgive my past sins, and to watch over me while in danger . . . and to receive me if I fell, while caring for those near and dear to me. After having done so all anxiety for myself, here or hereafter, is dispelled. I feel that my destiny is in the hands of the Almighty. This belief, more than any other fact or reason, makes me brave and fearless as I am. You might ask why, then, I have not become a member of some religious organization. It would take too long to tell. You are the first to whom I have ever made this explanation . . . I want you to know me as I am.

You ask for news. There is little to give. We are in readiness to advance. Weather and roads are favorable. Burnside's army, about 30,000, will co-operate with this. At the same time a movement on the James will be made by Genl. Smith who, in addition to Butler's men, has about 1,500 from Charleston. Do not be over-anxious. Remember: No news is good news.

Custer to Elizabeth, May 4, 1864, from Camp Libbie, Virginia:
This is probably the last letter you will get before the coming fight. The entire army moves to-night, and begins crossing the Rapidan at Germania and lower fords. Communication with Washington will probably be abandoned for several days, but do not borrow trouble.

No, dearest girl, of course I am not ashamed of you. . . . How could I be? for having declined to ride my horse? Before I received your letter I was chiding myself . . . but "She" knows me too well to think me careless of her safety.

In his *Memoirs* General Sheridan speaks of the superior wisdom of the Confederates in massing cavalry instead of dispersing it in scattered units, as the Union practice had been. Accordingly, he decided to join issue with them in their own fashion.

General Sheridan's Memoirs:
I sent for Gregg, Merritt, and Wilson, and told them "We are going out to fight Stuart's Cavalry. . . . We will give him a fair, square fight. . . . I shall expect nothing but success. . . . Our move would be a challenge to Stuart for a cavalry duel, behind Lee's lines, in his own country. [This great cavalry duel was fought at Yellow Tavern on May 11, 1864, completely justifying Sheridan's expectations. He gives a detailed account of Custer's participation in it:]

Early on May 9th the expedition started toward Fredericksburg. . . . About dark Merritt's Division crossed the North Anna. . . . Custer's Brigade proceeded on to Beaver Dam Station. . . . He met a small force of the enemy, but this he speedily drove off, recapturing from it about four hundred Union prisoners being taken to Richmond. . . . He destroyed the station, two locomotives, three trains of cars, ninety wagons, from eight to ten miles of railroad and telegraph lines . . . munitions, rations, supplies intended for Lee's army. . . .

By forced marches General Stuart reached Yellow Tavern on the 11th. The enemy, desperate but confident, poured a heavy fire from his line and from a battery. . . . Gibbs' and Devin's brigades, however, held fast, while Custer, supported by Chapman's Brigade, attacked the enemy's left and battery in a mounted charge. . . .

Custer's charge was brilliantly executed. Beginning at a walk he increased this to a trot, then, at full speed, rushed on the enemy. . . .

After Custer's charge the Confederate Cavalry was badly broken up. . . . The engagement ended by giving us complete control of the road to Richmond.

Extract from the Richmond Examiner, *May 13, 1864:*
. . . . Major-General J. E. B. Stuart, model of Virginia Cavaliers and dashing chieftain, is dead. . . . At Yellow Tavern, seeing a brigade preparing to charge upon his left, he dashed down the line to form troops to repel the charge. . . . The Yankees came thundering down. . . . "Of all our knights he was the flower. . . ."

Custer to Elizabeth, May 14, 1864, from Rexall's Landing, James River, Virginia:

We have passed through days of carnage and have lost heavily. . . . We have been successful. . . . The Michigan Brigade has covered itself with undying glory. . . . We destroyed railroads, &c., in Lee's rear, mentioned in Sheridan's report to General Grant. . . . I also led a charge in which we mortally wounded Genl. Stuart and captured a battery of three cannon and a large number of prisoners. . . . Genl. Sheridan sent an aide on the battlefield with his congratulations. So did Genl. Merritt: "The Michigan Brigade is at the top of the ladder". . . . Jim and Mr Baylis had their horses shot. . . . We were inside the fortifications of Richmond. I enclose some honeysuckle I plucked there. . . . Autie.

Custer to Elizabeth, May 16, 1864, from Rexall's Landing, James River, Virginia:

I have detailed Capt. Judson to proceed to Washington with a detachment of men. . . . He will deliver this to you, and will give you a full account of our late battles. Suffice to say that *our* brigade has far surpassed all its previous exploits, and that your Boy was never before the object of such attention, and has succeeded beyond his highest expectations . . . and is only sorry that he cannot be with you to tell you all. Wilson proved himself an imbecile and nearly ruined the corps by his blunders. Genl. Sheridan sent for me to rescue him (Wilson) from these, though I was in a different part of the field. And after a severe and bloody fight in which I had command of nine regiments I cut my way through the enemy's lines and opened a way for the Corps to safety. The 1st Vermont, now under Wilson, sent over to our brigade and asked if they could not obtain "a pair of Custer's old boots" to command them. One of Genl. Sheridan's highest staff officers said "Custer saved the Cavalry Corps," and Genl. Sheridan told Col. Alger "Custer is the ablest man in the Cavalry Corps." (This is for you only, my little one. I would not write this to anyone but you. You may repeat it to our own people in Monroe, but not to anyone in Washington). I thought of you in every battle, and was sorry you would be caused anxiety on your Boy's account.

I can tell my little one something that will please her: I have sworn far less during the late battles than ever before on similar occasions— all owing to the influence of my beloved darling. During the battles, while I was in the thickest, with the bullets whistling by me and shells bursting all around me I thought of you. You are in my thoughts always, day and night.

Elizabeth to Mr. and Mrs. Bacon, May 22, 1864, from Washington:
J. E. B. Stuart is really dead! But our men are sorry, for they consider Wade Hampton who will succeed him a superior officer.

Autie captured a book, on the raid: "Sketches of Hampton's Cavalry." In it is a description of Autie.

I hear nothing but praises of Autie's achievements. . . . One of the prisoners said he was splendid. They say he takes off his coat, rolls up his sleeves, sets the band playing, then, with a shout, the "Michigan Yell," the whole brigade rushes in. One prisoner said he never saw such a man as "That Custer." "When he goes for a thing he fetches it in." One of the rebels, when taken prisoner, asked to see "that d——d Custer and his band." Pardon me, Father.

The officers all tell the same story. But don't tell all this, dear Father, for you know Autie is unostentatious.

And you know Autie swears in battle, but in this last he did not hardly swear at all. When I think how free from other sin Armstrong is I cannot look on this as of such magnitude. He will cease altogether, some time, I believe.

And so Albert is dead! Albert! I had used to think anybody out of the army was safe. The dear boy . . . that day last summer when Mother had a chill he wept over her pillow and took such tender care of her.

Custer to Elizabeth, May, 1864, from Virginia:
I am deeply pained to hear that you have lost so near and dear a friend. I regret that he and I did not have an opportunity to become well acquainted. I am rejoiced to hear that you try to be as cheerful as possible. I would not have you shut yourself away from society and amusement. I am glad you saw Clarke in so admirable a comedy as "Toodles."

I continue to receive the most flattering compliments in regard to our late battles, but you need have no fears regarding my vanity.

I have ridden "Clift" in battle and he is perfectly splendid. At his first experience under fire he was almost indifferent to it. A real war horse, and all the more valued by me because he bears my darling's name.

Eliza has escaped capture several times. Once the Rebs were right around her carriage.

I am surprised and sorry you have not called on Mrs K. Col. K. is one of my best friends, and feels the omission deeply. He will attribute it to your being prejudiced by your fellow-boarders at Miss Hyatt's. I should rather you had failed to call on any other person in Washington. I really feel quite badly about it. For my sake please be good and do so, won't you?

Sheridan's first independent cavalry raid, lasting about a fortnight, had inflicted on the Confederates a deadly blow. By cutting Lee off from Richmond it enabled Grant and Meade to move the main command unmolested. Resisting a possible temptation to make a spectacular entry into the enemy's capital, Sheridan, with admirable good sense, realizing that the war was far from won, took his cavalry back to the main body, the Army of the Potomac.

Custer to Elizabeth, May, 1864, from Virginia:
We have rejoined the army. . . . I have been successful in two or three important movements and have added fresh laurels to the Michigan Brigade . . . have received compliments and congratulations almost daily. . . . Did you observe that in the headings in the *Herald* no cavalry General's name was mentioned besides that of Sheridan and your boy? Some of the Richmond papers also speak highly of me.

When I think how successful I have been of late and how much has been said of my conduct and gallantry I think, "*She* will hear of it, and will be proud of her Boy!" That is all the reward I ask.

Be brave as I know you are, and do not borrow trouble. Tell me, have you heard from home lately?

Elizabeth to Mr. and Mrs. Bacon, May, 1864, from Washington:
The *Star* spoke of Sheridan's raid and of the commendable conduct of his Generals, including Autie. In Army Square Hospital a man with his arm wounded told of seeing Autie lead a charge, and a lieutenant who was in the battle on the 6th saw his horse shot under him, and expected every minute to see him killed.

Custer to Elizabeth, May 29, 1864, from Hanover, Virginia:
I am well and unhurt. We had a fight yesterday. Jim had his horse shot and is seriously wounded in two places: thigh and thumb. Our

Brigade lost heavily but was victorious. The 5th Mich. Cavalry lost
5 officers. Captain Greene was struck on the head by a spent ball but
was not injured. My horse was shot under me, the handsome one you
rode.

Telegraph Hon. I. P. Christiancy: Your son James seriously
wounded, but not dangerously Saturday 29th. Telegraph at once.

A few days later Mrs. Custer replied from her Washington boardinghouse where she was caring for their young friend.

Elizabeth to Custer, June, 1864, from Washington:
Judge Ch. got his telegram right soon. Jim is so dear. I talk to him of
leading a useful life, of reformation, of a wife who would save him
from wrong and of a God Who came to save sinners, not righteous
men. No one but you and Mother was ever so tender of my comfort.
He would not let me lean out of window to shut the blinds for fear I
should fall out, and was as distressed over my finger when a needle
pricked it as if it were a battle wound.

*Custer to Elizabeth, May 31, 1864, from camp near Cold Harbor,
Virginia:*
I am safe and well . . . we had another severe engagement yesterday.
Lt. Granger received a slight wound in the shoulder. Lts. Baylis &
Nims both had their horses shot on Sat. at the time mine was shot. We
were victorious yesterday in the Cavalry. The Mich. brigade turned
the tide (as usual) in our favor but the infantry under Genl. Warren
was not so successful. Fighting is now going on. All is well.

Elizabeth to Custer, early June, 1864, from Washington:
I have been very happy because yesterday's "Extra" gave me news
of you. . . . I have been so anxious. Wasn't Col. K good? He will give
me a letter to the Sec'y of War in case I need it in his absence. Mrs K
did not feel hurt at all because I waited so long before returning her call.
I am going again shortly to make up for my negligence. Scarcely
anybody here likes Mr K. Some say he is dishonest and licentious. It
makes no difference to me. I see nothing but a gentleman and a kind
friend.

Autie, I am going to leave this house. You wouldn't want me to stay
if you knew the annoyance to which I am subjected. Yet they do more
for me than for Mrs W. I tell Jim it is because I am Mrs General Custer.
He says it is because I am Libbie Bacon.

Jim is doing well. Pieces of his pantaloon come out of his wound every day. I am glad I had him brought here, the hospitals are unbearable on account of the horrible odor. I shall never give up my friendship for Jim. He has a fine pliable nature but has been without the influence of good Christian women. I hope, my dear, you do not think I did wrong because when he came he had much fever and was very sick and I in my sympathy kissed the poor boy as I should have done had I been unmarried.

To-day Annie Stevens and I went up to the Capitol with Senator Hale. At the House we met Speaker Colfax and Oh he said lovely things about you. I like him best of all here, he is so polite but not a bit of a flirt. In the Garden we met Mr Kellogg who said "We are going to make him a Major-General, Mrs Custer." I came home so pleased.

Judge Wade told Miss Hyatt that Congress were determined to make you a Major-General as soon as a vacancy occurs. I was so indignant on reading Genl. M's report that he never mentioned your name. But of course he is jealous.

I have been spending the day with Mr and Mrs Sheldon. We had a nice home dinner; only Mr & Mrs S and myself and plenty of tomatoes. Mr S. talked so much of the entire devotion of the men to you. He was so polite as to call a carriage and bring me home when I was prepared to leave.

If I were a young unmarried lady here I should flirt, I am afraid, but I have no desire to do so. Tho still enjoying gentlemen's society nobody could misconstrue my laughing and talking as flirting. I know, my dear, that tho I have a pretty face it is my husband's reputation brings me so much attention.

The middle-aged lady next door told Miss Liz she thinks I behave so nicely, not flying around the way so many as young as I would do. I would rather hear that than have the greatest critique call me beautiful. Autie, I think it well that I see so many wives in name only idling around with other men, for I feel how much better it is to be a correct wife even more than when I vowed it in Monroe.

Mrs K called here this evening. She is a flirt. She and another lady asked for Col. G. I do not question her taste, for he is very pleasant. But it was very bold. She is an *intense* woman.

Custer to Elizabeth, June, 1864, from Virginia:
You know what ample cause I have had to be suspicious or doubtful in regard to the conduct of women. One would naturally suppose my

youthful experience would make me ever watchful. But I would as soon harbor a doubt of my Creator as of my darling little wife.

Elizabeth to Custer, June 10, 1864, from Washington:
The *Herald* says you are gone on a dangerous expedition, again. They tell me raids are not so bad as battles. Oh I hope they are not.

Col. Gray can't say enough in praise of you. He told Judge Christiancy you are the most perfect gentleman he ever met. He never heard you say a word against anyone.

Oh my darling, what have I not endured in torture for the past fortnight. I will learn to be brave, but you know, dear, I can't learn all at once. Father and mother write me I am not alone in anxiety—they bear it with me. I cried over their letter all afternoon and dear sympathetic Jim cried with me. Was it not dear of him.

Autie, I do get along so nicely with my sewing. I am surprised at the ease with which I can make my clothes. I think of the days of peace when little children's voices will call to us. I can hardly wait for my little boy and girl. I send you a little picture I have drawn. . . . Dear *Father*, do you think you will look that way?

A subsequent letter voices the young wife's grief and self-reproach that their hope of children showed no signs of fulfilment. The husband's reply is all sensibility and sweetest reassurance. In time they grew to think it cause for thankfulness, in view of the discomforts of childbearing and rearing in army life, with the separations involved. Parental love seems to have been sublimated into an intensification of the conjugal.

The "raid" ordered by General Meade was Sheridan's second expedition. Circumstances were unpropitious. The Confederate cavalry had been reorganized under Wade Hampton, Fitzhugh Lee, and W. H. F. Lee. Sheridan's forces were greatly depleted by hard service; he could muster only some six thousand officers and men, many lacking mounts. Nor was there proper provision for the wounded. Starting from Newcastle on the Pamunkey, rations were issued—three days' rations for the men, two for the horses, and all supposed to last five days. Custer, for one, had no illusions as to conditions.

Custer to Elizabeth, June, 1864, from Newcastle, Virginia:
Dear little "durl"—Again I am called on to bid you adieu for a short period. To-morrow morning two Divisions, 1st and 2nd, of this Corps set out on another raid. We may be gone two or three weeks. I will write, the first opportunity. Keep up a stout heart, and remember the successful issue of the past. God and success have hitherto attended us. May we not hope for a continuance of His blessing?

With thoughts of my darling and with the holy inspiration of a just and noble cause I gladly set out to discharge my duty to my country with a willing heart. Need I repeat to my darling that while living she is my all, and if Destiny wills me to die, wills that my country needs my death, my last prayer will be for her, my last breath will speak her name and that Heaven will not be Heaven till we are joined together. Write to Monroe and tell them of my absence. Yours through time and eternity, Autie.

Mr. Bacon to Elizabeth, June, 1864, from Monroe, Michigan:
Do not fail to telegraph if anything happens to Armstrong, Greene or Nims. Be calm, submissive and composed is the wish and prayer of your Father.

Apprehensions proved well grounded. To outmaneuver the enemy there were rivers to be forded, forced night marches made. Ammunition ran dangerously low. Sheridan was unable for nine days to hear from the main command. Also his progress was seriously hampered by his own wounded—four hundred—being hauled in buggies, carts—any vehicle obtainable, and his war captives—five hundred. Human kindliness was shown when some trooper would dismount to let a weary, footsore prisoner spell a ride. Then from all sides sprang up hordes of colored folk, their belongings tied in bundles, hastening to attach themselves to this visible sign of their new freedom.

Custer to Elizabeth, June 21, 1864, from White House Station, Virginia:
Under a tree, near the famous "White House" on the Pamunkey . . . we crossed this morning, but have been unable to advance from it more than two miles, as the enemy have us completely hemmed in. We have been fighting all day. The Michigan Brigade have discovered a gap by

which we will probably move out to-morrow. The firing has almost ceased and quiet is almost restored along our lines. Eliza is cooking my dinner. The staff are lounging on the grass. I reserve details for our winter evenings. The main incidents are: Little fighting till near Louisa Court House, when our two divisions met the entire rebel cavalry. As usual, the Michigan Brigade was detached from the main body, for the purpose of turning the enemy flank and, if possible, attacking him in the rear. I was ordered to go to Trevillian Station, there to form a junction with two other brigades. I carried out instructions to the letter, but the others were three hours behind time.

During this wait I was fighting every man I had against two Divisions of the enemy Cavalry. My Brigade was completely surrounded, and attacked on all sides. Had the others been prompt we would have struck the greatest blow inflicted by our cavalry.

I had captured over 1500 horses with saddles, complete; 6 caissons of artillery filled with ammunition, 250 wagons & several hundred prisoners, but, against overwhelming odds and lack of support, could not retain our captures. . . . Never has the Brigade fought so long or so desperately.

Five caissons belonging to Pennington's Battery followed by my headquarters wagon & Eliza's carriage, drove too far from our lines, and were taken. Eliza was taken upward of two miles when she made her escape, and after dark got back to our lines. Johnny who takes care of my horses, and several orderlies were taken. Captain Greene is a prisoner, at Genl. Hampton's headquarters. A prisoner here said that as his spurs were taken from him Capt. G said "You have the spurs of General Custer's Adjutant-General."

Tell Jim that, after all my joking about it, the rebs have taken Captain Greene's flute!

Would you like to know what they have captured from me? *Everything except my toothbrush.* They only captured one wagon from me, but that contained my all—bedding, desk, sword-belt, underclothing, and my commission as General which only arrived a few days before; also dress coat, pants and one blue shirt.

Poor Eliza, faithful to the last! When she saw she was to be taken she ran and got my valise, but the rebs took it from her. She succeeded in retaining her own, and brought it back with her. When one of her captors ordered her to get up on his horse behind him she said, "I don't see it!" On which he remarked to a comrade, "Ain't she d—d impudent!"

I regret the loss of your letters more than all else. I enjoyed every word you wrote, but do not relish the idea of others amusing themselves with them, particularly as some of the expressions employed . . . Somebody must be more careful hereafter in the use of *double entendu.*

They also took three of my horses including "Clift." But, determined to have one of the name, I have been so fortunate as to obtain a beautiful dark chestnut with curly mane and tail. Tell Jim we still have his pony, but horse and darkey have vanished into the unknown.

Sergeant Mashon was struck while gallantly carrying his flag at the head of a charge. He lived until morning. When shot he remained in his saddle till our lines began to waver, when he made his way to me, saying, "General, they have killed me. Take the flag!" To save it I was compelled to tear it from its staff and place it in my bosom.

Baylis was severely wounded. . . . At that point we lost over 400.

I was struck twice by spent balls, on the shoulder, and arm. Bruise and swelling soon passed away. One of my men of the 5th Mich. was shot in the heart by a sharp-shooter, and fell in a position as still exposed to enemy fire. He was even then in the death-struggle, but I could not bear the thought of his being struck again, so rushed forward, and picking him up, bore him to a place of safety. As I turned a sharp-shooter fired at me—the ball glanced, stunning me for a few moments. . . .

Your beautiful ambrotype was in my desk. . . . Write to Monroe; tell them I am too busy. Our men and horses are completely wearied out. Write to the boy who adores his darling little one.

Elizabeth to Custer, June, 1864, from Washington:
My darling Boy . . . Oh, I was so frightened, even after the raid was over. I kneeled down and thanked God. . . . When we are enjoying peace we must never forget His goodness.

I was so startled to hear of Eliza's narrow escape. Wasn't she thoughtful to seize your valise! And how ugly of the rebels to take it from her! When people told me of your saving the colors I realized what danger you had been in . . . and how jealous I was that a flag should take my place.

I suppose some rebel is devouring my epistles, but I am too grateful to feel badly about that. Let me unburden my mind about the matter, since your letter implies chiding, tho the slightest and kindliest. No Southerner could say, if they are *gentlemen* that I lacked refinement. There can be nothing low between man and wife if they love each other. What I wrote was holy and sacred. Only cruel people would not understand the spirit in which I wrote it.

How I laughed when I heard that the inevitable toothbrush had not been taken! . . . My dear, I have not cried for a week since learning that you came out of that Trevillian engagement alive!

I have had such a nice time to-day. Mrs Sheldon and I went with Dr. Bliss's horse and buggy to Mt. Pleasant Hospital. The household exclaimed at my going, with the thermometer at 104° in the shade. But I was fully repaid. Dr. Price was very polite and showed us round. Most of the cavalry wounded at Trevillian were there. Oh, Autie, if you could have seen how their faces lighted up when they learned who I was. . . . They shook my hand. . . . I can feel it yet. One little fellow said of the Michigan Brigade "Where *our boy* goes, we will go!"

There was one wounded rebel: I told him he was the best-looking rebel I had ever seen, and Mrs Sheldon told him he looked too good to be engaged in a vile cause and she would come again to convert him. He did not reply, but was very pleasant to us both.

I had only a basket of oranges which I gave the doctor for them.

Elizabeth to Mr. and Mrs. Bacon, June, 1864, from Washington:
Do tell any wife or mother or anyone with some friend in a Washington Hospital that the patient is better off even than at home . . . has better medical attendance, nursing, &c. Many windows make the wards light and airy. Food, beds, linen, men's clothes . . . all so neat. Each ward has a female volunteer nurse. They are delicate women, too, refined in manner. They see to the special diet, medicaments, and administering medicines. There is nothing for ladies to do in hospitals. Everything goes on so systematically, and there are so many nurses from the Invalid Corps there is no chance to do anything.

Elizabeth to Mr. and Mrs. Bacon, June, 1864, from Washington:
If Autie had not made me promise not to do so I should ask you for money. [Her own expenditures in Washington caused her to write them this.] Money simply melts away here. After all, I am still your daughter.

Letters to her husband tell that she has tried doing her hair "over a rat," emulating the style of Lady Washington, but abandons it as "people here think it makes me look too mature." Seeking to change her quarters she hears that "there is only one reputable boarding-house on Capitol Hill."

Elizabeth to Custer, June, 1864, from Washington:
Coming from the next room I saw Mr S. embracing Miss Liz. We sat on the sofa with him between us, and he put his arm round her and tried to put the other arm round me. But I sat so stiff. . . . I told him he might sit beside me if he wasn't afraid of *that man.* And I pointed to your portrait.

Captain M. and Miss B. have decided to be married in Washington. We had the advantage of them. A wedding in a small place like Monroe is far more important than in a wealthy, showy city such as this.

Mr. Bacon to Elizabeth, extracts from letters, June, 1864, from Monroe, Michigan:
The *Free Press* of yesterday had the most graphic description of Armstrong's position in the late fight. No man of his age has his reputation. Everybody knows all about him. Few letters I receive do not make allusion to my brave son-in-law. He makes no mistakes. Every battle endears him and his men to one another more and more. I have not written him, not knowing where to send.

I am glad you are changing your boarding-house. Old maids are selfish and unreliable.

Hearing that Mary Q was keeping company with a fast young man of questionable reputation, in her father's absence I deemed it my duty to speak to her. . . . This was not acceptable. You have no idea of the many compliments we receive on our watchful care of you, of your upbringing.

Prof. Boyd and myself have sent Mrs W. our written obligation to pay for her daughter's full course till graduation. This broke Mrs W. down more than the loss of husband and son.

Hattie Bacon, her father, and Albert's father, look to me for the settlement of Albert's estate. . . . She will be a rich woman. This does not pay for the loss of such a man as Albert. All speak well of him, especially the poor.

Yesterday was Commencement [at the Seminary] but not as interesting as usual.

Your Mother cannot live without company—and cannot live with it.

Custer, meanwhile, kept his wife informed as to his movements.

Custer to Elizabeth, June 25, 1864, from north bank of the James River, six miles below Harrison's Landing, Virginia:

We have just reached this point after a long and tiresome march, tiresome both to men and horses. We expect to cross the James as soon and as rapidly as we can be ferried over.

As the rebs captured my dressing-case I must ask my little Durl to make me another, also to get me hairbrush, soap, penknife for nails, &c.

Custer to Elizabeth, June 26, 1864, from north bank of the James River, Virginia:

We have been lying idle the entire day, waiting while our large wagons precede us in crossing. I have heard from good authority that our corps is to have ten or twelve days' rest. We certainly need it. My time will be completely occupied in attending to the wants and requirements of my command, supplying what they lack in clothing and equipment, but I shall be only too glad to know that my men and horses are having a little rest.

Custer to Elizabeth, June 28, 1864, from south side of the James River, ten miles below City Point, Virginia:

I am seated on the river bank. Eliza is near her tent, giving utterance to her peculiar and sage remarks. My tent is under a beautiful, wide-spreading tree on a bluff. The men are camped beneath. We began crossing at five this morning.

When some officer who is so fortunate as to obtain a short leave says, "General, is there anything I can do for you in Washington?" my invariable reply is, "I wish you would call on Mrs Custer and tell her you left me well." I live for you, dear girl, and seek to establish a name among our country's defenders that in after years we and ours may claim with pride. . . . But now I love and am loved— That is all I ask.

Autie

Elizabeth to Mr. and Mrs. Bacon, June, 1864, from Washington:

I hear that the mortality in the hospitals is something frightful. Sixty to a hundred a day. A new law gives every dead soldier some honor. Ambulances pass with coffins wrapped in the flag for which they died. They have a cavalry escort to the grave. There are numerous establishments for embalming the dead. This is the saddest city, with maimed and bandaged soldiers in the streets, and the slow-moving government hearses.

Did I tell you? At Trevillian Autie lost *everything*—except his toothbrush. Mother will be glad to know that he never parts from that. He brushes his teeth *after every meal*. I always laugh at him for it, also for washing his hands so frequently.

There was a day in the spring campaign when rumor had it that Custer was killed. Extras were rolled off the presses; newsboys cried it in the streets. Mr. Bingham tells how he received the word.

Mr. Bingham's Reminiscences:
George killed: In one of the battles of the Wilderness? I rushed to the War Department, into Stanton's office, asked if this terrible news were true.

"Killed? No," thundered Stanton. "He was hemmed in on all sides by the enemy—cut his way through with his sword—and covered himself with glory!"

Ah, how like my brave boy!

I went at once to see Mrs Custer. I found her pale and trembling. She had heard the newsboys under her windows crying "Custer killed. All about Custer being killed." She was waiting for some word, and, seeing me, feared the worst. But when I told her she broke down completely from relief and joy.

9: Major General

ESPITE HEAVY casualties and the loss, through capture, of artillery and men, Sheridan's second expedition was accounted by Grant a success in its results. After fifty consecutive days of marching and fighting, the exhausted cavalry were allowed a three weeks' respite in July for recuperation.

Custer to Elizabeth, July 1, 1864, twelve miles from Petersburg, Virginia:

My Darling—The papers have no doubt informed you of the disgrace brought upon a *portion* of the Cavalry corps by the upstart and imbecile Wilson. He left this army with over 8000 cavalry well-equipped and mounted, also 3 batteries of artillery numbering 12 guns. His instruction was to make a raid toward North Carolina and destroy the Petersburg & Lynchburg railroad. . . . He permitted himself to be cut off, lost all his artillery, burnt his ammunition and wagon trains, abandoned his ambulances filled with wounded, lost by capture a very large proportion—probably over half—of his entire force, and is now struggling through the country, followed by a small portion of his command—according to the latest intelligence—with the rebels in close pursuit.

It was Genl. Sheridan's intention to send the 1st Vermont to my Brigade on his return, but I fear there will be but few of that gallant regiment left.

Here is the result of consigning several thousand cavalry to the charge of an inexperienced and untrained officer. All who knew Genl. W. prophesied a disastrous outcome, but the most charitable never imagined the half of this. Even Genl. Grant in his high and responsible position cannot fail to learn wisdom from this disgrace.

Genl. Grant obtained the confirmation of W's appointment by the Senate, but it will require influence even more powerful to satisfy the people—above all, the Army, that this was a judicious measure, in view of his total ignorance and inexperience of cavalry, because he was a favorite staff officer of Genl. Grant, also it was he who wrote Genl. Grant's report of Vicksburg, and later has been engaged in writing a history of Genl. Grant's campaign in the West.

I hope the authorities have learned from this unnecessary disaster that a man may be a good engineer, but an indifferent cavalry leader. One might as well expect that a person with a good singing voice should necessarily have a talent for painting. But enough of this. You cannot imagine what a blow this humiliation is to our esprit-de-corps, and to the pride each member of the Cavalry feels in our organization. We, as individuals, as companies, as regiments, brigades and Divisions, have labored long and arduously to establish an honorable record . . . and our efforts have been successful, our career brilliant . . . and now to have this imbecile (in Cavalry), this Court favorite tarnish our fair fame is discouraging, to say the least. We of the 1st & 2nd divisions have the consolation of knowing that we were in no way connected with it. We also know, the whole Army knows, that it was not the fault of the brave men who compose the 3rd Division, but that the sole blame rests on W. and on those who, knowing his deficiencies, placed him in such a position of responsibility.

But my little girl may not be interested in such matters. My last letter was written when we were comfortably encamped on the James expecting a 10 or 12 days' rest. But this mishap has rendered it necessary for us to occupy our present position on the extreme left of the Army, near the Weldon Rrd. offices. Men and horses are worn out with long marches and absence of food. We need rest, and I hope will soon be granted at least a two weeks' respite from raiding.

While I am still as strongly wedded to the "noble profession of arms" as I ever have been and hope ever to be, I frequently discover myself acting as umpire between my patriotism and my desire to be and remain with my darling. I wonder at the strength of my love of country and my desire to serve her, in view of the sacrifices I make to carry out my idea of duty to my government. I do not enter the Army, as some do, leaving wealth, position, a comfortable home—but I do infinitely more, I separate myself from my heart's darling. But it will not always be so. A better time is in store for us.

Custer to Elizabeth, July 3, 1864, from camp six miles below City Point on the James River, Virginia:
. . . . And so "Somebody" thought her boy intended to chide her a least little bit about her captured letters? Ha, ha, dear one, you do

not know him if you suppose he intended to "chide" his heart's idol. I only wished to impress on you the need of more prudence in writing— but the effect was not lasting, for the very next letter would afford equal amusement to my Southern acquaintances as those now in their hands. Now do not think me exacting or too particular.

Mr Colfax's note was certainly complimentary and it affords me great pleasure that so able and deservedly honored a man should be at all interested in my career.

Mr Kellogg writes that he has engaged a boat from the Sec'y of the Navy to bring Senators Chandler & Wilkinson and several ladies down to the Army, and that my girl would be one of the party. If you can get no further than Fortress Monroe I can meet you there. And Oh wont that be nice!

If you need more money now let me know, and I will send you a "pay account" by which you can draw from Major Rochester, the Paymaster, all you require.

We expect to remain in camp here for several days in order to obtain rest.

To the gentle admonition about reticence in letters that might come under derisive scrutiny, Elizabeth replied with gentleness.

Elizabeth to Custer, July, 1864, from Washington:
. . . . I shall not again offend my dear boy's sense of nicety by departing from that delicate propriety which, I believe, was born in me— the lady in me inherited from my mother. . . . Trust me, my dear. I am glad you are so particular with me. With my much loved and honored parents I felt indignant at reproof, but when you express yourself as ever so slightly displeased I feel grieved and try to do better.

There is nothing to write you about, but I love to punctuate even a sentence of nothings, to you.

While the husband's energies in the field were concentrated on the stupendous task of warfare, so the wife's, in her boardinghouse, were devoted to the serious business of warding off masculine attentions.

Elizabeth to Custer, July, 1864, from Washington:
Mr Ph. mails my letters every morning and brings me mine. When he saw my spirits rise at getting one he called loudly for postage. I

gave him the answer I always give to gentlemen hinting at such a salute—I'm married. Had I not been. . . .

Mr K. was here to-night. Very cordial. Too much so, for I avoided his attempt to kiss me by moving aside and offering him a chair. Any lady can get that man to do anything. But all I want is that he shall take me on that trip, to you. . . .

She is one of the party to City Point. But first she writes her parents of Independence Day in Washington that year.

Elizabeth to Mr. and Mrs. Bacon, July 4, 1864, from Washington:
It has been noisy since twelve last night. In spite of the hosts of Secessionists in this half-rebel city there has been quite a show of patriotism. An immense flag is stretched across this street. Darkeys have taken possession of the city, never having had much liberty before. However, they are using it in an orderly manner. There are processions of them, ranging in color from pale to sooty black, all dressed in the gaudiest colors. The babies have black woolly heads and beady eyes. They are so good. I never heard a black baby cry. This is the only holiday clerks and business men have had all summer.

Col. T is very feeble. He is dying of consumption. But it gives little pain to see such a man die, for he is a sincere Christian. You dont know how barbarous the life is here, with family prayers and grace at table shut out. This city is a Sodom crowded with sin which the daylight sees as well as the night.

Elizabeth to Laura Noble, August 18, 1864, from Washington:
My Ever Dear Laura, you cannot tell how I wish for some sweet friend—you, Nettie, Anna—to talk to and walk and write with. Somebody under the sun who is not married, which means I don't like married people hardly a bit.

Think of Autie's and my happiness since Mr Boyd said those solemn words over our heads last February, and rejoice.

The night we were at City Point the Senator invited several officers on board. It was the President's boat and beautifully fixed up. Genl. Sheridan brought his band and they played for us to dance on deck. It was too solemn, within hearing of those dreadful sieging guns at Petersburg, but the officers seemed to ignore the fact that they have just been or are soon to be in battle, and enjoy the present.

You should have seen Genl. Sheridan dance; it was too funny. He had never danced until this summer and he enters into it with his whole soul. He is short and so bright— He is like Genl. Pleasanton except that Genl. P is quieter and has exquisite taste.

We arrived here Saturday but Autie had to leave me Sunday. I was so unhappy. But on Wednesday, as I sat here reading, up the stairs came someone with such a bounding step as no one else has, and I had nearly a week I hadn't hoped for with him. But he was far from well when he left. He hadn't taken long enough leave to recruit his strength.

Many of his friends, regular Army officers, were here at the same time. Laura, I never met such gentlemen in my life. They are perfectly charming. Such grace and carriage and such manners,—faultless. Oh they do enter and leave a room with such an inimitable air. And so finely educated. All West Pointers are so jolly and full of brotherly feeling. How I wish I might transport Genls. Torbert and Sheridan— both bachelors and so agreeable—to Monroe.

Washington is dull now, so far as society is concerned. Mrs Col. T and I pass these warm days as best we can, only venturing out to eat ice-cream and hear the Marine Band in the President's grounds. Washington surroundings are so pleasant, thickly wooded, with the old Potomac like a silver band, seen from the heights. Laura dear, I shall hail a letter from you with joy.

You see I am thoroughly a Cavalry woman by the color of my note-paper. And I have a hat trimmed with Cavalry yellow.

Custer to Elizabeth, mid-August, 1864, from Virginia:
Darling, Last night the band played in front of my tent by moon-light, "Virginia Rosebud." Then I asked Axtell to play "Then You'll Remember me."

I must tell you that, the day before yesterday, we had a severe engagement and a very trying one. . . . During the whole time I never used a single oath. My staff spoke of it afterwards. This is the first time I have not been remarkably profane during the heat of battle.

Elizabeth to Custer, August, 1864, from Washington:
The best news in your letter was of your having successfully overcome the fearful habit of using oaths. I feel that the angels in Heaven sang glad songs over your victory.

The siege of Petersburg was a major catastrophe to Union arms. Long and arduous preparations had been made to blow up the enemy fortifications, but by a mistiming the explosion was premature, and the attacking forces rushed into a burning crater, perishing in agony.

Custer, elsewhere, wrote of this with deep discouragement. His own news, however, is in happier vein.

General Jubal Early was threatening Washington. A redistribution of Union forces placed Sheridan in command of the Shenandoah Valley. With Torbert as chief of cavalry, Sheridan relied for direct support on his "bright young men," notably Merritt and Custer.

Custer to Elizabeth, August 21, 1864, from Berryville, Virginia:
The other day at the close of my successful fight near Front Royal I was riding with staff and escort near Ransom's battery, now with my brigade, and which was in a fight with me for the first time. . . . They are all regulars, who, you may not be aware, are stoical and undemonstrative. But imagine my surprise as I watched the retreating enemy to see every man, every officer, take off cap and give "Three Cheers for General Custer!" It is the first time I ever knew of such a demonstration except in the case of General McClellan. I certainly felt highly flattered. The commander is a graduate of West Point long before my time, and yet as enthusiastic over your boy as if he were a youth of eighteen.

After the battle I heard "By G—d Custer is a brick!" "Custer is the man for us!" And other expressions somewhat rough but hearty.

Genl. Merritt was present during part of my engagement, but never gave me an order or suggestion, even. The battle was called by many "the handsomest fight of the war," because fought on open ground, and successful.

Elizabeth to Custer, September 6, 1864, from Washington:
Col. T is very feeble to-day. He came home disgusted, last night. Said he would not put on his uniform unless necessary, so many officers in the city are drunk or carousing without restraint.

Major Kennedy walked home with me from church. He is so polite and without affectation. Autie, nobody tries to flirt with me. I pride myself they understand I do not desire such things.

The 25th N. Y. and the rest of your brigade with Lt. Wheeler passed by as I was coming from church this morning. Oh my heartstrings

warmed under the influence of the bright cavalry yellow. I was glad
that tho I wore no sabre nor yellow cord on my jacket I had yellow on
my hat. One of the orderlies looked at it.

I like to wear it at church on Sundays. I know you are thinking of
me at that time—and you said it was the prettiest bonnet you ever saw.

Mr Ch. was here with several politicians—quite sober for him. He is
in love with Mrs G. How can Major G stand by and see his wife
flirt? Her excuse is she is married to a dunce.

I have studied my accounts. Of the $500. you so generously gave me
I have spent $300. for myself apart from board. It seems a great deal,
but as I had to have a whole new summer outfit it was not extravagant.
Mrs T. spent $600. I want a new black silk dress. I do not think $60.
too much.

Mrs T told me of two young married men comparing notes. One had
laced his wife's dress for a party (A dear boy has done so patiently for
me). It was a yard and a half long to the points, & then he found he
had done it wrong and had to unlace it and do it all over again. These
married slaves . . . dont you wish you were not a Benedict?

Mr Ch has just made me a flying call, but as Mrs G was going out
of course he went with her.

I will *not* give way to despondency when I dont hear from you. The
ladies here think I do wonderfully.

Mr P who was near death's door is better. Mrs G has been a devoted
nurse. Oh but what a flirt she is. She was even having a sly talk with
the doctor—who is indeed very nice. But she was in the dark front
room by the window, when I went up, charming him. And idiotic
Major G sat quietly talking in the next room. Bah! I wouldn't give a
snap for a husband who would allow such goings on. He knows and
sees it all, yet is ninny enough to do nothing. I like her though.

Mr P's wife came to-day. I dont like her a bit. Autie it is rather the
exception than the rule that married people here care for each other.
She might live here, but no. She cant keep up the same style as other
people. And yet she has ample means. His salary is $2,000. I believe.

Old Mr P is so funny. He said, "I saw you coming upstairs, Mrs
Custer, and by the way you moved I thought it was one of our girls."
He explained he judges a woman as he does a horse, by its movements.
Blunt old fellow.

To-night I was so tired of staying in the house and it was so pleasant
I took a walk, up to the park by the President's. But the longer I stay

here the more I am afraid to go out by myself; I walk in terror for fear of being taken for one of the "ten thousand." I went in a street off the avenue because that is always filled with gilded sin. I might just as well be in Turkey, for, tho I despise a vail, I dare not go alone without one. I try to console myself thinking anyone would take me for a dress-maker or milliner I dress so plainly. But virtue is mistaken. I myself made such an error. I saw two girls with their dresses suspiciously long. I passed them, supposing them questionable, when I heard one say "What a pity that such a young girl as so-and-so should act that way!" So I concluded they must be good if they felt another's conduct so deeply. And yet I have to take exercise.

If you had come in to-day you would have found your little wife in a common, rather short dress—no hoops—and hair tucked up, busy painting. I cant sit at my easel with hoops on so I become rather primi-tive in style.

Mr P was worse last night. Mrs G came down for me. They thought he would die. The doctor was there nearly all night. I slipped on a wrapper and went up. The doctor saw me thus and I was a little ashamed, but in illness such things are unnoticed.

I saw Warren as "Dr. Pangloss." He is 65 but active and so comical. One sentence struck me; the hero said "The kiss of honest virtue is worth more than all the embellishments and luxuries of untold wealth."

I am half inclined to get me a black silk.

Mr P died this morning—perfectly well and strong till a short time before. I am afraid he was not prepared to die, for he relied on his morality for entrance into Heaven. When will men and women learn how useless it is to hope for entrance thus? I wish they would take warning.

I drove out early this morning into the country for cream for him. Poor man he ate some and enjoyed it before he died.

Elizabeth to Mr. and Mrs. Bacon, September, 1864, from Washington:
He [Mr. P] was never spoken to about death, and a short time before he died while in partial delirium he swore frantically. I understand they are Universalists.

How Autie's pay goes! Autie took $100. I took $190. Autie dont spend much out there; his commissary bill was only $70. for a good part of the summer. I have spent $600. since April. Autie never says a word regarding it. My washing is reasonable, only $3. a month. I am determined to be more economical for we wont always have the same pay. It is such a good idea to keep accounts. I dont wonder *now* that Father tried so faithfully to teach me. These victories have caused a great tumble in gold. Mother, would you get a plaid or plain goods for winter in my place? Everyone wears plaid but I like plain best.

I was told that in a hand-to-hand fight lately a rebel had his pistol pointed at Autie. Autie drew his sabre and just missed the rebel's head but slashed his nose. He was taken prisoner. He is getting well.

There is great excitement over the political campaign. We are between a Lincoln flag and an immense banner with McClellan's name on it and Pendelton's beneath. McC has lost many votes by this association. The soldiers make demonstrations as they pass, some cheering for McClellan and groaning for Lincoln and the reverse. I dont know how Autie feels. Mr Chandler makes speeches cursing the copperheads frantically.

Elizabeth to Custer, fall, 1864, from Washington:
Both war and peace Democrats claim McClellan. I think he will be elected and that would mean peace—perhaps dishonorable. Autie it is treasonable and unwomanly but way down in my heart I want peace on any terms, for much as I love my country I love you more. Why is it your Brigade has to do everything? Why cant Genl. Torbert give some other Brigade what he crowds on you?

Robert N called on me and told me how well I was looking. I was so pleased, for I am not indifferent to compliment and have feared of late I was growing right homely.

Major K walked home with me last night and we talked election. He is thoroughly McClellan. He asked your politics. I said if you had any I didn't know them, but I am for Abraham.

It is generally thought now that Lincoln will be elected. But I never say so, for fear people will think I am repeating your sentiments—and I dont even know them.

Elsewhere she expresses a fear that Mr. Lincoln's neglect of social duties will count against him.

Custer to Elizabeth, fall, 1864, from Virginia:
My darling—Only think of the hundreds, the thousands of cases more aggravated than Mrs C's. Look at Mrs Pennington. She has known Mr Lincoln for years, yet he has never called on her, never left a card,

and yet I doubt not she has cast many a vote—an indirect one—for his election.

I believe that if the two parties, North and South, could come together the result would be a union closer than the old union ever was. But my doctrine has ever been that a soldier should not meddle in politics.

In early September husband and wife met for a day at Harper's Ferry. On the morrow Custer wrote her from camp.

Custer to Elizabeth, September 11, 1864, from camp at Berryville, Virginia:
My dear little Army Crow—following me around everywhere. . . . Not even the supposed proximity of Mosby's gang could drive away my happy thoughts of you. During the 16 miles' ride back I spoke but once, and I fear the two officers with me deemed me unsociable, or wrapped in my own importance. But I did not think of that till later.

That officer of mine who was captured by Mosby escaped under strange conditions. He is a Mason, and found his guard to be one also. So it was arranged between them that at night he should get away. Then, to avert suspicion from himself, the guard fired two shots, carefully aiming wide of the mark. Our man was pursued by rebels some miles over the mountains, but made his way safely into camp.

September found Sheridan making preparations to end Early's control of the Virginia Valley. His epic ride took place October 19. Prelude to this was the battle of the Opequon a month earlier, the success of which called forth from President Lincoln his telegram: "God bless you all, officers and men," while guns at the War Department fired a hundred shots in salute. Meanwhile, in the field there could be no pause for rejoicing. There is reorganizing to be done.

Custer to Elizabeth, September 30, 1864, from Headquarters, 2nd Cavalry Division, Army of West Virginia:
My Rosebud—Before this "She" will have learned that her Boy General has been assigned to permanent command of a Division. . . . Mine is the largest. Am I not fortunate?

I had to leave my old brigade and staff, all but two aides. Fought and Eliza also come with me, But Genl. Sheridan has promised I shall trade one brigade for the old as soon as practicable. You would be surprised at the feeling shown. Some of the officers said they would resign if the exchange were not made. Major Drew said some actually cried. Axtell, the band leader, wept. Some of the band threatened to break their horns.

I have a tent almost as large as a circus tent. When I get back my old brigade I shall have almost every wish in regard to a command gratified.

Now Father Bacon is writing his daughter for news.

Mr. Bacon to Elizabeth, October, 1864, from Monroe, Michigan:
I have been in suspense regarding Armstrong . . . I have not heard since the Shenandoah fight . . . only partial accounts of the Michigan Cavaliers . . . I read that General Custer with his brigade made a successful counter-charge when the rebels were within pistol-shot. . . .

Elizabeth to Mr. Bacon, October, 1864, from Washington:
Autie told me to write you. . . . He first was given Genl. Averill's Division, the 2nd, but, as Genl. Wilson was sent to Sherman's Army, Genl. Torbert sent Autie a note that Genl. Sheridan would transfer him to his old Division, the 3rd. . . . Autie says when he gets his old brigade he will have the best Division in the Army. . . .

Now I can see you hold the letter down as you are reading it, and look over your spectacles at Mother and say, "I knew it!" And then beg her not to interrupt.

Mr. Kellogg has just returned from the front. He wants to go to Monroe and deliver a speech telling them what a man General Custer is. Now, Father, do have some of your friends invite Mr. K. to do this. But don't let anybody know you did so. For when he praises Autie they might think us proud. We have a right to be, but not to be "set up."

Do write often, Father. Your letters comfort me.

Mrs. Bacon to Elizabeth, October, 1864, from Monroe, Michigan:
My Darling Child—I am so relieved to get your news. We have had such fears for our dear boy.

You speak of expences. I am glad you are trying to be more economical, for that is the duty of any wife. I do not think you naturally extravagant. But you cannot expect always to have money so plenty as now. Money goes easy when one has it. You must make some sacrifices and take care of everything, then you will always have good cloaths without getting everything new.

I am like you; I think a plain dress more genteel than a plaid. Please write me what kind of winter hat to get, when you go to New York. I must have a nice one, but my conscience will not let me go over $12.

I think your coat will be very pretty—all the nicer for your making it yourself. It will please Armstrong. All husbands like to' have their wives ingenious as well as industrious.

Elizabeth to Mrs. Bacon, October, 1864, from Washington:
Mother, I never think of you without gratitude. . . . I thank God for you more and more, and long for your sweet society. I look upon my dear home as a paradise, and only restrain myself from fleeing to it because of the hope that Autie and I may come together . . . to be near him and ready for any emergency. . . .

I have made me a light basque out of my last winter coat. And my neapolitan hat is trimmed sweetly with blue and green plaid ribbons, with a chenille crown, and scarlet flowers inside.

I shall get me a winter poplin in New York.

Elizabeth to Custer, October, 1864, from Washington:
Remember, I cannot love as I do without my life blending with yours. I would not lose my individuality, but would be, as a wife should be, part of her husband, a life within a life. I never was an admirer of a submissive wife, but I wish to look to my husband as superior in judgment and experience and to be guided by him in all things.

Did I tell you that I bought Mrs G's bonnet ribbon? She is in mourning . . . and have trimmed me the sweetest hat I've seen this fall. It's a right becomming bonnet, and indeed I look nearly good enough to kiss when it's on.

Mr Stires has just been here. I could not let him in as I was ready to retire for the night, but talked to him through the door. He says when the railroad to Strasburg is opened he will go down to the front. Oh Autie, if only I could go with him. He read me a piece from the papers. It is terrible to think that you are the mark of sharpshooters. Autie darling, your arm has been raised often enough in defence of your country. You can make yourself more useful in directing and planning for others.

The first task assigned to Custer in his new command was to avenge the murder of Lt. Meigs by burning the houses within a certain area and to bring back all able-bodied males as prisoners. His first battle was at Strasburg, where Sheridan's orders to Torbert were, in effect, "Whip the rebel cavalry or get whipped." Custer's division went into action against his friend and classmate General Rosser.

Custer to Elizabeth, October 10, 1864, from Virginia:
Darling little one, Yesterday, the 9th, was a glorious day for your Boy. He signalized his accession to his new command by a brilliant victory. I attacked Genl. Rosser's Division of 3 Brigades with my Division of 2, and gained the most glorious victory. I drove Rosser in confusion 10 miles, captured 6 cannon, all his advance trains, ambulance train, all Genls. Rosser's, Lomax's & Wickham's headquarters wagons containing all their baggage, private & official papers . . . recovering Major Drew's commission captured at Buckland Mills, and the case of my little girl's ambrotype captured at Trevillian. . . . I am now arrayed in Genl. Rosser's coat. . . . My new command is perfectly enthusiastic. . . . Genl. Torbert has sent me a note beginning "God bless you. . . ."

Elizabeth to Mr. and Mrs. Bacon, October, 1864, from Washington:
Oh, that last battle was a magnificent affair. Father I send you the newspapers with accounts of it. Autie only wrote a few lines. Wasnt it splendid that his first move with his Division was to recapture what Genl. Wilson had lost? And he got his Division by merit, not by hinting and begging.
Mother I had the most splendid success with my basque I cut out from my cloak. I think of hanging out a sign. . . .

Elizabeth to Custer, October, 1864, from Washington:
I guess you'd like to know who's been taking your little girl around? Well, he's very nice, but he's Mrs G's beau. I like Major P. very much; he is intelligent and refined, but he cannot really love his wife or he wouldn't be taking other ladies to the theatre.
Last night Mr Ch. called—tight as usual, and disgusting when he has taken too much. I had to keep moving from place to place to keep him

from kissing me. It makes me enraged that one has to endure these old
fellows when a younger one can be sent off so readily.

Do you think I write stupid letters, darling? I would not be stupid
if somebody were here.

I got $140. from Mr Stires; $40 for my board and the rest to go to
New York.

Custer to Elizabeth, October, 1864, from Virginia:
A few days ago Dr. Ruliston, the Corps surgeon, was congratulating
me on my successful fight near Front Royal. . . . He is a religious man
and withal a perfect gentleman . . . after speaking of my narrow escape he asked if I felt grateful & had returned thanks for my preservation. How glad I was to reply in the affirmative and to add that I
invariably offer my thanks to Him Whose shield protects me and
Whose wisdom guides me and directs my judgment.

Major Rochester, Paymaster, has sent me pay accounts to sign. I will
return them to you. I will write him to call on you and cash the accounts. He will give you $291.30. You can use what you want and
send for the rest.

Mr. Bacon urged Custer to invest in land in the Traverse area at
$2.50 an acre, with timber "for which there is always a market in
Chicago," and suggested his saving $1,000 for the purpose. There is
no record of his doing so.

Custer to Elizabeth, October 15, 1864, from Virginia:
Tony Forsyth is sitting in Genl. Torbert's tent getting shaved. I am
writing at Genl. Torbert's desk. There will soon be a movement of the
Cavalry but the 3rd will not participate, as it is necessary to have some
reliable cavalry remain with the Army. I am living in daily hopes of a
movement which will bring me nearer my darling little girl. Poor coon.
Since your letter came disapproving of her sharing my pillow Dixie has
to sleep at the foot of the bed, and Dixie does not like it. I captured a
squirrel also from Genl. Rosser's collection. Eliza's goat and the coon
have great times together.

Among the papers I captured from the rebels are all of Genl. Mum-
ford's private correspondence (He captured all mine at Trevillian)
including his wife's letters. I have tied them in a bundle, neither reading
them myself nor allowing others to do so. I think the relation of husband and wife too sacred to be violated, even in war.

Have you seen the Sec'y of War's letter of thanks to Genls. Torbert, Merritt & Custer? Your father will be delighted.

Elizabeth to Custer, October, 1864, from Washington:
. . . . We went to see Booth—Brutus Booth from California—in Richard III. It was rather tiresome tho the man did well and showed cultivation. That magnificent scene where Richmond stands before his tent and prays on the eve of battle was quite spoiled after hearing McCullough last winter.

I have heard from Nettie that she has dismissed Jacob, and am glad. He is unworthy of such a pearl. Oh, and John R is married at last to that sweet Frankie M. But she must be lacking in sense to marry him.

I am about to start for Newark. I am going alone— That is, in care of the sleeping car agent.

In October Elizabeth visited Mrs. Bacon's relatives in Newark, N.J., and wrote her husband of the journey there.

Elizabeth to Custer, October, 1864, from Newark, New Jersey:
My beloved darling—The conductor was very polite. Through trains do not stop here so I had to go five miles through Philadelphia in a horse car. He took me to the car and gave me directions. . . . I was so frightened in the sleeping car all alone.

Mr Bagg says I am "very well preserved." They all think I look just as I did. I know you will be glad your vain little wife has passed muster with such critics. Oh, Autie, they are all surprised I am such a sempstress. To think I made and fitted a calico myself. They think it so commendable, now that I have plenty of money to get it done.

From the news there has been another engagement in the Valley. Autie if you were here you would be spoiled with admiration if that were possible after all you have already had. When will those Valley rebels learn it is useless to make any more attacks? Mrs Bagg and I went to New York shopping. The silks are such fabulous prices I would not think of buying one till they come down in spring. I got me a purple poplin, worsted and silk, for $35., very beautiful and not expensive for the quality. A fashionable dressmaker on Broadway is to make it also a black alpaca. We had lovely times looking in the shop windows. Such lovely ladies too and stylish. But I think they embellish a little.

I don't care if fifty rebels read this letter. I miss your kisses. . . .

Meanwhile Custer was not idle. On October 19 the redoubtable Early met crushing defeat from Sheridan's cavalry at Cedar Creek, Virginia.

Account in the New York Times, October, 1864:
Custer who, since the arrival of Genl. Sheridan, was authorized to act according to his own judgment in an emergency, by a single dash opened the way for the final success attained. It was a critical moment. . . . Rosser was forced to retire precipitately across the Creek . . . and here Custer, young as he is, displayed the judgment of a Napoleon. He considered a moment, then, quick as thought, saw that the time for a dash had arrived . . . with a small command pushed through a rocky ravine, striking the Creek at a blind ford, one fourth of a mile from the pike. . . . The rebel Artillery could be heard rumbling over the pike, a prize too great to be lost. . . . "Charge! Charge!" Custer fairly screeched . . . and the small but gallant band did charge. . . .

For over fourteen miles the ground was littered with the small arms the fleeing Rebels threw away, while the take made a fine showing in Sheridan's report. Sheridan himself came up and fairly dragged Custer from his horse and, as if nothing else could express his feelings, threw his arms about the other's neck and hugged him, in the revulsion from previous defeat and the intoxication of complete victory.

When the official report was being prepared, a staff officer heard General Torbert say, "Hadn't some of the guns better be credited to Merritt?"

Sheridan replied, "No. I saw Custer taking them."

Custer declared the men were heartened by feeling that this was the beginning of the end, for, as the Army advanced up the valley, they were met by squads of men on all sides returning from the mountains, whither they had fled to escape Jefferson Davis's order for "every man who could shoulder a musket to go to the defence of Richmond."

Elizabeth to Mr. and Mrs. Bacon, October 25, 1864, from Washington:
My dear Father & Mother—Armstrong is now a *Major-General*. His taking 51 guns in 10 days is said to be without a parallel in history. I

send you the Star's account of his interview with the Secretary of War.
. . . But let me tell you how I came to see Autie. I was in Newark. On
Sunday at breakfast someone brought in the N. Y. Times and read that
General Custer had arrived in Washington with the captured flags. I
thought they were joking and went round to read it over Mr Russell's
shoulder and read it and began to cry, for I thought he would have
gone back to the Army. I ran upstairs and cried for about ten minutes
as you never saw me cry. Then some of them came and condoled with
me for my lost chance of seeing Autie. Then the children and some of
the girls began to scream "He's come. He's come!" And come indeed he
did and dried my tears. It seems the Sec'y of War was ill, so the flag
presentation was postponed till Monday, and so he was able to come
here to see me. They all flocked round him and were as proud of him
as if he were their own flesh and blood. And indeed I was proud of
him myself, for you know if a person passes muster with and delights
the exquisitely critical taste of the Wells family (Mother the chief in
nicety) he must certainly be very worthy of admiration. I cut short
my visit to return to here with him.

At ten o'clock this morning Autie walked to the War Department
with the soldiers who had captured the flags bearing them. . . .

Account in the Washington press:
The party took a locomotive and ran forty miles an hour [to Wash-
ington]. When they reached the Capital they took a street omnibus,
and with a rebel flag flying from each window, went up Pennsylvania
Avenue amid a storm of cheers. Washington has not had many such
sensations. The soldiers in the city were jubilant, and when they met
Custer and his men in the street, would give the soldiers a jubilant hug,
and some of the old soldiers would kiss Custer's hand.

The story of each trophy was related at the presentation, in reply
to the secretary's kindly questioning. One, torn from a rebel staff,
was mounted on a jointed fishing rod. Another was taken by a lad
not yet eighteen, named Sweeny. With a comrade, Fred Lyons, he
had ordered a rebel ambulance on the field to stop. They were wearing gray jackets and were obeyed by the driver. In this way they
captured General Ramseur's own flag—with its motto "On to
Victory"—and himself.

Ramseur and Custer were old West Point friends. When Ramseur was captured he asked for his old classmate. "Custer," he said, "I knew if I fell into your hands you would treat me kindly." Custer did for him all he could, but to no avail. The captive had been shot through both lungs, and his time was short. The two chatted of old cadet days. Then Ramseur bade Custer cut off a lock of his hair for his wife and the child he had never seen, and asked that his remains be embalmed at Winchester and sent through the lines to his home.

When every trophy had been duly acclaimed, Secretary Stanton told the delegation that each member would receive a medal from the Government in appreciation. Custer then asked that they should receive their pay as if on duty while awaiting their medals in Washington and should have their way paid to their homes and back to the command. These requests were gladly accorded by Stanton.

Account in the Washington press:
"To show you how good Generals and good men work together [said the secretary] I have appointed your commander, Custer, Major-General."

Taking him by the hand, the Secretary continued, "General, a gallant officer always makes gallant soldiers."

This announcement was received with tremendous cheers by the assembled throng. One boy who had captured a flag spoke out:

"The 3rd Division wouldn't be worth a cent if it wasn't for him!" All laughed, and Mr. Secretary patted the boy on the head. The embarrassed looks of General Custer, as he bowed his thanks, showed that his modesty was equal to his courage.

Another incident, also recorded by the press, followed. Mrs. Custer wrote of it to her parents.

Elizabeth to Mr. and Mrs. Bacon, October, 1864, from Washington:
After the presentation Mr. Stanton asked Aut if he wasn't a son of Emmanuel Custer. Aut said Yes. "Well," said the Secretary, "he was once a client of mine. If he should come here I would do anything to make it pleasant for him. I have been trying to find his son. But learning you were from Michigan I thought it could not be you." Mr Custer has frequently told Aut "Go see Stanton. He'd be glad to see you." But Aut never would, for fear he might be thought to be seeking something. So when Mr Secretary asked, "Why have you never been to see

me?" Aut replied "Because I never had any business to bring me to your office, sir."

People are beginning to call me Mrs Major-General. But I have been too well-trained by you to be "stuck up."

Elizabeth to Custer, 1864, from Washington:
. . . . Mr G was here to-day to get a bundle he is to take for me to Monroe. As he is a private I did my best to entertain him, but he stayed so long I got tired. When he was in Libby prison he heard one of the doctors say he had been reading General Custer's wife's letters. I felt deepest chagrin . . . but I shall not let it trouble me when I have everything to make me happy.

I thought Col. Smith must be a Regular because he wore kid gloves and was so polite. Now you'll laugh at my definition of a Regular.

Custer himself at the time was not wearing kid gloves, nor did he invariably appear clad as a Regular.

Account in the Washington press:
. . . . In a former pursuit of the enemy among Custer's captures was a wagon containing the wardrobe of Genl. Rosser. In this was a fine new uniform, much better than any Custer had on hand, accordingly he appropriated it. Knowing Rosser well he thought it would be a good joke to notify him of the fate of his toggery. So, as we were retiring, he left a note with a family in the Valley, telling Rosser that he had received his clothes and worn them; that they fitted excellently, but it would suit him, Custer, better, if in ordering the next suit Rosser would have the coat made a trifle shorter in the tails. Later he learned that the note actually was delivered to the foe his friend.

Custer to Elizabeth, October 28, 1864, from Martinsburg, Virginia:
Dear little Durl . . . We arrived here after several hours' delay, the engine of the train ahead having been thrown off the track. General Seward is such a gentleman and has been so kind to your Boy. He insisted on my staying the night, wanted me to bring my entire party— two Aides and Mr Stires—and when I refused sent one of his staff to find comfortable quarters for them.

A bounteous supper was served of which I partook heartily, having eaten nothing since morning.

As the General has a fine house and all the comforts of civilization

I said, "Why, General, I should think you would have your wife with you." He replied, "I would, but my wife has one small child and is expecting another, and must remain at home." I could scarcely refrain from exclaiming Thank God my little girl is not so burdened yet, but is able to come and go. . . . It is only one of our many pieces of good fortune that at present she is spared the discomforts which would attend such an event.

The mail brought me letters from Father and Mother Bacon which I enclose. Is not your mother's charming? The best I have received from her. And so your father thinks your Boy should be promoted. How delighted he will be to learn the facts. Do not fail to send them the N.Y. papers of the 24th. I enclose a slip from the *Baltimore-American*. The Secretary used the words quoted.

I am sending for you to visit camp. You must make up your mind to fewer comforts than you now enjoy. You will lead a real soldier's life. Do not come if you do not desire it. Retain your room. Bring riding-habit, one small trunk. You will not need any nice dresses this time. I will come or send Fred Nims with a party to meet you at Martinsburg.

Good-night and a kiss from your devoted Boy Autie.

Elizabeth to Custer, October, 1864, from Washington:
I love luxury, dress, comfort. But, Oh, how gladly I will give them up. I can be ready in a day or two. I can hardly wait.

There are incidents in the Custer story not told in Custer letters but recorded later. One concerned a beautifully carved conch-shell button with silver shank that Custer had had set as a brooch among his wedding presents to his bride. How he came by it, Mrs. Custer has set down.

Elizabeth in her diary:
One of my husband's classmates at West Point left the Academy when his State, Virginia, seceded, and as Lt. James B Washington fought in the Confederate Army. Captured, he asked for Custer, at the time a Captain on the staff of General McClellan. The greeting was affectionate, and Custer asked for, and received, permission, from the kindly McClellan, to make the prisoner his guest for what time he would be kept in Union lines. A camp photographer, seeing the two seated on a log, chatting, was preparing to photograph them when

young Washington called out to a small darkey standing near, and placed the child between them, saying "The picture ought to be called "Both Sides. The cause." And so it appeared (in *Harper's Weekly*).

Lt. Washington was exchanged, and was fighting with the enemy again when Custer, now a General, was campaigning with Sheridan in the Shenandoah Valley. One day a servant came from an estate they were passing, to Custer, saying that his mistress would like to speak with him.

Mrs Washington had sworn that she never would speak to a Yankee, but her son had told her that she must make an exception of Custer should he ever come her way, and now she wanted to thank him for his kindness to her son. She did more; she forced him to accept a gift, a precious heirloom in the family, one of a set of buttons from a coat made for and worn by George Washington.

Then, though her hospitable instincts would have detained him she hurried him away to catch up with his column, lest the Confederates should get him.

1 0 : Closing Scenes of the
Civil War

Elizabeth to Mr. and Mrs. Bacon, November 6, 1864, from Martinsburg, Virginia:

My dear Father and Mother—I came to Martinsburg by cars, and was met by Autie in his old rebel hat, overcoat, gloves, pants, looking every inch a rebel. Genl. Seward had sent his ambulances for us. We spent the night at the house of a Union lady. Loyal people in the border States have to endure all sorts of misfortunes. Next morning at 7 we set out, going through 40 miles of country infested by guerillas, and scene of Mosby's barbarities . . . travelling in a light spring wagon, with an escort of 150. Father used to show up the horrors of army life for a lady. . . . "Gypsying, no better than riding on the plains in a covered wagon". . . . But, Father, I assure you, in this age of delicate females none is better adapted to army life than your daughter.

Our tents are in an enclosure of evergreens, one for bed-chamber, the other reception-room with floor made of barn-doors, while Eliza has a near-by tent which also serves for dining-room. Genl. Sheridan is looking for winter-quarters near Winchester, and we hope soon to settle there.

Elizabeth to Mr. and Mrs. Bacon, November 13, 1864, from Winchester, Virginia:

Such a stirring week. Wednesday before daylight the cavalry were ordered to fall back, the rest of the army having moved the day before. After breakfast by candle-light I went out and sat by the camp fire while my tent was being packed. I rode in my Virginia carriage, just in the rear of Autie, his staff and color-bearers. The escort rode behind. I had the honor of moving with the army.

We halted in a field, and I sat in the carriage while the tents were being put up—floors down, stoves set up. Next morning we uprooted, and moved on a mile to the right. We were accommodated with parlor and bedroom in a large house, with the basement for Eliza to cook in. I thought I was fixed for a week at least. But . . . the fortunes of war. The enemy cavalry under Genl. Rosser made an attack which forced the Division to go out and engage them. I rode in my carriage to Genl. Torbert's headquarters where I remained all day, lonesome and anxious. At two a dispatch came from Autie—the Asst. Adj.-General let me read it—saying the enemy had been driven several miles. Also it reported the death of Col. Hull.

I feel very badly about Col. Hull. He was one of the best of Autie's officers . . . only 22, risen from a private, the only son of his mother, a widow, and devoted to him. I had urged him to send for her to come to camp this winter. He was shot in the neck and never spoke afterwards. When I came back here and found my boy safe and well I was very grateful.

For headquarters Autie has a large, roomy Virginia mansion. The owners, Mr and Mrs Glass, are delightful people. They treat us as if we were special guests. I have never felt so much at home since leaving my own dear home.

Mother, if once you had colored servants you would never want any other. Mrs Glass used to have 19, now she has but two, and has to do without many things we think indispensable. It is so pleasant here, but for all I know we may be off in a few hours and away.

Armstrong and his staff went out again about 10 or 12 miles to Cedar Creek. I do not know if they have been fighting. I am so anxious. . . .

Elizabeth to Rebecca Richmond, November 15, 1864, from Winchester, Virginia:
My dear Rebecca—If you could only know what an exciting life I lead, hurried from one place to another with such rapidity . . . ! But as these changes are to be with or near my husband I am always ready to move at a day's notice.

It seemed so strange at first to sleep in a tent, like sleeping out of doors; almost no furniture, the free winds of heaven playing with the walls. But Oh, so exciting, a fascination about it. A soldier's life is glorious.

We are now staying with such nice people. They are so glad to have an officer in the house. It protects them from the rough element found in every army. We have such gay times.

How I should like a visit from you and Mary this winter. I am sure, Rebecca, you would make some very agreeable acquaintances, mostly gentlemen of course, but such gentlemen . . . such as one only finds in the Regular Army. There is a difference between one of these and a Volunteer officer.

I have a nice little saddle-horse, also carriage and horses. Aut's brother Tom has received a commission in a Michigan regiment and is with us. Such an open-hearted boy, he adds much to our family circle—for as such I consider the staff. In fact, Rebecca, no happier woman lives than your cousin Libbie.

Custer to Mr. Bacon, November, 1864, from Winchester, Virginia:
My dear Father—Libbie and I are most comfortably settled in this old Virginia mansion. . . . My Division is posted on the extreme right of the army. Genl. Sheridan's headquarters are about a mile to our left and rear. My line of pickets, about 8 miles in length, is about 5 miles from the main body.

This Division is now the strongest of the three, and will become stronger before the opening of the campaign. I have made some important changes. I believe in the principle enunciated by Secretary Stanton that "gallant officers make good soldiers." Acting on this I have secured the appointment of some of the most experienced officers as field officers. Two are from Genl. Sheridan's staff, a third from Genl. Torbert's, another from among the instructors at West Point but with a brilliant and extended experience in the field. A fifth will probably come from the Army of the West, now on Genl. Stoneman's staff, who, prior to the war, served in European armies, in the late Italian war. . . . None will occupy a position lower than that of Major, while several will rank as Colonel or Lt. Colonel. Then I have my time-honored associate Pennington as one of my brigade commanders—I have had frequent occasion to strengthen my early confidence in his ability and gallantry. As Adjutant-Genl. I have a German of noble family and military education, and an accomplished gentleman, Col. Pope, of the 8th N.Y. cav., a position second to none in importance, Inspector-General. Mustering officer, Capt Barnhart from my old brigade, and Capt. Lyon Quarter-master. My Surgeon-in-chief is an excellent physician and withal a perfect gentleman. A promising young man, Capt. Earle, is Commissary. Other positions—Provost-Marshal, Ambulance officer and Ordnance Officer are competently filled. I have four aides. Tom, with a little more experience will make a valuable and most efficient aide.

An order has just come— My Division is to start at 7 to-morrow morning. You may see news of an extensive raid in the telegrams. Libbie will be left in a safe and comfortable place near the main body of the army, Eliza with her.

Elizabeth to Mr. and Mrs. Bacon, December 4, 1864, from Winchester, Virginia:

Only three weeks to Christmas. I hope we will be able to get 30 days' leave, but Autie fears only 20. How I wish you would return with us. You can come without fatigue, now that the railroad is completed within 5 miles of Winchester and 9 of us. Our carriage is easy and the pike is good. You could come through to Baltimore in a day and two nights. And tho everything is raised enormously in these war times, travelling is no higher unless one stops at hotels.

Oh, *do* come. Mother will want to, but Father will pull up his chair to the fire and cross his legs and say, "Now, Wife, we have been away all summer . . . and then Armstrong and Libbie are coming home."

Now, Father; two weeks from us will be nothing of a visit. But if you come here Autie will introduce you to all the Generals, infantry and cavalry, and he will describe all the battles he has been in that you're dying to hear about. If you say No, we'll take Mother away from bed and board. Oh, Mother, I'll make it the pleasantest visit. I promise you the officers will do you the same homage as if you were unmarried and twenty. You only need your home dresses. I wear my black basque and blue merino skirt for afternoons, calicoes for mornings, and my riding-dress.

I am the only lady in the Army. The wives of line officers have been ordered out. I feared it might be a general order, but I believe Genl. Sheridan thought wives interfered with officers' duties in Winchester. But Mother and Rebecca may come.

Autie started with his Division for another raid on Monday night at two. They returned Friday morning. Autie always gets back ahead of his command. When within five miles he lets his black horse fly, and 'tis all the staff can do to keep up with him. They had frightful weather, good roads and fighting. Autie said before starting that Rosser would go back a different road from that by which he came, and so it proved. I'm glad he had the sense to retreat when he heard our command was coming.

I have a lovely little horse (loaned). I jumped a ditch with it yesterday.

Mother dear, the officers and the lady whose house we occupy notice my dressing so plain. But I do not think the army an appropriate place for display. As I happen to belong to the dignitaries I can do as I please.

Elizabeth to Mr. and Mrs. Bacon, December 25, 1864, from Winchester, Virginia:

We were delighted to get your letter, but amused. Father, you seem to think we can get a leave as long as we want and whenever we want it. But it's quite a hard thing to get. We had hoped to spend the day with you, but in the army everything is so uncertain. Autie went off on a raid. He sent me back notes by the scouts who brought despatches to Genl. Sheridan . . . thin scraps of paper sewed up in the hem of their pantaloons.

As for any reception of a public character when we do come, if we get a hearty welcome from our friends it is all we ask.

I am still the only lady in the army. I receive a great many calls and much polite attention from the officers. I never enjoyed so much respect as I do now. Being so occupied with company even your chatterbox daughter sometimes gets tired of talking.

A dark hour clouded the New Year when by order of Sheridan two deserters were shot, convicted of furnishing information to the enemy. There is no record of their being connected with Custer's division.

The hoped-for leave was deferred, as Custer was appointed president of the military court, with several important cases to try. Mrs. Custer was surprised to find that her husband was "quite a lawyer."

Then there came news of seasonable merrymaking.

Elizabeth to Mr. and Mrs. Bacon, January, 1865, from Winchester, Virginia:

On Sunday night Genl. Sheridan, his staff, and several Winchester ladies gave us a surprise party. We had learned of it in time to be prepared. Our walls were decorated with crossed sabres, regimental flags and evergreens. A Winchester baker supplied our tables with cake, turkey, biscuits, coffee, candy, nuts, oranges, &c. Genl. Sheridan is a beautiful dancer and enjoys himself greatly at such entertainments.

Tuesday sees us in Washington, Wednesday in New York. Then Ho for our beloved home! We shall have a jolly party . . . Capts. Lyon,

Earle, Barnhart; Lts. Nims, Worrell . . . Tom, Aut and I. Tom is a
fine boy. He has improved so much. Accept a daughter's love. Libbie.

Mrs. Bacon and Rebecca Richmond were of the return party.

Custer to Mr. Bacon, January, 1865, from Winchester, Virginia:
Mother and Rebecca are enjoying army life and, I am happy to say,
are acquiring army appetites. There are rumors of a movement, but I
do not place much reliance on them. I think you had better not delay
in your coming. I will send you a pass. We are enjoying the box of
vegetables given us by our friends at home. It has been suggested that
you might take up a collection of like kind and bring with you.

On the return journey Elizabeth accompanied the departing
guests as far as Washington. Mrs. Bacon went to Baltimore to visit
friends.

Elizabeth to Custer, March 8, 1865, from Washington:
On the journey we received the most polite attention from Colonel—
I forget his name. He telegraphed Genl. Seward who sent a Lt. of his
staff and two ambulances for us. Father is so inexperienced in army railroads we should have been lost without such help. Mr G. kindly carried
the bird-cage and the plants for us.
Senator Chandler kindly took Father and I to see Sec'y Stanton. I was
charmed with his dignity and elegance. He spoke of his friendship for
Father Custer, and said of you "I am glad he has been as judicious in
love as he is wise in war!" When I thanked him for his kindness to you
he said, "Not at all, Madam. He has deserved it."
Rebecca and I saw the Inaugural ceremonies from the Senate gallery.
We heard the farewell of Hamlin and the Inaugural of Andy Johnson.
He was drunk unfortunately. Mr Lincoln appeared with great dignity.
We could not hear him distinctly.
Monday evening I attended the Inaugural Ball with Senator Chandler.
I went solely as a spectator, and danced with him simply out of eti-
quette.
I promenaded with him and he introduced me to some of the distin-
guished people—Admiral Farragut the most so; he is right jolly and
unaffected. The ladies' costumes were superb;—velvets, silks, diamonds
dazzled my eyes. We were fortunate in getting out to the supper-table

before it was disturbed. It was a miracle of confectionery, and substantials were not wanting.

I wish you could have had some of the nice turkey and celery we had for dinner to-day. Oh, I have been so glad for the confirmation of the good news about your army. I am so anxious to hear particulars. I expect a letter from you brought by the officer who comes in charge of the prisoners.

Col. Mann is so polite. He sent me a lovely basket of violets and camellias. It reminds me of my boy last spring. You would come in with your hand behind you, then hold up a boquet. Those dear ways of yours. . . .

At the beginning of March, 1865, Custer's division made a surprise attack on Early's cavalry at Waynesboro with sensational results.

The New York Times, March, 1865:
Merritt had the lead, marching on through Staunton without asking questions. Custer asked questions, found that Early had turned to the left, going towards Waynesboro. This he reported to Genl. Sheridan, and received orders or permission to follow. The fight was ended when Merritt joined them. Early was whipped.

When Custer got back into camp after chasing Early into the mountains the rebel prisoners waved hats and cheered him.

The *Times* correspondent, Paul, decided to accompany Custer's division, the 3rd, for the remainder of the campaign, as the best command for news.

In Sheridan's reorganization of forces preparatory to cleaning out the Shenandoah Valley, Torbert was replaced by Merritt as chief of cavalry. Two divisions—the 1st under Devin, the 3rd under Custer—were sent by different routes to destroy the James River Canal and the Virginia Central Railroad. Scouts were sent to Grant asking that supplies be sent the exhausted forces at White House on the Pamunkey.

At Charlottesville Custer was met by a delegation of citizens headed by the mayor, who handed him the keys of the city and of Thomas Jefferson's own University of Virginia, in token of surrender.

At Fredericks Hall Custer had the "luck" of the man who over-
looks no detail and leaves nothing to chance. In the telegraph office
he found dispatches from Early to Lee disclosing plans for attacking Sheridan from the rear. Custer forthwith pursued Early and
broke up the projected sally so effectively that Early escaped only
by swimming the South Anna (going thence to Richmond) with
but one orderly, having lost everything "except his life."

We pause at Charlottesville to insert here a memorial written for
Elizabeth Custer forty years after the event by her old friend General Pennington, who had been in command of a Civil War battery.

General Pennington's memorial:

Long years after the great conflict had ended some members of our
family were seeking a place near Charlottesville, Va., for a summer sojourn, and found ourselves in a charming old mansion kept by two
charming elderly gentlewomen. Some word set the chord of memory
vibrating—and the tale of Captain Tom Farish was retold.

Early in March, 1865, Sheridan's Cavalry left Winchester to rejoin
the Army of the Potomac. On March 2nd our Division—Custer's—
defeated Early at Waynesboro, and that night crossed the Blue Ridge
at Rockfish Gap, and on the 3rd entered Charlottesville, followed by
the rest of the cavalry corps.

Captain Tom Farish, then on the staff of Confederate General
Walker, at the time stationed in Halifax County, not having heard from
his family for some time, started for home. About 12 miles from it he
stopped at a mill and changed his uniform for a miller's garb. So disguised he made his way to the house of an old friend, Col. Randolph.
As the Colonel was away in the woods with his cattle and horses, Farish
wrote him a note, asking him to come to meet him, as he had important
information for him—probably he intended to borrow a horse. This
note he entrusted to a servant, George. But George was captured by
Custer's scouts and taken into Union lines and the note found on him.
(He was brought to Custer's headquarters—Farish's own home).

Mrs Farish knew nothing of this until wakened at midnight by a
servant, Martha, whispering "Marse Tom's near by." And she told her
about the note and George.

Captain Farish grew tired of waiting for an answer to his note, and,
tho greatly fatigued, set out on foot. Arrived at his home he found his

father in the smoke-house, giving out ham to Yankee soldiers. Impossible to retreat, so he put a bold front on it. His father, too, betrayed no surprise, merely saying, "Tom, you'd better go to the house. Your mother is expecting you."

He went out, accordingly, but the Union officer in charge of the foraging party put a hand on Mr Farish's shoulder and said, "You have a Confederate officer in your house."

"That man who was here just now? Why, he's my son."

This the Union officer did not believe. He thought young Farish was General Early, and had him arrested and sent to Col. Wells' headquarters.

To Col. Wells Farish made himself known. On which Col. Wells sent him under guard to Custer's headquarters—the Farish home.

I was sitting with some of the staff, with Custer, when we saw mounted men approaching with a civilian.

"What's this," said Custer. "They seem to have a prisoner."

They halted. The officer in charge saluted. "General, I have a prisoner. He says his name is Farish, Captain Farish, and that he lives here."

"It that so, Captain?" asked Custer.

"Yes, General."

"Well, Captain, you don't need a guard. You can go to your room." And he dismissed the guard.

You can imagine the consternation of the household. Captured—in disguise. . . . He might be treated as a spy.

After the Captain had been with his family a short while Custer went up to them. Finding them in great distress he soothed them, told them he would do all in his power to have Farish paroled and treated as an ordinary prisoner. He could promise nothing, but would do his best.

He wrote a letter to Sheridan, accordingly, and Captain Farish, who had changed his miller's garb for a suit of civilian black, carried it, accompanied by two staff officers, to the General.

Sheridan asked him many questions about the location of the enemy troops, which Farish declined to answer. "Why, General, I cannot answer those questions. Did you expect me to?"

"No," replied Sheridan, "but I thought I would ask them." He enquired about the General on whose staff Farish had served, then exclaimed, "Why, that must be 'Mud' Walker. We always called him Mud at West Point."

He paroled Captain Farish who returned home, and assumed the duties of host until we left, a few days later.

When we departed Farish called out, "Custer, as an enemy I hate you. But I love you as a brother!"

Does it not seem strange that after all these years I should go back, and occupy the room where the family had gathered in their distress? And then that I should photograph the front porch where Captain Farish, now dead, had been brought, disguised, a prisoner?

One of the ladies showed me a photograph I had given her at that time. Another remembered it all distinctly, though a child of eight at the time. All had the pleasantest remembrances of Custer and spoke warmly of his kindness to them.

When Captain Farish came downstairs in his black suit he had slippers on. Custer said, "Captain, you can't go before General Sheridan that way!" "But, General," said Farish, "I have nothing else. My boots are wet." Custer said, "Well, your feet look about the same size as mine. Take mine." And he pulled off his boots and gave them to Farish who wore them to present himself to General Sheridan.

With the formidable Early disposed of, Sheridan sought to rejoin the main command besieging Richmond. Fears that he might be intercepted by Confederate General Longstreet were dispelled, and he proceeded to the Pamunkey where, at White House on the north bank, supplies from Grant would reach him. There, too, his weary forces would have a chance to rest after a march exceeding anything they had ever experienced: sixteen days and nights of drenching rains, swollen streams, roads deep in mire. They pulled through, buoyed by the knowledge that they were homeward bound. They no longer were a detachment on a raid but an integral part of the main army.

Custer to Elizabeth, March 11, 1865, opposite White House, on the Pamunkey River, Virginia:

Well, thanks to the care of a kind Providence, your Bo is safe and well. We will probably cross to-morrow. Meanwhile my command is drawing forage and rations from the loaded vessels in the river. Our raid has been a chain of successes, and the 3rd Division has done all the fighting. I wish you could see your boy's headquarters now. My flag is floating over the gate, and near it, ranged along the fences, are 16 battle-flags, captured by the 3rd Division. Neither was Genl. Sheridan nor Genl. Merritt within 10 miles when these captures were made. Nor did they know what I was doing. You will see Paul's account in the N.Y. *Times*. (Send a copy to your father, and one to Father Custer.) The 3rd stands higher than ever, in advance all the time . . . 3,000 prisoners and our own loss not exceeding 30. Your Bo has won new laurels. Never have I witnessed such enthusiasm. . . . I thought they—men and officers—would throw themselves under my horse's feet. Genl. Sheridan said "Old Custer is a trump." And "Custer, that command is just crazy at being with you, &c.&c." Oh, my angel, I have the most glorious Division. They behaved splendidly. I am more than repaid for the trouble I took last winter. Genl. Sheridan and others speak of the difference between it and others.

Write to our parents. Tell them I am well. Tom also. . . .

Custer to Elizabeth, March 16, 1865, twenty miles from White House, Virginia:

We had an engagement with the enemy at Ashland, and there my preservation from death, or being maimed, crippled, for life, was miraculous, and strengthens my grateful dependence on the Merciful Being Who has so often shielded me. . . . May I live to glorify Him and keep His commandments!

I was riding with my staff and escort to a distant part of the field, when the fight began. I was riding my new horse Jack Rucker who behaved splendidly . . . when his foot slipped into a hole and he fell, turning a complete somersault, rolling over, then lying with his full weight upon my back. Had he struggled I should have been crushed to death. But the noble animal seemed to comprehend the situation, for he lay perfectly still, without motion. The staff sprang from their horses, rolled mine off me, expecting to find me crushed or crippled. But, as soon as released, I called for another horse—mine being stunned—and was up again in a moment directing the fight. I am very sore and stiff today, but shall soon recover.

Chaplain Holmes—he is one of my aides now—exclaimed "Thank God." To which my grateful heart responded Amen.

The evening after Waynesboro I invited Chaplain Holmes to my tent, for prayers and to read a Chapter. He and I alone with God gave thanks for the victory He has vouchsafed our arms.

I read a chapter every night—except last night when it was raining and I had no light.

This crossed a letter from his wife, who had learned of his victory from the press.

Elizabeth to Custer, March 13, 1865, from Washington:
Oh, Autie—How delighted I was to hear of your success. Oh, you dear glorious warrior—my warrior. The *Herald* has quite an account of your taking Early's army. To-day's despatch from Sheridan I gladly hailed. What wonders you have accomplished in two weeks. But, my Darling, how fatiguing it must have been—and in such unpleasant weather. The mud so fearful, too. I expect you have been riding inside your waterproof coat ever since I saw you last.

Custer to Elizabeth, March 20, 1865, from White House Landing, Virginia:
My Darling—We are now resting our horses and obtaining such supplies as are needed after a march of 500 miles. The staff are gathered about the camp fire singing: "It's a Way we have in the Army," and "Let every old Bachelor fill up his glass, And drink to the health of his Favorite Lass."

Col. Capehart sent his band to serenade me this evening. They played "Auld Lang Syne" and "Home, Sweet Home." And Oh, how lonely I felt for my little one. I do not complain, for that I should deem a sin. God has been more than kind to me, and I humbly trust I may ever have a grateful spirit for His goodness. . . . Oh, I forgot to tell you: I have not uttered a single oath, nor blasphemed, even in thought, since I saw you, so strictly have I kept my resolution.

Mr Stahl will bring you a set of chessmen captured in General Early's headquarters wagon—probably belonging to him. I am learning to play. It is a beautiful game, much like a battle. If you will learn, it will be a great source of pleasure to us hereafter.

Tell me what you hear of Captain Greene—whether he has been exchanged. I miss him greatly.

I long for the return of peace. I look forward to our future with earnest hope. Our state may be far below our present one. We may not have the means for enjoyment we now possess, but we shall have enough and to spare. Above all, we shall have each other.

I think of you, even in the excitement of battle, and at night I dream of my darling.

Chaplain Holmes received such urgent calls from his congregation that he left the service. On the eve of his departure he addressed a letter to Custer.

Chaplain Holmes to Custer, March 21, 1865, from White House, Virginia:
General—Will you allow me an informal word before leaving. I feel deeply indebted for the privilege of the relation to you afforded by the past weeks, as it has enabled me to know you better, and has made me respect you even more heartily than before. I cannot express my gratefulness to the Almighty that He should have made you such a General and such a man. I rejoice with the 3rd Division, with the army, with the whole country in the splendid military genius that has made your name glorious in the history of War. But even more I rejoice in the position you have taken deliberately, and, I believe, finally, in regard to a moral and religious life. You cannot know what a great power you are exercising in this way upon your staff, your command and upon the whole army.

May God strengthen you in every right purpose, arming you ever for the good fight of faith, giving you at the end the Heavenly crown.

Praying that during the perils you yet must pass through before the war shall close, you may be safely kept by the Power that has so strangely shielded you in the past, I am, with great respect,

Theodore J. Holmes
Chaplain 1st Conn. Cavalry

Proud of this letter, Custer sent it to his wife, asking her to forward it for perusal to Bacon parents, Custer parents, Dr. Boyd, and the Reverend Mr. Matson in Monroe.

A letter to his daughter-in-law from Father Custer shows his strong religious bent.

Mr. Custer to Elizabeth, March, 1865:
Well, Libbie, I received your welcome letter. I need not tell you of our anxiety . . . you know from experience. Also you know to Whom to look for help. I feel every day more and more under obliga-

tion to my Savior for such good boys. I have all the confidence in the world in my dear son Auty, surrounded, as he is by temptation. Counsel Thomas. I want my son above all to be a good soldier of our Savior. We send our love and you send it to the boys. Your affectionate Father

E. H. Custer

Elizabeth to Custer, March, 1865, from Washington:

I am so grateful for that beautiful set [of chessmen]. Rebecca and Major Farnish have been playing, she representing Early and his staff, and Major you and yours. Of course you came out victorious. Rebecca compared her defeat to Early's retreat with but a single orderly. I have taken one lesson. You will always beat me. Rebecca said, "Well, wouldn't you rather have it that way?" "Yes," I said. "I wouldn't want a husband who wasn't my superior."

I left the others in the parlor singing hymns. I had to write my darling. To-day I actually had to leave the room when Mrs C and Mrs W welcomed their husbands. Of course I want them to enjoy their happiness, but it hurt me when Genl. C took his wife's hand on the sly under the tablecloth. It made me think of you.

Col. and Mrs Chipman called. She is lovely. Also she loves her husband—a rare thing in this horrid city.

I must tell you about my hunt for a new boarding-house. I hesitated about one because of a remark you made concerning Major P. But, my dear, I should only see him at table in the presence of his wife. And I have met any number of men a hundred times more attractive. Mr H told Cara I was enough to drive a whole brigade of officers wild because of my indifference to mankind. I compare them all with you.

Last evening Rebecca and I spent with such a nice little couple, Mr and Mrs J. Then Mr W came in, and immediately Mr J got out whiskey and offered it to him. I do think it such an ill-bred thing for gentlemen to drink before ladies. When people ask me what you drink I tell them, Water, coffee—no intoxicants, they think it wonderful.

Don't expose yourself so much in battle. Just do your duty, and don't rush out so daringly. Oh, Autie, we must die together. Better the humblest life together than the loftiest, divided. My hopes and ambitions are more than a hundred times already realized in you.

It will be recalled that the battle flags captured by Custer's division at Cedar Creek in October, 1864, were sent by Sheridan to the

War Department in charge of Custer, who on that occasion was made a major general by Secretary Stanton. The flags captured by Custer's division at Waynesboro in March, 1865, were no less distinguished a triumph, but at that time Sheridan could not spare his right-hand cavalry leader from the field; he therefore sent the flags and their captors in charge of General Townsend. Mrs. Custer being present, the secretary paid her a charming compliment, knowing no surer way to compliment her absent husband. Custer learned of this from the press, then from her letter to him.

Elizabeth to Custer, March 26, 1865, from Washington:

So you heard that I was present at the Presentation. Oh, what a happy day that was—the proudest of my life. Rebecca and I were down town shopping when we saw flags approaching and learned that they had been sent by General Sheridan. So we rushed into a street car, and arrived at the War Office just in time. I sent in to Secretary Dana, but he was not there. However an usher, hearing my name, took us in to Stanton's room. I thought no one had a better right, so was not one bit afraid. The room was full, but Mr Stanton perceived me and extended his hand most cordially. He introduced me to Senator Harris, then, as the men and officers presented the flags, he introduced me as "the wife of the gallant General."

As every flag was presented General Townsend read at the end, "Brevet Major-General Custer commanding . . ." every time, from first to seventeenth. . . . I could hardly keep from crying out my praise of my boy. But I knew it was a conspicuous place, so tried to behave as quiet and unassuming as I could.

To hear each soldier's story, and to know that my boy. . . . It was too much to bear unmoved. But when I saw tears in Senator Harris's eyes I was not ashamed of my own. I was so proud I walked on air. People in the hall stared and pointed me out to each other: "Custer's wife. . . . That's the wife of Custer!"

Before leaving I told the Secretary I had waited a long time for a letter from you, but was more than repaid by having witnessed this. Mr Stanton replied, "General Custer is writing lasting letters on the pages of his country's history."

The brief space allowed the weary troops for rest and reprovisioning at White House was over.

Custer to Elizabeth, March 24, 1865, from White House, Virginia:

We move to-morrow morning at six, to the James, to form a junction with the Army of the Potomac. We are delighted at the thought of seeing the Army again—provided we are not compelled to stay in it too long.

We shall then receive daily mail regularly.

I am sending the brown colt home. . . . I purchased him at government sale— He was considered too young for service. Superior blood, I expect to make a handsome profit on him, the Army having drained the country of such stock.

Tell me about your boarding-place, your landlady. Tell me about home.

Custer to Elizabeth, March 28, 1865, near Petersburg, Virginia:

Gen'l Sherman arrived last night at City Point, for a consultation with Genl. Grant.

I am sending by Mr Stires a black dress pattern, captured with other dry goods in one of Genl. Early's wagons. All desire you to have it. I think it will make a very nice dress.

Custer to Elizabeth, March 30, 1865, six miles from Dinwiddie, Virginia:

My Darling—To-day it has rained almost continuously. We have been on the march toward Dinwiddie Court House, starting yesterday. Last night I slept on the ground by the roadside, the rain coming down in torrents, our wagons several miles in the rear. Nothing to eat since daylight. My only protection was the fine rubber poncho given me by Captain Lyon. For pillow I had a stick laid across two parallel rails. Before I got the rails I slept a little, then woke to find myself in a puddle about two inches deep. Later I slept soundly. When the wagons came and I told Eliza about it she said, "Oh, I 'spect you wanted Miss Libbie with you . . . and she just as willing, and she'd have said 'Oh, isn't this nice!' "

We have halted to allow the wagons to overtake us again. We will resume the march in about an hour.

I am delighted you are pleasantly situated, and near so many army ladies. I shall feel less anxiety than I did last winter.

I received the package of clothing. I like the color of the drawers and socks.

To-day there has been but little fighting. The great battle is probably near at hand. I am hopeful and confident that the God of Battles will reward our efforts with a much-desired victory.

My little girl was misinformed when told that I was rash and reckless. . . . At Waynesboro I acted with caution—more for the sake of Her than from any other motive. Now good-night, beloved. Soon we must mount our good steeds and away.

Elizabeth to Mr. and Mrs. Bacon, April 2, 1865, from Washington:
These last few weeks Rebecca and I have had so much company. . . . Then, too, I have been making a flag for Autie to take on this last raid. It really is beautiful, like the old one, only larger—red and blue silk with white crossed sabres on both sides, and edged with heavy white cord. Lt. Boehm took it to him.

Chaplain Holmes called and told me about Autie—that his example is splendid to his men . . . and how he is almost alone in his determination to lead a Christian life.

Rebecca is such a comfort to me with her cute ways—laughing and singing so merrily. Glorious news of Sheridan. Still I am very anxious.

Custer to Elizabeth, March 31, 1865, 6 miles from Dinwiddie, Virginia:
Owing to the almost impassable state of the roads we are still at the point from which I wrote yesterday. Last night Lt. Boehm arrived, with what all pronounced "the handsomest flag in the Army . . ." and I do think it the handsomest flag I have ever seen. What renders it infinitely dear to me is that it is the work of my darling's hands. It could not have arrived at a more opportune moment. It was attached to the staff when battle was raging all along our lines. Cannon and musketry saluted it as its folds opened to the breeze. I regarded it as a happy omen. We have planned to procure a new staff for our beauty.

Lt. Boehm had to pass through enemy country for a considerable distance without an escort. He is extremely venturesome, and was determined to join us. Fearing capture he wrapped the flag about his person under his clothes, and in this way brought it to your Boy.

Nearly half a century later Major Boehm (Retired) modestly recalled for Mrs. Custer young Lieutenant Boehm's exploit.

Major Boehm to Elizabeth, September 15, 1910, from Chicago:
My dear Mrs Custer—I am highly honored to be still in your remembrance. I do indeed remember taking your flag to the General. The flag was the incentive which gave me strength to carry out my mission which resulted in my most highly prized honor.

The General had despatched me with letters to the War Department, also with one to you. You entrusted me with the Cavalry guidon on one of the points of which you had embroidered your name.

The command to which I had formerly belonged was now Genl. Grant's bodyguard, and, knowing the old men pretty well, I appealed to their sergeant who procured me a horse—a splendid animal. Pass and countersign enabled me to pass the pickets—the two lines were very close to each other—having wrapped your guidon round my body. And so I reached the General.

Being extremely tired I lay down to sleep, but shortly the General received orders to push forward to reinforce Merritt and Crook who were being driven back from Five Forks . . . March 31st.

The General rode ahead of the command with a few men, including myself, reaching Dinwiddie Court House about 4 in the afternoon. We found our lines in considerable confusion, being driven back. I took your guidon from the color-bearer, and with an orderly, Huff, rode with the General along the lines. We succeeded in rallying the men and re-forming the line, checking Pickett's advance. This enabled the General to place his command in position that evening.

It was during this engagement your name must have been shot off the guidon, as we were under very heavy fire. Huff was mortally wounded while riding alongside of me, and died that evening. My arm which was almost shattered at Five Forks next day does not trouble me to speak of, except when occasional pains make me a judge of weather. I am married, have a son who is himself father of two nice children.

Pickett's infantry had come to the aid of the enemy cavalry, and Custer had been ordered to check their advance.

Sheridan's account:
They—the Confederates—opened, but Custer's repeating rifles poured forth such a shower of lead that nothing could stand against it.

Northerners were gratified at the turn of events, but still were uneasy so long as Lee was at large. With Petersburg and Richmond no longer to be defended, Lee might escape, form a junction with other Confederate forces, recoup, retrieve. Sheridan would take no chances. Sheridan realized—none better—that Lee must at all costs be isolated, pressed, cornered, and forced to surrender or face annihilation. He selected Appomattox as most favorable to his project. On his cavalry, he could count as on himself; also, he enjoyed the confidence of Grant. Recorded in terms of battles, his Appomattox campaign comprised Dinwiddie, Five Forks, and Sailor's Creek, but this takes no account of the innumerable moves and countermoves, shiftings, and feeling-out processes involved. He never made the fatal error of underestimating his enemy.

The fighting on both sides was frenetic, desperation pitted against grim determination. Neither side spared men. Colored troops won high commendation. Morale was held at tautest, was even strained lest the slightest advantage be lost. And both sides were war weary, hungry—unable to be reached by provender.

On April 1 a dispatch from Sheridan stated: "I am holding in front of Dinwiddie Court House, on the road leading to Five Forks about three quarters of a mile with Genl. Custer's Division."

Custer himself had no time for letter writing in those crescendo days, and it was not till later that he told his wife the story. But here we are indebted to Lt. Blackmar for details. This young officer himself came out of the struggle unscathed, with a "rebel Major-General's dress-coat and shot-gun" as trophy. He wrote of days and nights of fighting without food or sleep. No fires were lighted for fear of revealing positions to the enemy. He tells of a running clash of fifteen miles, a blinding volley from pursuers which set the pursued Rebels to waving drawers, shirts, towels—anything white —in token of surrender. Custer charged and the band played "Hail Columbia" to spur on the men when temptation arose to give in to overwhelming lassitude. Then on bad ground they were forced to dismount and fight on foot—"hard work for cavalry-men."

Beyond a swamp they came upon a road lined with Rebel wagons and artillery, which "Custer worked nobly" to secure. Every moment his men expected to see him go down before the grape that came crashing through the bushes. But high above the din, clear above the clarion note came his order, "Forward, charge!"

Now came two days of strangely unopposed marching, weary and cautious. Suddenly came an electrifying sound . . . not the "rebel yell" but a tentative train whistle . . . carloads of supplies for Lee from Lynchburg.

On April 6 Sheridan sent Grant two dispatches:

> Genl. Custer, who had the advance, made a dash for the station, capturing four trains of supplies . . . then pushed on toward Appomattox Court House, driving the enemy who kept up an incessant fire of artillery, charging them repeatedly, and capturing twenty-five pieces of artillery. . . .

> Genl. Custer reports that his command has captured in all 35 pieces of artillery, 1000 prisoners, including one general officer, and from 150 to 200 wagons. . . .

A detail also was sent to destroy the tracks to Lynchburg and cut off retreat that way.

The battle of Sailor's Creek has been so overshadowed by Lee's subsequent surrender that, according to Sheridan, history has failed to recognize its significance in terminating the war. The Custer story rests for the moment and gives place to two important matters of record: Custer's testimonial to his brother Tom's valor on that occasion, and the first-hand account of the capture of Confederate General Kershaw. The latter account, with its tribute to Custer, is Kershaw's own. He dictated it to his wife, since his eyes were causing him trouble, and signed it himself. The document was unsolicited, being volunteered by the gallant Kershaw for Custer's widow when he heard the "heart-rending news" of the battle of the Little Big Horn.

The testimonial to Tom Custer was occasioned by Daniel Bacon's paternal interest in all the Custer children. Having heard that Tom was wounded, he expressed a fear that his wounds might have been purchased at the expense of proper caution. This fear was allayed by word from Tom's commanding officer, his brother Armstrong.

Custer to Mr. Bacon, 1865, from Virginia:
My dear Father—It was at Sailor's Creek . . . Tom led the assault

upon the enemy's breastworks, mounted, was first to leap his horse over the works on top of the enemy while they were pouring a volley of musketry into our ranks. Tom seized the rebel colors and demanded their surrender. The color-bearer shot him through face and neck, intending to shoot him through the head. So close the muzzle Tom's face was spotted with burnt powder. He retained the colors with one hand, while with the other he drew his revolver and shot the rebel dead. By this time our men were by his side and the fight was over.

My horse was shot under me on the same ground.

This is the second battle-flag Tom captured within one week. The other was in the cavalry battle at Namozine Church. Tom led the charge, captured the flag, 14 prisoners—3 officers. He was several rods in advance. His horse was shot—the second in three days. With blood pouring from his wound he asked that someone might take the flag while he continued with the assaulting column. Only my positive order forced him to leave the field.

You might infer that Tom lacks caution, judgment. On the contrary he possesses both in an unusual degree. His excellent judgment tells him when to press the enemy, and when to be moderate. Of all my staff officers he is quickest in perceiving at a glance the exact state of things. This trait frequently excites comment.

When he first joined me I was anxious concerning his conduct. But now I am as proud of him as can be, as soldier, brother. He has quit the use of tobacco, is moderate in drink, is respected and admired by officers and all who come in contact with him.

Another word on Tom's marked faculty of percipience comes from the New York *Times* correspondent, Paul. When the circumstances of Lincoln's assassination were being discussed in a military group, someone exclaimed, "Why, Tom Custer was in Washington at the time, in charge of the battle-flags; he may have been in the theater that night."

Paul replied, "Impossible. Tom would have taken in the situation at a glance and the assassin would never have escaped."

The rest of Custer's letter to Mr. Bacon is quoted, since it indicates his attitude toward alcohol:

You will be pleased to learn that I have induced Jim C and young N to sign the pledge of total abstinence during the time they are in the

U. S. service. Willie C bears himself to my entire satisfaction, attends to duty promptly, faithfully. In most of our late battles he has been near me, often by my side, under hottest fire of shell and musketry. He has never quailed. He even offered to carry my flag, knowing what is wanted of a color-bearer. He is as gallant an officer as I have in my command.

"Intoxication when on duty"—often charged to subordinates older than himself—was the bane of Custer's career from start to finish. His patience was sorely tried by "Jim C and young N." These culprits received an ultimatum: to sign the pledge, or dismissal. They chose to sign the pledge, doing so in the presence of their fellow officers, "a condition," reported the adjutant general, "with which they cheerfully complied."

Confederate General Kershaw's story follows upon the complete defeat of Ewell. Kershaw, in command of one of Ewell's divisions, with a small party tried to escape. Riding through a dense wood toward a clearing, they beheld ahead of them one of Custer's brigades, "drawn up in precise and orderly array." Hastily retreating unobserved, they were confronted by another peril—a single Union trooper "jauntily herding a group of unarmed Confederates into camp."

Trusting to superiority of numbers, Kershaw demanded the trooper's horse for one of his party who lacked a serviceable mount. He might have enforced his demand but for a signal from one of the prisoners. Sure enough, screened by trees stood a group of Union infantry.

Surrender was the only course. The trooper was a corporal in Custer's 3rd Division. Kershaw introduced himself and his companions, an introduction acknowledged "by a soldierly salute." His surrender was conditional upon his being taken to General Custer's headquarters without molestation.

The promise was readily given but not so easily carried out. Near headquarters an officer halted them and demanded the captive's sword, a graceless act which the corporal was powerless to prevent.

Deprived of that which he had been prepared to yield to the commander, the vanquished went to meet the conqueror.

General Kershaw's account:

At headquarters there was little to indicate the importance of the spot. Not a tent spread; not even a fly. No staff. A single young officer, not more than 23, was sitting on the carriage of one of the two guns, section of a light battery. On receiving a communication from the corporal he stepped forward, extended his hand, begged us to dismount, saying that the General would not be there till night. Meanwhile he would do his best to entertain us.

In the saddle, on the march for two days and a night, without refreshment of any sort, such hospitality lingers in the memory. Next morning when Lt. Woodruff was preparing to depart I took off my spurs, a splendid pair, captured at Manassas, and begged him to accept them. Ten years later they were sent back with a note that gives them unfailing lustre, recalling the moment when he rode off with his battery, with a wave of his hand in kindly adieu.

Shortly after, three Brigadier-Generals, my friends, of Pickett's Division, were brought in, and from these I learned the fate of Anderson's command—also that Colonel Ruger of the Artillery with his entire battalion—guns, horses, caissons—had been gobbled up by the wily Custer who had completed his day's work by holding the road against Anderson's advance.

The sun had gone down, peaceful evening settled on the scene of recently contending armies, when a cavalcade rode up briskly. A spare, lithe, sinewy figure; bright, dark, quick-moving blue eyes; florid complexion, light, wavy curls, high cheek-bones, firm-set teeth—a jaunty close-fitting cavalry jacket, large top-boots, Spanish spurs, golden aiguillettes, a serviceable sabre . . . a quick nervous movement, an air telling of the habit of command—announced the redoubtable Custer whose name was as familiar to his foes as to his friends.

He was met by Lt. Woodruff who introduced us.

"Why, General!" Custer took my hand with a kindly smile, not without humor. "I am glad to see you here. I feel I ought to know you."

"True, General. We have often met. But not under circumstances favorable to cultivating an acqaintance."

This made us quite at home, and the conversation became free, general, and kindly. With soldierly hospitality our host made us feel welcome. And, despite our misfortunes, we enjoyed not a little the camp luxuries of coffee, sugar, condensed milk, hard tack, broiled ham, spread on a tent-fly converted into table-cloth, around which we sat on the ground, Custer and his Rebel Guests.

After supper we smoked and talked of subjects of common interest, dwelling on the past. Our host, with true delicacy, avoided the future, which to us was not an inviting topic.

We slept beneath the stars, Custer sharing his blankets with me. We lay in the midst of Custer's squadrons. Thousands of men with their horses lay about us within easy call. As the last bugle call sounded "Tattoo" and "Taps" silence reigned, broken only by the neighing or snorting of a horse, the cough of some wakeful soldier. Custer was soon asleep. As I lay there, watching the glittering hosts of Heaven, I buried my dreams of Southern independence. The God of Battles had deserted our banners. I bowed my spirit in submission. Mine, thenceforth, the task to help bind my bleeding country's wounds.

The sun was shining bright when I awoke. All was bustle and activity. My host gave me cheery greeting as I joined him standing by the fire.

He wore an air of thought, receiving and sending many communications. While we breakfasted some thirty troopers rode up, one after another within a few rods. Then, dismounting, aligning, horse held by bridle, each carried a Confederate battle-flag—all except my captor, and he carried two. Also, as he caught my eye, he bowed, and pointed with an air of pride to my own sabre at his belt.

I asked, and Custer explained: "It is my custom after each battle to select as my escort for the day those men who have most distinguished themselves in action, bearing for that time the trophies they have taken from the enemy." I counted. Thirty-one banners—thirty-one of our regiments killed, captured, or dispersed, the day before. It was not a comforting thought.

Corporal Lanham's possession of my sword was at my own request. I had told Custer of the officer's conduct in regard to it. Custer had said nothing, but he had done the right thing. May that good soldier's—that Corporal's descendants wield it in defence of their country, even as its master had sought to do his duty according to his conscience and convictions!

Custer's whole Division was now drawn up in columns of squadrons in full view, a spectacle to a soldier of keenest interest. Finally he turned to me. "You will remain here a few minutes when horses will be brought for you and your companions, and you will be conducted to Burkesville where you will find General Grant. Good-bye!" He shook my hand, mounted a magnificent charger, and rode proudly away, followed at a round gallop by his splendid escort bearing "the fallen flags."

As he neared his conquering legions cheer after cheer greeted his approach. Bugles sounded. Sabres flashed as they saluted. And the proud cavalcade filed through the open ranks, and moved to the front, leading that magnificent column in splendid array. Methought no Roman victor had ever a more noble triumph.

I saw Custer no more. And now

> On Fame's eternal camping-ground
> His silent tent is spread,
> And Glory guards with solemn round
> The bivouac of the dead!

In his report to Grant of the issue of Sailor's Creek, with the names of the generals captured there, Sheridan said, "If the thing is pressed I think that Lee will surrender." This message, relayed by Grant to President Lincoln at City Point, brought back the classic answer, "Let the thing be pressed."

Elizabeth Custer lived only for her husband. To be with Autie, no hardship was too great, no danger—from Mosby's gang, from guerilla-infested country, was to be considered. And she had learned that soldiers must sometimes travel and even fight on the Sabbath. But for herself, a civilian, to disregard the Divine pronouncement, she had no excuse. Accordingly, on April 9, 1865, when arms were laid aside and great commanders were taking stitches to close a nation's wounds, in Elizabeth's diary we find this entry:

Sunday—and I have been *sewing* today, mending my dress and slippers. Oh, I *hope* I shall be forgiven!

11: Appomattox and After

AT LAST Sheridan had maneuvered Lee into the place chosen for the final showdown. Still there was the possibility that Lee, though trapped, might cut a way through Sheridan's cavalry. To prevent this, Sheridan proposed to take the initiative.

Custer's division was in the advance, awaiting Sheridan's word to proceed against Lee's cavalry, when galloping across the field came the harbinger of peace, an officer waving a towel tied to a stick. He came to the division directly confronting the Confederate lines—Custer's.

An aide received the messenger and took him to Custer, who, as always, was at the front. Custer followed the prescribed procedure. He received the flag—no more, no less. Then he dispatched one aide to escort the messenger back to his own lines, another to report to his superior. Sheridan, in another part of the field, received the winged word: "Lee has surrendered. Do not charge. The white flag is up."

In after years Custer's widow was so annoyed by an absurdity in the surrender story that had gained credence by repetition that she appealed to an old friend to relate the precise facts. This was Brigadier General Michael V. Sheridan, at that time a captain, and serving as aide to his brother General Philip H. Sheridan.

Michael V. Sheridan to Elizabeth:
X. reminds me of a man who, having bought a saddle, had to invent for himself a horse. Custer certainly would have had more sense than to *demand* the surrender of the Confederate Army of Northern Virginia when General Sheridan was in the field (but not near Custer) and in command.

The surrender had been *demanded* the day before by General Grant.

On receipt from Custer of the information Sheridan stopped all firing, and sent for Genl. Grant to come over to Meade's army. And he, Grant, came. That is all there is to it.

Custer's aide, sent to escort the truce bearer back, did not return in due time, and Custer determined to investigate. A breach of faith was feared, since some of the enemy had at the time failed to respect the request for armistice. Sheridan, riding about the field, was fired on. General Merritt was forced to spit fire on a group that, boasting "South Carolina never surrenders," fired on his command. One Union officer was killed. Custer's own handkerchief, chosen by his wife in replacing his captured wardrobe, being blue, he borrowed a white one of an orderly and, waving this about his head amid whizzing bullets, dashed across the field into the Confederate lines. He returned almost immediately, shouting breathlessly, joyfully, "It's all right, boys. Lee has surrendered."

A calm descended on the field, though there might yet be more fighting, for General Meade had set a time limit on the truce. The men, ordered to remain at their billets, relaxed gratefully. Where opposing lines were near enough, there was brisk interchange of repartee, jibes, insult, with gifts of tobacco and food.

Some half-dozen dwellings made up the village of Appomattox. The largest had been borrowed for the occasion. In its pleasant parlor two gentlemen met by appointment. They were not strangers to each other, professionally or personally. Both were graduates of the same Military Academy, both spoke the same military language and had served under the same commanders in Mexico. But for scruples of conscience, Lee might have been occupying the position held by Grant—at the outset of the war Generalissimo Winfield Scott had strongly urged his appointment as leader of the Union forces. Of the two, he was the older by about fifteen years. Grant was forty-three.

The usual amenities were observed. Each general presented to the other the members of his staff. Then they came to the business in hand. Lee took his seat at the center table, marble topped in the style of the day. Resplendent in full uniform he was the magnificent protagonist of an epic tragedy. Grant took his place somewhat to one side. His garments looked as if he had bivouacked in them— as indeed he had. His dominance of the group owed nothing to externals. It owed everything to achievement and force of character.

When Grant took out his manifold notebook to draft the surrender terms, Colonel Horace Porter brought from a corner a small, pine, varnished stand and set this beside him. The terms then were shown to Lee for his approval. Copies had to be made in ink. The McLean inkwell having run dry, Lee's military secretary, Colonel Marshall, offered his, a boxwood container he always carried with him. For a good handwriting Grant called upon Colonel Parker of his staff, a full-blooded Seneca Indian.

Colonel Marshall's account:
Col. Parker then took the little table back to the corner of the room, and made a copy of the terms in ink. I then took my seat at that table, and wrote Genl. Lee's reply to Genl. Grant. The table was then carried back by Col. Parker and placed by Genl. Grant's side with the ink copy which he then signed. I laid the draft of Genl. Lee's copy on the marble-topped table, and he signed it.

It was over. Lee made the obligatory offer of his sword to Grant, and Grant by a gesture declined it. He readily gave Lee his promise that provisions would be issued to the Confederate soldiers. There was no reminder that these would be the provisions which had been destined for Lee's army and which, as General Kershaw put it, "had been gobbled up by the wily Custer."

There was a cordial handshake between the principals, and salutes of profound respect from all present. The vanquished withdrew, to be heartily cheered by his own men waiting outside. Grant also departed. Reports were to be made, dispatches sent to the President.

The tension over, there was a change of mood, and the formal scene turned into a frantic auction. Mr. McLean reaped a harvest from bidders for souvenirs. The victory was unquestionably a cavalry one, and to Sheridan was unanimously accorded the first choice. He spoke for the little pine stand, the "surrender table." He paid for it with two ten-dollar gold pieces he had carried on his person throughout the war, thinking "they might come in handy were I taken prisoner."

This symbol of victory he gave forthwith to Custer, bidding him take it, with Sheridan's compliments, to Mrs. Custer. "How tender-hearted the great Sheridan," a friend once remarked to Mrs. Custer, "that in such a moment his first thought should be for a woman!"

"But I feel I deserved that table," replied the recipient of the gift, "for Sheridan frequently asserted that my husband was the only one of his officers who had not been spoiled by marriage."

Doubtless Sheridan's real motive was not so much to compliment a woman as it was to reward his invaluable Custer. Speaking to the Illinois Commandery of the Loyal Legion in Chicago, Sheridan told how "the delighted Custer rode off, like a boy, balancing the table on his head."

Sheridan to Elizabeth, April 10, 1865, from Appomattox Court House, Virginia:

My dear Madam—I respectfully present to you the small writing-table on which the conditions for the surrender of the Confederate Army of Northern Virginia were written by Lt. General Grant—and permit me to say, Madam, that there is scarcely an individual in our service who has contributed more to bring this about than your very gallant husband.

Yours very respectfully
Phil. H. Sheridan
Major General

The news spread fast: surrender—prelude to peace. Old friends arrayed against each other in the morning were clasping hands by sunset.

Colonel Woodruff's account:

I was taking a short ride from my battery. . . . I had not gone far when an officer in gray called to me, and, as I drew near, said, "I would like to see General Custer. George and I were classmates. We last met in '63, in Williamsburg." I then recognized him. "Why, then you must be 'Gimlet' Lea. I belong to Custer's Division, and will take you to the General." The meeting between the two was very interesting.

Custer to Mrs. Reed, April 21, 1865, from Virginia:

At Appomattox I met my old friend and classmate Lea. He was in Lee's army which surrendered. He came to see me, and took dinner with me.

It was reported that when Custer returned Lea's call, the Confederates cheered him heartily.

Another former classmate came into the Union lines seeking Custer—his distinguished cavalry opponent General Fitzhugh Lee. Captain Lyon wrote home about it, telling how he laughed to see the two, arms about each other, rolling over and over on the ground like exuberant schoolboys.

Custer worked far into the night compiling his report and making preparations for the next move. For the war was not over. Sherman had yet to force Johnston's army to come to terms. Early the next day Sheridan was to take his command to Petersburg, ready for what might be required of him.

Bodily fatigue was not to be considered. One observer wrote: "On the eve of the surrender . . . in one of those last strenuous days I came upon General Custer, sitting on a log, upright, a cup of coffee in his hand, sound asleep."

But before Custer rested on that memorable April 9, there was a letter he had to write—not to wife or parents—they would learn the news from dispatches—but to his men, his beloved 3rd Division. If to modern ears the language seems flowery, it is to be remembered this was the fashion of the day. Did not Grant, most direct of men, when he wrote to Lee demanding surrender, speak of "effusion of blood," when "bloodshed" was simpler?

Custer to the soldiers of the 3rd Cavalry Division, April 9, 1865, from Appomattox Court House, Virginia:

With profound gratitude toward the God of battles by whose blessings our enemies have been humbled and our arms rendered triumphant, your Commanding General avails himself of this, his first opportunity, to express to you his admiration of the heroic manner in which you have passed through the series of battles which to-day resulted in the surrender of the enemy's entire army.

The record established by your indomitable courage is unparalleled in the annals of war. Your prowess has won for you even the respect and admiration of your enemies. During the past six months, although in most instances confronted by superior numbers, you have captured from the enemy in open battle, one hundred and eleven pieces of field artillery, sixty-five battle-flags, and upwards of ten thousand prisoners, including seven general officers. Within the past ten days, and included in the above, you have captured forty-six pieces of field artillery, and thirty-seven battle-flags. You have never lost a gun, never lost a color, and have never been defeated; and notwithstanding the numerous engagements in which you have borne a prominent part, including those memorable battles of the Shenandoah, you have captured every piece of artillery which the enemy has dared to open upon you. The near approach of peace renders it improbable that you will again be called upon to undergo the fatigues of the toilsome march or the exposure of the battlefield, but should the assistance of keen blades, wielded by your sturdy arms, be required to hasten the coming of that glorious peace for which we have been so long contending, the General commanding is proudly confident that, in the future, as in the past, every demand will meet with a hearty and willing response.

Let us hope that our work is done, and that, blessed with the comforts of peace, we may be permitted to enjoy the pleasures of home and friends. For our comrades who have fallen let us ever cherish a grateful remembrance. To the wounded, and to those who languish in Southern prisons, let our heartfelt sympathy be tendered.

And now, speaking for myself alone, when the war is ended and the task of the historian begins—when those deeds of daring which have rendered the name and fame of the Third Cavalry Division imperishable, are inscribed upon the bright pages of our country's history, I only ask that my name may be written as that of the Commander of the Third Cavalry Division.

Official   G. A. Custer
 L. W. Barnhart   Brevet Major General Commanding
  Captain and A.A.A.G.

Not till two days later did Custer find a moment to write to his wife.

Custer to Elizabeth, April 11, 1865, from Prospect Station, Lynch-burg and Petersburg Railroad, Virginia:

My Darling—Only time to write a word. Heart too full for utter-ance. . . . Thank God PEACE is at hand. And thank God the 3rd Divi-sion has performed the most important duty of this campaign. . . . Night before last 24 more pieces of artillery captured and 7 battle-flags. I have now 40 at my headquarters. The 3rd Division has always been in the advance. Oh, I have so much to tell you, but no time. The Army is now moving back to Brandy Station. . . . Hurrah for Peace and my little Durl. Can you consent to come down and be a Captain's wife?

Custer's rank as major general was in the Volunteer Army. As a Regular, his rank was that of captain.

Custer to Mrs. Reed, April 21, 1865, from Virginia:

. . . . I hope that the last shot has been fired in this war. At least, I hope I shall not hear another. I feel confident that the end of the war is near at hand, and that we shall soon be enjoying the rich blessings of peace.

I never needed rest so much as now. However I feel more than re-paid for risk and labor.

General Sheridan did not ascertain until the end of April that his command would not be needed to aid Sherman in bringing the Johnston army to terms. When that was brought about, his com-mand proceeded to Washington.

Mr. Bacon to Elizabeth, April 10, 1865, from Monroe, Michigan:

All day yesterday failed to get news at the Telegraph Office. Went to bed intending to get up early, feeling that something important im-pended. At five o'clock heard the bell, and, the day being dark, thought it was six o'clock. Then it occurred to me it was Fire, and I went to ascertain the locality of this, but saw a crowd of men who told me the news. An official paper had been brought from the depot. I joined in the general rejoicing with a grateful heart.

All praise to the Army, for, under God, the most formidable re-bellion that ever was has been crushed. It makes a great man of Sheri-dan and has added new laurels to the *greatest young general of this or of any other age.*

Mr. Bacon to Elizabeth, April 11, 1865, from Monroe, Michigan:

Until final word came of Lee's surrender my nerves were more un-strung than at any other time of my whole life. Father Custer was in the post-office when your letter came, and he called Reed in and I read it to them. The news of Tom was such I went with his father and read it to the family. How gratifying to parents to have two such sons. How much better than wealth or honor.

Your marriage relations bring a corresponding happiness to me, to say nothing of being father-in-law to a man whose reputation is second to none anywhere. A returned prisoner from the 7th Cavalry stayed here overnight—in the Humphrey House. In conversation with me he said he understood that Custer's father-in-law was a boarder here, and that he would like to see him. Whereupon I said "Look upon my face!"

Armstrong needs rest and quiet. Obtain leave. Come home.

It was a standing joke among the Custers that Elizabeth reached Richmond before her husband, who had been four years getting there.

Elizabeth to Mr. Bacon, April 11, 1865, from Richmond, Virginia:

Father dear, when you heard of Lee's surrender didn't you *cry?* The salute was fired yesterday morning at five. At the first gun I was out of bed, and running all over the house.

At two in the afternoon we started, the Committee on Conduct of the War, their wives, a Philanthropist, and myself. We travelled by the President's gunboat, the "Baltimore." Admiral Porter sent a pilot, and we ran through the blockade safely, and were guided through the torpedoes after dark. At City Point we met the Admiral, a man of style, social, but not free and unassuming like Farragut. He sent Autie a telegram: "Mrs. Custer will be in Richmond to-morrow." The telegraph is completed to Burkesville, Grant's headquarters, and I presume the message will be sent on to Autie by orderly.

Father, do write Mr Chandler one of your good letters, to thank him for bringing me.

I can scarce realize I am in the city so many thousands died to conquer and where brave Union men languished in prison.

Elizabeth to Laura Noble, April, 1865, from Richmond, Virginia:

The party left me at headquarters, as guest of Genl. and Mrs Weitzel, the White House, till recently home of Mr and Mrs Jefferson Davis.

It is a box-like structure, but handsome, and furnished with an abundance of mirrors and draperies.

I slept one night in Mr Davis's bed, the next in that of Mrs Davis. There is a grand piano in the parlor. The china—Sèvres, I believe—is handsome. Silver and linen Mrs Davis took away. They left sewing-machine, also a little black-and-tan dog that had belonged to the small son they lost. The housekeeper remains and guards things jealously.

The second morning Autie came before I was awake. He is tanned, but thin and worn. Genl. Sheridan is very tired after all those battles.

A few days later Mr. Bacon began a letter to his daughter.

Mr. Bacon to Elizabeth, April 14, 1865, from Monroe, Michigan:
Armstrong's beautiful black horse "Phil Sheridan" arrived yesterday. I gave up my barn for his use. I had hay and oats on hand. Not a bad speculation, since horses known to have been used by Genl. Custer will command high prices. . . .

In the middle of his letter Mr. Bacon dropped his pen. He had just heard that President Lincoln, while attending a performance of Tom Taylor's comedy *Our American Cousin* at the Ford Theater in Washington, had been shot. Lincoln died the following morning. Mr. Bacon took a fresh sheet of paper to resume his letter:

Oh, Daughter, Daughter! What is to become of us as a nation and as Individuals? This is the most gloomy day in the history of the continent. The thought that a man, such as Andy Johnson, lunatic, drunkard, is to be at the head of the government at this, the most critical period of our national existence is *awful* beyond words.

I may be one of those who will ask Grant to take the government in his own hands.

This morning the rumor came from Toledo. We immediately put the wires into requisition, and found it true as regarded the assassination. Then came the Detroit papers in mourning, with details as far as known.

I hope for the country Seward will recover. He has been and is yet, the Government.

Custer took his wife with him from Richmond to the army, on its way to Petersburg.

Daniel Stanton Bacon, Eleanor Sophia Page Bacon, and Elizabeth
Clift Bacon

Elizabeth Bacon,
about 14

Elizabeth, General
Custer, and Tom
Custer (*standing*)

Brigadier General Custer,
probably 1863

Elizabeth Custer

Black Hills Expedition, 1874, from a photograph by W. H. Illingworth

Custer at Aldie, 1863   (COURTESY BETTMANN ARCHIVE)

Custer receiving the first flag of truce on the surrender of Lee, 1865
(COURTESY BETTMANN ARCHIVE)

Battle of the Little Big Horn, from a painting (COURTESY BETTMANN ARCHIVE)

Sitting Bull

Chief Gall

Custer in civilian clothes, 1872

Custer and Grand Duke Alexis
of Russia, 1873

Elizabeth, General
Custer, and a friend

Custer to Mr. Bacon, April 20, 1865, from Petersburg, Virginia:

My dear Father—Libbie will have informed you of her arrival in the Army. We reached this point day before yesterday, having marched 44 miles in two days from Nottaway Court House, Libbie riding in a spring wagon at the head of the column with me. She endured the fatigue well, and enjoyed the novelty. She was the first lady to pass over the South Side R. Rd. . . .

Elizabeth to Mr. and Mrs. Bacon, April, 1865, from Petersburg, Virginia:

I marched with the Army two days, riding in an ambulance. Father dear, remember how you used to try to frighten me out of marrying a soldier, "No better than gipsying . . . in a covered wagon on the trail"? I think it grand fun.

To-morrow I return to Washington to prepare to come to the Army again. Genl. Sheridan says I make no trouble, and he is always willing I should come.

Elizabeth to Mr. and Mrs. Bacon, April, 1865, from Washington:

Mother, I sent home two skirts to be tucked. Please have a wide hem and several small tucks. It is so expensive here. Everyone loops up their dresses, and one must have handsome white skirts. Will it be too much trouble to have them starched and done up?

Mother, won't you have Rose make me some thin nightgowns? I have no sewing woman. I have just made me a spring bonnet of blue silk.

In Richmond our party was the admiration of hundreds of darkeys who bowed profoundly as we passed. They seemed delighted to see us. Our bonnets amazed them. They had never seen any so small.

. . . . Tom is a hero. He will tell you the news. I wanted to go home with him, but could not be so far from Autie. The last campaign has surpassed all others in desperate fighting. Autie has been exposed to fire constantly for so long.

Mr Chandler said lately to the Secretary of War, "Don't you think Custer has done enough to have a full commission?" And Mr Stanton answered, "My God, what hasn't he done!"

Father, take good care of the table I sent. Don't give away a splinter even. They tell me I might sell it for a million dollars. I send you a copy of Genl. Sheridan's letter. I like it better than the table, even. I have Lee's flag of truce, also Autie's when he went into their lines.

To her husband she had written after the surrender, "Now I hope nothing will ever separate us again."

A grand review of the victorious army was held in Washington on May 24 and 25. Two persons who should have been there were absent. One was the dead Lincoln. The other was the great cavalry leader whose military prowess had brought the issue to a triumphant close. Who more richly entitled to the cheers of the multitude that lined Pennsylvania Avenue than Sheridan, whose "Rienzi" had borne him agallop to Winchester, twenty miles away?

Grant, scenting danger in delay, feared mischief from French and Austrian intriguing in Mexico. He believed that the states so recently in rebellion should be under military control until Congress could take measures to restore them to Union status. For this work he needed Sheridan. Sheridan's feeling of frustration is understandable. Nothing vital would have been lost and something personal would have been gained by according him a breathing space, his meed of applause, the opportunity at least to take leave of his men. There was loss to the populace, too, in not seeing victory duly objectified, in not testifying to their gratitude.

After Sheridan, none could be so popular in the triumphant cavalcade than his division commanders, and of them, none more vividly than Custer. People went wild as he passed by. "Custer . . . Custer!" they shrilled.

Among the spectators were groups of schoolchildren trained to sing patriotic ditties. One young girl, who was to become Mrs. Robert Underwood Johnson of New York, later told Mrs. Custer: "We were massed along the sidewalk waving flags, throwing flowers as we sang. Custer had always been my hero, so as he rode by I tried to throw a wreath of flowers about his horse's neck."

Others, too, were paying this tribute. But the beautiful horse, which had never quailed under fire, shied at this floral bombardment and attempted flight.

Colonel (later General) Horace Porter's account:
Conspicuous among the division leaders was Custer, his long golden curls floating in the wind, his low-cut collar, crimson neck-tie, buckskin breeches—half General, half scout, dare-devil in appearance.

Within 200 yards of the President's stand his spirited horse took the bit in its teeth, and made a dash past the troops like a tornado. But Custer was more than a match for him. When the Cavalry-man, covered with flowers, afterwards rode by the officials the people screamed with delight.

That same afternoon Custer met his beloved division to bid officers and men farewell. The parting was heartfelt on both sides. They had fought, dared, endured together. "Old Curley" was cheered wildly. Mrs. Custer, in black velvet riding cap with scarlet feather contrived for the occasion, was called for and cheered.

Custer was not to have the rest and quiet Father Bacon had prescribed for him. Sheridan still had need of his dependable cavalry leader. They were under marching orders.

Lieutenant General U. S. Grant to Major General P. H. Sheridan, May 17, 1865, from Washington:
. . . assigning you to command west of the Mississippi. . . . Your duty is to restore Texas and that part of Louisiana held by the enemy to the Union in the shortest practicable time, in a way most effectual for securing permanent peace.

Sheridan's Memoirs:
. . . . The surrender [of Kirby Smith] was not carried out in good faith, particularly by the Texas troops. . . . Because of the desire of the Government to make a strong showing of force in Texas I directed one column of cavalry to San Antonio under Merritt, the other to Houston under Custer.

In *Tenting on the Plains* Elizabeth Custer describes their journey to Texas—first by train, then by boat down the Mississippi to New Orleans and up the Red River past Shreveport to Alexandria, Louisiana.

Custer to Mr. Bacon, July, 1865, from Alexandria, Louisiana:
My dear Father—We have been waiting for stores. When the wagons are loaded we will start for Texas. I have had a spring wagon prepared for Libbie, so fixed that she can lie down in it, curtained, fitted up as a dressing-room with adjustable seats; india-rubber roof, rain-proof, with

canvas covering over this; a lunch-box in front of her seat . . . drawn by four handsome matched grey horses. The saddler has covered a government canteen with black leather. . . . [Elizabeth interpolated an item: "And he has worked my name on it in yellow silk . . . Lady Custer."]

She will ride horseback part of the way. We shall march in the cool of the morning and evening. We have a pontoon train to enable us to pass over any river. However Libbie is accustomed to ford rivers on horseback. . . .

This country is wholly unlike Virginia. It is more like notions formed from "Uncle Tom's Cabin." Slavery was not as mild as in States whose proximity to Free States made kindness desirable to prevent the enslaved from seeking freedom across the border. The knowledge that runaways would have to traverse thousands of miles of slave or hostile country placed slaves at the mercy of their owners, in the Red River country, and every plantation had its Simon Legree and humble Uncle Tom. In the mansion where I now write is a young negro woman whose back bears the scars of five hundred lashes given at one time, for going beyond the limits of her master's plantation. If the War has attained nothing else it has placed America under a debt of gratitude for all time, for removal of this evil.

I expect to reach Houston in thirteen days. Genl. Fitzhugh is to report to me, also a regiment of Texas cavalry.

Libbie bids me tell you my hair is cut short. She cut it for me. I find it more comfortable in this climate.

I advise you to visit this country and invest in land. Land before the war brought from one to three hundred dollars the acre. Now, owing to the absence of slave labor and current money it is far cheaper. Immigration from the Free States to the southern and south-western country is likely to come soon. The soil is rich. A wealthy planter informed me that land bought at $150. per acre paid for itself in two years.

Elizabeth to Mr. and Mrs. Bacon, July, 1865, from Alexandria, Louisiana:

My dear Parents—We are still delayed here. The roads are good, and we ride between hedges of white double roses. We live well, with abundant fruits and vegetables. Our mess bill for six weeks is not more than I had to pay for myself alone in Washington.

Mother, won't you make me a fruit cake? Oh, for some of your sugar cookies!

Everything here is so behindhand. "Ancestral Halls" and "Parental Mansions" are nothing but old-style roomy houses, not so good as that of a Michigan farmer. No wells are dug, the lime water is considered unhealthy. There are immense cisterns for rain-water at the back of a house, but with no invention for drawing it. It spouts from a wooden plug. They need the advent of the thrifty ingenious Yankee.

J is so extravagant. If he should get his wife down here and the troops were then mustered out he wouldn't have enough to pay their way home. If he would only pay his debts . . . especially that $100. a poor soldier entrusted to his care. . . . He has bought himself three expensive hats since he came here. When I remonstrate he says "I know." But he don't really care. It makes me so mad.

Father Custer is coming down here as forage agent. Little to do and fine pay. The government now has to buy all that the men and horses eat.

Custer's notebook shows that August was spent on the march. Custer habitually went ahead with an aide to find a suitable site for the camp. The pontoon bridge was requisitioned for river crossings. Few houses were passed on the way. Mrs. Custer's narrative describes Reveille before daybreak—daytime rest in the blistering heat of a southern pine forest—nights drenched with dew—poor water—fears of shico and scorpion—and when not in the spring wagon Autie had prepared for her so sedulously, riding "side-saddle" in a habit so heavily weighted at the hem that a woman could hardly lift it over her head unaided. All these discomforts Custer's wife bore more than willingly, for she was with her husband. Nor has she any scruples about Sunday letter writing.

Elizabeth to Mr. and Mrs. Bacon, October 22, 1865, from Head-quarters, 2nd Cavalry Division, near Hempstead, Texas:
My dear Father and Mother—Another week gone, and we are still here. We expect to go to Austin next week. Orders were sent some time ago, but were lost on the way. Autie received second orders yesterday.

I am most interested in the renovation of the "Bacon Mansion." I was sufficiently pleased with its appearance before I left, but am glad Mother is going to be pleased with the fixing up.

Autie was much pleased with what you said about its being "fortunate under the circumstances" of your "limited income" that I am "no charge" to you. It is customary for the wives and children of regular army officers to live with their parents and to be supported by them, also, often. For the pay of an officer is hardly enough to support him decently in the field without the additional expense of a family. Very, *very* few officers but what drink, and it is the custom in entertaining brother officers to offer liquor and cigars. The bills for these two luxuries Autie by his prudence and good habits entirely avoids.

I am sorry your income is not larger, dear Father. It seems hard that one who has always been so charitable as you, and who has handled so much money as you have in your lifetime should be limited. Autie and I were saying that if you had all your land in ready money and could invest it down here you would make yourself wealthy in a short time. I wish you could get some of the money that is floating around in Texas. Captain S. who left Autie's staff last week to go into the wool business in New York was here last week to buy wool. Wool was so high, so he waited, and, while he was waiting, cotton went up six cents. So he invested in cotton and in three days made five thousand dollars. But cotton is not the only way of coining money down here. Land is so cheap. Improved plantations are selling for one third their value, because planters are disgusted with free negro labor. I hear the officers talking of these matters. I received a letter from Rebecca yesterday. Uncle Richmond wants to invest some thousands here, and wants Autie's opinion.

Autie has fine opportunities every day for making a fortune in land, or cotton, or horses, or in buying government claims, but he feels that so long as the government needs his active services he should not invest.

We are saving all our money now, and yet have all we want. Since leaving New Orleans we have lived on less than $150. a month. And now we will live on less. Autie will not receive a Major-General's pay much longer, and we are trying to get accustomed to living on less.

I am very glad that I am no expence to you in "sere and yellow leaf" time. I often think it would be so pleasant to be getting my clothes from home, and still partially dependent on my parents, for then I should not feel so entirely cut off—but fortunately I am married to an independent, high-minded man who would not let others support his wife. As long as his health remains he will support me handsomely, and, if necessary I could help support myself. My health is firmly established.

You would hardly believe in the short time we have been here what a favorite Autie has become. He could be elected to Congress. There seems no honor too high for them to bestow on him. The soldiers are now in an excellent state of discipline, and the planters live undisturbed. The soldiers do not fancy having so tight a rein, but they know enough to obey. And we have been treated with more kindness than had we lived in Monroe for *years*. Our own relatives (aside from the home ones) would not do so much for us as some of these Texans who were prominent and active rebels. We shall never forget their kindness to us. No country in the world can equal the South for hospitality.

Personal kindness from strangers once politically opposed—trouble within his own ranks—such was Custer's experience. He was forced to report an official.

Custer to Major Lee, assistant adjutant general, Middle Division, 1865, from Texas:
Major McA. Paymaster U.S.A. while at this point paying off troops under my command . . . frequently under the influence of liquor to the extent of rendering him unfit for duty. Once, when intoxicated, sent his deputies to pay off the men of the pontoon train. He has kept his hotel room in Hempstead as a gambling resort for officers of this command, often for high stakes. It has been reported to me that Capt. D., recently mustered out, left with several thousands of dollars won in this way. Statements of officers and certificates of hotel-keeper are enclosed.

A paragraph intended to injure Custer appeared in the press, accusing him of having obtained his horse "Don Juan" illicitly. This was retracted the day after publication, but not before Custer had received a government order to return the animal to its owner. On this he cleared himself by documentary proof, with the following attestation:

On the march to Danville Genl. Sheridan ordered all horses found in the country to be seized, and Genl. Merritt, commanding the cavalry, ordered them to be branded for the use of the command, except such as officers who had lost their own in battle might desire to purchase. A Board of Appraisal fixed prices according to the serviceable value of the animals. "Don Juan" did not qualify as a war horse. Custer paid the asked price, $125.

Custer appended this statement of his own:

I have had 8 horses killed or disabled under me in battle during the past three years, three of them my own property, without making any claim on the Government for indemnity.

Also submitted was the receipt: "Rec'd for one bay stallion, 12 years old, 15 hands high, white saddle marks, &c. $125."

In the three military departments into which the seceding states had been charted, according to the three surrenders, there was serious disaffection among the soldiers in the armies of occupation, amounting at times to actual mutiny. Volunteers felt aggrieved at not being permitted to return to the civilian life which a national emergency had disrupted. In Washington bureaucracy acted sluggishly. Consequently, desertions among the soldiers were frequent, deserters joining with the outlaws who were preying on the exhausted conquered regions.

Courts-martial were not sufficient to meet the situation. Custer adopted drastic measures. Here is one of his orders:

Every enlisted man committing depradations on the persons or property of citizens will have his head shaved, and, in addition, will receive 25 lashes on his back, well laid on.

This provoked comments from his enemies. He was denounced for "brutality, for flogging men who had fought for their country, while favoring those who had turned traitor to it." An enquiry into the matter was addressed to Major Lee.

Custer to Major Lee, 1865, from Texas:
Regarding the report that Genl. Custer issued orders to flog any soldier who shall forage, altho the troops under his command complain that they are not properly subsisted, and have no money wherewith to purchase supplies, that they are in a rebellious district, surrounded

by rebels who have plenty, &c. &c., I respectfully submit: The time referred to was when that command was in camp near Alexandria, La. Part of this time the rations issued were of inferior quality, and deficient in quantity—a fault in my opinion attributable to the officers of the Subsistence Depmt in New Orleans. Every effort was made to remedy this, and now such evils do not exist. The stores, deficient or damaged, were such as could not be replaced by foraging on the surrounding country—beans, rice, salt pork. Beef could be obtained by organized and authorized foraging parties, also by contract, amply to supply the wants of the command.

Authorizing for independent foraging parties has never been done in this command. No soldier is permitted to leave camp for this purpose. Necessary foraging is conducted by an organized body, under an officer —often more than one, who is responsible for the good conduct of the men. Foraging by soldiers not so controlled is practically highway robbery, burglary, house-breaking—often murder.

[Custer goes on to describe conditions when he assumed command late in June in Alexandria.] Regiments arriving, and those arrived, in a state of greatest dissatisfaction, from disinclination to remain longer in the service, and fear of being ordered to Mexico.

Owing to disagreement among the officers, the 2nd Wisconsin Cavalry in a state of insubordination and mutiny. A mob of the enlisted men, abetted by several of the officers, assailed the commanding officer, Lt. Col. Dale, in his tent, demanding his resignation on threat of forcible expulsion or his life.

To quell this I placed sixteen commissioned officers of the regiment in close arrest, and reduced 76 non-commissioned officers to the ranks.

. . . . Indiscriminate foraging of daily occurrence. Citizens assailed, knocked down, robbed in open day; houses broken into, ransacked, women insulted, maltreated. Yet no steps were taken by regimental officers to check these outrages.

My instructions from the Major-General Commanding [Sheridan] were to "treat the inhabitants of the country in a conciliatory manner, and to establish a rigid discipline among the troops, and to prevent outrages on private persons and property."

Since my order—head-shaving and lashes—not flogging, discipline has been restored. Men caught stealing have been required to pay the owner. . . . Complaints of outrages have ceased.

In my opinion conditions were such nothing less severe would have had effect.

At first disposed to resent the presence of the troops, inhabitants of the occupied districts learned to rely on them for protection. A local official wrote Custer to that effect:

The Rowdies who incited the mob have disappeared. I earnestly entreat you to permit the detail to remain a considerable time, to preserve the lives of innocent persons and allow them to go about their occupations.

Never would mischief-makers let Custer alone. By putting a false construction on an official act of his, an attempt was made to discredit him with his friend General Sturgis. Hearing of this, Custer sent a statement of the facts, to which the general replied. The reply is worthy of both, writer and recipient:

General Sturgis to Custer, July 3, 1865, from Austin, Texas:
My dear General—It is with unfeigned satisfaction I acknowledge your note of this morning, and I beg to assure you that our happy personal relations have not been (so far as I am concerned) for one moment endangered by any official action it may have been necessary to adopt. As you justly remark, I was not aware of the circumstances, and, had I had any fault to find touching the manner it reached yourself, it would be completely disarmed by the frank and elevated character of your note which has but increased the high esteem in which you have always been held

by Your Friend
S. D. Sturgis

Custer withheld his official worries from his wife so far as he was able. In Alexandria, since her knowledge of the soldiers' disaffection caused her fear for his life, he kept a revolver under his pillow at night. Later she learned it was never loaded.

Custer to Mr. and Mrs. Bacon, October 5, 1856, from Hempstead, Texas:
My dear Father and Mother—If you knew what a source of pleasure your letters are to us you would write more frequently. We are leading a quiet, contented, normal life. Horseback riding is one of our chief pleasures. Libbie—I never saw her in better health—is now an expert horse-woman, so fearless she thinks nothing of mounting a girthless

saddle on a strange horse. You should see her ride across these Texas prairies at such a gait that even some of the staff officers are left behind. Nettie goes riding with her, but they soon part company. Tom is doing very well; Libbie and I are delighted with his conduct. My father enjoys himself, more than in Monroe, having pleasant and lucrative employment, and is in better health than for years. He hunts a great deal. I keep six hounds. Libbie's love for dogs is second only to her affection for horses, those ranking next to her nearest relatives.

I wrote Hough he could have "Roanoke" at the price he offered ($250.) and to pay the money to you. Invest it, dispose of it, as you see fit. Use it for your own purposes if you so desire.

You mentioned your intention to sell your farm. Let me know the price you fix on, and all details.

A large number of troops are mustered out in this State. I trust these men will be enabled to return to their homes, as they claim with justice, in my opinion. Negro troops are also being mustered out rapidly. I trust this will continue until they can lay down musket for shovel and hoe. There are white men, veterans, anxious to fill up the Army, to whom preference should be given.

I am in favor of elevating the negro to the extent of his capacity and intelligence, and of our doing everything in our power to advance the race morally and mentally as well as physically, also socially. But I am opposed to making this advance by correspondingly debasing any portion of the white race. As to trusting the negro of the Southern States with the most sacred and responsible privilege—the right of suffrage—I should as soon think of elevating an Indian Chief to the Popedom of Rome.

All advocates of giving suffrage to the southern negro should visit these States and see for themselves. From the few northern papers we receive here I read good accounts of the industry and good conduct of the Freedman, and of the happy working of the new order of things.

I would not place too much reliance on these statements. I have travelled over a considerable portion of this State and of Louisiana, and have found no recognized system of labor. Planters are losing extensive and valuable crops because negroes refuse to work. To deprive one of wages has no effect, so long as he gets enough to eat and drink.

I regard the solution of the negro problem as involving difficulty and requiring greater statesmanship than any political matter that has arisen for years.

Tell Fred and Jim I hope to secure them appointments in the 3rd
Michigan. Libbie and Nettie [Annette Humphrey was now Mrs.
Jacob Greene] are in the tent with me "jabbering" of old times.

Custer's command at this time was larger by thousands than at
any period during the Civil War. His jurisdiction extended over a
vast territory. In January, 1866, he dispatched the valuable Assistant
Adjutant General Captain Jacob Greene as an intelligence agent to
ascertain the temper of the people in remote districts toward the
new order of things and toward the practicability of withdrawing
the troops. Mingling with all kinds of people who did not suspect
his mission, Captain Greene made a fair survey.

Captain Greene's report:

The German element in general is loyal and attached to the government. They and others of like stamp are keenly apprehensive of the
designs of participants in the Rebellion, or sympathizers with its aims.
These dissidents deem it due their self-respect to accomplish by political
power what they failed to do by arms. They are submitting to what is
forced on them with an intense hatred.

A minority—but a large one—boast of their intention to "pay the
Yankee back." They say, "We'll run the nigger ourselves." And "The
nigger must clear out." This attitude complicates the withdrawal of the
troops. The Government has admitted the Freedman to his natural
rights as a human being—but he is without legal rights under the legis-
lation of the State in which he finds himself, and is therefore, without
protection or defence where the power of the Government is constantly enforced.

Self-interest no longer demands consideration for the negro. As
Freedman he is disliked, despised. Murders of negroes are frequent,
and actual slavery exists in regions remote from the troops.

A war of races, indiscriminate murder and destruction of property—
every outrage would result were Government protection now withdrawn. This is feared by many who were active in the Rebellion, but
who are fair-minded enough to consider the matter truthfully.

Organized plots against the Government; demonstrations against
those who were accepting defeat and conforming to authority; un-
bridled outlawry—to suppress these things in Texas and Louisiana

had been Custer's task. It was made the more difficult because of the elements of discontent in his own command. That he fulfilled his assignment with success is evidenced by letters from persons of all affiliations. Provisional Governor Hamilton testified to his "wise and efficient conduct of an affair as much administrative as military."

Custer's term was completed in March, 1866, and he was mustered out. His pay as major general in the Volunteers—$8,000— ceased. He automatically reverted to rank and rating in the Regular Army at $2,000 a year, with a small allowance for living quarters.

He was concerned now for his future. He had made for himself a distinguished record during the war and its aftermath. He was twenty-seven, and his experience of men was extensive. He was dynamic and full of enterprise. If nothing was offered him to challenge his abilities as a soldier, he would resign and make his way in civilian pursuits. He decided to look about. Elizabeth went to Monroe.

Custer to Elizabeth, March 12, 1866, from Washington:
Dear Old Sweetness—I am *so* lonesome. I arrived here Friday morning. I have a nice room. Friends I have met express regret you are not with me. *So do I.* Senator and Mrs Chandler are here; Mr and Mrs Sherrill, Mrs and Miss Stevens, Major and Mrs Grant. They all say such nice things about you and are extremely polite to me. Mrs Chandler and I attended Dr. Sutherland's church Sunday evening, and heard a very fine sermon.

You know how fond your boy is of the theatre, and of course you imagine me a nightly attendant. The opera is here also. But . . . I do not feel the slightest desire to go to theatre or opera . . . a certain Somebody is not here to go with me.

Sec'y Stanton enquired very kindly after you, said I ought to have brought you along. Said he would not have believed me disloyal if all the papers in the U.S. had said so. He seemed so glad to see me. He looked at me, then came over to where I sat in his office and said, "Custer, stand up. I want to see you all over once more. It does me good to look at you again!"

He gave me a very cordial invitation to call on Mrs Stanton.

I telegraphed you that Tom has been appointed to the regular army.

In speaking of this the Secretary said, "I tell you, Custer, there is nothing in my power to grant I would not do, if you would ask me." I replied that this was offering a great deal. He said, "Well, I mean it."

Tell Tom he must study Tactics all the time now.

I had scarcely arrived before the Sergeant-at-Arms of the Senate summoned me to appear before the Reconstruction Committee. Much of my time has been spent in giving testimony before this Committee. . . .

I am so anxious to return to the "bosom of my family. . . ." I think if I stay here much longer and Andy Johnson remains firm, the Constitution will be able to stand alone. . . . At least, that seems the present policy.

I have adopted the motto of the Father of our country: "In time of Peace prepare for War." Which means to keep a standing army. I have plenty of standing but very little army. This does not trouble me, however.

It is after midnight and I must go to bed.

Custer to Elizabeth, March 16, 1866, from Washington:
My table is covered with cards. I am in demand with artists, cast of head for bust, photographers . . . Miss Vinnie Reams for a medallion, &c.&c.

To-day at dinner Mrs Sherrill wore a water-green silk trimmed with velvet a darker shade.

Eliza has gone to visit her "ole Missus." She will then start for Monroe. Col. Greene has decided not to enter the regular army, but will travel for an Insurance Company through New England.

A lady, wife of Senator C. of Mo. said, from hearsay she inferred that you are beautiful. I told her that by actual observation you are a beauty.

Custer to Elizabeth, March, 1866, from Washington:
. . . . A grand political meeting is to be held next Wednesday evening to endorse President Johnson. I should like to attend, but business will prevent.

Urge Tom to study his Tactics, Cavalry and Infantry. He was most fortunate in his appointment considering the number and rank of applicants. Several of those appointed Lieutenants in the regular army had been brevet Major-Generals in the Volunteers. (Tom was the lowest, of course). So the "Custer luck" has again prevailed. . . .

I send you some pictures of guests at the dinner-party at Chief Justice Chase's. Slightly Dundreary-ish. Please do not show except to the family.

Political combinations. . . . I dare not write all that goes on underhand. . . . I never knew political excitement to run so high. Even the ladies are excited and engaged in these matters.

Custer to Elizabeth, March 18, 1866, from Washington:

Still undecided when I can leave for N.Y. Am waiting the action of Congress on an important bill (Not the Army Bill which passed the Senate last week) in which I am interested as to my future. I think it probable that I shall leave the army, but shall not decide till assured of success. I can obtain the position of Foreign Minister, with a salary in gold of from 7 to 10 thousand dollars per annum. This would be best for a few years, after which I should have to look for some other pursuit. I would like it for many reasons.

Yesterday I went to Baltimore as guest of the Union Club. . . . I was introduced by the Hon. Mr Thomas to many prominent citizens many of whom were enthusiastic over your boy. We visited many public buildings, and then sat down to an elegant dinner. . . . I never was more handsomely treated.

Genl. McCook invited me with other friends to "Fidelio." To-morrow I am to see Mr and Mrs Charles Kean open in "Henry VIII."

I called on Mrs Genl. Williams. I think she is perfectly magnificent. There is so much woman about her.

I dined with Jim Martin and saw the baby. Mrs Martin is if anything more beautiful than ever.

My confidence in the strength of the Constitution is increasing daily while Andy is as firm and upright as a tombstone. He has not uttered any speeches lately, but I am nightly expecting an outburst of his peculiar eloquence. However, I'm not partial to speechmaking. I believe in acts, not words. But, unlike some public characters, he does not swallow his own words. He has grown. . . . He is a very strong Union man. . . . Union now and forever, one and inseparable.

I am sending by express a box of books, all military. Tell Tom to study Casey's Tactics, Cavalry, Infantry.

I procured Yates' appointment to the regular army, from Sec'y Stanton. I had obtained from Sec'y Seward a clerkship for him, in the State Depm't. But he greatly prefers the army, and is delighted over it. You would be surprised, considering the number of applicants, for how many I have procured appointments.

Tell Tom to study his Tactics.

Birds of all colors are worn in the centre of fine fans. There is a new style of hair-nets.

Custer to Elizabeth, April 1, 1866, from New York:

My Darling—In accordance with orders I have the honor to report on the operations of my command this day. It being Sunday I did not attempt to engage in business, but rose late—result of late hours last night. I was awakened by Hamilton coming to enquire if I would like to ride in the Park. Three of us started in a fine open carriage up Broadway. . . . Sunday is a great day for riding, here. We saw many vehicles and fine horses, and enjoyed a drive on the Harlem Lane and the famous Bloomingdale Road.

I called on Maggie Mitchell, at the house where she lives with her mother, a handsome residence in 54th Street, near Fifth Avenue. A delightful visit. Her manners are so pleasing, her conversation so refined you would not suppose she had been on the stage. Spent the evening writing to "mein leedle Frau."

To-morrow Cara and I go shopping. I am in luck. Silks at A.T. Stewart's have come down fifty cents a yard in a week, and other articles in proportion.

At six to-morrow evening Genl. Pleasanton and I are to dine as guests of Genl. Davis at the Manhattan Club. Oh, these New York people are so kind to me. I would like to become wealthy in order to make my permanent home here. They say I must not leave the army until I am ready to settle here.

At the Hotel we have a military table. One of the waiters is one of my old soldiers. You should see how he supplies me with "rations." "Giniral, will ye have some of this?" Or that. And, "Giniral, that was a mighty fine horse ye rode at the Parade." Or, "That was a hard ingagement we had at . . . Giniral!"

Custer to Elizabeth, April 3, 1866, from New York:

My Darling. . . . after some business I listened to a rehearsal at Niblo's of "A Child of Fortune." Afterwards walked down Broadway with Maggie Mitchell. Left her at the Winter Garden. Called to take Mrs Chandler and Minnie to see Mr Balling's "Heroes of the Republic" at his studio. Mrs C. was too tired with shopping, but Minnie went with me, and then to the Art Gallery, 625 Broadway. We saw "Oriental Princess. After the Bath" . . . a superb painting, but calculated to make a schoolgirl blush. Had I but know beforehand. . . .

After dinner went with a friend (he had a box) to see "Little Beaufort."

No letter from Her to-day.

Matinée, with Cara, at the Academy of Music . . . Miss Kellogg in "Faust." She was superb.

Several West Point officers were here. . . . After the theatre several of us went out on an expedition in search of fun—visited several shooting galleries, pretty-girl-waitress-saloons. We also had considerable sport with females we met on the street—"Nymphes du Pavé" they are called. Sport alone was our object. At no time did I forget you.

You can read of the Bal Masqué at the Academy of Music in *Harper's Weekly* of April 14th. Cara wore white domino and mask, Fannie B, blue. I was the Devil, the only one. You can see my picture, but I assure you I was not so horrid. My costume was elegant and rich. Cape and coat, black velvet with gold lace. Pants the same, reaching only to the thighs. Red silk tights with not even drawers underneath. Red Velvet cap with two upright red feathers, for horns. Black shoes with pointed toes upturned. Handsome belt. Mask, black silk.

Much as I admire New York I feel that our fancy-dress party at the Humphrey House was more choice. While many a costume here cost more than all ours put together, yet as to quality of guests, here were all sorts—good, bad, indifferent. At ours none were bad nor indifferent.

Custer to Elizabeth, April 18, 1866, from New York:
Early this morning went down on lower Broadway, called on Mr Russell. Then went with Col. Howe into Wall Street, the financial heart of the country, and was introduced to some prominent capitalists. Then went by invitation to the Brokers' Board . . . a full session, and much excitement. I had scarcely taken my seat when a member unknown to me rose and stated that they had present "one of the bravest and most gallant generals of the War," and proceeded to compliment your boy, ending by proposing three cheers for Major-General Custer. Not three, but six, were given, with a tiger. I was then conducted to the President's chair from which stand I returned my thanks, saying "I am no speaker, as you know" . . . To which a voice from the floor replied, "You are a fighter!" I was most kindly received by all.

A very distinguished breakfast was arranged for me . . . frustrated in a laughable manner I will tell you about. . . . Among those who had accepted invitations were Bancroft, the historian; Wm. Cullen Bryant, the poet; Mr Charles O'Conor and other celebrities. . . .

In Monroe, Mrs. Custer had been practicing economy in view of their probable reduction in income. On her birthday in April she wrote her Aunt Eliza, Mrs. Sabin.

Elizabeth to Mrs. Sabin, April 8, 1866, from Monroe, Michigan:
I am twenty-four. Would you believe it? But people do not think my looks changed in spite of all I have been through. Autie is too necessary to my happiness for me not to miss him every hour he is away.

Do you remember how you used to try to get me to sew nicely? Well, now I love it, and occupy myself with my clothes.

Custer's homecoming was all a returned hero could desire. While he shunned parades—for which he was ever in demand—he delighted in meetings with his old soldiers. He was constantly urged to enter politics.

He had promises of strong support should he be put forward as candidate for the governorship of the state. But a political career did not appeal to him. He would engage in business unless pending military matters might offer the scope his abilities demanded.

In May the household was saddened by Judge Bacon's death.

Elizabeth to Mrs. Sabin, May, 1866, from Monroe, Michigan:
Mrs Thurber helped nurse him. Father Custer stayed with us. He knew of his approaching end, and was prepared. He sought to avoid the confusion found in settling Albert's estate. He seemed triumphantly happy, so near Heaven, so contented in regard to me: "Elizabeth has married entirely to her own satisfaction and to mine. No man could wish for a son-in-law more highly thought of!" He seemed stronger, and as Autie had to be in New York for a few days when he returned it was too late.

The Choir sang "Cast thy burdens on the Lord." The Dutch say they have lost their best friend. One old German says he cannot pass the house without crying.

Elizabeth to Mrs. Sabin, May, 1866, from Monroe, Michigan:

Our house is not the same. Mother is visiting in Clinton. I do not think she will ever be strong enough to keep house again. I should be far more miserable but for Armstrong's care. He keeps me out of doors as much as he can. I do not wear deep mourning. He is opposed to it.

Walter Bacon is here as Administrator. I have not seen the Will, but Walter says Father left Mother the interest on $5,000. This, with her own money will support her well. Property will have to be sold to get the sum on interest. Most of the estate is in land which does not sell readily just now. Fortunately I do not need any more than what my generous husband gives me.

When I come I will bring you Grandfather's cane which Father always used.

Armstrong is thinking of going to Mexico. The government there offered him handsome inducements. I am opposed to it. I do not want him ever to go into battle again. But if he goes I shall go with him.

In the spring Custer had been in correspondence with Carvajal, head of the military party in Mexico in Brownsville, Texas, regarding temporary service across the border, if requisite leave from the U. S. Government could be obtained. He could have the rank of major general and serve also as adjutant general at a salary of $10,-000 in gold. He consulted his chief, Sheridan.

Sheridan to Custer, June 30, 1866, from Headquarters, Military Division of the Gulf:

My dear Custer—I thank you for your kind letter which gave me much information about civil and military affairs.

In regard to Mexico, I could tell you much, if I could see you. Scarcely a native Mexican is in favor of Maximilian, and his position is becoming precarious, whether the French and Austrians are withdrawing or not. Ten thousand Cavalry would take the country from him in six months, backed, as it would be, by a Mexican force.

The Liberals have 6,000 men on the Rio Grande frontier, but want of money and a good bold leader made them non-effective till the 16th of the month, when they captured the Imperial convoy, and killed or captured two-thirds of the escort which numbered 1600 men. They will probably also get the specie train coming from Monterey with about $2,000,000.

In fact, Custer, if they have any vim they will take Matamoras and the whole of Northern Mexico inside six weeks. There are but 300 soldiers left in Matamoras and I think it would require about 10,000 to man the fortifications. I expect to hear by the next steamer of the occupation of the place by the Liberals. The city would then be turned over at a moment's notice, if the merchants could get any security for their property. I advised Carvajal to give that security, as a matter of policy.

Carvajal told me about you and the permission Genl. Grant would give you. If you conclude to go you would have my warmest support. But I do not advise the introduction of Americans. Unless they can be well paid and well rationed they would get disgusted. The country is different from the rosy colors in which it is painted to them.

If you do anything it will be necessary to do it soon. Maximilian's power is a farce, and he has no troops to sustain it.

Thus Sheridan. Grant's letter to Romero, Mexican minister to Washington, commended Custer "in a high degree" and promised to endorse his application for the needed leave.

This leave, however, the United States Government denied. And somewhat over a year after Appomattox, Custer is again in Monroe "awaiting orders."

12: Lieutenant Colonel

WHILE AWAITING orders in Monroe during the summer of 1866, Custer received unofficial word that he would shortly be appointed lieutenant colonel in one of the cavalry regiments being formed for service on the western frontier under General Sheridan.

At the close of the war in the spring of 1865, Sheridan had been sent by Grant to bring the seceding states into line and suppress outlawry. One department of this work he assigned to Custer. Now, in 1866, he was transferred to the Department of the Missouri. This was one of the four military districts into which Lieutenant General Sherman had divided the geographical area under his control. It included Missouri, Kansas, Indian Territory, and New Mexico. Its task was to deal with the Indians. Savage hordes were harassing settlers, attacking the surveying and construction parties of the Kansas-Pacific Railroad, subjecting isolated families to unspeakable tortures. They resented the intrusion of the white man on their hunting grounds and were retaliating. Treaties made with the several tribes were violated by the Indians, nor is it to be forgotten that the bureaucrats themselves did not always show good faith.

Sheridan, in his province west of the Missouri River, with headquarters at Fort Leavenworth, Kansas, had to handle these perplexities. And the remaining decade of Custer's life was to be closely related to the military aspects of the country's expansion westward.

While Sheridan's plans—which included Custer—were being developed, Custer was active in reconstruction measures. While so engaged, he was bitterly assailed by some of the newspapers.

Custer to J. W. Forney, Secretary of the United States Senate, August 30, 1866, from Monroe, Michigan:
A few of the most extreme Radical journals, prominent among these the organ controlled and edited by yourself, have pretended to discover

an inconsistency between my views expressed before the Reconstruction Committee, last March, and my present action as delegate to the Philadelphia Convention, and supporter of the principles enunciated in the resolutions adopted by that illustrious national and patriotic body, composed of representatives from every State and Territory in the Union—the first truly national assembly in our country during the past six years. . . .

I will not reply to the seditious epithets you have applied to the Convention of which I am proud to have been a member, nor will I expose your baseness in calling disloyal those gallant soldiers taking part in it— men who periled their lives to defend, restore, perpetuate a constitutional government which you are laboring to destroy.

What have *you* done to justify you in traducing those whose patriotism has undergone the test of battle . . . ?

As to the propriety of my attending the National Union Convention, if I satisfy my God, my country and my conscience I achieve my highest aim.

Along with the victories won on many a hard-contested field by our noble and patriotic armies, and in which I am proud to have been an humble participant, I place, as crowning victory, the assembling of that Convention of men, for years opposed in principle and policy, but who, casting aside personal feeling and prejudice, came together for one purpose—to secure prosperity and preservation of the country, inspired by one sentiment—Union, Concession and harmony. Everything for the Cause. Nothing for men.

When in September the Cleveland *Leader* got out an extra designed to injure Custer, the *Plain Dealer* countered by printing the above letter under the heading "Custer's Reply to the Atrocious Attempts of the Corrupt or Insane Radical Press to Pervert his Testimony." These were the concluding words of Custer's letter:

You know with what earnestness I engaged in the late struggle, fought till it was ended, victory won. With that same earnestness I desire Peace—that peace for which our armies contended.

. . . . The platform and principles adopted by the Convention may be stated in six words: National Integrity, Constitutional Liberty, Individual Rights.

General John A. Dix, presiding at the first meeting of the Convention on August 14, 1866, spoke of the parallel between this convention and that of 1787 . . . to assert the supremacy of representative government over all within the confines of the Union. They had come together to assert this basic doctrine and protest against its violation by Congress: The seceding states had been called on to accept certain conditions for readmission to the Union —ratification of the amendment abolishing slavery, repudiation of debts contracted to overthrow the Government. Thirty-six states were being governed by twenty-five; eleven were without representation in the legislative body.

When it came to choosing individuals to represent a state in Congress, Custer believed firmly that preference should be given those who had not participated in the rebellion or in any way favored it. A stranger soliciting Custer's views respecting two rival candidates was answered with a detailed letter.

Custer to a correspondent, October 23, 1866, from Kansas:
. . . . With regard to the two Congressional candidates . . . under no circumstances would I vote for a man who in time of war had sympathized with the enemies of the government. I class Mr G. whom you champion, as among the men of the North who opposed the Government in its efforts to suppress the late Rebellion.

Regarding the Congressional Plan of Reconstruction— In my opinion, as victors we have a right to name the terms on which peace shall be established and the Union restored. During hostilities I supposed the National authority would bring to punishment the leaders and instigators of the Rebellion. I would deem it a breach of faith on the part of our Government were the terms of parole violated or disregarded on our part.

I believe that every man who voluntarily engaged in the Rebellion forfeited every right held under our Government—to live, hold property. But I do not agree with you that it is "a flagrant violation of our Constitution not to exact those penalties in full." I believe this position —not to exact such penalties—lies within the provisions of that instrument.

For the Government to exact full penalties, simply because it is constitutionally authorized to do so, would, in my opinion, be unnecessary, impolitic, inhuman, and wholly at variance with the principles of a free, civilized and Christian nation, such as we profess to be.

On the eve of an election politicians seek to alarm the people. . . . Our Union has withstood attacks from front, rear, without, within. . . . I do not believe the adoption of either plan of Reconstruction can destroy it. Whatever plan put forward, adopted, *Union* will be the result. For that purpose the North went forth to fight, and only that object will satisfy the people.

We who, as soldiers, have performed our part, knew that a difficult task—saving the Union—remained for other hands than ours. That question is now presented to the people and to soldier-citizens. I speak for myself alone. I think it the height of inconsistency to alarm intelligent citizens, many of them who have been soldiers, with the cry "Union—or Dis-Union" when the candidate put forward to "save the Union" was a prominent opposer of the war.

President Johnson likened the Union to a circle that has been grievously disrupted by the war and must be mended by legislative action backed by the people. To bring this idea home to a citizenry divided in sentiment and torn by factions and often led by an unscrupulous press, he planned a tour—"Swinging Round the Circle" —with speeches at strategic points. The Custers were invited to join the presidential party and accepted. It was a carefree time for Elizabeth Custer, for the Mexican venture, which she had dreaded, was no longer in question.

Elizabeth in her diary:
My husband had known for some time what his future position would be—years of monotonous service on the frontier—so that he had no axe to grind, and we both could make the most of the pleasure offered us.

It seemed to me we gained more enjoyment than the rest of the party. Mr Johnson had a most harrowing and perplexing position. Tho he met many friends and supporters also he encountered bitter opposition.

The Cabinet officers who accompanied him also had their trials, for even in relaxation they could not cast off their responsibilities. I frequently wondered that Mr Seward could rise above them, and chat with us, while he took in the beauties of cities and country as we flew through the broad West.

His face and throat bore ineffaceable marks of what had been so nearly his tragic end [he had been marked as a victim in the plot by which Lincoln was assassinated]. But instead of his nerves being unstrung by that night of horror when his life hung in the balance, he was so calm and bright one could not imagine he was mentally revolving questions of diplomatic import, and that for five years he had given his wonderful statesmanship to our relations with other lands. In my father's house I had been so accustomed to hear veneration for his intellect that, when he invited me to lunch, I was almost surprised to see him eat and drink like other mortals, and enjoy the good things our car supplied.

But the happiest men of the party were those of Army and Navy.

I recall Admiral Farragut's genial sunshiny face as he went among the people who surrounded our train at stopping-places returning to his wife whose eyes rested on him with such affection—perhaps to introduce some admirer—a sweet remembrance of a distinguished man receiving the homage of a grateful nation.

Secretary Seward paid tribute to President Johnson as "an absolutely honest man." Speaking at Toledo and Detroit he said:

Six years ago Andrew Johnson, a Southern man, a slave-holder, Democrat, met me in Congress, a Whig and Abolitionist. . . . God bless him for the stand he took. He gave up fortune—everything, for the preservation of principles that patriots hold sacred.

Johnson defended his veto of the Freedman's Bureau Bill on the grounds that he felt it designed to exploit the Negro. At Cleveland he was faced with a frantic mob. When some admirers cheered him, a riot ensued in which a man was killed and several persons injured.

Challenged to "hang Jeff Davis," he reminded his audience that this was a matter for the courts, for Chief Justice Chase, not for the Executive. He made a strong plea that "passion, prejudice, be laid aside" and that reason should resume empire. He pointed out that much opposition to measures for reintegration came from those who had stayed at home to speculate in the profits of war, sending substitutes to fight.

Army and Navy were the heroes, Grant and Farragut their spokesmen. When, as not infrequently, indisposition kept Grant from some public appearance, the President deputed Custer to take his place.

At New Market, Ohio, near Custer's birthplace, the Executive was insulted by a radical group. This was atoned for by the hospitalities of Cadiz, causing Custer to remark that as a Harrison County man he was glad for the President to meet some respectable citizens of the district, having had to encounter some of the worst. "Not worse than the Rebels," someone shouted. "Oh, worse by far," retorted Custer, "for the rebels have repented."

The presidential junket over, Custer was ordered to Fort Riley. He received a generous send-off from his friends and rode in a private car to St. Louis, where an exposition was in full swing. Here Custer formed a lasting friendship with the actor Lawrence Barrett, who had left the boards to become an infantry captain during the Civil War.

Fort Riley was ten miles beyond the railway terminus, and primitive. Elizabeth Custer was amazed to find that storey-and-a-half buildings about a parade ground constituted a fort on the plains, but she speedily turned their quarters into a home. Their party included the ever-faithful Eliza and her colored swain Henry, and a Seminary schoolmate of Elizabeth's, a pretty girl whose mother did not share the usual parental dread of having a daughter marry into the army. Even with her to set an example, the Custers could not always secure attractive young women to help brighten garrison life "outside the States." (Though Kansas had been admitted to statehood in 1861, it still was considered alien land.)

Sheridan's policy was to keep small movable columns always alerted to protect or avenge. They were not to engage in long pursuits, because the Indian ponies, with riders who knew the country, could outdistance their best mounts. His main business was to bring the tribes west of the Missouri into the Indian reservation allotted to them—peaceably, if possible, but effectively. Certain that an outbreak by the young braves was contemplated, he prepared to take the initiative during the winter, when the hostiles would be at their weakest, and conciliate during the autumn. Food, he learned, was the unfailing peacemaker in negotiating with the Red Man.

When duty called Custer to Fort Hays, where Sheridan had his temporary headquarters, Elizabeth would join him there. As an "army lady"—often the only lady—with the Army of the Potomac, she had often lived in luxury. Even the Texas experience, despite the hardships of the march, had offered comforts at the centers of population. But this was roughing it. Kansas was the real test of fortitude.

Elizabeth to Mrs. Sabin, 1866, near Fort Hays, Kansas:

Dear Aunt Eliza—I am never happier than when sleeping in a tent. It is so comfortable. Storms are our only trouble—thunder, lightning, freshets, wind. But our tent is well staked. We were at Ft. Leavenworth lately, but could not get back for three weeks, as a storm had destroyed culverts, railroad bridges, also six miles of the railroad.

Even after the road was repaired the country was flooded. There was another storm like it last week. It will cost the company about $4,000. to repair the damage.

Streams rise about a foot a minute. A few nights ago the creek near-by began to rise. All hands were set to work to bring cook-tent, dining and servant's tent up the hill, a rapid move at night.

There are drawbacks to Kansas, but it is a fine spot to begin life in, with good farming land.

There is some trouble with Indians, within twenty miles from us, coming down from the North. A part of the regiment is still in camp, so that I am not afraid, near such a large body of men.

Mails come irregularly, on account of freshets. Also sometimes the Indians cut the tracks.

The most pernicious enemy was the traitor within. Squabbles as to whether Indian affairs should be managed by the War Department or a special Bureau—dishonest Indian agents on the reservations—dishonest contractors who applied the army with provisions —bacon weighted down with stones—mildewed hardtack—these were some of the outpost troubles. The telephone had not been invented. The telegraph reached only certain stations, not the most remote. Mails came irregularly. Complaints were readily dismissed at the center, which concerned itself all too little with matters that did not affect its own well-being. There were no amusements, no shops near at hand, no ways of supplementing official shortages by

purchase. Small wonder that soldiers at those frontier posts deserted
when rumor reached them of gold for the picking up, high wages in
the newly discovered mines of Colorado and New Mexico.

In the United States Army and Navy Journal an old soldier
wrote:

Without fresh vegetables, in a life of monotony, away from home,
what was there for a man to do—but desert or get drunk?

In Texas, Custer had been accused of brutality when resorting to
stringent disciplinary measures. And now, for putting down insubordination in a unit from Iowa, it was suggested in the legislature
of that state that he "should be brought to trial and subjected to
condign punishment." It came to nothing. But it had been seriously
considered.

The spark of mutiny, kindled by the neglect of bureaucrats and
fanned into flame by profiteers and professional mischief-makers,
forced Sheridan to issue an order that deserters, when taken, should
be shot without benefit of court.

Drunkenness among officers was, from first to last, one of Custer's
major problems. On the frontier, with such limited scope for their
activities, men of intemperate habits gave way to excess. Sullen-
ness was the next stage. Then deterioration of quality was likely to
set in. Resentments, fancied slights, when brooded over, became
obsessions. Men by nature sane, in an abnormal situation were likely
to show themselves not sane. To establish and maintain a rational
standard was by no means least and lightest of a leader's task. As a
girl in Monroe, Libbie Bacon had deplored seeing local swains occasionally "politely tight." But Mrs. Custer had to find out that
in military life drunkenness was rule rather than exception among
the men in positions of authority.

One officer, newly appointed to the command, when paying the
obligatory call on his commander's wife, fell in at the door of the
parlor, where Mrs. Custer was waiting to welcome him—though
not, as she observed later, "with open arms to receive his collapsing
form."

Elizabeth in her diary:

In civil life people are too much occupied with their own concerns to pay much heed to the woes of others, but in a military existence one is often forced to play the part of listener. I never had serious sorrows of my own to air, and my husband had a horror of parading trouble, so that I was deprived of the satisfaction of paying back in their own coin those who bored me with recitals of injuries from which they smarted.

In civil life a gentleman, tight, at a dinner-party, fills the ear of the lady, his partner, with sentimental outpourings. At a military banquet the drink-loosened tongue recounts some tale of past injustices—never too long past for the slightest detail to be forgotten. What injustices? Oh, having been thwarted when on the point of being assigned to a post where duty was light and pleasure perpetual. Or having had baseless charges preferred against one. Or having been overslaughed.

At a military dinner there may be little to eat, but never a lack of grievances.

At such festivities as we were ushered to table according to rank, owing to my husband's position I was generally partnered with an old officer who tolerated me for the grim patience with which I heard his oft-told tale. Also because when the soldier waiting on the table came round with wine, he begged me not to refuse, as was my habit, "the gift of the gods," as that enabled him slyly to substitute my filled glass for his so rapidly emptied. Fortunately the soldier soon noticed the speed with which the wine vanished, and on his next rounds passed us by.

One officer—and his grievance was not imaginary—worked off his resentment by naming each chair in his room for one of the officers who had overslaughed him, then, sending them, each with a resounding kick and an equally resounding expletive, hurtling down the hall. After this outburst he went about his duties faultlessly, for he was an excellent officer.

I learned my lesson, once and for all, from my husband, so that hurt feelings ceased to disturb me. "Leave him alone for a few days," he would say. "He's sure to come to himself soon." And this is what invariably happened. In a small circle it was a loss to have a friend drop out, even for a day, but people soon grew tired of sulking and were only too glad to join again in the sociabilities.

When separated from the brother he adored, it was Tom Custer's habit to apply for a transfer to Armstrong's command. On one such occasion, when there had been an official delay, he manifested such resentment that Elizabeth wrote to enquire the reason.

Thomas Custer to Elizabeth:
Well, I will divulge the secret, but I expect you will feel very badly. I have now got into the habit of taking my daily cocktail with the rest. The temptation has been very great. I get along very well when I am with you and Autie. I hope your love for me will not be weakened, though I may not be worthy of it.

You ask if I think you unsympathetic about the transfer. My Dear Girl, I love you for it, more, if possible, than I always do. Tom.

Gallant and brave, an admirable soldier, Thomas Ward Custer lacked Armstrong's self-control, his iron resolution, and he had the sense to fly to sanctuary when temptation grew stronger than resistance.

Miss Libbie Bacon of Monroe had prided herself on her "exclusiveness," but on the frontier Mrs. Custer found that her standards had to be revised. With regard to masculine attentions she consulted her husband.

"Dance, ride, walk, with whom you choose," he told her. "But never allow any one officer to feel himself your special cavalier." As for officers' wives: "Friends, intimates, as to these follow your own preferences, of course. But when receiving company formally, officially, treat all alike. You must not snub Mrs So-and-so because you do not like her."

"But—she's not a lady."

"She's an officer's wife. At our house she's our guest. She is one of our official family. Look, Libbie. This is how you behaved when she came up to shake hands with you."

"Oh, Autie. As uncordial as all that?"

Custer reminded her of the serious trouble arising from pettinesses, how often a man's career had been spoiled by dissensions among wives, by false report, senseless gossip. Above all, in a small community as they were, isolated, dependent on one another for companionship, it was essential to the general good will that small preferences be sacrificed. Once this was made clear to her, Elizabeth Custer wholeheartedly fostered the spirit of harmony in their military family. She was richly rewarded. Gratitude from the homeless, the assuaging of many a nostalgic pang, helping turn a weak impulse into wholesome channels—these would always be among her most cherished memories. Elizabeth also learned to admire women who bore hardships uncomplainingly so they might contrive a home wherever a husband's lot might be cast. She developed a high regard for women who bore cheerfully the complications, along with the enrichments, of motherhood.

Had her New England mother lived, Elizabeth would have been more thoroughly schooled in housekeeping, but her indulgent stepmother had spoiled her in that respect. Yet her husband would not have her assume any tasks that could be delegated to others. He felt that his wife's gifts could be put to better uses than coping with the hardships of frontier housekeeping.

Custer's chief occupation was to make a fine implement of service out of the incongruous elements that formed the 7th Cavalry. It eventually won high renown through his tireless efforts, even in the face of his comparative youthfulness, bureaucratic neglect, difficulties of communication and transportation, the remoteness of frontier life from civilized centers, and the comparatively unfamiliar problems of warring with Indians.

Fort Riley was on a plateau swept by winds from two river valleys—the Republican and the Smoky—and as the women crossed the parade ground, their skirts ballooned about their heads. To enjoy an evening stroll, Elizabeth weighted her hems with lead. Amusements at the fort seem naïve indeed. They would laugh derisively when a man newly appointed to the cavalry showed lack of skill, or complete ignorance, when it came to mounting a horse or even keeping his seat once he was astride. *Harper's Weekly* and *Harper's Bazaar*, passed from hand to hand and devoured by everyone, were lifesavers on the frontier at a time when there was no radio, no motion pictures, no telephone. As for books, Custer carried an assortment of history and military studies everywhere, but apart from these, books had no place where men and women had to travel light and be prepared to move on short notice. In any case, sports and entertainments, however primitive, were wholesome and without malice.

Custer began writing at this time, and his leisure hours were spent in the library, happiest when his wife sat sewing beside him. From time to time he would look up and say, "Aren't we happy, Libbie?" Perhaps there was an unconscious foreboding of peril lurking nearby.

As the railroad thrust further into the "American Desert," the East became more curious about the West—as the present-day Middle West was called then. In 1867 a correspondent for the *United States Army and Navy Journal* wrote from Fort Harker, Kansas, the most recent railroad terminus:

On June 27 the locomotive went whistling by us. Excursions to the end of the line are becoming fashionable among Congressmen.

Dangerous to go beyond the Fort. . . . No one is permitted to go without an escort. Several dead and wounded settlers were recently brought in. The only man among the corpses not having been scalped was bald.

Settlers swarm about the Fort for protection.

Often excursionists brought letters of introduction to Custer. His hospitality was sorely taxed but never stinted. Travelers came sometimes merely to stare at Custer—the only assault from which he ever ran away. Once Eliza discovered him hiding in the hen house, the only available refuge.

Visitors in many cases assumed that an officer's quarters were a kind of free hotel, to which all citizens had the right of entry, with free food. On the other hand, memorable friendships were formed on the plains.

Charles G. Leland has given a picture of the Custers in those days, emphasizing Elizabeth's charm and the unostentatious Custer hospitality. Of Custer he wrote:

He left me rich in impressions, both as man and gentleman . . . one I never could forget . . . not only an admirable, but an impressive personality. One would credit anything to his credit because he was so frank and earnest. . . . Such a man is as rare as the want of such in the world is great.

13 : Court-Martial

CUSTER WAS preparing his 7th Cavalry Regiment for a type of warfare new to the army in general. There had been sporadic battles with the Indians, fought by trial and error, but the Indian ways of waging war, the Indian psychology were all too little known. Nor were there reliable data on their numerical strength. Then, too, tribes differed from one another; many were in perpetual warfare against other tribes, while not a few were friendly to the white man. The Coast Indians, the Yakimas, with whom Sheridan had dealt successfully in past years, were not like the Indians of the plains—the Cheyennes, Arapahoes, Kiowas, Comanches —whom he sought to coax or coerce into the Indian reservation or, when barbarity called for punitive retaliation, to destroy.

Some commanders were versed in Indian warfare from experience. Others, though they had distinguished records in the Mexican and Civil wars, knew nothing of it. The old rules did not apply in matters military. And human values were on another, often inhuman, basis. New techniques were the order of the day.

In the spring of 1867 Custer was ordered to Fort Hays to be in readiness for an expedition under Major General Hancock. Elizabeth remained at Fort Riley, and Custer wrote her letters which were in effect a diary.

Custer to Elizabeth, May 1, 1867, from Fort Hays, Kansas:
. . . . With rifle, glass and revolver I galloped to a spot about a mile and a half distant, a knoll commanding an extensive view of the surrounding country. From the east two dark spots were approaching, two carriages or buggies, an unusual sight in these regions. Who should it be but Johnnie and the Division Agent, followed by a conveyance belonging to the stage company. "How did you leave them at Fort Riley?" "All well," to my relief was the reply.

Back in my tent I read your dear letter. How beautiful the selections you sent me.

> "A guardian angel o'er his life presiding,
> Doubling his pleasures and his cares dividing. . . ."

You are indeed my guardian angel, not doubling my pleasures, but creating them.

Your other letters are doubtless at Genl. Hancock's headquarters, or Genl. Smith's. Nothing has been heard of either for days. It is rumored that they are on the march for this post . . . the original plan.

Nothing heard of Indians for days. "All quiet on Smoky Hill."

Yesterday Captains Hamilton & Benteen, and Lts. Moylan & Nolan and Drs. Coates, Lippincott with half a dozen men went buffalo hunting, intending to return about 5 P.M.

Capt. Benteen shot his favorite horse dead, also a large buffalo dog belonging to "E Company" just as it had the buffalo by the nose. The dog will recover. Captains, men and meat reached camp just at Tattoo, the others, tho but four miles from them, got lost and did not get in till noon to-day.

I trust we shall not be separated this summer. Take a dark view: if we have an Indian war we must have a base of supplies, either here or at Wallace, and at either place you could be safe and comfortable. You could be here now, if Anna were as used to camp life as you are.

Johnnie is to be promoted to Commissary of the road—a very responsible position. That will increase his pay and permit him to sleep in a house.

Tell Eliza I am in search of an Indian husband for her—one who won't bother her to sew buttons on his shirts and pants, nor would his washing be heavy. And one dish at a meal would satisfy him.

Johnnie, the strayling who had adopted the Custer outfit during the Civil War, was one of the unsung heroes of the day. The home he had left, so Custer ascertained, was not a happy one, nor was he missed there. Custer had him put to school, but he always came back to serve the man he worshiped, under Eliza's sheltering wing. Employment was found for him with the Wells Fargo Express Company, where he was highly valued for his probity and resourcefulness. He died gallantly in youth, defending the property in his care against an Indian attack on a stage coach.

Custer to Elizabeth, May 2, 1867, from Fort Hays, Kansas:

Come as soon as you can. "Whom God hath joined. . . ." I did not marry you for you to live in one house, me in another. One bed shall accommodate us both.

I intend to forward charges of slander to Ft. Riley against Genl. Gibbs. Tying knots in my socks to darn them? There are but two holes to a pair, and these are for the entrance of my feet.

I have not yet heard from the General about the band. When I do I will send him every man that can play on an instrument, from curry-comb to threshing-machine.

When we surrounded the Indian camp we found dogs of all sorts, sexes, sizes and colors. Dr. Coates and I found a little girl, not more than eight or nine . . . almost insensible, covered with blood. When able to talk she said "Those Indian men did me bad! . . ." Woe to them if I overtake them. The chances of this, however, are slight, once they are forewarned.

I wrote a very strong letter recently *against* an Indian War, depicting as strongly as I could the serious results that would follow . . . putting a stop to trains on the Overland route, interfering with the work on the Pacific Railroad, all of which would be a national calamity. I regard the recent outrages as the work of small groups of irresponsible young men, eager for war. The Indian stampede, I said, I consider caused by fear of our forces. . . . I ended with the hope that my opinion would be received as intended; that, should a war be waged, none would be more determined than I to make it a war of extermination . . . but I consider we are not yet justified in declaring such a war.

Genl. Hancock is expected here the day after to-morrow, when I shall know more of his plans, than at present.

I am glad that your views coincide with mine regarding Walter Bacon's letter. I regard it as a gross insult to the memory of our dear departed father to suggest that the child he idolized should sign a statement implying that he had been guilty of injustice toward his wife. . . . He who would have forfeited life sooner than have sanctioned an unjust act.

The Will, I believe is just. The law would not provide for her as advantageously as I can and will. Justice does not require anything at your hands. If you grant your mother anything it will not be justice; it will be generosity on your part.

I can well imagine how some of those drawling, canting hypocrites in Monroe to whom Walter refers have fawned on your mother, insinuating that she has been badly treated—probably under the impression that the estate was valued at thirty to forty thousand dollars, without knowledge of the true condition of affairs. If all Monroe should raise voices against the Will it would not shake my 'confidence in the justice of your Father's provisions as set forth in it.

I have notified the Companies that on the Fourth we will have a foot-race; distance, 300 yards, the Company producing the winner to be excused from guard and fatigue duty for one week, the winner from same duties for twenty days. I hear much excitement about it. I want to give the men exercise, innocent amusement, something to do.

It is also proposed that the officers of the 7th Cav. match those of the Postmaster's Division, the party that kills the smallest number of buffalo to pay for a champagne supper for the entire group. How I wish you were here. You would enjoy a buffalo hunt.

I am glad Anna's mother has sent Anna her summer dresses, as now she can come with us. I impose but one condition—that she, as well as yourself, shall heed the counsels of le bon père, myself, for, though young in years, he is old in experience and knows men, women, too, for that matter, for what they are worth.

Anna's horse will be a splendid buffalo-horse, a rarity. You both will be carried away with excitement . . . there is nothing so nearly resembling a cavalry charge as a buffalo chase.

As the post-office is established at Hays mails will come regularly, and I shall take the couriers off.

That stove is just what we require. Outdoor cooking is impossible in high wind and rain and storm. Fuel on the treeless Plains also is a consideration. Why, you evidently were created to be an Army officer's wife—provided that officer was Me.

So the sergeant is an admirer. I should like to see any man setting eyes on you who was not.

Comstock messes with Moylan and I. A worthy man, I am obtaining from him most valuable information in regard to Indians, their habits, &c. He brought with him a large dog he has named "Cuss" . . . short for . . . ???

Comstock was one of the scouts or interpreters engaged by Sheridan because of familiarity, from hunting and trapping, with plains Indians. Sheridan's hope was that by such influences the hostile tribes might be inducted without warfare into the Government-allotted reservation. Turkey Leg, Cheyenne chief, was an intimate of Comstock's, but whether through Turkey Leg's treachery or that of the young braves of his tribe, Comstock was betrayed and killed in a raid shortly after this letter of Custer's was written.

Custer to Elizabeth, May 4, 1867, from Fort Hays, Kansas:
I have just returned from Genl. Hancock's tent. He leaves at six for Ft. Leavenworth. Genl. Smith will go with him as far as Harker, perhaps to Riley. If so, you could come back with him. He is delighted at the idea. He will give you as many wagons as you need, and an ambulance fitted up with all conveniences. Should he go no farther than Harker I will start for you on his return here. So look for Genl. S or me within seven days, and commence packing.

Genl. Gibbs and all the 7th Cavalry, including Band, are to be here. Col. Parsons is to command at Ft. Riley all summer.

Col. B (He has just been released from arrest) will shortly go fetch his wife. Captain Barnitz has written Mrs Barnitz to join him. All the Companies, except Sheridan's, are to be concentrated here. We have a most beautiful camp. You will be delighted with the country.

Bring a good supply of butter—one hundred pounds or more; three or four cans of lard, vegetables—potatoes, onions, &c. You will need calico dresses, and a few white ones. Oh, we will be so, *so* happy.

Custer to Elizabeth, May 5, 1867, from Fort Hays, Kansas:
Please read enclosed letter, then deliver it to Tom. This is a matter I will not trifle with. Tom's conduct grieves me.

. . . . I wish you knew how very kind Genl. Smith has been, and how freely he has offered everything to facilitate your coming. When Depmt Headquarters broke up here, the finest sibley tent with circular floor used by Genl. Hancock was given to him. He now insists that you shall have it. I declined, while thanking him, but he insisted: "I don't care about you, but Mrs Custer must have this tent." He also said that if a hospital tent could be had at Hays, Harker, or Riley, you should have it, adding, "Oh, I am going to do it up brown." He promised that, if he got to Riley, you should have all the packing boxes you need. (I would not ask him for transportation of the clothes-press, in your place. Bring what you need, but nothing else, on account of the scarcity of wagons.)

Custer to Elizabeth, May 6, 1867, from Fort Hays, Kansas:

Only think, your letter came in less than thirty-six hours. You re-member how eager I was to have you for my little wife? I was not as impatient then as now. I almost feel tempted to desert and fly to you. I would come if the cars were running, this far. We will probably go on another scout shortly, and I do not want to lose a day with you.

Bring a set of field-croquet, and one of parlor-croquet.

Our camp is not only beautiful, but so clean. This evening we had our first dress parade, all the eight companies. They looked well and made a long line. We are all anxious for the Band to join us.

Yesterday I put White in the guard house or tent, for not getting up at reveille. This evening I saw a sergeant leading him to the guard tent by the ear. W. had given an impudent reply to an order. Stark was tied up the other day with his hands behind him, for washing my table-cloth in the Creek (this being against orders). Hale was officer of the day. It was all right, but in half an hour I released him.

Genl. Hancock took dinner with me the last day of his stay. After-wards we went up the hill to witness the foot-race between eight men, picked, one from each company. They wore only shirt, drawers and stockings. It was quite exciting. An "A" Co. man was winner. An "E" Co. man was in advance, but tripped and fell just before reaching the goal.

Then came a quarter-of-a-mile horse-race, between an "H" Co. horse of the Cavalry and an Infantry horse from the Post. The Infantry were very sanguine, their horse never having been beaten, but luck favored the Cavalry handsomely. I have made arrangements to acquire the In-fantry horse; I believe him to be the better, only requiring care and management.

If you come here under Genl. Smith's escort you had better invite him to mess with you en route.

Custer to Elizabeth, May 7, 1867, from Fort Hays, Kansas:

Will Her be content with a very brief letter, from her boy? Cause Why? He went buffalo-hunting. Seven officers in our party; the other goes to-morrow.

Major Pope was sent back to camp, drunk, so beastly drunk he could scarcely sit on his horse. His friends desired him to be placed in one of the ambulances taken along to carry the meat. But I told them this wd. not be permitted, that if he chose to act in that disgraceful manner and could not ride his horse he must be left behind. His friends then placed him in charge of a Cavalry private and sent him back to camp. Had I been on duty I should have placed him under arrest, but it was a social occasion. He became drunk before we were three miles from camp, to the surprise of the other officers, none of whom had been drinking.

Our party killed twelve buffalo. I was riding a strange horse, one loaned me by Capt. Hamilton. He could not run as fast as the buffalo, and after about five miles developed blind staggers, and was about to fall with me when I dismounted. In doing so my pistol accidentally discharged into his free shoulder, entirely disabling him. Soon Sergeant King who always accompanies me came, looking for me. Together we took off my saddle and fastened it atop his, and so footed our way toward the column. On our way we came upon a small herd. The Sergeant then carried my saddle while I rode his mount, bringing down a fine one. My horse—or rather, his—was too fatigued for a second run.

The tongues were to be exhibited as evidence. When we arrived in camp Mr Hale immediately asked how many we had. But we kept it a secret. Asking an orderly he was told "Four." He smiled his peculiar smile and said he expected his party to bring in six, on the morrow, adding "Won't you all feel badly if we should bring in ten!" Well, we had twelve to our credit.

I wish you would bring your boy a broad brim hat, very broad, the broadest you can find—felt, soft, not stiff, black. Your money has held out remarkably. I wish someone were going to Riley that I might send you another $100. in addition to the $150. I sent by Genl. Davidson.

Custer to Elizabeth, May 10, 1867, from Fort Riley, Kansas:

> By all kind words and gestures that I might,
>   I call her my dear heart, my sole beloved
> My joyful comfort and my sweet delight,
>   My mistress, goddess, and such names
>   As loving knights apply to lovely dames.
>
> Whate'er is pretty, pleasant, facile, well,
>   Whate'er Pandora had she doth excel.
> Thou art my Vesta, thou my goddess art,
>   Thy hallowed temple only is my heart.

These lines, so truly expressing my sentiments, are from a most interesting volume I am reading . . . a work of nearly 700 pages, written about 1620—Burton's "Anatomy of Melancholy." Written at so early a date there is less restraint than now obtains. It goes beyond "Don Juan" in rich and racy terms, yet without a single immoral sentiment.

I am sending this letter by Col. Bannard who asks me to send him in an ambulance to Harker on his way to Riley.

Keep me informed. . . . Have writing materials that you may send me reports by every passing stage. You will probably stay one night at Harker. If so ask Col. Hart to send it through that night to me by one of my couriers.

Elizabeth, her friend Anna, and the cook Eliza joined Custer at Fort Hays, where he installed them before starting on his "scout." This real business of Indian scouting began for Custer on General Hancock's departure from Fort Hays. On June 1, with a column of 350 men of the 7th Cavalry and 20 wagons, he set out for Fort McPherson on the Platte, 250 miles away. His orders were to scout the country between the two posts, move southward to the headwaters of the Republican, touch the Platte again at Fort Sedgwick, where supplies would be replenished, move southward to Fort Wallace on the Smoky Hill River, and return to his starting point, Fort Hays. He kept pencil notes in a daybook along the march.

Custer's notes, June 6, 1867:
Reached this point 6 P.M. having halted and grazed our animals two hours at White Horse Creek. Struck an Indian trail at Horse-Stealing Crk. Party abt. 30 strong, going east, probably a war-party. Grazing better than on Salmon. Wood abundant, water good. Wind blowing straight from South all afternoon.

Custer's notes, June 8, 1867, at Medicine Lake Creek, thirty miles from the Platte River, Kansas:
The officers of the 7th—the entire camp, is wrapped in deep gloom by the suicide of Col. Cooper while in a fit of delirium tremens. We reached present camp after a march of 17 miles over a broken country. I had just risen from dinner-table where I had been discussing with Tom Col. Cooper's actions, when Col. Myers came rushing in. . . . Calling Dr. Coates we hastened to Col. Cooper's tent, and found him ly-

ing on knees and face, right hand grasping revolver, ground near him covered with blood . . . body still warm, pulse beating, the act having been committed but 3 or 4 minutes before. Placing him on his back we saw how well the shot had been aimed. Only the eyes wore the ghastly look of death. Conversation with other officers showed he had contemplated the act under the influence of rum. One by one all came to gaze on one who but a few minutes before had been companion of our march.

Actuated by what I deemed my duty to the living I warned the officers of the reg't of the fate of him who lay there dead. All felt deeply, particularly his intimates who shared his habits. May the example be not lost on them.

Another of rum's victims. But for intemperance Col. Cooper would have been a useful and accomplished officer, a brilliant and most companionable gentleman. He leaves a young wife, shortly to become a mother.

I thank God my darling wife will never know anxiety through intemperance on my part. Would I could fly to her now . . . but a wise Providence decrees all.

Custer's notes, June 8, 1867, twenty miles from Fort McPherson:
Marched 25 miles to-day, reaching present camp abt. 5 P.M. Passed through beautiful, broken country. Grazing good, along the line of march. Horses and mules marched better than in past days.

Col. Cooper's body brought in ambulance for burial at Ft. McPherson.

Arrested all but two herd teamsters, replacing them with enlisted men. Anticipate no further trouble. [This brief note, Custer amplified later in the following account:]

In the vicinity of the Platte River 35 of my men deserted in 24 hours. I was accordingly apprehensive for the whole command as I had before me a long march through a hostile country. When breaking camp, about 5 P.M. on the 7th, I caused Boots and Saddles to be sounded, when 13 of my men deliberately shouldered their arms and started off for the Platte, in the presence of the entire command, in open day. As I intended camping but about 10 miles from the place, and not knowing but that the remainder of the command, or a considerable portion of it, might leave during the night, I felt that severe and summary measures must be taken. The horses of only a few of the officers were saddled in addition to those of guard & picket. I directed Major Elliott and Lts.

Custer, Cook & Jackson, with a few of the guard, to pursue the deserters who were still visible, tho more than a mile distant, and to bring
the dead bodies of as many as could be taken back to camp.

Seven of the deserters, being mounted on our best horses, and having
two miles' start, made their escape. One, a dangerous character, presented his carbine at Major Elliott, but, before he could fire, was
brought down by another of the pursuing party. Two others were
brought down by pistol shots. The remaining three, by throwing themselves on the ground and feigning death, escaped being shot. Six were
brought back to camp. From there to Wallace wounds were treated,
but did not prove serious.

The effect was all that could be desired. There was not another de-
sertion as long as I remained with the command.

Custer's notes, June 10, 1867, at Fort McPherson:
Reached Ft. McPherson at 2 P.M. Encamped abt. half a mile below
the Post on the Platte. Invited to dine with Col. Carrington. Declined
on account of duties in camp. Col. Carrington desired me to report to
him with my command, which I peremptorily refused to do, it not being in my instructions.

Made arrangements for burial of Col. Cooper at 10 A.M. to-morrow.
Funeral as quiet as possible, suicide not being entitled to military
honors.

Learned that Genl. Sherman is at Ft. Sedgwick. Telegraph wires
down at this point. No opportunities to send despatches east or west.

Wrote letter to my little girl to be sent by courier to-morrow.

Where telegraph wires were down, or the line incomplete, couriers carried dispatches and mail to their destination. The skill of
these fleet-footed messengers in evading capture by concealed enemies along the trails was extraordinary.

Custer's notes, June 11, 1867, at Fort McPherson:
Breakfast with Col. & Mrs Ransom. Spent delightful morning at the
Post inspecting stables and storehouses.

Dined at 5 P.M. with Col. & Mrs Merrill, afterwards enjoyed hearing
Mrs Merrill perform on the piano and sing.

At 6.30 the officers of the Post came down to our camp, Col. Carrington very kindly having sent his Band to serenade the 7th. A very pleasant feeling subsists between the officers of the Post and those of the 7th.

Called at the Post in evening to thank Col. Carrington.

Rec'd telegram from Genl. Sherman in regard to Indians and a movement against them. The command is to move at 6 A.M. to-morrow.

From Riverside Telegraph Station Custer wired Fort Sedgwick to enquire if further instructions from General Sherman were awaiting him there. To his surprise he learned that Lieutenant Kidder of the 2nd Cavalry Regiment, with ten troopers and a friendly Sioux guide, Red Bead, had been sent out to him with dispatches and should already have caught up with him. These dispatches, he was further informed, directed him to strike across country to Fort Wallace.

Supplies, which he had been expecting to supplement at Sedgwick, were running dangerously low. He had eighty miles of savage-infested country to traverse before reaching Fort Wallace. And what had become of the brave but inexperienced young lieutenant Kidder and his detail, sent to intercept him? Custer consulted with his Indian scouts and the white guide Comstock. All agreed that traces of the Kidder party would most likely be found along their own route, the trail to Fort Wallace.

They set out. Indian pony tracks were discovered, then the stripped carcases of mounts marked with the United States brand. Finally they beheld a scene of indescribable horror, the mangled victims, and about them evidences of torture by fire, of obscene mutilation. There was nothing to do but bury the poor remains.

Custer's notes, June, 1867:

The march to Wallace from the Platte was a forced one, for altho my train contained supplies for my command up to the 20th, yet, when the stores came to be issued, they were found to be in such a damaged condition that it would be difficult to make them last until reaching Wallace. And I take this opportunity to express a belief, supported by facts, as well as by the opinion of officers under me, that the gross neglect and mismanagement of the Commissary Depmt. throughout the District has subjected both officers and men to needless privations, never intended by the Government.

When my command left Fort Hays for the Platte the officers were only able to obtain hard biscuit and bacon, coffee and sugar, for their private messes, tho it had been known for weeks, months, indeed, that a large command must be provisioned for an expedition to the Platte.

On the return march to Wallace all hard bread not damaged was required to subsist the enlisted men, while the officers were actually compelled to pick up what they could from the condemned and abandoned bread for their own maintenance.

That this bread was damaged will not appear remarkable when it is known that many of the boxes were marked "1860."

That desertions will occur under the most stringent and prohibitory laws I have no doubt, and I am equally certain that many that have taken place can be attributed to the mismanagement of the Commissary Department.

They arrived at Fort Wallace, and it was a sorry state of affairs they found there. Themselves weary, sun scorched, famished, they had looked forward to some creature comfort, to a satisfying meal. But they found the garrison in a virtual state of siege, cut off from relief. The country had been ravaged by Indians. Stage stations were closed, dugouts abandoned. Mails had ceased. Supplies were almost exhausted. Sickness was rife, and there were no medicines. There was no certainty that help would ever come, or that it would not come until too late—when the pestilence breaking out had seen the last of them alive.

Instructions? Orders? The latest that had been issued to Custer had been in the care of the Kidder party, now massacred. General Sherman was not there, nor was General Hancock, organizer of the Indian scouting expedition. Custer did the only thing possible. He arranged to go forth and obtain food, fodder, medicines, surgical appliances. Picking a hundred of his least exhausted men and mounts and leaving the others to recuperate, he organized an expedition to the nearest supply depot, Fort Harker. Fort Hays would be a halting place on the way. Custer placed Captain Hamilton in command. He accompanied the party himself in his capacity of pathfinder and for the purpose also of reporting to his superiors, Sherman and Hancock.

It was 150 miles, more or less, through ravaged country to Fort Hays and 60 miles beyond that to Fort Harker.

Custer's notes, June, 1867:

My march from Ft. Wallace to Ft. Harker was without incident, except the killing of two men about 5 miles beyond Downer's Station. A sergeant and two men had been sent to bring up a party who had halted at the last rancho, and then returning, had been attacked by between forty to fifty Indians, and two of whom were killed. Had they offered any defence this would not have occurred. Instead, they put spurs to their horses and attempted to escape by flight.

When Fort Hays was reached, Captain Hamilton and the main body of his command halted there for a brief rest. The tireless Custer, with his two indefatigable aides, Colonel Cook and Tom Custer, and two troopers, pressed on to Fort Harker.

At that depot Custer requisitioned wagons and supplies—all that was needed at Fort Wallace. He reported by wire to General Sherman, whose instructions from Fort Sedgwick had been lost with the Kidder party, and to General Hancock. This general had been expected to be present at Fort Wallace when Custer first arrived there, but he was absent and had sent no instructions for Custer.

Custer reported also to the district commander, General Smith, who was replacing Sheridan, away on sick leave.

The loaded wagons would be ready by the time Captain Hamilton, refreshed, should arrive from Fort Hays to escort them to Fort Wallace. Custer, with a little time on his hands and wishing to attend to his personal concerns, set out for his "family" at Fort Riley.

He had, he thought, installed them in comfort and security at Fort Hays before he set out on his scouting trip. But not long after his departure, the creek rose suddenly and inundated the surrounding country. Men were swept away to death on the raging waters. Elizabeth and Eliza rescued more than one with a clothesline and with their ministrations saved those half drowned. Then they and Anna, with Mrs. Gibbs and her two children, were dispatched in ambulances to Fort Harker, only to find there was no room for them there. They spent a night in the ambulances, which, being badly tethered, rolled down a sharp incline. Their screams brought help and the wagons were pushed uphill and safely moored.

But cholera was raging at the Fort. Sisters of Mercy were arriving to nurse the sick. The two ambulances were sent under escort to Fort Riley. On the way, some members of the escort bought the poisonously adulterated liquor of the plains, became hopelessly drunk, and were ignominiously lifted from the mounts they could not ride and dumped into the wagons.

A soldier's family had no official standing, but at every post there were quarters suitable for married officers. A limited number of enlisted men had wives, generally with children, who lived in "Laundresses' Row." During the Civil War Custer had called his wife a "little Army Crow," following him from place to place, and Sheridan had been willing she should be with her husband, since she "gave no trouble." But at Fort Riley, since that was not Custer's post in June, 1867, she was somewhat on sufferance through the courtesy of the post commander. There were vacant quarters he was able to put at her disposal until Custer should make other provision for her. She was awaiting word from him when suddenly Custer himself appeared before her.

While at Fort Hays, Custer had heard of the flood. At Fort Harker he learned of the cholera outbreak and of the banishment of his family to Fort Riley. On his arrival he placed everything in order. It was something of a shock, therefore, suddenly to find himself placed under arrest by order of General Hancock and faced with court-martial. Every instruction concerning his scouting expedition had been punctiliously fulfilled, and Custer had taken no independent action until instructions ceased. The specifications of the charges against him were "leaving Fort Wallace without permission, marching his men excessively, allowing two of them to be killed; and losing several U.S. horses—all on a journey on private business; excessive cruelty and illegal conduct in putting down mutiny in the 7th Cavalry by shooting deserters."

Elizabeth Custer's letters at this time contrast sharply in mood with the seriousness of her husband's situation.

Elizabeth to Rebecca Richmond, September, 1867, from Fort Riley, Kansas:

This Post is almost perfect as a garrison. No place could be cooler or more agreeable as a summer residence. But I am hoping we will be stationed at Leavenworth this winter. It is considered the third best post in the U.S., and Genl. Sheridan and his staff will be there.

Elizabeth to Rebecca Richmond, September, 1867, from Fort Leaven-worth, Kansas:

I can hardly wait for your arrival, it is so lovely here in the fall. This wonderful Western country will surprise you. Needless to tell you of our care-free life. Had I ever had any housekeeping desires they would long have been quenched, so frequently do we move. What things we retain from our many movings are put down in quarters never in re-markable repair. But you are so adaptable you will not mind, while giving us great pleasure.

We are longing for Genl. Sheridan's arrival. He will not come until after Genl. Forsyth's marriage.

The garrison, composed mostly of officers permanently stationed here, with their families, is just now blessed with several young officers summoned as witnesses. You would soon find how little the trial troubles us. We never were treated with more attention.

It is progressing finely for Aut. He has for counsel Col. Parsons, an old West Point classmate, a fine military lawyer, and a Christian gentle-man. And a Churchman, Rebecca. Most West Point graduates are Epis-copalians, and so are most Chaplains in the service. Only two are Pres-byterians.

Custer to Mr. Walker, September, 1867, from Fort Leavenworth, Kansas:

My dear friend—During a recess of the Court I drop you a line. Slow progress is being made. The Prosecution have examined about half their witnesses, including the most important. I would not hesitate to go to Court on the evidence adduced thus far.

I have obtained evidence that, last spring, when desertions were so numerous, General Hancock telegraphed General Sheridan to shoot deserters down. Genl. Sheridan has been summoned to testify that he ordered me to shoot without trial for the same offence. He himself called my attention to this, and urged me to introduce it in evidence.

He assured me that in any and all circumstances I could count him as my friend, and that, further, the authorities in Washington regard my trial as an attempt by Hancock to cover up the failure of the Indian expedition.

West is drinking himself to death, has delirium tremens, to such an extent the Prosecution will not put him on the witness stand. Parsons is conducting my defence most admirably.

We return to Mrs. Custer's correspondence with her cousin, which points to a weak point in the defense.

Elizabeth to Rebecca Richmond, September, 1867, from Fort Leaven-worth, Kansas:
Autie made the trip from Fort Wallace on horseback. . . . He took a leave himself, knowing none would be granted him, and Genl. Hancock ordered his arrest. It sounds quite solemn to unaccustomed ears, but officers look on it as an ordinary occurrence, especially when one has done so little worthy of punishment as Aut has. When he ran the risk of a court-martial in leaving Wallace he did it expecting the consequences . . . and we are quite determined not to live apart again, even if he leaves the army otherwise so delightful to us.

This sounds as if the young wife were carrying off a poor situation jauntily. Custer had written repeatedly he was "tempted to desert" and fly to her, that he would resign sooner than consent to lengthy separation from her. But these sound like love's exaggerations that never would be translated into action. As to his leaving Fort Wallace without permission, he had to leave Fort Wallace and get to Fort Harker in order to obtain permission to leave it.

Deposition for the defense:
Major Elliott, of Custer's detail . . . testified: Upon reaching Fort Wallace, Kansas, and not finding Maj. Genl. Hancock there, the accused (Custer) stated to the witness (Elliott) that he, Custer, was ordered to report to Hancock, and was disappointed at not finding him here.
And that, owing to the closing of the mail route, he, the accused (Custer) felt it his duty in the absence of further instructions to follow Genl. Hancock to Harker, or the nearest telegraph station, and report to him, and ascertain what orders were awaiting him. After two days' rest the accused so set out.
Further . . . that at the time the accused (Custer) left Wallace, it was the opinion of the deponent (Elliott) and, so far as he can testify, of all the officers of the command, that the command would not be

engaged, or in condition to be actively engaged, for three or four weeks after its arrival at Wallace, and that the energies of the deponent (El-liott) were fully employed in recuperating the command and preparing it for the field, for nearly a month.

And, further, that when reaching Wallace, the horses of the command were nearly all barefoot and requiring shoeing, and that the first horse-shoes in sufficient quantities for issuing to the command reached the Post about the 4th or 5th of August, by a train escorted by Capt. Hamilton, 7th Cavalry.

That freedom of action was accorded Custer when precise orders were lacking was shown by an order offered by the defense in evidence, dated Fort Harker, July 16, 1867, and signed by Acting Assistant Adjutant General F. B. Weir:

The Brevet Major-General Commanding directs me to forward to you the accompanying communication from Depmt. Headquarters for your information and guidance, and to say that he expects you to keep your command as actively employed as the condition of the animals will permit. You will see by the communication referred to you are not restricted in your movements in the vicinity of Fort Wallace, but are to operate wherever the presence or movements of Indians may lead you.

The results of the court-martial are of official record, but for the Custer story, told in letters, we turn again to Mrs. Custer's letters.

Elizabeth to Rebecca Richmond, October 13, 1867, from Fort Leavenworth, Kansas:
Dear Rebecca—We were greatly pleased to see your father, but long for you. Can't you muster up courage to travel alone? It is such lovely weather for riding and driving. Autie has a new buggy, and promises himself the pleasure of taking you driving.

We have a guest, an illustrator, an insufferable bore. His conceit overwhelms me. But we have a delightful time. The Court called so many of our friends as witnesses.

The Court closed yesterday. The final decision may not be heard for some time, from Washington, but Autie will hear by telegram from friends. The trial has developed into nothing but a plan of persecution for Autie.

I can't write much. In two days this week I copied about fifty pages of foolscap for the defence—a labor of love, of course.

Elizabeth to Rebecca Richmond, November 20, 1867, from Fort Leavenworth, Kansas:

Armstrong has received official notice—He had already heard by telegram—the sentence is unjust as possible. Autie merits acquittal. Suspension from rank and command; forfeiture of pay proper for a year. It does not disturb us, for now we can be together for a year and a half, for the next Indian campaign (which he will not participate in) will be over in the summer, it is believed, and by the expiration of his sentence all will be in winter quarters.

Pay proper is $95. a month, but a soldier's emoluments amount to more than his pay, so that we have enough to live on. We have bought a new carpet for the front room, and put the old one in your bedroom. We anxiously await a telegram announcing your arrival.

Autie and I are the wonder of the garrison, we are in such spirits.

Custer to Mr. Walker, November, 1867, from Fort Leavenworth, Kansas:

My dear friend—You have doubtless learned from the press the results of my trial. . . . All with whom I have conversed deem the verdict not sustained by the evidence, as I have been adjudged guilty on some specification on which the Judge-Advocate declined to take testimony. I will go into particulars when we meet.

I must apologize for retaining the books you so kindly lent me. I thought some revising or reconvening of the Court might make it necessary to consult them. I shall never forget your kindness since my arrest, and trust I may have an opportunity to requite it.

I have written Genl. Sheridan to make no effort to obtain a remission of any portion of my sentence. I would not accept it.

All charges and specifications were dismissed for lack of evidence, except his journey to Fort Riley to fetch his family. It was argued he lacked the authority.

For a time it seemed a second trial impended when a private letter of Custer's was published. Written in answer to a friend asking for details of his arrest, it denounced certain officers as "pickpockets." But the "pickpockets" preferred letting the matter drop to having the matter aired in court. Custer expressed his readiness to face them there.

Custer to Mr. Walker, 1867:

I am like Macawber, waiting for something to "turn up," meanwhile I am preparing to execute a long-projected plan—to write a memoir of my experience from West Point to Appomattox. Arrangements for this are concluded with Messrs Harper & Brothers. I have fifty pages of the script completed.

14: Reinstatement

SHORTLY AFTER the sentence the Custers went home to Monroe, where Custer gave his time almost entirely to writing. In September, 1868, with two months of his rustication still to run, he received a communication that was a salve to wounded pride. It was a telegram from Sheridan, who was again in command of the Department of the Missouri.

Sheridan to Custer, September 24, 1868, from Fort Hays, Kansas:
Generals Sherman, Sully and myself, and nearly all the officers of your regiment have asked for you, and I hope the application will be successful. Can you come at once?

He could and did come at once. Red tape was cut, for the need was urgent. Sully's meridian was past, and Sheridan knew what he could get from Custer.

Sheridan's instructions to Custer:
Eleven companies of your regiment will move about Oct. 1st against the hostile Indians, from Medicine Lodge Creek toward the Wichita Mountains.

Medicine Lodge was in the lowest third of the Kansas oblong, south, on an eastward slant from Fort Hays, the Wichita Mountains somewhat north and east. In 1876 Congress had created a peace commission to treat with Sheridan's problem tribes—Cheyennes, Arapahoes, Kiowas, Comanches. But serious outbreaks were occurring, instigated by the young men of these nations. Trouble was fomented when an Indian agent attempted reprisals for a minor offense by withholding from the Indians the arms and ammunition that accompanied annuities; when the Indians feigned penitence, he gave the weapons over to them.

Parties of Sioux were joining the malcontents. Savageries passing description were frequent. The United States Military, instead of merely policing peace conferences, were going into aggressive action. Custer's experience and qualities of leadership were made to order for the situation.

Custer to Elizabeth, October 4, 1868, from Fort Hays, Kansas:
I breakfasted with Genl. Sheridan and staff. He said, "Custer, I rely on you in everything, and shall send you on this expedition without orders, leaving you to act entirely on your own judgment."

Two weeks later Custer was at Fort Dodge, three easy marches, or about a hundred miles, from Fort Hays.

Custer to Elizabeth, October 18, 1868, from Fort Dodge, Kansas:
We have been on the war-path but one week . . . within two hours the Indians attacked our camp.

When Custer had organized the 7th Cavalry Regiment in July, 1866, he had spared no pains to unify it and train it as a powerful instrument of war. Now he found it demoralized and depleted by desertions. Vacancies had been filled by raw recruits. He thereupon started a course of intensive training to bring it once more into fighting condition.

Custer to Elizabeth, November, 1868, from Fort Dodge, Kansas:
Some of the officers think this may be a campaign on paper—but I know Genl. Sheridan better. We are going to the heart of the Indian country where white troops have never been before.

Sheridan had confined his summer activities to protecting the settlements on overland routes. With the approach of winter he was preparing for relentless warfare on the enemy. That it would be no campaign on paper, Custer rightly surmised.

Custer to Elizabeth, November, 1868, from Fort Dodge, Kansas:
Yesterday my twelve Osage guides joined me, a splendid set of warriors, headed by a Chief, Little Beaver. They are painted and dressed for the war-path, and well-armed with Springfield breech-loading guns. All are superb horsemen. [Indian guides and white scouts in govern-

ment employ received $75 a month and rations, with a bonus of $100 for anyone leading the regiment to an Indian village.]

A white woman has come into our camp, four days without food. I suppose her to have been captured by Indians, and rendered insane by their barbarous treatment. I sent her to-night, by the mail-party, to Fort Dodge.

Custer to Elizabeth, November, 1868, from Fort Dodge, Kansas:
I suppose you have seen considerable excitement over the Presidential campaign. Out of the hundreds of men here I doubt if a dozen remembered that this is Election Day, so little is the Army interested in the event.

Custer's own interest in the event would have been quickened could he have foreseen what Grant's election to the presidency would cost him—possibly his life.

Now the Indian campaign was on. Custer's instructions were "to seek the winter hide-out of the hostiles, and administer such punishment for past depredations as his force was able to."

Custer to Elizabeth, November 21, 1868, from Beaver Creek, Indian Territory, one hundred miles from Fort Dodge, Kansas:
The day we reached here we crossed the trail of a large war-party; the guides report that they have evidently come from the village which must be 50 miles from us in a southerly direction.

Custer to Elizabeth, November 22, 1868, from Beaver Creek, Indian Territory:
To-day Genl. Sheridan and staff with two Companies of Kansas Volunteers arrived. I move to-morrow morning with my eleven companies, taking thirty days' rations. I am to go south to the Canadian River, then down the river to Fort Cobb, thence south-east toward the Washita Mountains, then north-west back to this point, my whole march not exceeding 250 miles. The snow is five or six inches deep, and falling rapidly.

It snowed all night, and when reveille wakened us at four we found the ground covered to the depth of one foot, and the storm still raging. Little grooming did the shivering horses get from the equally uncomfortable troopers. While they were saddling I galloped across the narrow plain to the tents of Genl. Sheridan who was awake and had been listening attentively to our preparations. His first greeting was to enquire what I thought about the storm. All the better for our purpose, I told him, for we could move in it while the Indians could not.

"To horse" was sounded. Then "Prepare to mount." "Mount." With guides and scouts in the lead, the Band at the head of the column, "Advance" set the column in motion to the strains of "The Girl I Left Behind Me."

Nature's signs, on which the guides depended, were effaced by the snow, but with pocket compass Custer found the trail. By evening they had covered fifteen miles, and they made camp according to schedule. Fresh buffalo meat, easily obtainable there, compensated for many discomforts.

The next day there was the Canadian River to be forded. Its icy waters, treacherous currents, and quicksands were bad enough for men and horses but to heavy wagons were a serious obstacle. Major Elliott was sent on a down-river scout to hunt for Indian traces.

Custer to Elizabeth, November, 1868, from Indian Territory:
The last wagon had crossed the ford, was safely parked on the plain to the south, when a courier from Major Elliott came dashing in to report the fresh trail of a war-party, 150 strong, leading nearly due south, evidently the last of the season, disgusted with the cold weather going home.

They were in the heart of the Indian country now and were so far undetected. Accounts of the historic battle of the Washita that followed were pieced together by Mrs. Custer from her husband's fragmentary letters, supplemented by notes made by Sheridan.

They had twenty minutes to prepare. Leaving eighty men with the poorest horses to guard the wagons, Custer moved southeast with the rest. At sunset he cut into Elliott's march on the Indian trail. They took time out to feed themselves and their mounts, then continued on into the valley of the Washita. This river, whose name is also spelled "Ouachita," flows through Arkansas and Louisiana and into the Red River.

Ten o'clock found them still in their saddles, four abreast. At the head were two guides, gliding pantherlike over the snow, three or four hundred yards in advance. Then, single file, came the other Osages and the white scouts, among them the noted California Joe.

Custer to Elizabeth, November, 1868, from the Washita valley, Indian Territory:

With these I rode, so as to be as near as possible in the advance. The Cavalry followed, from a quarter to a half mile distant, lest warning should be given by crunching of the crusted snow.

Orders prohibited a word above a whisper, a match struck, pipe lighted, great deprivation to a soldier. Thus, silently, mile after mile, until it was discovered that the guides had halted, were awaiting my arrival. Word was passed back to halt, pending enquiries.

"Me smell fire," one of the Osages informed us.

Not so keen is the white man's sense of smell, but soon it was ascertained that the guide was not mistaken. On the edge of the timber were embers of a blaze, kindled, no doubt, by Indian lads set to guard the ponies. Scarcely a handful of glowing ashes, but sure sign of the nearness of our quarry.

Volunteers were called for, to investigate. These, led by Little Beaver and Hard Rope, stole toward the timber.

Moments seemed hours as we sat on our horses in the open moonlight, within easy reach of a hidden enemy.

Soon the guides reported that we were, in all probability, within two or three miles of the Indian village.

The command resumed the march, myself mounted, now with the guides who were afoot, in the lead.

At the crest of a hill the Osage who had scented the fire crept forward, and, shielding eyes with hand, peered into the valley below.

"Heaps Injuns down there."

Dismounting and crouching, Custer likewise peered. Those dark forms—might it not be a herd of buffalo? To his whispered enquiry the Osage shook his head. "Me heard dog bark." That meant Indians, but not on the warpath. When out for a fight they would leave their dogs at home. Custer also heard the familiar sound and, still more significant, an infant's cry.

Stealing back to the advance, he halted the column and ordered all officers to report to him immediately. It was after midnight. Complete silence was to be observed. Custer requested his officers to remove their sabers, that the clank of metal might not be heard. He outlined his plan. He was going to divide the command into four detachments of equal strength. One was to move to the woods below the village, another downriver to the timber above it, a third to occupy the crest north of the village, and the fourth, his own, to remain at the point of discovery. The attacks would be simultaneous, and the enemy, being surrounded, would have small chance to escape. Everything depended on accurate timing and the element of surprise.

Custer's detachment would have four hours to wait while the others found their positions. The troopers were permitted to dismount, but the suffering was intense—even foot stamping and pacing back and forth to maintain circulation would have been fatal to the plan. The troopers stood about or lay on the frozen ground, each holding his horse's rein.

The Osages had scant faith in the white man's loyalty and expected to be used as hostages in the event a pact was made. But California Joe was optimistic: "As the deal now stands we hold the keerds."

It was two hours before dawn. The moon had gone down and the night was perfectly black. A brilliant light appeared. It was not a signal from the village. It was the morning star. According to the schedule, the other detachments must by now have reached their stations. This was the moment to advance. Half frozen as they were, the troopers had to discard overcoats and haversacks and anything else that might impede action.

They reached the level of the valley. Immediately behind Custer was the band, each player with instrument in readiness to sound out the moment the leader—the cornet player—should give the sign. A rifle shot cracked from the far side of the village—the farthest detachment was in place. Custer gave the word. The band broke into "Garryowen," the regimental tune. Cheers resounded from the other detachments. The entire command rushed into action, four units as one. The battle of the Washita was on.

Custer's notes:

Accessions to our opponents kept arriving, mounted warriors in full war-panoply, with floating lance-pennants . . . Cheyennes, Arapahoes, Kiowas, Comanches, and some Apaches, hostile tribes from some twelve miles off. . . .

In our temporary hospital improvised in the village the wounded were being cared for. Hamilton fell. His last words to his squadron as he rode by my side to the attack were "Now, men, keep cool. Fire low, and not too rapidly." Colonel Barnitz was seriously wounded. Of Major Elliott nothing had been heard, nor did we at the time know his fate, nor that of the Sergeant-Major of the regiment. . . .

From being the surrounding party we now found ourselves surrounded, Indians on all sides closing in on us.

Help arrived, a fresh supply of ammunition with which the Quartermaster, Major Bell, by heroic efforts had contrived to reach us. Despite their vast numerical superiority the Indians fought with less confidence than their wont. . . . Vain their efforts to draw us from the village. We applied the torch to this with all the captured property.

I now determined to take the offensive. It was about three in the afternoon. . . . I knew that the officers in charge of the train and eighty men would be following us on the trail, and feared that the Indians, reconnoitring from hill-tops, might discover this helpless detachment, and annihilate them, at the same time leaving the command in mid-winter, in the heart of enemy country, destitute of provision for horse and man.

Eight hundred and seventy ponies, wild, unused to white man's control, were on our hands. Such wealth, from the Indian standpoint, would cause us to be waylaid, night and day. This, with sixty prisoners to convey, our own wounded to care for, the exhausted condition of our troops, might have resulted in the loss of all we had gained. Having caused the best ponies to be selected for our captives, I issued an order as painful to decide on as to carry out—that the unwanted ponies should be shot.

The sad side of the story is the killed and wounded. Captain Hamilton . . . Major Elliott who with 15 men charged after a small band of Indians and pursued them too far . . . nineteen enlisted men . . . three officers and eleven enlisted men wounded. . . .

Band playing, colors flying, Custer marched down river, intending by this bold move to intimidate Indians from other villages while diverting attention from his approaching wagon train. The ruse succeeded. At ten that night he retraced his steps. At two o'clock the command bivouacked in the conquered territory, the valley of the Washita. Here the men built bonfires to warm themselves in the absence of their overcoats, which with other impedimenta had been discarded and which escaping Indians made off with.

Next day they met the wagons and turned back to Camp Supply, where Sheridan would await their return.

The bodies of Major Elliott and his party were not discovered for some weeks. When first they were missed, it was supposed they had lost their way back to the command and would find the nearest route back to Camp Supply. When Custer was later criticized for not sending them relief, he replied with the obvious fact that in the wild turmoil of the battle it could not have been ascertained that any detachment had gone off in an independent pursuit into unknown regions.

Custer had sent a preliminary report of victory by California Joe and another scout to Sheridan at Camp Supply. By the same messengers the general sent a message to the returning column.

Sheridan's message:
The energy and rapidity shown during one of the heaviest snowstorms known to this section of the country, with the temperature below freezing, the gallantry and bravery displayed, resulting in such signal success, reflects highest credit on the 7th Cavalry . . . and the Major-General Commanding expresses his thanks to the officers and men engaged in the Battle of the Washita, and his special congratulations to their distinguished commander Brevet Major-General George A. Custer for the efficient and gallant service opening the campaign against the hostile Indians north of the Arkansas.

As the triumphant column appeared over the distant hills at evening, the scouts celebrated the victory by yelling, firing, throwing themselves on necks or sides of their horses to exhibit their marvelous skill, and chanting their war songs. Behind them came the troops in orderly platoons, the band playing. Each officer, as he rode by Sheridan, gave him the sword salute. The general spoke of it later as "one of the most beautiful and interesting scenes" he had ever witnessed. His joy was mingled with intense relief.

Sheridan's account:
. . . . Besides being greatly worried about the safety of the command in the extreme cold and deep snows I knew that the immediate effect of a victory would be to demoralize the rest of the hostiles, and to expedite our ultimate success.

For Sheridan, it had been a tremendous hazard. He had invested his future in Custer's leadership. Failure would have meant loss of prestige. Also it would have given mastery of the situation to the Indians. The battle of the Washita had demonstrated to them that their hideouts could be discovered, penetrated, occupied by the whites and that future savageries would meet with sharp reprisals.

Custer had been magnificently supported by his officers and men and had enjoyed the full confidence of his superior. He had justified his reinstatement. As to the accusers who had brought him to trial, against their names the records read "Arrest for intoxication while on duty."

Victory in the first action of Sheridan's aggressive campaign called for a speedy follow-up. On December 7, a few days after their return, the 7th Cavalry Regiment set out again for their recent battleground. Sheridan accompanied the regiment, attaching to it a special force of Kansas cavalry. This made a total force of fifteen hundred. They had provisioning for a month.

Custer to Elizabeth, December, 1868, from Fort Cobb, Indian Territory:
Here we are, after twelve days' marching, through snow and an almost impassable country where sometimes we made only eight miles a day, following an Indian trail. . . .

Custer to Elizabeth, January, 1869, from Fort Cobb, Indian Territory:
Yesterday a grand council was held near my tent. All the head chiefs of the Apaches, Kiowas, Arapahoes, Comanches, Cheyennes, were present. I was alone with them except for an officer who took stenographic notes.

Sheridan's plans were seriously hampered by commissariat mismanagement. Supplies he had ordered to be accessible in the autumn of 1868 were stalled some hundred miles away in January, 1869. Custer's supplies at Fort Cobb were running low.

Sheridan to Custer, January 24, 1869, from Medicine Bluff Creek, Indian Territory:

My dear Custer. . . . I have just received your note. Col. Cook will start at once with the rations. Nothing new. No mail. Keep close watch to prevent Cheyennes and Arapahoes from getting the advantage of you.

Sheridan to Custer, January 31, 1869, from Medicine Bluff Creek, Indian Territory:

In receipt of yours of the 26th. Have ordered the 10 days' rations and 3,000 lbs of grain. If the Cheyennes do not come in at once I will move out against them. I hope this will not be necessary, but if so let me know. If the Kiowas or others have any of your party I will make them feel lightning here.

Sheridan to Custer, February 3, 1869, from Medicine Bluff Creek, Indian Territory:

Rations are between here and Arbuckle. Will get here in two days.

Custer to Elizabeth, February, 1869, from camp thirty-five miles from Fort Cobb, Indian Territory:

. . . . to remain here till the Indians all come in. Cheyennes, Arapahoes, and remaining Kiowas due in four to five days. Chiefs come in almost daily reporting progress. I hold Satanta and Lone Wolf under strong guard. [Satanta and Lone Wolf were Kiowa chiefs taken prisoner as hostages, since their good faith was open to suspicion. Sheridan threatened them with hanging if their bands were not "brought in" to the reservation at the appointed time. This worked. Their bands were brought in at the appointed time.]

Sheridan thinks this is the last Indian war in this department. I sent to Camp Supply for ten wagons loaded with clothing and officers' stores. They should be here in 10 days. They will not bring in as much as we require, but, as Genl. Sheridan says, "Enough to last us home."

Custer to Elizabeth, February 9, 1869, from Indian Territory:

I have made a long march since writing you. . . . We have been to try to bring in Indian villages. But our provisions became exhausted; there was no game. . . .

Genl. Sheridan and staff just rode up to my tent. He got here a day before us. I selected my camp site about a mile from him, then what does he do this morning but pick up his tents and come over beside me. He has done this before.

To-day is our wedding anniversary. I am sorry we cannot spend it together, but I shall celebrate it in my heart.

Tell Eliza I have a robe for her, one of those presented to me, also one for Henry. For my birdling I will bring back her dear Bo.

My command has been living on quarter rations of bread for ten days. Genl. Sheridan has been worried almost to distraction. I wish some of those responsible for this state of affairs who themselves are living in comfort and luxury, could be made to share the discomforts and privations of troops moving in the field.

None of us feel that we could or ought to leave here until the Indian matter is settled.

Tom has just come in. He is cuter than ever, but he is becoming more profane, and a little vulgar. I have not spoken to him about it, but am leaving that pleasant duty for you.

In going "home" to Leavenworth we shall move due north, or nearly, to Fort Harker, and thence by rail. Col. McGonigle, Chief Quartermaster, recommends this as most economical for the Government, as the loss of horses by marching would exceed the cost by rail. Our horses have done nobly. You know how critical and severe Tony Forsyth is on duty. Well, he says no lot of horses ever received better care. But they have done all that horses can do, and are beginning to fail, so can do nothing till we get shelter and plenty of forage for them, not to be obtained out here.

We are now in the Wichita Mountains . . . a high level plateau, with streams of clear water, and surrounded by a distant belt of forest trees. Tom and I sat on our horses as the view spread before us, worthy the brush of a Church, a Bierstadt, the structure of the mountains reminding one of paintings of the Yosemite Valley, in the blending of colors—sombre purple, deep blue, to rich crimson tinged with gold . . . while the valley below showed a rich grass, a kind unknown to me, from six to twelve inches high, varying in color from that of ripe wheat to that of beet leaves and stem. . . .

Have I told you how shamefully the Commissary Depmt. has treated the command? Genl. Sheridan is terribly enraged at Genl. X and curses him not a little. Says that X had positive orders to send rations to Arbuckle last October . . . and they have not reached there yet.

We have considerable flour, but men marching cannot carry facilities for making bread. They are put to every strait, sitting up at night, baking unwholesome stuff upon shovels over a camp fire. We feel that troops undergoing the severities and unusual hardships of a winter campaign, such as ours, should receive every comfort the Government can give.

Neither are there officers' stores on hand. Officers are living on the same fare. If Genl. X could only hear the execrations heaped on his head. . . . Some of the officers say he has not an idea beyond running the Leavenworth bakery, and keeping his own Commissary bill down to the lowest figure. I do not believe he has the ability to run the Department for a large command.

Also Genl. Sheridan says "He is the d—dest old gossip. Can't keep anything to himself."

We are without candles.

Keep these personal comments to yourself.

While unstinting in praise of courage and efficiency, Custer never allowed the morale of his command to deteriorate during periods of inaction.

Custer to Elizabeth, February, 1869:

. . . . I have been very strict with the officers, have no favorites where duty is concerned. I have had Tom in arrest, also Y. The latter is "huffy" but I hope will soon get over it.

Several officers refer to the pleasant times they have had at our house, masquerades, euchre parties and the like.

That the Indian question was not settled and could not be settled by arms alone was Custer's firm opinion after his Washita victory and the ensuing conferences with tribal chiefs.

Custer to Sheridan, winter, 1869:

. . . . Without delicate handling by persons of experience in Indian affairs we are liable to lose all the benefits of the winter's campaign, and be plunged into another war with the Southern tribes. However I think this can be avoided.

Sheridan's work was grievously undermined by negligence and dishonesty in the controlling powers.

Sheridan to Custer, March 2, 1869, from Camp Supply, Indian Territory:

My Dear Custer—On my arrival I found a letter from Genl. Sherman, and a wire from Genl. Grant, requiring me to report at Washington without delay. I start to-morrow.

I send out F. to-morrow, to meet you at the crossing of the Washita, with 24,000 rations and 200,000 lbs. of forage.

I have thought best to let the 19th Kansas go back for muster-out. In the movement I spoke to you about, marching with this regiment would greatly embarrass me in rations. I think I will draw in the 7th, and terminate this campaign, unless the views of Genl. Sherman differ very much from my own.

I considered the campaign ended when Little Robe and the delegates from Arapahoes and Cheyennes hollered Enough! This was on the 1st of January. I think they had only been kept out by the influence of the Indian Ring and other authorities, a view in which I was confirmed by my interview with Little Raven.

Should you be able to strike the rascals on your way up, so much the better. But, should you not, it will only hasten their final surrender here or at Medicine Bluff. At all events I do not anticipate further trouble.

I will push your claims on the subject of promotion as soon as I get to Washington, and, if anything can be done, *you may rely on me* to look out for your interests.

I feel very anxious to hear from you.

Sheridan to Custer, April 7, 1869, from Chicago:

I am very much rejoiced at the success of your expedition, and feel very proud of our winter operations, and of the officers and men who bore privations so manfully.

I presume you will want a leave, and so spoke to Genl. Schofield [Secretary of War] and, if you desire such, you can have as long as you please.

15: New York and Kentucky

THE EXHAUSTED 7th Cavalry Regiment went home. "Home" was summer camp on Big Creek, between two and three miles below Fort Hays, Kansas. In her *Following the Guidon* Elizabeth Custer tells of domestic encounters with rattlesnakes, prairie dogs, and other denizens of the plains, but she dwells also on the compensating welcome and real kindness afforded by the post commander, General Nelson A. Miles. She bestows on him the highest encomium in her repertory: "Though an Infantry Commander he was at heart a true Cavalryman." During the Civil War he had, in fact, been a cavalry officer.

At Custer's behest she accompanied him on visits to the Indian prisoners being held as hostages in camp. His purpose was to accustom her to Indian ways, so far as possible, and to engender comity between the races.

November of 1869 found Custer in Chicago, staying with General Sheridan, who was convalescing from a protracted illness.

Custer to Elizabeth, December 2, 1869, from Chicago:
. . . . I never had so nice a time in all my life—except when I am with you. Everybody does so much for me, I can only accept a few of the invitations I receive.

Mike [Sheridan's younger brother Michael V.] has returned from a tour out West. The General is improving but requires "setters-up" with him at night.

Last night I saw Joseph Jefferson. . . . You know how I fairly squeal when laughter becomes impossible. I laughed till my sides ached. Oh, he was splendid.

Tony and the rest of the staff are enjoying what they think a good joke at my expence. We had seen a performance of Lydia Thompson's "Blondes" at the Opera House, and the "Times"—a bitter, copperhead sheet, informed the public that I was pursuing blondes instead of the dusky maidens of the Plains. Sandy says he will send the slip to you.

The paper never fails to pitch into the military. It criticized Genl. Sheridan for a speech he made at Louisville, saying he might "burn a haystack, but would never set the river on fire."

On his journey there had been a stop at Detroit.

Custer to Elizabeth, November, 1869, from Detroit:
Barker took charge of me till the train started. . . . While in the city I went to the Club and played a few games of euchre. The Detroiters had planned a grand dinner and reception for me at the Biddle House, which I declined. A Committee of five gentlemen was appointed to meet me at the depot, but this I avoided, having been told of it, by not arriving at the expected time. Barker told them it would not suit me, but they insisted on showing me some courtesy, so I compromised on a friendly evening at the Club at some future time. I have been treated with the most polite attention by all.

During the inaction of the cavalry following Sheridan's roundup of Indians, Custer was summoned to Washington in regard to upheavals and reorganizations in the army.

Custer to Elizabeth, December 18, 1870, from Washington:
An authority beyond question in the War Department told me that some officers are using the Board to gratify personal resentments . . . so that, after Jan. 1st., the Army will probably be kept on the Qui Vive by court-martials. My own suspicion is that the majority of the officers ordered before the Board deserve to be, and that the Service will benefit by their discharge. Nevertheless there are several instances of injustice having been done.

Washington is greatly improved. Pennsylvania Avenue has a new pavement.

In New York I went with Mrs Cram to see Jefferson in "Rip Van Winkle." The acting surpassed anything I have ever seen. I have read that to an actor's heart the most gratifying tribute is deathly silence. From opening to close of one Act there was not a sound to be heard. The house was packed, and this was the 136th consecutive performance. The acting compelled laughter one moment, the next drew tears. When the daughter, grown to a young lady, recognizes in the decrepit, tattered old man her lost father, there was not one person not affected by it. . . . I never saw the play before, nor, so deep an impression has it made on me, do I desire ever to see it again.

Custer visited Monroe to help clear up some matters regarding Daniel Bacon's estate. Through overinvestment, as well as incompetence and dishonesty on the part of subordinates, the estate was nearly insolvent.

Custer to Elizabeth, December 15, 1869, from Monroe, Michigan:
All ready money is needed to make up the $5,000. for Mrs. Bacon. John Rauch has put house and lot on the market for $5,000. or $5,500. Tax on house $87. Highest offer for lot $500.

Eventually Elizabeth derived some benefit from her inheritance, but considerably less than she expected.

Custer to Elizabeth, December, 1869:
The fifth of this month—December—added another year to my calendar. I hope I may profit by the experience it carries with it. I have employed the time since that day with reference to my future. I have formed a resolution. In this I have not been influenced in aught but my own judgment. I have acted on suggestion or advice of no one, only according to my conscience and idea of right.

From the 1st of January, and forever, I cease, so long as I am a married man, to play cards or any other game of chance for money or its equivalent.

This is a resolution, not the result of impulse, but taken after weeks of deliberation. And in considering, and finally adopting it, I experience a new-found joy. I breathe free'er, and I am not loath to say I respect my manhood more.

Custer's own prospects were not too satisfactory. An effort was being made to get the 7th Cavalry Regiment away from the Department of the Missouri, because a regiment on the Pacific Coast wanted to take its place. Nothing came of the proposal. Then Custer heard that the 7th Cavalry might be broken up. He made formal application to accompany its headquarters, in such an event, to whatever post it might be assigned. This request was warmly endorsed by General Sturgis, who had succeeded the retiring General A. J. Smith as colonel of the regiment. Nothing came of this, either. Custer accordingly took stock of his prospects.

As to continued service with the army, he would wait and see what the future might hold. With an extended leave in which to look about, Custer went into the New York financial district.

Custer to Elizabeth, 1871, from New York:
Dear Old Standby—I arrived at 7 last night. A good-looking young lady boarded the train at Syracuse, occupied seat next mine, said she had known you at school in Auburn, and spoke very kindly of you. Which did not please me. Oh, no.

This is a fine hotel; everything new, clean, of best quality, I have a bedroom and bathroom . . . Brussels carpet; walnut wardrobe with hooks enough for two.

Within an hour I had received more invitations than I can accept. One from the Northern Pacific to join an excursion of Eastern Press representatives—over the Erie Railroad to Buffalo, special steamer to Chicago, Duluth, special train to terminus of line, returning by way of St. Paul. About two weeks, without cost to myself. But business will prevent.

Mr O. and Mr George's wives are in Europe. The former had told me that if a certain woman, not his wife, should become troublesome and threatening, he would rid himself of her by taking his family abroad.

A friend has taken a box at the Academy of Music for ten nights, paying for it $120. He has invited me to occupy a seat in it whenever I choose. Miss Kellogg also expects me behind the scenes.

Is it not strange to think of me meeting to confer with such men as Belmont, Astor, Travers, Barker, Morton and Bliss?

Genl. Young would like to have us stationed at Atlanta. Is it not nice to have prominent Southern people desire to have us with them?

I have just heard from Bos [Boston, youngest of the Custer boys, employed in the forage department of the regiment, on the plains]. He has sent home $25. almost half his month's salary. I at once wrote him a letter of encouragement. I am proud of the way he is beginning life.

Tell Mother [Bacon] on no account to consent to sale or transfer of the house. I am suspicious of the party interested in it, where money is concerned.

I dined last night at one of the handsomest houses I ever saw. Not large, but filled with works of art. One that took my fancy was a music-box playing sixty tunes, chosen by the lady of the house.

The dinner was for me. The gentlemen, stockbrokers, represented millions. One, a Greek, the first I ever saw. The dinner was elegant,— new potatoes, strawberries, cucumbers among the dishes. We sat down at table at half past seven, and rose from it at half past one.

Everything was perfect, except that the lady of the house, with whom I am acquainted, was not present. The guests were told solemnly that she was indisposed. On my expressing sincere regret the host said in an undertone, "To tell the truth, General, there is nothing the matter with her, and she is disappointed, but I thought we would have a better time without her, so bade her remain upstairs. . . ." A lady who can command almost unbounded wealth, kept in her room, out of the way of company, like a child. . . . I thought of a little girl without money whose Bo would not want anyone at his table without his Bunkey. . . . Married life in New York does not seem married life to me.

We are the luckiest people in forming nice acquaintances and friends. A gentleman, living in the country, offered to send a pair of fine horses and light carriage into town for me, placing them at a livery stable without expence to me. Were you here I might have been tempted to accept, but I declined as I do not want to get into the habit of driving with any person in particular.

The "Herald" announces the death of Col. Myers. My sympathies are moved. No wife to cheer him . . . a true soldier and a gentleman.

Custer to Elizabeth, July, 1871, from New York:
Darling Standby . . . The old Irish servant who takes care of my room looks at me with suspicion when I return, sometimes not till morning, the bed not having been touched. I think she believes I do not pass my nights in the most reputable manner. In fact, circumstances, as she sees them, are against me.

Would Somebody appreciate my letters more if they were less frequent? Perhaps like immense riches they are less enjoyed because they leave nothing to be desired.

A married man here told me—in the presence of a young lady—that he loved no one, nor ever had, except his child. He described the relations between himself and wife as "No nonsense about it." Few wealthy people seem to enjoy their married life. Only think, little one, how much pleasure we have, planning to procure this or that article, make this or that journey. I have yet to find husband and wife here who enjoy life as we do.

Genl. Miles writes that he would like to buy the flanigan. It is yours. Sell it, and buy a basket-phaeton, if you like.

Oh, something astounding . . . a married gentleman took me to call on a married lady, her husband being away. Two young ladies, her intimates, were present. He told me her illness was the result of an abortion—a condition for which he was responsible. . . . Is it not terrible?

Do not leave my letters lying about.

Genl., Mrs and Miss Howard are here. Mrs H is most agreeable, having banished all coldness from her manner. The daughter is charming—pure, innocent. She will make a true wife for some man, a good woman, able to withstand temptation, flattery.

I have just come from Booth's Theatre—"Richelieu." I sent you a despatch: the Morton & Bliss firm have taken $10,000. worth of [mining] stock. $60,000. now disposed of. Don't perseverance accomplish a good deal?

Crosby said Mr and Mrs Belmont speak very highly of me, Mr B. most encouragingly of my business prospects.

Dined at 6.30 with the McKeenes at the Gramercy Park Hotel. Genl. McK. told me that Captain Chandler, formerly of Genl. Hancock's staff, who was Judge Advocate at my trial, is now in an insane asylum, in Washington.

To-night I am to sit with Miss Kellogg in her box at the Academy of Music—She does not sing—At her request I am sending you a paper with an account of her, with her compliments.

This morning I took a walk with Miss Kellogg on Broadway. I do not think she likes Mrs. C. as well as she did at first . . . doubts her sincerity. Miss Kellogg cannot endure affectation in man or woman.

To show you how careful Miss Kellogg is in her conduct with gentlemen, she told me she has never ridden with a gentleman alone but twice in New York, and on one of these occasions her coachman was along. How many ladies even in a private station could say as much.

She was talking to me about Bierstadt whom she does not like as much as does her mother. Miss Kellogg is very dainty in regard to gentlemen. She became disgusted with B because he appeared before her in brown stockings, and also because he mis-spelled a word in the first letter he wrote her.

What would you think of a Bunkey grown so corpulent about the waist he cannot keep his pants up without suspenders? I have had to buy a pair.

At the theatre with the Howards. Shakespeare's "Winter's Tale. . . ." Beautiful beyond words. There was a storm at sea. Mrs. Howard said it gave her cold chills. But to me the crowning beauty was the closing Act, the "Statue Scene," arousing the same emotions as "Othello."

"I'd rather be a toad and live upon the vapors of a dungeon than keep a corner in the thing I love for others. . . ." A fear from which I am free, for if ever husband had unlimited confidence in his wife's purity. . . .

I have bought some new musical selections: "Champagne Charlie," the "Letter Song" sung by Aimée in "Perichole" and "Lui Dit," Persigni in "La Grande Duchesse. . . ."

About to call on Col. Jerome Bonaparte. . . . He is a West Point graduate.

Mr Newell is to have the Presbyterian Church, corner of fifth Ave. and 42nd St. at $5,000. if pew sales warrant. Larry Jerome says he can keep an Opera Box more cheaply than a pew, and prefers it.

Pongee parasols are the style, some with colored border, some with small ruffles at the edge.

Chignons are unpopular. The prevailing style is to wear the hair in two braids in the morning, and in the afternoon tuck these up, the ends concealed with little curls.

Gentlemen's hats are worn very high. One most becoming style at a summer resort is straw, with broad band of light blue velvet and brim bound to match.

There is a beautiful girl, eighteen or nineteen, blonde, who has walked past the hotel several times trying to attract my attention. Twice for sport I followed her. She lives about opposite Mr. Belmont's. She turns and looks me square in the face, to give me a chance to speak to her. I have not done so yet. At her house she enters, then appears at a window, raising this for any attention I may offer. I called on Mrs Hough. She has the clearest, ringing laugh. I told her about the young lady.

I went on to Miss Kellogg's. She was not dressed, but sent word for me to wait. I could hear her moving about overhead, and it reminded me of you in Monroe days when I sat in the parlor below, waiting.

She sang some beautiful songs for me . . . "She's waiting, I'm Coming" . . . And so I am.

I see that young Black who killed a man for seducing his sister is acquitted. But I fear Mrs Fair will be let off, I think she is an awful wretch and should be put out of the way. Such women are dangerous to society.

Custer to Elizabeth, 1871, from New York:
. . . I have received a characteristic letter from Col. Keogh. He thanks me for calling on Miss Hf. "since she must feel lonely since I left." He wants me to send her "a handsome collection of flowers" in his name, and to Mrs Cr. "a basket of flowers as handsome as can be made, sparing no expence." Also I am to order fifty-dollar sleeve buttons for Cook, won in a bet. A bouquet costs at least $5., a basket, such as he contemplates, not less than $25. I shall order the sleeve-buttons and have them sent him C.O.D. He must think I am made of money.

You know I bear not the slightest animosity toward him, tho I think he treated me unfairly. I do think him rather absurd, but would rather have him stationed near us than many others.

Tell Maggie I appreciate her having answered my letter. Usually I never hear from her unless Jimmy gets into trouble.

But this letter I enclose from Jimmy shows he is not lacking in gratitude. Do not show it to Maggie. He would not want anyone to know what he says of Col. K. It would be just like K's suspicious nature to suppose that I prompt Miss Hf. to write the sharp letters she does . . . for she wrote him finally that his complaints were monotonous and uninteresting. So sensitive a man I wonder he can endure it. One of his letters to her that she showed me was full of poetry and very touching.

Margaret ("Maggie") Custer was engaged to James Calhoun, known later as the Adonis of the regiment, and of undoubted bravery. His early derelictions—though of a minor nature—sometimes put Armstrong to not a little trouble. As seen from a later letter, Calhoun was not ungrateful.

James Calhoun to Custer, April 23, 1871, from Bagdad, Kentucky:
My dear General—I have just received my commission as 1st Lt. in the 7th Cavalry, and it reminds me more vividly than ever how many, many times I am under obligations to you for your very great kindness to me in my troubles. I shall do my best to prove my gratitude. If the

time comes you will not find me wanting. . . . Col. K. went to Louisville yesterday as he was becoming lonesome. Letters from a certain
party in New York do not content him much. This for yourself.
Good-bye.

Custer to Elizabeth, 1871, from New York:
My Darling . . . Mr Osborn took Mr George (his partner) and myself to Wallack's where he had a box, to meet three ladies . . . Saw
Wallack in "The Liar." He wore a wig of long light hair like mine
during the war. He was so funny in the part.

One of the young ladies has evidently taken a strong fancy to your
Bo. She makes no effort at concealment. She said, "Oh, why are you
married?" I said, "Well, I found a girl I loved. And if you knew her
you would love her too." This fancy of hers was not induced by any
advances of mine. She is not fast, is refined and educated. I really think
she is a good girl but cannot control herself. She can cause my little one
no uneasiness, no regret.

Mr O took Mr George and myself to supper at Delmonico's. Afterwards he asked if I had been in a faro bank since coming to New York,
and since I had not, offered to take me to a first-class one. It was understood that I would not play. . . . One run by Johnny Chamberlin, a
splendid fellow—the most fashionable in the city, near the Fifth Avenue Hotel. Oh, the magnificence and the luxury! We met some of the
most prominent men of New York. All sorts of games went on. . . .
Baccarat, a new game. Even Rouge-et-Noir. And, would my girl believe
it? I remained nearly two hours without the slightest desire to succumb
to my old foe.

. . . . Girls needn't try to get her dear Bo away from her, because
he loves only her, and her always.

O will have to tone down a great deal when his wife returns. I wish I
could repeat his quaint sayings. . . . "Well, boys, school begins on
Wednesday. No more vacation pour moi. . . . I've had one good
winter. I expect I shall never get the old lady to leave me alone for another." Still, from what I hear Mrs O is very exacting.

As I wrote you at the outset, I do not expect great results from my
trip, but hope to close the business satisfactorily. I asked Mr Travers
if the results could not be communicated me by telegraph, but he
thought I should remain. Col. Hull has left, leaving all the business
to me.

The streets are full of policemen anticipating a grand riot between

Protestant and Catholic Irishmen, the former celebrating a victory (Protestant) won over two hundred years ago. A few broken noses are already in evidence.

Custer to Elizabeth, 1871, from Saratoga, New York:
Darling Standby . . . Here I am in the midst of enjoyment, only lacking you. Such a jolly party. . . . The two Jeromes, Larry and Leonard, sing negro melodies like professionals. Johnny Chamberlin . . . The Knights Templar highly honored me, sending a Committee to escort me to their ball. I only stayed a short time, being in traveling clothes.

In the race between Mr Belmont's Kingfisher and Longfellow, belonging to Mr Harper of Kentucky I feel certain the latter will win. [The winner was Longfellow.]

How I wish you were here to "double my joys and quadruple my expences" in this enchanting place. Pardon the quotation—it seemed the place to bring it in. But you never seem any expense to me.

Custer to Elizabeth, 1871, from New York:
Back in New York. Col. Hay tells a story admirably. . . .
I have donned a light stove-pipe. You do not see one black in twenty.
Whom should I see alight from a Fifth Avenue omnibus but Genl. Merritt with a stylish handsome young lady. He registered as "Genl. and Mrs." He invited me to call on the madam which I shall do.

A letter from the Commissioner of Parks, accepting the bear for the Zoological Gardens. I am sorry to part with him, and only do so because of change of stations.

In referring to *the* young lady you ask if I told her about you. If you will look over my letters you will find I told her I love you and you alone. She frankly said she would only ask me to love her next to you, which I did not consent to do. It is as she says: she does all the liking. How she can keep it up. . . . When tickets were sent for the Opera, finding I was expected to be her escort I did not go.

As for *that* young lady—Her dear Bo don't care if She did tear up the photograph he sent her. He never could care for a woman who so far forgot herself as to make the advances. I care for no one in town but Miss Kellogg, and I respect her and she respects me. My girl should be grateful that, seeing so many people as I do, to me she stands all the higher by contrast, in bright relief, true womanhood.

Genl. Torbert has invited me to visit him at his Delaware home. He says he will take my halter off and turn me loose in a peach orchard.

Custer to Elizabeth, 1871, from New York:
Darling Standby . . . Genl. Sheridan arrived late last night, the "Russia" being a day overdue. I was in a box at the Opera with Miss Kellogg—she left early to rest for her performance on the morrow. I went straight to the Fifth Avenue Hotel, to the General's room and stayed till one in intimate talk. He told me all about his European visit from beginning to end. The descriptions of the war [Franco-Prussian] and the armies differed from accounts he gave reporters, these being colored by the Hospitalities he had enjoyed. He said, "Custer, I wish you had been with me." And "Custer, you with that 3rd Division could have captured King William six times over."

He wants me to accompany him to Boston, will telegraph Genl. Terry about it. I shall do so, as it would be an unusual way for me to visit that city.

Custer to Elizabeth, 1871, from New York:
I was at a dinner-party—one I never can forget, for the talented and distinguished men I met there. It was for representatives of the Press, editors-in-chief. . . . Your boy the only outsider. On the right of the Presiding officer sat Mr Horace Greeley, and your Bo next him. On my right, Mr Bayard Taylor, and next him Whitelaw Reid. Opposite, Mr Dana of the "Sun" with the Poet Steadman on his left. Twenty-five, in all. Mr. Taylor related to me many incidents of his travels in Central Africa. Mr Steadman, who sought for an introduction to me, told me that during and since the war I had been to him, and, he believed, to most people, the beau ideal of the Chevalier Bayard, "knight sans peur et sans reproche" and that I stood unrivaled as the "young American hero." I repeat this *to you alone*, as I know it will please you. Another said no officer holding a commission was so popular with the retired men. . . . I was so complimented and extolled that, had I not had some experience, I should have been overwhelmed. . . .

I presume you have seen the announcements of the War Department in the papers. Personally I should have preferred the Plains, but for your sake. Duty in the South has somewhat of a political aspect, which I always seek to avoid.

Elizabeth to Mrs. Sabin, 1871:

Autie has sold his mine. We go to Elizabethtown, Kentucky. There will be little to do there except keep the mobs down. . . . We expect to stay there till the close of the Administration [Grant's first term, beginning March, 1869].

He preceded his wife to the new post.

Custer to Elizabeth, September 4, 1871, from Elizabethtown, Kentucky:

Darling Standby . . . I think "Betsy" [town] and I will not be out. The climate is pure and healthful, the citizens so far have been cordial, no one churlish or unfriendly. Col. Thomas called on me at once.

I enjoy this old-fashioned hotel, its quaint landlady who is everything in one. The meals are not so dreadful; apple-sauce and hot biscuit at each meal, and I have appetite for both. The table runs the length of the room, the landlady has placed me at the head. On my left is an ex-member of Congress, survivor of many duels, carrying in his person as many bullets, as mementoes. The system of bells passes comprehension. Four are rung for breakfast, also a small darkey knocks at the door to say "Ready an' waiting." The Army ladies "Made" for me at once . . . a party to visit the Mammoth Cave, to be absent three days. I will wait for it till you come. No, I had no physician for my cold. You know my distrust of the profession. The bracing mountain air here will cure me.

With commutation, and odds and ends and if Uncle Sam persists in giving us $200. a month we ought to live nicely and have a little money for an occasional trip.

After our house is paid for and we are square with the world I would like to stay so, always having two months' pay due. Wouldn't you?

Mrs. Custer joined her husband and shortly wrote her sister-in-law, Maggie Custer, now Mrs. James Calhoun, about her new environment.

Elizabeth to Mrs. Calhoun, 1871, from Elizabethtown, Kentucky:

Imagine yourself your grandmother to get an idea of this place. Everything is old, particularly the women. The old madam, landlady, entered into conversation with me at the first meal. I, smiling, trying to keep up with what I hoped were well-studied remarks. When mistakenly I said "I don't think many ladies have fine suits of hair" the old false front I was addressing nearly dropped off. The old standing corner clock has not been allowed to run down for forty-five years. The dog is sweet sixteen and can scarcely walk. An old gentleman boarder of the old school is equally unsteady on his legs. But, tho over seventy, wishes to marry again. . . . No, not the landlady who was his old sweetheart, but a young girl.

To keep flies off the table an infernal flying machine runs its length— pieces of board about three feet square, attached in a series to a rope with a red rag hanging from it. This a little darkey pulls in order to agitate the boards, so that we dine to music.

The most active inhabitant of the place is a pig.

Autie is going to Louisville. I have offered to stay behind for $120.— the price of our board for a month. It would be enough to have my new dresses made and trimmed.

Apparently she accompanied her husband, for next she wrote her cousin Mary Richmond (married to Mr. Charles Kendall).

Elizabeth to Mrs. Kendall, 1871, from Elizabethtown, Kentucky:
We have returned from a two weeks' visit to Louisville, Lexington and Cincinnati—expositions at the first and last, where we were much entertained at both. Ohio is so far advanced Kentucky can't stand the comparison.

All you bought for me in New York is lovely . . . new notch in rosettes. . . . I will make up my black cashmere with a vest.

Maggie is on her way to her husband, the sweetest most satisfactory sort of a girl. I hope poor Annie will feel better when her baby comes. She is always anxious about her husband when away from him. How grateful I am Autie does not drink. When the gentlemen ask him what he will take—Everybody in Kentucky drinks—He says "A glass of Alderney," and toasts in that while they take whiskey, brandy, wine.

Elizabeth to Mrs. Sabin, 1871, from Elizabethtown, Kentucky:
This is a rest after our late excitement. But it is the stillest, dullest place. No sound to be heard but the Sheriff in the Court House calling "Hear ye," three times as each case comes up. This part of Kentucky is very poor, the people low and uneducated. Three or four ride the same horse. A mother and two big children just passed, mounted that way.

Autie would like to be on the Frontier, but spends his leisure reading and writing.

Autie has been helping his brother Nevin, married, with five children, buy a farm in Monroe to be near his parents.

Autie has bought me a sewing-machine, I make it fly. I enjoy making my own clothes.

One of Custer's duties was to purchase mounts for the regiment.

Custer to Mrs. Calhoun, 1871, from Elizabethtown, Kentucky:

We sent Tom's troop 24 very handsome black horses. "M" is to be mounted like "D" on black. Mr My. went in charge, his wife with him. The horses reached the troops with manes and tails cut off. Tom is awfully put out about it. Col. Cook thinks Mr My. cut the hair off to make "waterfalls" for his wife.

I will take up the matter of Mr Calhoun's transfer with Genl. Terry.

I must tell you a joke on Libbie. My friend the actor, Lawrence Barrett, sent me a very handsome ring, a cameo, a beautiful female figure. Libbie opened both note and case, and was delighted, thinking the ring would be too small for me and that she would get it. Imagine her disappointment when it slipped on my finger quite easily.

A good sister-in-law, Mrs. Custer occupied herself with the wardrobe of Tom Custer, with her new sewing machine. In a characteristic letter he acknowledged her gift of nightgowns and underwear.

Tom Custer to Elizabeth, 1871, from Oxford, Missouri:

My Dear Libbie—The Drawers are better than the first pair. But you did not make the strap so that it wouldn't twist the lag half-way round, and bring the inside of it on my instep. The nightie is very nice indeed, but you did not get the collar as I wanted, to lie down all around, like the collar of a dressing-gown. Try and make the others that way. And don't put so much lace on them, but ruffles, as I would like that better, and just one false plait for button.

And I would prefer you to make the button-holes yourself instead of the person who made these, and have them run up and down instead of Crosswise. I will draw—if I can—the shape of cuff or wristband. Don't think I am finding fault. I am very proud of this one, and have shown it to the Doctor and to French who think it very grand.

We received a telegram yesterday, saying that Genl. McDowell would be here in the afternoon to inspect the Fort. French and I were at the depot to meet him. After looking at us dismounted we had to saddle up and come out mounted. By that time it was dark. He intends to inspect all the Kentucky Posts. Tell Armstrong.

Tell Armstrong that when the sale comes up to buy a fine horse for me and one for French. I have a stable all fixed up for them.

Now Libbie if Armstrong is too confounded mean to write I wish you would and Libbie I wish you would keep your eye on that old hag that is doing the sewing and make her be more careful and write oftener to your devoted brother Tom.

Mrs. Custer went off on a visit with dressmaking its object.

Custer to Elizabeth, 1872 (?), from Elizabethtown, Kentucky:
I expect my Sunbeam is so deeply interested in the mysteries of clothes that all thoughts of her dear Bo are vanished. The little bouquet-holder you gave me stands before me holding a delicate pink rose with buds, and a spray of white flowers—reminding me of you.

> Love born only once in living,
> Truth that strengthens in the giving,
> Constancy beyond deceiving. . . .

Custer to Elizabeth, February 9, 1873, from Elizabethtown, Kentucky:
I have been rambling through the house. I have gone through my extensive and classical repertory on the organ, from "Oh, Who Will Care for Mother now?" to "Put me in my Little Bed," also beautiful and expressive lines announcing that Annie Yates has a baby, but that it is barefooted on top of its head, like some other member of its family.

After an intermission to allow applause to quiet down, and consuming nearly a peck of apples, I have responded to encores, and gone through my list with variations, till even the wheezing old organ cried "Let us have Peace!"

This is the last leave you get from your headquarters. Or next time you are to take your command with you—one long-haired cavalryman in serviceable condition.

This place is called Elizabethtown, but that is a mistake. The town is here, but not Elizabeth.

The Methodists are holding a revival. Capts. Moylan and Smith and Lt. Varnum attended last night, and will go again, from the same motives as if attending a circus.

I have almost completed my "Galaxy" article, but am waiting for a paper for which I have telegraphed Genl. Sherman.

Enjoy yourself to the utmost. Now that you are away I want you to have enjoyment enough to pay for it.

General Mitchell (of Hancock's staff) to Custer, March 1, 1872, from St. Paul, Minnesota:

My dear Custer—I have been reading with much interest your "Galaxy" articles about Indian matters and the Plains. In the N.Y. *Times* of Dec. 25, 1868, you will find an editorial concerning Genl. Hancock's expedition that may be of service to you.

Three years later General Sherman wrote Custer in regard to the latter's plan for writing his recollections of the Civil War.

Sherman to Custer, December 14, 1875, from St. Louis, Missouri:

My Dear Custer—I assure you I thoroughly approve of your idea of writing your War Reminiscences. Your articles on the Plains are by far the best I have ever read, and every member of my family has read the volume with deep interest.

Somehow these personal observations have a freshness, lifelike, lacking in more sober history. In time they will be of infinite use when a Napier collects all facts and breathes life into the actors—as various as could be developed of men aroused by vehement passions. Therefore I approve your purpose and will read what you write with intense interest.

I also thank you for the copy of Genl. Lee's letter of July 27 '68. It confirms my conviction that the advance of my Army from Savannah, north, was a direct attack on Richmond which he, no one, could ignore without certain defeat.

I have received such hard knocks about my Memoirs that I should suppose you had been warned. Still, I hope they will also help in the Grand Compilation when done.

Lawrence Barrett, the actor, deplored the fate that would take Custer far away, but he felt that Uncle Sam had a better use for him than to employ him as a mule inspector. Heartily he wished he himself might escape the servitude of "the starched horror of a hotel-table" for the free life of a Cavalryman, forgetting that the soldier himself was not a free agent. Certainly Custer's new assignment was not to be one of ease. His two-year term in Kentucky over, he was to go again into the field. The 7th Cavalry had been broken up, distributed among small posts in the South, mainly to suppress illicit distilleries and eradicate the Ku-Klux Klan, though there was small need of this at Elizabethtown. Now it was to be reintegrated, reunited, prepared for active operations in Dakota Territory, "outside the States."

16: "Outside the States"

CZAR ALEXANDER II of Russia sent his third son, the Grand Duke Alexis, on a world tour of education. In January, 1873, he arrived in the United States and was welcomed by delegations at every train stop between New York and Chicago. From Chicago he was taken to North Platte, Nebraska, where a buffalo hunt was planned at his request.

This came within the jurisdiction of General Sheridan, who was host to the ducal party on the special train that carried it to the scene. General Custer was summoned to conduct the proceedings in collaboration with Colonel Cody—"Buffalo Bill"—the famous Government scout whose aid was needed to persuade the Indians to participate in the hunt. All Cody's diplomacy, backed by Sheridan's promise of liberal largesse, was invoked to bring the great Sioux chief, Spotted Tail, and his village to the rendezvous. This was to be no ordinary buffalo kill; it was to be a spectacular display of the "Wild West" at its most sportive.

Under Custer's coaching the young Alexis learned the difference between buffalo and boar hunting. A good rider and a good shot himself, the duke brought down a buffalo and cabled the news to the Czar. Indian war dances closed the entertainment. When camp broke up, Cody as a parting touch drove the distinguished guest at breakneck speed in a four-in-hand as if pursued by Indians. Custer also was a passenger.

The grand duke asked Custer to remain with the party to New Orleans, his point of embarkation. Mrs. Custer and some young ladies joined the party en route.

Elizabeth in her diary:

February 5

Took charge of Miss Nina Sturgis and Miss Duncan, starting for Memphis. At the Overton Hotel took dinner in the Grand Ducal Suite.

From the outset it was clear that the less formal, the more desirable our society. The gentlemen wore everyday clothes, the ladies were dressed as they would be at home. No ceremony observed except that the Grand Duke goes in to table first with whichever lady he selects, and leaves first. As he changes the lady every night, we have the pleasant opportunity of becoming acquainted with all.

Luncheon (or breakfast) at noon, and we are becoming so Russian in our habits as to take rolls and coffee when we rise. The meal begins with eggs on toast, and ends, as at dinner, with coffee.

They like Rhine wine, sherry, claret. It is a real pleasure to sit next them, for, should American gentlemen take the amount of wine they do, the lady would be forced to listen to the idiotic mumbled sillinesses a man, politely tight, inflicts on her. The cold climate of their country enables these Russians to drink what seems to us a vast quantity without effect on them.

At Memphis we were joined by Mr Vance, a cultivated Southerner with moderate liberal views, and his two charming daughters. Also by Mr D., Chairman of the Reception Committee, a tall pallid widower who at once succumbed to Miss Nina's charms. At a plantation we visited he showed his sense of her fitness to become the mother of his children because she called a darkey with a pickaninny to the carriage to talk with her. But Miss Nina assured him that, having younger sisters and brothers, she cares for all children.

Admiral Poisset and Mr Machin are ranking, managing members of the Grand Ducal party. Mr Machin is a highly cultivated Englishman who has had charge of the education of all sons of the Tsar. He has keen merry brown eyes, that nothing escapes. He has noted many of our peculiar provincialisms. I am surprised we have so many.

Also I am surprised that the Imperial children have to master their tasks, just as if they were students at our own high schools.

The Admiral is all sunshine and sweet simplicity. He strives to interest Alexis in the towns we pass, length of rivers, and the like. But in boat or on the train Alexis is not concerned with the outside, only with the pretty girls, with music—he sings magnificently, and has already learned Lydia Thompson's Music Hall ditty—which he renders "If efer I cease to luf . . ."—in his eternal cigarette, and in joking with his suite and with the General.

This was a spring interlude. Summer was to see Custer in his new post "Outside the States." Custer hailed his new assignment with joy. It meant work and was in every respect far removed from his lethargic existence in Kentucky. The 7th Cavalry Regiment was to be reunited and go into the field to guard the engineers of the Northern Pacific while they surveyed the route to the Yellowstone.

With a faith hardly justified by the facts the Custer party packed its limited equipment and set out for the Dakota Territory. The train took them from the bland Kentucky breezes into a region under heavy snow where they almost perished from the icy winds. It was only with some difficulty they were rescued alive.

In *Boots and Saddles* Elizabeth Custer tells with admirable restraint how little foresight the Government exercised in safeguarding its servicemen in these distant regions. They were in Yankton, in the extreme southeast corner of what is now South Dakota, and had before them a five-hundred-mile journey to their destination, Fort Rice. When the regiment reached that tiny post, they found there were no accommodations for the army wives who had accompanied their husbands to that wilderness spot. There was nothing for it but to go back the way they had come. Elizabeth Custer and her sister-in-law Mrs. Calhoun sought refuge in Monroe, their home town.

Custer to Elizabeth, June 26, 1873, from camp on Heart River, Dakota Territory:

My Darling Sunbeam—This is our sixth day from Fort Rice. We expect to remain in camp, as it is somewhere in this locality we are to meet the engineers, and the four companies of infantry.

Capt. Moylan started at five this morning with his troop and an Indian guide to look for them. He took two days' rations, but expects to return this evening.

Our march has been delightful. Such hunting I never have seen. We have encountered no Indians, but yesterday we saw the tracks of fifteen ponies.

Lt. De Reuter is just in from the engineers with 17 men. He brought doleful accounts of their progress. They encountered a severe hailstorm, and all their stock stampeded. This they recovered, but several of their wagons were so badly damaged they had to be abandoned, two men were injured seriously, one fatally. His own head is covered with bumps from the hailstones. Three antelopes near their camp were killed by them.

I start at five in the morning with all the cavalry to join the engineers who are supposed to be twenty-five miles from here. Genl. Stanley with the infantry and main train will follow.

Marched 30 miles over a bad country, besides building a bridge over a stream 30 feet wide and 10 deep. . . . 180 men worked on it. It was completed in two hours. It was necessary first for someone to cross the stream. I detailed McDougall and twenty of his men to do this. They had to strip to swim it. You should have heard the laughter of the young officers on the bank as McD led his "Light Brigade" across.

Well, I have joined the engineers. The day we arrived I was lying half asleep when I heard "Orderly, which is General Custer's tent?" I sprang up. "I know that voice, even if I haven't heard it for years!" It was my old friend Genl. Rosser. Stretched on a buffalo robe, under a fly, in the moonlight, we listened to one another's accounts of the battles in which we had been opposed. It seemed like the time when, as cadets, we lay, huddled under one blanket, indulging in dreams of the future.

Rosser said the worst whipping he ever had was that of Oct. 9th (Well do I remember it) when I captured everything he had, including that uniform of his now in Monroe. He said he had been on a hill, watching our advance, and, through his field-glasses, recognized me, so sent for his Brigade-Commander, and said, "Do you see that long-haired man in the lead? Well, that's Custer, and we are going to bust him up" . . . "And so we should have only you slipped another column round us, and soon my men were crying out 'We're flanked, We're flanked.' "

Col. Grant visits me quite often. I find him most congenial, so modest and unassuming, withal sensible and manly. We talk over West Point experiences. One reason I like him is because he has such respect for the wishes of his mother. He did not bring any of his fine rifles, because she feared he would be tempted to wander off hunting. Lt. Adair, her cousin, was killed that way on last year's expedition.

Captain Z came back from his visit to his wife and sat up all night, playing and losing over four hundred dollars and getting very drunk. He remained so two or three days, much of the time out of his head. He owed me $25. and this he came and paid me, then, in an hour returning, trying to pay me again, and then going to Capt. Smith, trying to get him to take it to pay me. He is now on the sick report. I fear he will be a confirmed drunkard, and see but little happiness for his poor wife.

The officers have been sitting night and day, playing, since we left Fort Rice. They are now in Dr. H's tent, next mine. I carry Tom's funds now. Mr C began playing as soon as we left Rice, and only stopped, night before last, from lack of funds. He borrowed $20. from me, but cannot get any more from me, nor any from Tom, since Tom has to borrow in order to play. I hope C. will lose every time he sits down. Otherwise he will return to winter quarters with nothing to go on with.

I have been in Dr. H's tent while the game was going on, and I congratulate myself daily—as often as the subject enters my mind— that I have told Satan to get behind me so far as poker is concerned. Notwithstanding the pleasure and excitement I used to find in it, it no longer possesses the slightest power over me, and I never feel tempted to take a hand. You often said I could never give it up. But I have always said I could give up anything—except you.

Elizabeth to Custer, July, 1873, from Monroe, Michigan:
My Darling Boy—Your magnificent letter of 42 pages sent me into the seventh heaven of bliss. I had declined an invitation to the Lake, preferring to wait for the one o'clock train with mail. Ten years have so changed me in some respects that though I enjoy even the simple pleasures of Monroe I no longer go into ecstasies over anything but your letters. How we have managed to preserve the romance . . . after nine years of married life and all our vicissitudes. . . . But, though we have had our trials, you have the blessed faculty of looking on the sunny side of things. Dear Autie, you are the richest of men.

I hope we can get our affairs in order. Our interests are too scattered now to look after them properly. And now we must assume the burden of this family [the older Custers]. I now feel ready for any amount of saving since you have given up gambling. That you can watch play and forego all personal excitement in it is a mystery to me.

I am dreadfully sorry about Jimmy. I simply told Maggie in an off-hand way that everyone, even Mr Godfrey, was at the old game. But now, Autie, I fear he will take to drinking. I hope Maggie may be able to restrain him. She and I are perfectly despondent about Captain Z. I feel trebly sad about it because it was at our house his wife saw him so often. Do, Autie, write him a strong letter, reminding him how she proved her love by marrying him in the face of family opposition. Now, Autie, we must redouble our efforts to befriend her, sweet sensitive soul that she is.

How delightful that General Rosser and you are such company for one another. I am glad Fred Grant takes to you. I think his character remarkable, to be unspoiled by all the adulation he receives. I wish for our own sake he weren't a President's son. He would not credit our disinterested friendship. How nice for the Grants to be so fond of one another—a united family.

Monroe seems determined to spoil me. But I find it hard to rise above depressing surroundings without your help. There are not many joyous people here. The women are so fagged with domestic cares, kitchen drudgery, leading a monotonous life, the men without bright women to cheer them up. . . . No Civil life for me, except as a visitor.

Mrs Bagg has sent Mattie to Germany with her sister. Mattie is a dangerous girl here where there is so much liberty with beaux. Emma Reed is sweet, Autie. She has a nice little beau from Detroit, but is quite fascinatingly indifferent. . . . Gifted with the Custer trait—an inclination to coquette.

The clergyman here is such a talented man. It is a privilege to go to church again. But, oh, so hard to be plodding along without you.

I had a nice old-fashioned visit from Mary Dansard. Poor Mary, lingering along with childbirth illness. She said, "Just think, Libbie, in ten years I have had seven children—and you not one." And she seemed to envy me.

Maggie and I are trying to remember all the new games, and the round and square dances, for our winter evenings.

Elliott Bates came in to say good-bye. I miss him, for he and Maggie are the only ones with whom I could talk army talk. But if he had stayed it would have caused remark, had he spent an evening a week at our house, and I am more than ever anxious to be above suspicion of reproach.

He told me he had often enquired about me in an off-hand way, knowing of my being surrounded by temptation, and was satisfied that I was, and am, the good woman he had expected me to be.

Autie, I try to improve to keep up with you, be worthy of you. God keep you, my precious darling. I kiss you a hundred times.

Custer to Elizabeth, June, 1873, from Dakota Territory:
We are now encamped 15 miles from the infantry. Rosser is desperate about conditions, and cannot speak too highly of the Cavalry. General Stanley is acting very badly, drinking, and I anticipate official trouble with him. I should greatly regret this, but fear it cannot be

avoided. Rosser has told me how badly General S behaved last year, some days being so overcome the expedition could not go on. One morning the engineers started at the appointed hour, but Rosser, looking back, from a high bluff, saw that the infantry camp was still standing. On going back he found the officers searching for the General, but in vain. Finally Major Worth told Rosser confidentially that, having found Genl. S. dead drunk on the ground outside the camp, he had carried him into his own tent, though he and the General were not on good terms, for the honor of the service. He was then lying there in a drunken stupor.

Rosser said he told General S. in St. Paul before starting that he would have a different man to deal with this year, in command of the 7th Cav.—one who would not hesitate, as second in command, to put a guard over him, S., if incapacitated. Genl. S., Rosser said, acknowledged that he knew this and would try to do better. But whiskey has too strong a hold on him.

Our officers are terribly down on him. One day, when intoxicated, after leaving Rice, he abused Mr Baliran [the sutler] in such coarse terms, calling him foul names . . . and threatened to hang him, should he seek to come into camp at any time. Mr Baliran, who is a great favorite with our officers, asked me what he should do. I bade him come into camp with me . . . and no one has been hanged as yet. [The sutler's store was outside the camp proper. Mr Baliran came, accordingly, as guest of the officers.]

Genl. S. in one of his fits of ill-humor, ordered Col. Grant to go to the 7th Cavalry, and inspect Mr Baliran's wagons and stores, and, if he found any spirituous liquors there, to take an axe and spill the contents of barrels. This would have injured Mr B. financially, as he had thousands of dollars' worth on hand. Col. Grant was greatly mortified, but fortunately Mr B's wagons were so far in the rear it was hours before they arrived. So, after chatting with me on pleasant topics Col. Grant said, "Well, my tent leaked last night, so I guess I will go back and take a nap. By that time the wagons may be in. And I hope the Sutler will have anything of the kind hidden before I come to inspect."

Our officers regarded Genl. S's order as persecution, and were eager to help. So Mr B loaded his drinkables into one wagon and made the rounds of our temperate officers, leaving with each a keg of brandy, case of rum, or barrel of Bourbon, for temporary keeping. Never were temperate officers so well provided with intoxicants.

Then Genl. S reconsidered, canceled his order to Col. Grant to inspect. But, fearing this might be a trap, the officers retained the kegs, &c. for a few days, till the excitement was over.

Poor Mr M. was so fearful that a barrel of whiskey might be found in his possession he never slept a wink till B. took it back.

I shot another antelope beside some curlews, from which Mary made a delicious pot-pie. Whenever pot-pie is mentioned Tom, Mr Calhoun and I all begin, "I'll tell you where you get the best pot-pie you ever tasted. . . ." And then, "At Mother's!"

Mary says, "Tell Miss Libbie I like it better out here than I thought I would." She is a great favorite, never complains, and takes things humorously. All are kind to her. [Mary was successor to Eliza, who had married one of her swains.]

Genl. Rosser and I have again been talking over war experiences, with Moylan an attentive listener. Rosser once took him prisoner.

I have just answered Mr Rauch on business matters. He will call on you for some old papers he says he needs. You should be present when these are overhauled, and should keep a list of those taken.

This letter would make an article for the "Galaxy." It is for my Gal. Don't you think you should send me a cheque?

Custer to Elizabeth, July 1, 1873, from Dakota Territory:

Good morning, my Sunbeam. . . . Infantry and trains still 15 miles in the rear, stuck in the mud, they say, but probably through lack of energy, for Capt. Smith took our wagons back to the main line for supplies, and returned with them loaded.

The officers continue to sit around the festive board. Mr C's luck is bad; he cannot hold his own with good players. Tom and Fred try to dissuade him from playing, but he refuses. He tried to borrow from Tom who said "Relationships don't count in poker. Bunkey or no Bunkey, keep your hands out of my haversack."

Genl. Rosser considers this expedition too unwieldy to perform the work well, and I agree with him. But he thinks we are not going to have Indian troubles.

Give my love to Mother, Father, Ann and Nev, and their families, and kind remembrances to all friends.

Custer to Elizabeth, July 19, 1873: from the Yellowstone River, Montana Territory:

My Precious Darling—Well, here we are at last, at the far-famed— and to you far-distant—Yellowstone. How I have longed for you during our march in what seems a new world, a Wonderland.

The engineers have been escorted daily by the Cavalry, so found themselves progressing far more rapidly than when dragging along with the "Web Feet" as heretofore, accordingly we arrived sooner than anticipated at the Little Missouri, and concluded to push on here, as the engineers are employed daily in locating their lines in this valley, returning to camp each night.

The Yellowstone is the largest affluent of the Missouri, flowing in a general northeast direction. Fort Rice, from which post the cavalry started, is on the Missouri, in South Dakota, 500 miles above Yankton. The cavalry's march was westward, and the Yellowstone was come upon in Montana, then a territory. A steamer with supplies was to meet the expedition at Glendive Creek, and to find this creek in an unknown region was now the problem. Custer, as wontedly, was pathfinder.

Custer to Elizabeth, July, 1873, from the Yellowstone River, Montana Territory:

When we arrived within, as was supposed, about fifteen miles of where the steamer would be found, I volunteered to go on a steamboat hunt, as I had secured almost every other kind of game. So, taking two troops, Hall's and Moylan's, and leaving tents and wagons with the main command, I started, looking for the "Key West." Everybody wanted to go along, first Tom, then Mr Calhoun; then Dr. Harvey hinted that someone might be taken ill and need medical attention, so all three were added to the party. Then Genl. Rosser who is always ready for a trip of this kind accepted my invitation to accompany us, bringing three of his assistants, including Fred and Genl. Meigs' son. The men carried one day's rations in their haversacks, the officers simply a lunch in their saddle-pockets. Mary had made me some doughnuts, and these, wrapped, were given to my orderly to carry, but unfortunately I killed an antelope, and in strapping it behind his saddle, the blood dripped on the doughnuts.

Each step was a kaleidoscopic shifting of views, sublime beyond description. Much of our journey was necessarily made on foot, our horses being led in single file, except my own noble little steed Dandy who seemed to realize our difficulties, and who, altho untethered, followed me as closely and carefully as a well-trained dog.

Sometimes we found ourselves on a high summit, at others wending an uncertain way along the treacherous and craggy sides of cliffs with barely a foothold. Again, we found a way impassable and had to retrace our steps. Genl. Rosser and I led the advance.

It was a picturesque sight . . . the half-dozen men in the lead, ascending or descending the broken heights, first a man, then a horse. Then a man, then a horse. And so on, sandwiched. Often the route was so steep the horse seemed standing on hind legs. A mis-step would have imperiled those behind. If I were in the lead I would call to Rosser to hold on till I could determine the practicability of the route, and then would call "All right"—and the word would be passed back. Once when Rosser had the lead he called out "By George, Custer, we can get no further. Old Jim (his horse) says the Northern Pacific can go to the devil, but that he can't and won't climb this mountain!" And, sure enough, a steep acclivity rose before us.

But we could not turn without great danger to our horses. Looking around, to our left I saw a possible ascent, but barred by a huge rock. Bidding Tuttle look out, and with a caution to Dandy,—who seemed to grasp the situation and say "All right"—I set to work to get the rock out of the way, and soon had the satisfaction of seeing it go bouncing down into the valley, some hundreds of feet below.

Once on the summit we were well repaid by the grandeur of the scene before us.

I am told no country equals this region in the number and character of its petrifactions, animal and vegetable. What would you think of passing through acres of petrified trees, some with trunks several feet in diameter, and branches perfect?

Dr. Harvey offered Capt. Smith $20. for a fossil fish, but failed to obtain it. I have a similar one.

I intend to make a collection of petrifactions, fossils, &c. and present it to Ann Arbor University. The wagons being light on our return, boxes can be easily transported.

To return to our steamboat hunt:—After struggling through beds of deep cañons, and climbing heights we finally emerged into the Valley of the Yellowstone—a valley varying in width from nothing to many miles. I say "nothing" as the high ridge occasionally extends abruptly to the water's edge.

But we were not simply searching for the Valley of the Yellowstone. We were searching for a particular point in that valley, at the mouth of Glendive Creek, a stream flowing into the river on the east side. We found ourselves about twelve miles above this.

The day was hot, but the waters, as we quenched our thirst, icy cold, from melting mountain snows at the source.

We moved through a beautiful grove. Everything seemed to favor until we came to a dense grove of underbrush, impossible to penetrate.

Changing our route we ran into a swale of uncertain depth. I tried out a way with Dandy. . . . When all were safely across we saw Genl. Rosser, now in the lead, on a bluff, waving us to halt. An impassable range barred our way. Nothing for it but to go back, and find a way around it. Then a ride of ten miles took us to the mouth of the Glendive Creek, and there, down among the forest trees, we beheld the depot of supplies, and, tied to the river bank, the "Key West"—all guarded by 180 men of the 6th Infantry, under Lt. Thorne.

Mrs. Thorne and half a dozen little Thornes were on board.

The meeting was mutually agreeable. They had been there since July 1st, and had been awaiting us long and earnestly. We, for our part, were glad not only to have been successful in our search, but, in the condition of our larder, to see a well-stocked table and to be bidden to help ourselves. Which indeed we did.

What a contrast. The 6th Infantry—Lt. Thorne and officers, 8 or 10 —reveling in change of linen, dress coats, access to barber. And our party reveling in the effects of hot sun and hard exercise, in the coarsest of garments. . . . All laughed heartily at table. But they looked like invalids, beside our young, hearty, healthy fellows.

Knowing that the rest of the expeditionary force could not reach the depot the way we had come, I ordered the "Key West" to get up steam, and, loading the horses on her and the "A" and "K" troops, we proceeded up stream for fifteen miles, till it became too dark to go further.

I wrote a long despatch to Genl. Stanley, and sent Lt. Varnum with his men to carry it back to Genl. S's camp.

That night I slept without undressing, under a huge tree, by the river, Tuttle and my trumpeter-orderly near me, with Dandy picketed near by. The two troops bivouacked somewhat further from the river. Tom and Mr Calhoun slept on the boat, Moylan on deck, while Hall and Godfrey were near the troops. It rained during the night, but that did not disturb us, so fatigued were we with our exertions of the preceding day.

At three o'clock we were in the saddle on our way to a point five miles up the river where we expected the command would—and did —strike the river, the steamer mooring there. This was on the 17th.

We are now encamped at this point, the Cavalry in a forest of cottonwood trees, Infantry and trains on the open bottom, about a mile distant.

The boat is now busily employed night and day, transporting stores from Glendive Creek to the new depot. This will take about three days, then probably as long to ferry troops and trains to the other side, from which point the railroad survey will be resumed. Genl. Rosser accompanies the expedition no further, returning by the "Key West" and leaving his assistant, Mr Eccleston, a most agreeable young man, in charge. Both think the further survey will not take more than forty to forty-five days. Then, on our return, we shall start from this point on our return march, to the crossing or Fort Rice. This will be rapid. We shall carry only needed supplies, and, as our wagons will be empty, the Infantry can ride.

Soon you will be counting our separation by weeks instead of months, and will be on your way to a post on the frontier of Dakota.

Rosser and I were sitting on a log in front of my tent when we descried the advance of a train some five miles distant . . . Yates and Baker. Tidings from the outside world. You see that my prediction came true—that letters would make their way through from time to time.

I enjoyed your telling me the pleasure Father and Mother derive from our presents. In no way could I find a greater pleasure than in placing money at the disposal of those I love, and to whom I owe so much.

Capt. Yates brought Col. Benteen word of the death of his little girl at Fort Rice, fifteen days before.

Genl. Rosser has given Fred Nims a place with the engineers at $60. a month, with expences and prospects of advancement. Fred has become acquainted with the members of the party, all youths under twenty-five. How I wish some of our Monroe boys with talent and education, but lacking opportunity, would cut loose and try their fortunes in this great, enterprising Western country, where the virile virtues come out and a boy finds himself a full-fledged man.

Much as I dote on my profession and am devoted to it, yet, should accident cut me adrift, I have no fear but that energy and a willingness to put my shoulder to the wheel would carry me through to a reasonable success.

In this country no man of moderate education need fail if determined to succeed, so many the opportunities for honorable employment.

The mail brought many newspapers with allusions to the expedition, and references to your "Boy General." I send you an extract from the Chicago "Post" calling him the "Glorious Boy." I wonder if you think he is a "Glorious Boy"?

The Cincinnati "Commercial" of June 30 has an article on the expedition by G. A. Townsend, interesting and instructive. I regret I cannot send you a copy, but there is but one, and that is going the round of the officers.

The mail brought Col. Grant word of his grandfather's death. He will go back by the "Key West," visiting his mother at Long Branch, and then may go to Europe. Reticent as he is on personal matters, yet one day, when lying on the grass, I took out a little purple velvet case to show him the portrait inside, a few days later he said "You showed me a picture of your sweetheart, now I'll show you mine," and from an inside pocket drew out, first an unframed vignette of his father, then one of his mother, then a picture of a most beautiful, pure-minded-looking girl, of perhaps twenty, with large, lustrous eyes full of intelligence and sincerity—worthy of a President's son. As I read her traits he said, "Yes, she's all of that."

If he—Col. Grant—goes to Long Branch from Chicago by way of Monroe to see you, you will, of course, do all in your power to make his stay agreeable. If you know of his arrival in advance you and Maggie should meet him at the depot with a carriage. Have his father's picture hung in the parlor in compliment to him.

I have killed several antelope at long range, supplying our mess with game and that of several officers, and have given quantities to the men. But, to relieve your anxiety, I don't go far from the column, and always have from 20 to 30 men with me, old soldiers, good shots. Tuttle and another got lost recently, and did not find their way back to camp till an hour after reveille.

Have you invited some young lady to stay with us next winter? Do not let it be of a past generation. Moral worth is superior to beauty, but a young lady visiting a garrison should be possessed of both, else young officers might regard escorting as fatigue duty.

The Louisville Agent of the Insurance firm has acknowledged my final assured payment on the policy on behalf of Father and Mother. I have asked him to send Father a duplicate. Also I am sending him a check for $125. payment for the additional $5,000. policy drawn on your behalf. I am disposing of horses in Kentucky, as I cannot properly care for them, here.

Writing to others seems difficult, but to you not so. When other themes fail we still have the old story which in ten years has not lost its freshness . . . indeed is newer than when, at the outset we wondered if it would endure in its first intensity.

Custer to Elizabeth, July 22, 1873, from the Yellowstone River, Montana Territory:

The steamer is still transporting stores from Glendive Creek. Wind in the tall tree-tops above my tent rustles, and the days, though warm, are never unendurable, while the nights are glorious for refreshing sleep. The health of everyone is improved. Mr Larned, most delicate of our officers, has gained 15 pounds. Mr Aspinwall the same. Mr Wallace has regained his health. Those who came as invalids now are robust. One soldier of my command, deemed "consumptive" in the south, had made application for discharge, but this arriving too late, had come here with his company. In this bracing climate he is now a vigorous man.

You know how easily I get the "snuffles." Here they are unknown, and my throat, so sensitive elsewhere, gives me no discomfort.

The officers and men of the 7th are behaving admirably. Not one has been intoxicated since leaving Fort Rice, while scarcely a day passes without one seeing an Infantry officer too intoxicated to be fit for duty.

Custer to Elizabeth, July 25, 1873, from the Yellowstone River, Montana Territory:

Another steamer has been seen down the river, the "Josephine." To-morrow we resume our march. Col. Benteen's squadron ("H" & "C" troops) will remain at this point, guarding the depot. Also a Company of Infantry, the whole under command of Col. Pearson of the 17th. They remain in a stockade on the east side of the river.

Lts. Gibson and Harrington (whom I like exceedingly) have just ridden up to say good-bye.

Dr. M. returns to Memphis from this point, to the general satisfaction. Not that he is viciously inclined—quite the contrary—but because he peddles all the gossip afloat. Gossips are not welcome in the 7th Cavalry, as each is intent on minding his own business.

A yawl is going down the river to Fort Buford—120 miles. We may send mail by it.

Capt. Smith lost his pocketbook in the woods yesterday, with $500. in private and public money. Fortunately, retracing his steps, he found it intact.

Here is something you will hardly credit. Here we have been encamped several days, surrounded by guards and pickets. Our march through a difficult and dangerous country, almost unknown, said to be infested by hostile Indians. Imagine our surprise at seeing a white-covered wagon drawn by two mules, driven by one lone individual—a humble priest who, having started seven days before from Fort Rice, had traversed more than two hundred miles thus, each step in peril of his life.

Yesterday we marched at noon, but only five miles before going into camp. Everybody is chafing at the delay. We have been thirteen days at one point when three would have sufficed. Whiskey alone is the cause. You have no idea how this has delayed the expedition and added to the government expences. The steamer has been detained here needlessly for ten days, at $500. a day—$5,000. Genl. Rosser says it is a disgrace to the service.

I enclose $100. which Tom asks you to add to his deposit. I am to tell you it is money some of the officers owed him.

The priest called on me yesterday. I invited him to dine and he spent the whole afternoon with me. Forty-two; native of Alsace; came here in '64. He is a counterpart of the actor Joe Emmett. . . . And such a talker, hardly giving me time to replenish his plate. He kept us in a roar of laughter, and seemed greatly to enjoy his dinner. His description of his journey was most interesting even to experienced campaigners.

There is one party in this expedition, I think a scientist. His friends call him John. He has travelled much, observed much, leads a quiet, regular life, is simple, unpretentious, and, though evidently having seen better times, is uncomplaining. He is perfectly bald, with a luxuriant growth of blond whiskers. Should I go east when the expedition breaks up I shall invite him to accompany me to Monroe . . .

Tell Mother I shall try to get home this fall. Tell Maggie Mr Calhoun makes a splendid Adjutant.

There would have been no Cavalry left at the stockade and depot, on the Yellowstone, but Infantry alone, had not, from whiskey or some other inexcusable cause, somebody had been guilty of gross miscalculation, as to the amount of supplies and forage in our train and boat. It was discovered at the last moment.

General Stanley's report to the War Department, August 4, 1873:
. . . . I had sent Lt. Col. Custer ahead to look up the road, a service for which he always volunteered. . . . Three scouts and a Cavalry

straggler ran in, and said they had been pursued by Indians. . . . I sent all the Cavalry to support Custer, but an hour before, he had driven all his opponents miles away. . . . He had gained 8 or 10 miles ahead of his train, had unsaddled to graze his animals, when his pickets signaled the approach of Indians. These were only a decoy. When Custer with a few of his officers who had watched their movements declined to follow this decoy to the adjoining thicket of cottonwood, 250 to 300 warriors rode out to the attack. The squadron was about 80 strong, and, the Indians being more numerous, Custer fought defensively on foot, till, finding the Indians had nothing new to develop, he mounted his squadron, and charged, dispersing them in all directions.

On the 5th, 6th, and 7th, Indians watched the column, from the bluffs. On the 8th, approaching the mouth of the Rosebud River, we discovered a large Indian village fleeing before us. Pursuit was resolved on. Custer with all the Cavalry, Indian scouts (7 days' rations and 100 rounds of ammunition per man) left to try to overtake them. On the 10th they discovered that the Indians had crossed the Yellowstone in skin boats, rafts, three miles below the mouth of the Little Big Horn.

Custer tried industriously to cross, but the river is deep and swift, and American horses do not take it.

Next morning the Indians fired across the river (about 700 ft. wide) and Custer found himself assailed from a bluff, 600 yds to the rear. Pushing up a skirmish line in that direction, he formed each squadron into a separate column, and charged, driving them [the Indians] 6 to 10 miles from the field.

General Rosser to Elizabeth:

The time I would rather have had a picture of George was on the Yellowstone Campaign, when he had a horse shot under him. As the orders were issued and he was making a charge George sat on his horse out in advance, calmly looking the Indians over, full of suppressed excitement, but also with calculating judgment and strength of purpose in his face. . . . I thought him then one of the finest specimens of a soldier I had ever seen.

Custer to Elizabeth, September 6, 1873, from stockade on the Yellowstone River:

Darling—Thus far safe and well. Three Indian scouts will go from here to Ft. Buford, 150 miles by river, 80 by land, with mail, and to bring mail in return.

I am here with 6 companies of Cavalry, having separated from the main command six days ago at Mussel Shell River and marched direct to this point, about 150 miles. The Railroad engineers came with me. The nucleus of the long train began giving out, forage almost exhausted, horses only allowed 3 lbs a day—14 the regular allowance. Country unknown, no guides knew anything of the route before us. . . . I addressed an official communcation to Genl. Stanley offering to take the main part of the Cavalry and strike through to the Stockade direct. Glad to be relieved of responsibility Genl. S gave his consent, written. I left "F" & "L" with him as he requested a squadron to be left, and the weakest horses with Yates. In the official order I was authorized to "burn or abandon" all my wagons or other public property, were this necessary to preserve life. What was the result? With "Custer luck" we struck the most favorable country for marching, and brought in every wagon. I am going to send Capt. French with his squadron in charge of 14 wagons loaded with forage for Genl. Stanley's command.

The steamer to ferry us over is expected about the same time as the main command. Then, as soon as over and our wagons loaded, we start the march to Ft. Abraham Lincoln, about 12 days from this point.

I am ordered to despatch four companies to Fort Rice, and to command the six at Lincoln. The new quarters are to be completed by the time we arrive. This settles our location for the winter, and is satisfactory to me.

I presume you wish you were here, to give the Lt. Colonel a little advice about the designation of these companies. For this reason I am glad you are not here. I should not wish it thought that I had been influenced in the matter. Several officers have applied for long leaves, but, Lincoln being first choice with all, it would hardly be fair to give preference to officers who had spent the winter in the States, over those who had remained with their troops. It is a difficult and undesirable task to make these decisions. Personally I should like to have every one of them with me at Lincoln. My relations, personal, official, are extremely agreeable, and I know those going to Rice will be disappointed.

I shall not relax my caution on the homeward march. I do not forget that on last year's expedition two officers were killed. . . . I shall hunt less, and always with an escort. . . .

I have killed a fine buck elk, larger than Dandy, and weighing, dressed, 300 lbs. with the handsomest antlers I ever saw, and such a beautiful coat. At camp a perfect reception awaited him. Some of the gentlemen of the scientific corps, particularly zoologist and taxidermist have kindly made me their pupil. In return I have given them many specimens. I will present my collection to the Audubon Club. . . . The elk would be too large for a private collection. . . .

Mary continues to get along admirably. Capt. French says he has lived better than ever before, the last four or five months. Nearly every day she prepares something special for Lt. Braden. Think of him, with his shattered thigh, having to travel over a rough country some 300 miles. He is not carried in an ambulance, but on a long stretcher on wheels, pushed and pulled by men on foot. It requires a full company every day to transport him. He is now with the main command. When the command divided I had the band take a position where he would pass, and when his escort approached they struck up Garryowen. . . . He acknowledged the compliment as well as he could. . . .

Custer to Elizabeth, September 10, 1873, from stockade on east bank of the Yellowstone River:

We are just crossing the men by the "Josephine" which arrived yesterday. My headquarters and about half the troops are over; the rest will be over by sundown.

Finding there would be a delay of several days your Bo proposed to Genl. Stanley who arrived with the main command yesterday, that the main portion of the Cavalry cross at once and set out with the engineers in order that these may complete their work between this point and Ft. Lincoln, thus saving delay . . . and, this being done, your Bo with 6 troops of the 7th and two companies of Infantry, with the engineers, will set out at once.

The reports brought by Major Dickey, Sutler at Lincoln, and others who came by the "Josephine" present our new quarters in the most favorable light. Major D says no quarters being built in the Department compare with those being prepared for the 6 troops—and the Commanding Officer's house is described as "elegant."

The railroad will be completed 27 miles on this side of the river to some valuable coal-fields. This will keep railroad communication with the east open all winter.

It is assumed that I will go on a long leave, but I will not. You remember this was offered—and refused by me—after the Washita campaign.

The "Josephine" will leave for Lincoln to-morrow, arriving there in 4 or 5 days, so that you should get this in about a week. Tell Ann I have not forgotten her request for a pair of antlers for a hall-rack, and have a handsome pair for her, large enough to hold half the hats in Monroe. Tom says don't tell Miss B about the buffalo head he is bringing her. I have one for you.

If Dell comes with you I will arrange for her railroad passes. Let no false ideas about wardrobe stand in her way. If you want two girls with you why not bring Mollie T? Our social life will depend on the life within the garrison—and how much this is enhanced by girls attractive and intelligent of fine character. It is a shame such should be kept in the dark in nice, pleasant, but dull old Monroe.

Custer to Elizabeth, September, 1873, from camp in Montana Territory:

. . . . Great was our joy at receiving a large mail. You call me to account for not telling you I miss you. You know the old adage, "You can lead a horse to water, but cannot make him drink." Now I, for the nonce, am the obstinate steed. Famished, athirst, but, as Falstaff says, "On compulsion Never." You argue, "Yes, I know you know I love you without being told so every minute, but I am a woman, and want to hear it constantly." When we get to Lincoln I will tell you. . . . The scout has just called for the mail. Love to Father, Mother, Ann, Nev. Hasten the time when I can see my Rosebud.

Custer to Elizabeth, September 11, 1873, from camp in Montana Territory:

Good morning, my Sunbeam. . . . I must tell you what comfort I have enjoyed through this long march from the tender foresight of one who so fitted up her Bo that no one in the expedition could vie with him in such appointments. Was ever man so blessed as I?

How the boys do tease and devil Mr Calhoun! When a poor old horse died they accused him of starving the animal that a mare might have double portion of oats. When the theatrical ventures of Buffalo Bill and Texas Jack were discussed Tom said it might be a good speculation to back our own "Antelope Jim"—on which Mr C rushed out indignantly from the tent.

Mr Eccleston told me he has been writing the railroad authorities to whom the success of the expedition is due: "When others saw obstacles and turned back you went forward and led the way. As an act of justice I want our people to know this." My girl never saw people more enthusiastic over her Bo than these railroad representatives.

I must end this letter. We will have all winter to talk over particulars in our bran spankin' new home. Tell Emma Reed she must make as much advance in her studies as possible, also her music, as she is to spend next winter with us.

General Stanley in a fit of intoxication caused Custer's arrest for taking over as second in command when he himself was unable to do so. Mrs. Custer learned of this.

Custer to Elizabeth, September, 1873, from camp in Montana Territory:

In regard to my arrest and its attendant circumstances, I am sorry it ever reached your ears, as I hoped—not for myself, but for those who were the cause of it, that the matter should end here.

Suffice to say that I was placed in arrest for acting in strict conscientious discharge of what I knew to be my duty—a duty laid down expressly in Army regulations.

Never was I more confident of the rectitude of my course, and of the official propriety of my position . . . so confident that I was content to wait, knowing that I would be vindicated in the end.

Within forty-eight hours Genl. Stanley came to me, and apologized in the most ample manner, acknowledging that he had been in the wrong, hoping I would forget it, and promising to turn over a new leaf.

Twice did he repeat "I humbly beg your pardon, sir. I not only make this apology to you, but, if you desire it, will gladly do so in the presence of all your officers."

With his subsequent faithful observance of his promise to begin anew in his intercourse with me, I banished the affair from my mind. Nor do I cherish any but the kindliest sentiments towards him, for Genl. Stanley, when not possessed by the fiend of intemperance, is one of the kindest, most agreeable and considerate officers I ever served under.

Looking back I regard it, as do other officers, as a necessity that an issue was forced on us, and that by my opposing, instead of yielding, the interests of the service were advanced.

On one occasion whiskey was destroyed by friends of Genl. Stanley as the only means of getting him sober. This was publicly avowed. It had no connection with my difficulty with him, although the papers have coupled the two incidents together.

Since my arrest complete harmony exists between Genl. Stanley and myself. He frequently drops in at my headquarters, and adopts every suggestion I make.

At last Custer writes his wife (still in Monroe) from his new home.

Custer to Elizabeth, September 23, 1873, from Fort Abraham Lincoln, Dakota Territory:

My Darling Bunkey—Where are the numerous bridges you have been crossing as regards delays in our return? Well, here we are, not only as good as new, but heartier, healthier, more robust than ever. I have not drawn a sickly breath since we started, and if ever a lot of hardy, athletic young fellows were assembled in one group it is found in the officers of the 7th Cav.

I left Genl. Stanley with the balance of the expedition on the other side of the Yellowstone, enjoying a spree.

We made the march here in eight days, taking everybody by surprise.

The expedition is considered over, and I am relieved from further duty with it.

You will be delighted that Mrs Carlin will be here, Genl. Carlin preferring to remain, even though under your Bo, to being in command at Fort Wadsworth.

The Infantry portion of the garrison is nearly ¾ of a mile from the Cavalry.

Before we arrived Genl. Carlin sent an orderly to meet me with an invitation to go straight to his house. I declined, as I had to see to the disposition of the camp. Then came another orderly with the message, "Supper's on the table and waiting." So, knowing Mrs. Carlin, as an Army lady, would understand, I went, in my buckskin suit. . . . They invited me to make my home with them, but while grateful I declined, as it would be too far from camp. They want you to stay with them till we are settled in the new quarters.

Custer to Elizabeth, September 28, 1873, from Fort Abraham Lincoln, Dakota Territory:

I open my letter of the 10th of this month, and sent by the "Josephine." She should have have reached here by the 16th, but ran aground and was delayed ten days, finally having had to unload and abandon on the bank sixty tons of government stores.

I have received a telegram from Genl. Sherman, "Welcome Home."

Genl. Shannon called with some other Yankton gentlemen who are up here, holding court. I cannot tell you how many elegant and well-appearing people have come across the river to pay their respects to your Bo, and congratulate him on his successful work.

Mrs Carlin is surprised at the number of people who come here from the east.

The "Galaxy" people are stirring me up for more articles. They will get Davis of Harper's "Weekly" to illustrate them. A telegram from the N.Y. *Times* asks me to write up the trip. I enclose a slip from the "Army and Navy Journal" with a complimentary reference to your Bo. [The new post stood on the west side of the Missouri in what is now North Dakota, with Bismarck across the river.]

Genl. Dandy, Quartermaster, is so obliging, making every change we need. There was no wardrobe in our room; I have induced him to put in two large ones, otherwise I knew I should find the hooks at my disposal dwindle until I found my garments hanging over the back of a broken chair.

I am comfortably housed in my large railroad tent, given me by Genl. Rosser. . . . I am sending you for deposit between four and five hundred dollars, saved from my summer's pay.

During the expedition I killed and brought into camp 41 antelopes, 4 buffalo, 4 elk, 7 deer, &c. &c. also captured alive a wild-cat and a porcupine, amiable creatures I still possess.

Genl. Stanley and his staff with the 22nd Infantry are just going on board the steamer about a mile above here, preparatory to leaving for Fort Sully. And your dear Bo has just sent the band to serenade Genl. Stanley as the boat is about to leave.

I suppose you think I am of a very forgiving disposition. Well, perhaps I am. I often think of the beautiful expression uttered by President Lincoln—"With malice toward none; with charity toward all . . ." and I hope this may ever be mine to say.

Your devoted boy
Autie

17: Fort Abraham Lincoln

CUSTER AND his 7th Cavalry Regiment had left Fort Rice in the summer of 1873 to guard the advance of the Northern Pacific Railroad to the Yellowstone. The return march took them to the new Fort Abraham Lincoln. When the railroad reached Bismarck, territorial capital of Dakota, General Sheridan had caused this stronghold to be built on the west shore of the Missouri and strongly garrisoned by cavalry capable of pursuing the hostile Indians, who resented with increasing fervor the white man's advance.

To Custer was granted a leave when he reached Fort Abraham Lincoln, but he did not take nearly the time allotted. He knew active service might soon be required of him, and he was zealous to foster the esprit de corps that had grown in the 7th Cavalry during their long march. He contented himself with a brief visit to Monroe to see his parents and to fetch his wife and sister to their winter home.

There was danger. The fort was a military island surrounded by hostiles, it was remote, it was bitterly cold in winter. But it was regarded as home, and at last Elizabeth could again be with her husband. The journey was long and arduous, even up to the final phase, the crossing of the Missouri. When the swirling current was frozen hard enough, they walked; when the ice gave out, they rowed. They were cordially welcomed, to the tune of the regimental band. It was November, 1873.

Elizabeth to Mrs. Sabin, March, 1874, from Fort Abraham Lincoln, Dakota Territory:
Dear Aunt Eliza—When we came out here in November I made a resolution to write regularly to my friends. I thought I should have so much time. But I am more occupied than ever. We have company constantly. After the four months spent in Michigan when Sister Mag-

gie and I got here, we found this one of the largest Posts in the country, and our houses, substantial, wooden, all ready for us, all ready for housekeeping, made so by our husbands. But, woman-like, I found a thousand things to do, a thousand-and-one alterations to be made.

You see, Aunt Eliza, it cost the Government so much to send our Regiment up here from the South, we think this will be our home for years to come. So I thought I would take pains to give it a permanent character. So for three months I kept painters and carpenters at work steadily. We curtained about twenty windows, carpeted almost all the floors, and we had made a beautiful billiard-room with rented billiard-table. . . . This being the house of the Commanding officer it is much the largest, more entertaining being done here than in all the others put together.

Well, about a month since, in February, the house was burned to the ground. . . .

A committee of officers was ordered to convene at the fort to investigate the origin of the fire. The findings were that the blaze had started in the attic, an explosion having been caused by a carelessly built, ill-pointed chimney in close proximity to the coal-oiled paper linings of the walls. Also, it was cautioned, the other chimneys offered a like hazard.

In the opinion of the Board [the report read] it was a loss that might have occurred at any time, and possibly sooner if the continued caution exercised by General Custer had not been observed. And the Board has the honor to report that evidence shows that he had exercised every precaution, and that he is in no way responsible for the fire and the consequent damages.

The young lady visitor spending the winter with them was Miss Agnes Bates, later Mrs. Wellington, of Monroe.

Elizabeth in her diary:
The ladies of the Post kindly outfitted Agnes whose entire wardrobe was destroyed except for one party dress. I am busy renewing mine. We now have new quarters, next to brother Tom's, with archways cut in the dividing wall, so that we have the use of his as well as our own. Eliza's successor is as good a servant as Eliza was, so that I

have no housekeeping cares, for she manages the other servants and attends even to the refreshments we offer on Friday nights for our reception hops. It is no light social care to be wife of the Commanding Officer of so large a Post, and I find my time fully taken up with entertaining. And just now I have to make needle and sewing machine fly, for I can get no one here to help me.

As soon as the railroad opens again no doubt we shall have a great deal of company from the States, for this is not only a new country, but so interesting, tourists are seeking it. We are delighted with the climate. Autie hunts a great deal. He is very busy with his official duties, for there are over eight hundred troops here, also many civilians are partly under his control as they live on the Reservation.

Among the Custer papers is a testimonial signed by the leading citizens of Bismarck to the moderation, promptness, and efficiency with which Custer put down an outbreak of gangsterism that for a time threatened the existence of that community. His sense of civic responsibility, which lay behind his use of military force in this instance, had been demonstrated also in Texas after the Civil War, when public and private encomiums likewise testified to his prudent and effective measures in preserving order.

Where the present-day state of South Dakota impinges on Wyoming, the Black Hills rise. They cover an area of about six thousand square miles and their highest elevation is two thousand feet. The Black Hills held considerable mystery in Custer's time, since they had not been scientifically explored. There were rumors among the Indians of great hidden wealth. Well timbered, well watered, the Hills were known to contain valuable mineral deposits, and adventurous settlers were being drawn to the region by the lure of gold.

The Sioux Indians regarded the Black Hills as their inalienable birthright, and in their view this was recognized in existing treaties with the whites. But while on the one side the Indian chief was the brain and the executive of his obligations, on the other, United States commissions drew up the treaties and a separate agency, the army, carried them out. This was one of the reasons for the frequent misunderstandings that arose over treaties. The military often were ministers of punishment for Indian behavior although they were at the same time unfamiliar with the covenants drawn up with tribal chiefs.

Woeful misunderstandings were general respecting the Black Hills region. In any case, it was decided to be a matter of military necessity that there be some armed surveillance there for the protection of the railroad and other advancing American interests. General Sheridan advised setting up a series of army posts in the regions not actually embraced in Rosser's Railroad Engineer survey. Preliminary reconnaissance was required, and Sheridan directed Custer to take his 7th Cavalry on such an expedition.

Sheridan to Custer, May 17, 1874, from Chicago:
Dear Custer—I sent instructions a day or two ago for the expedition to the Black Hills. I limited the number of teamsters to 80. I did not say when to start, but presume you cannot do so before June 15, or perhaps later.

Would it not be well to send out a scout for 25 to 100 miles to ascertain something of the country in a direct course to Bear Butte? The portion of the Belle Fourche River most interesting to explorers is toward head waters.

I will send Fred Grant and Sandy [Forsyth] with you. Write me if I can do anything more for you. I will write again.

Sheridan

Sheridan to Custer, June 2, 1874, from Chicago:
Dear Custer—Forsyth and Grant will leave here next Sunday or Monday to join you. I have given permission to Whitelaw Reid to send a correspondent subject to such conditions as you may impose on him, expences to be reimbursed to the Government. I have requested Prof. Marsh of Yale to go, but he cannot and will send an assistant, Mr Grinnell, in his stead.

These are the only burdens I will place on you, because I know how pinched you are in transportation.

Sheridan

Sheridan to Major Forsyth, June 10, 1874, from Chicago:
Major—The reconnaissance to be made by Lt. -Col. George A Custer to the Black Hills will leave Ft. Abraham Lincoln on or about the 25th

June, and I wish you to proceed to that point and to report in person to Genl. Custer, to accompany it.

It is especially desirable that these Headquarters should have a complete and detailed description of the country passed over, so it is desired that you will devote yourself to the collection of such information, and embody it in a daily diary.

This should embrace distance travelled, character of the soil, wood, water and grass, and topography of surface and geological formation, as well as incidents which may occur.

On the return of the command to Ft. Abraham Lincoln you will proceed without delay to report in person to these Headquarters.

Vy Respectfully
P. H. Sheridan

Custer to Elizabeth, July 2, 1874, from camp near Harney's Peak, Dakota Territory:

My Darling Sunbeam—Your dear Bo can't send a very long letter, tho with volumes to say. After dinner, when we reach camp, I usually take an escort to search out a few miles of road for the following day, and when I return I am ready to hasten to my comfortable—but Oh so lonely—bed.

Reveille regularly at a quarter to three, so that it behooves one to go to bed early. Reynolds leaves in the morning for Ft. Laramie, so to-day is letter-day. I am going to explore in that direction some 25 or 30 miles. I take five companies with me. Two companies left this morning in another direction. Both absent three days.

Breakfast at four. In the saddle at five. First I have my official despatch to attend to, then a letter to the "World."

The expedition has surpassed most sanguine expectations. We have discovered a rich and beautiful country. We have had no Indian fights. We have found gold and probably other valuable metals. All are well. I did not expect my wagon-train . . . and here it has followed me all the way.

Autie

Custer to Elizabeth, July 15, 1874, from Prospect Valley, Dakota Territory, twelve miles from the Montana line, 103° 46' west, 45° 29' north:

My Darling—We are making a day's halt at this beautiful spot, to rest our animals and give the men a chance to wash their clothes.

Everything satisfactory; officers, men, civilians, in best of health and spirits. Country thus far traversed beautiful and interesting.

We are now encamped on a tributary of the Little Missouri. I directed Col. Ludlow to name this Prospect Valley.

Three days ago we reached the cave referred to by the Indian called "Goose." It is about 400 feet long, its walls covered with drawings of animals, and prints of hands and feet. I cannot account for the drawings of ships.

No signs of Indians till day before yesterday, when about 20 were seen near the column by Capt. McDougall. They scampered off when they found they were observed. Yesterday we came where they had slept. Capt. Moylan who was in the rear on official duty saw about 25 following our trail. Signal smokes were sent up around us during the afternoon. Also Indians were seen watching us after we reached camp, but there were no hostile demonstrations. Some of the guides think the signals were to let their village know where we are, and to keep out of our way.

We expect to reach the base of the Black Hills in about 3 days. Yesterday Prof. Winchel and Mr. Grinnell discovered the remains of an animal of an extinct race, larger than the largest size elephant. I am gradually forming my menagerie; Rattlesnake, jack rabbits, eagle, owl.

Everybody pronounces this the best trip ever had. Col. Ludlow is a great favorite.

I have not written on the march, my hand and arm are tired, and all the time in camp I give to rest and sleep.

I am more than ever convinced of the influence a commanding officer exercises for good or ill. There has not been a single card party, not a single drunken officer, since we left Ft. Lincoln. But I know that did I play cards and invite the officers to join there would be playing every night.

Sandy is delighted with the 7th, says there is no Cavalry regiment to compare with it except perhaps the 4th. Our mess is a gratifying success; Johnson is not only an excellent cook, but also is very prompt. We breakfast at four. Every day I invite some officer to dine with us. Yesterday we had Mr Wallace. I ride at the head of the cavalry and *keep inside the lines all the time* . . . a great deprivation not to go outside to hunt. I feel like a young lady fond of dancing who is only allowed to sit and look on at some elegant party. But I try to render strict obedience to the orders of my Commanding Officer, issued when I started. In looking for a road I sometimes get a mile or so ahead of the Command, but have seventy or eighty men with me and Indian scouts in front.

I have killed 6 antelopes. Bos has killed one. In his report to Genl. Sheridan Sandy Forsyth speaks of Lt. Wallace as a young officer of great promise.

A fifth of our time has expired. A third will have passed when this reaches you. I am not certain if it will be possible to send back scouts hereafter. This will be carried by two Rees: Bull Bear and Skunk's Head. Bloody knife is doing splendidly.

There is not a man on the sick report, which the Medical Officer thinks unprecedented.

We move into the Valley of the Little Missouri to-morrow, and will probably follow the stream to the Black Hills.

Keep press notices of the expedition; they will be interesting, and of value, later.

You may judge how fertile the country when I tell you that our mules, also our beef herd, are in better condition than when we started.

Capt. Smith is the best Quartermaster I ever had in the field, and wins praise from all sides for his management of the trains.

Bos and Mr Calhoun are writing to Monroe, so I will write only to my girl.

We have travelled over 227 miles from Ft. Lincoln. 170 in a straight line, our bearing South, 62° West.

The Indians have a new name for me, but I will not commit it to paper.

Yr devoted Boy
Autie

Custer to Elizabeth, August 3, 1874, from the south fork of the Cheyenne River, Dakota Territory:

We marched 45 miles to-day in a Southerly direction from Harney's Peak. We are now encamped on the South Fork of the Cheyenne River, about 90 miles from Laramie. All are seated round the camp fire, writing home.

Custer to Elizabeth, August 15, 1874, from Bear Butte Creek, Dakota Territory:

My darling Sunbeam—I cannot tell you how hard and earnestly I have worked to make this expedition a success. I have been, not only Commanding Officer, but also guide, among other things. We have been in and through the Black Hills—and I have the proud satisfaction of knowing that our explorations have exceeded the most sanguine expectations, but that my superior officers will be pleased with the extent and thoroughness of these.

The camp Photographer has a complete stereopticon view of the Black Hills Country.

I have reached the hunter's highest round of fame. . . . I have killed my Grizzly.

We reach Lincoln about the 31st. There has been no drunkenness, no card-playing on this trip.

Your devoted Boy
Autie

A young 1st lieutenant accompanied the Black Hills expedition. Later, as General E. S. Godfrey, he was one of the best-informed authorities on Custer's last stand, in which he participated, though not in Custer's own detachment, none of whom survived the fighting. After the expedition returned, he wrote Custer a letter of appreciation.

Lieutenant E. S. Godfrey to Custer, September, 1874, from Fort Rice, Dakota Territory:

Dear General—I am disappointed not to have seen you to thank you in person for your kindness to me during the summer. I gained, through you, not only a practical knowledge of routine camp work, but also a knowledge of the country we passed through, and of a more genial society. I endeavored to show my appreciation by my entire willingness to do everything in my power to help make the expedition a success. I thank you for these benefits and for your unfailing kindness and consideration.

Letters on the march were carried to Fort Abraham Lincoln by the "Black Hills Express"—Indian scouts on ponies.

"At last," wrote Elizabeth, "the long wagon-train appeared . . . the instruments were battered, tarnished, but the Band returned to the strains of Garry Owen, the regimental tune. . . ."

Husband and wife were together again, and there are therefore no letters to record their doings. But from her own writings and Custer's, one learns of garrison life in Dakota Territory; of sporadic

Indian troubles such as the capture of Rain-in-the-Face by Captain Yates and Colonel Tom Custer and the escape of that brave to join the hostile Sioux in the last fatal encounter; of the fight for life and health in a climate where fruits and vegetables were unknown. As for Custer himself, while concerned preeminently with his military duties he turned to study and professional writing. His hope that the summer following their expedition should be spent in the Black Hills was not to be realized. Fort Abraham Lincoln was to be Custer's military home to the end.

The Custer story, as found in the letters, finds them after a long exile sojourning briefly in the States. At the close of 1875 they took a long-planned holiday in New York. Tom Custer was with them for a time then returned to Dakota.

Elizabeth to Tom Custer, December, 1875, from New York:
The holidays have been rainy, gloomy. I did not have half the fun I had anticipated, looking in at the shop windows. On Christmas morning I went to church, but came back, weary, disgruntled. Episcopal, but the extreme of ritual—intoned prayers, chanting and processions. Autie always finds the day somewhat of a bore and is glad when it is over. I missed the home atmosphere, all of you. And then the presents. Last year you all gave me presents because the year before I had had the fun. Autie gave me a black silk dress which I am making, as I have no one to help me. I gave him a solid silver table-spoon and tea-spoon, Maggie gave him fork and dessert spoon to match.

Autie has so many invitations, I have to drive him to accept them, as it is a privilege to meet such interesting people. One night he dined at three places. One night a dinner at the Lotos Club, another at the Stoughtons to meet Sir Rose Price, a noted sportsman . . . and, greatest treat—a lunch in Mr Bierstadt's studio, where we met the Earl Sunracen. Then we dined twice with the Barretts.

Mr Barrett is making an enormous success in "Julius Caesar" at Booth's Theatre. The scenery is perfect, and, added to this, the stage is full of people . . . three hundred, sometimes. And at the close there is a grand tableau. Brutus is burned on a funeral pile. Why, Tom, it makes you want to scream to see the funeral pile blazing, and Mr Brutus rising above it.

We have seen Oakey Hall in his own play, sensational and lawyer-like, but imagine an old man of fifty starting as an actor.

Autie and I have a room opposite the Hotel Brunswick (where we have our meals and get our mail). We live cheaper than at Fort Lincoln.

We are waiting to hear about the journey back. The stage-man said he would put our sleigh on with his horses, and get us through in four days. I enjoy New York, but I miss you all. . . . You, dear Tom, Maggie and Jim.

Don't spend more money than you can help at the Sutler's, drinking and card-playing. Don't be influenced by the badness round you. Oh, Tom, if I find that the boy I have loved, and prayed over, has gone down-hill. . . . Oh, if only you had a companionable wife!

Libbie

Custer to Tom Custer, January, 1876, from New York:
Libbie has been with me nearly a month. We have delightful rooms, at the back, quiet, opposite the Brunswick. We are having the most delightful and interesting time possible. I have the entree to all the theatres in the city. At a reception at the Historical Society its President and a group of other young men over eighty flocked around Libbie. . . . At a reception of the Palette Club the President took her in to supper. Dancing afterwards. The ladies danced in hats. Bird-pictures by Tait were exhibited.

The latest in regard to Army reduction is that the House will not interfere with the Cavalry, but will cut off 5 regiments of Infantry, and one of Artillery.

I have no idea of obtaining my promotion this spring or summer. On the contrary. I expect to be in the field, in the summer, with the 7th, and think there will be lively work before us. I think the 7th Cavalry may have its greatest campaign ahead.

For years I have been approached to deliver a series of lectures, throughout the country, but circumstances have prevented. Since my arrival in New York Mr Pond, manager of the Redpath Agency (in Boston), has come to see me and offer a contract. When I tell you the terms you will open your eyes. Five nights a week for from four to five months, I to receive $200. a night. My expences would amount to about $10. a day. They urged me to commence this spring, but I declined, needing more time for preparation.

These lectures were never given, since 1876 was the last year of Custer's life.

About this time an effort had been made—without result—to discredit Custer with the War Department. Throughout his short, spectacular career he constantly aroused envy among other men and was frequently the object of schemes to embarrass him. In this case it was intimated that an official act of his, the transferring of an officer at that officer's request, had been actuated by personal animosity. Custer, when apprized of this, placed the facts of the case before The Adjutant General of the army in a letter which concluded with this statement:

I stand upon the official course I deemed proper to pursue, as right, not only at the time, but justified by subsequent events, so that what I now write will not be considered an apology for doing my duty.

In disproof of the report that I was unfriendly to Lt. Weston, I offer the following: when a few years ago he desired to attend the Artillery School at Fortress Monroe, as my letters to the War Department will show, I exerted all the influence I could command to gratify his wish.

Again, when he sought promotion to one of the Staff Corps, I wrote the Hon. Secretary of War, commending him in highest terms, as one of the most promising and deserving young officers of the Army.

. . . . What I did at the time, in view of information available and attendant circumstances, I believe was right, proper, and just to all concerned. I was actuated by no personal motives, but solely for the good of the Service.

And while I regret no part of my action I do regret that my Commanding Officers should not have considered the facts and circumstances which caused me, as Regimental Commander, to recommend the transfer.

To Custer, Lieutenant Weston had already written: "I am very fortunate in getting the appointment—which is solely due to your kind interest in my behalf."

Custer further asked that a court of inquiry be instructed to look into his action, since this had been so misconstrued. But General Terry, to whom this request was referred, replied such action would not be necessary, Custer's explanation having fully vindicated him in his, Terry's, opinion.

The New Year holiday was over. Even had the Custers been able to procure an official extension, their means did not permit their staying further. The problem was how to get back to Dakota. The railroad from St. Paul to Bismarck had been completed, but trains would not be running until April. And this was February. Mindful of Custer's services, however, the railroad officials put on a special train for him. Again he, with Elizabeth, was landed in deep snow. And again they were rescued alive through heroic efforts.

They had scarcely arrived at Fort Abraham Lincoln and thawed out before Custer received an official dispatch summoning him to Washington. This meant he would be forced to retrace a long, weary journey, 250 miles of which presented great hazards. His presence in the capital was desired so that the building of new forts on the Yellowstone River might be discussed. Custer felt that this could well wait till the summer campaign was over. General Terry had informed Custer that the Dakota column was to be under Custer, since Terry had wisely decided that his own experience against the Indians in the field was inferior to that of the leader of the 7th Cavalry. The 7th was to be an essential element of the expeditionary force and would have to be at once primed for action. But Custer had no choice. He must go to Washington. Terry, who realized the importance of Custer's work, entered a plea, but to no avail.

Washington being adamant, Custer set out, refusing to let his wife accompany him. So long as he was heading for Washington, he thought he might be able to turn the visit to profit for the Service outside the States. The whites, Custer knew, had not always been above reproach in the matter of observing treaties with the Indians. Of complicity in these matters, Sheridan and his generals must be acquitted wholly. It was their function to act under orders from above. But now, as Custer had reason to believe, the Indian was being used as a pretext for white man to cheat white man. It resolved itself into a question of Government civilian employees on the reservations and the military posts. For such positions, only men of absolute integrity should have been appointed. Custer and other Generals in the field knew only too well that shady characters were permitted to hold down important places. While in

Washington, he thought, he might be able to effect some reform.

In the meantime, Washington did not realize it was playing into the hands of an enemy. It was giving the enemy, the Red Man, time to plan, organize, play the white man's game—which the white man was neglecting.

The Indians used primitive weapons, bow and arrow. But they could use firearms, the white man's invention, with equal skill. The Government, careless of its own, allowed the military to make the best of outmoded guns. The Indians could make their bargains with the agencies and obtain the newest and the best. In the art of warfare, the white man had certain techniques. The Indians would study these and meet them accordingly. This all took brains, and while myopic Washington could not see "outside the States," the Indians were planning under the leadership of one of their race of no ordinary caliber. He was the son of Jumping Bull, and his name was Sitting Bull.

18: Politics

Custer to Elizabeth, April 1, 1876, from Washington:
My Darling—This will be unsatisfactory as a letter, so pressed am I for time and sleep. I spent Sunday in Monroe, arrived here Tuesday night, went before the Committee on Wednesday . . . am also summoned before Banning's Committee on Military Affairs, and next week am to testify concerning Ml.

He—Ml—will be put on the stand to tell all he knows about how the South Carolina Legislature passed a Bill by which he drew $20,000. from the State Treasury. He has been released from duty at the Centennial, in consequence of an article in the N.Y. "Herald" in which he tried to make his fall easier through having been made to suffer by being caught in bad company. He went to Sherman and tried to have the order set aside, but Sherman said "Ml, in your ascending scale you chose to ignore me. Now in your descending scale I do not propose to interfere." This Sherman told me himself when I breakfasted with him yesterday.

I spoke a good word for H. and Sherman promised to find a place for him.

I have been treated with utmost consideration and courtesy by all with whom I have come in contact. The privilege of the Floor has been granted to me during my stay.

Genl. Banning gave me a copy of his Bill asking for my suggestions. Among others I thought that sergeants should not be the only noncommissioned officers to receive $40. a month.

I called on the President but he was abed with a cold. I left my card.

Genl. Sherman and I called on Mr Alphonso Taft, the Secretary of War. He received me with great cordiality. Genl. Sherman complimented me to him highly. He (Mr Taft) promptly returned my call. Genl. Banning told me later that both Genl. Sherman and Mr Taft had spoken of me in highest terms.

Genl. Ingalls wants me to stay at his house. He is in great anxiety. Not that he has done anything, but he has been threatened. He wants me to ascertain what the Clymer Committee can have against him. I have promised to enquire and hope soon to relieve him of an unmerited burden.

I sometimes walk from here to the Capitol with Mr Clymer, an elegant and highly cultivated gentleman. A widower of six years he speaks of his lost wife beautifully.

Passing through the Congressional Conservatories—a rare treat—he asked me if there were not some young lady in Washington to whom I would like to send a bouquet. After mentally reviewing my lady acquaintances here I selected Miss Nellie H who is staying with her mother and sister at the National.

Washington was in a state of ferment. Custer's letters to his wife give some idea of the investigations and exposures that preoccupied Congress and in connection with which Custer was to be summoned as a witness. Custer's personal popularity was enormous, and he would be a star witness in any court or in any inquiry. His uncompromising rectitude would always impel him to tell the truth as he saw it, regardless of whom it hurt, regardless of the consequences to himself. Correspondingly he was a shining mark of detraction. The obloquy heaped on him by a hostile press seems out of all proportion to his military rank or political importance. The papers went to such lengths to discredit him that one might well wonder at their fear of what one plain-speaking individual had it in his power to reveal.

Some understanding of this personal factor gives at least a clue to the reason for the premature end of a career of military achievement that was brilliant, authentic, valid, spectacular. True, that end did come because Custer was overwhelmed by numbers on the Montana hills that summer. His tremendous personal courage, his genius for organization and meticulous preparation were not equal to the overriding odds. Whether or not the charge generally leveled against him today is true—that his resentment at not being put at the head of the expedition against the Sioux aroused in him a desire to defeat them singlehanded and so regain his prestige—it is certain that his chances of success against the Indians were considerably weakened by personal animosities in Washington. This will come out later in connection with traderships on the reservations. In the meantime, he writes Elizabeth about his stay in the capital.

Custer to Elizabeth, April, 1876, from Washington:
Rufus has gone completely to pieces. Grant has not stood up for him as he should have done.

The Army Ring is completely broken up. The late members of it are glad to hide their heads.

I am over-run with applications for help. Applicants come before I am up. Three to-day before breakfast. One, a widow, whose son was killed in '67 on the Arkansas. She wanted a position in the Treasury. I went with her at once, and procured her an appointment. She left, showering blessings on you and me.

Custer to Elizabeth, April 8, 1876, from Washington:
My Precious Darling—I cannot tell you how overwhelmed I am with engagements, but I cannot let my little girl's birthday pass without a word from her dear Bo. I have only telegraphed you once on account of the cost. My pass is not good over Western Union lines, and I cannot use Government rates.

I have been recipient of kindest attentions from all papers except a few radical. I am surprised if a morning passes without abuse of myself. But leading papers throughout the country commend my courage.

Ml seeks to gain sympathy by intimating that I am persecuting him. I have neither suggested nor instigated any steps against him. The order relieving him of his Centennial duties may be revoked. All the carpet-baggers are seeking to induce the President to do this.

One of the Majors of the now-broken-up Army Ring has been ordered to California. E is relieved as O.M. in San Francisco on a charge of defalcation—$60,000.—found by forcing his desk.

I am ordered to return via Detroit, to visit the House of Correction, in order to examine the Bismarck convicts and take testimony in the matter. The order came from the Atty-General's office to the War Department.

Senator Bayard gave a dinner in my honor. His daughter, a lovely young lady of nineteen acted as hostess. Though there were Senators and Members present and some Southern generals I was placed on her right. On her left was Mr Clymer. Among others was the "Duke of

Sonora"—a title bestowed by Maximilian, and General Bradley Johnson who had fought me at Trevillian and elsewhere. Senator Bayard's
noble bearing entitles him to be called Chevalier. He is spoken of for
the Presidency, but I fear he is too remote from political bias for that.

I am invited to dine there again, informally.

I have been invited to a dinner at the Manhattan Club—*the* Democratic Club of New York, with the promise that it would be non-politi-
cal with no speeches. Congressman Robert Roosevelt signed the invitation. My duties here prevent my accepting.

Senator Gordon of Georgia has been extremely courteous to me.

Sunset Cox made an elaborate speech on the Indian question, citing
the Battle of the Washita, Garryowen, &c. After it he came up to me
where I was standing and said, "Well, Custer, I guess I have taken your
scalp." To which I replied, "Wait till I get you on the Plains! Then I
will turn you over to those gentle friends of yours."

This recalls a letter written by Mrs. Custer, at Fort Hays, to her
aunt at a time when Eastern papers were denouncing severity toward the Indians.

Elizabeth to Mrs. Sabin, from Fort Hays, Kansas:
My dear Aunt Eliza—Surely you do not believe the current rumors
that Autie and others are cruel in their treatment of the Indians? Autie
and others only do what they are ordered to do. And if those who
criticize these orders could only see for themselves. . . . As we see.
. . . A woman rescued from Indian captivity who has suffered degrada-
tion unspeakable; the brutalities of the men, the venom of the squaws.
. . . People in civilized conditions cannot imagine it. But we who have
seen it know.

Death would be merciful in comparison.

Any military detail escorting white women on the plains in
those days had one standing order: the leader was to shoot the
women in his charge sooner than let them fall captive to the Indians.
The women fully concurred in this order. They considered themselves better dead than so degraded they would be unfit, if by remote chance they were rescued, for life again among their own
people. If an officer's hand should falter, the woman herself would
unhesitatingly have aimed a gun at her own heart.

Custer to Elizabeth, April 10, 1876, from Washington:

I have been instrumental in getting four companies up from the South. They are ordered to proceed at once to Fort Lincoln. Col. Ledyard Brown also is instructed to report for duty with the expedition.

I dined recently with Genl. Banning . . . a Buckeye dinner, all eight being born in Ohio. Genl. Banning has prepared a long speech on the issue shortly to come up: transferring the Indian Bureau to the War Department. He took many arguments in favor of it from my book, but asked me not to mention this till afterwards, lest others also might use it.

When some papers from Fort Lincoln arrive I do not expect to be detained more than forty-eight hours. . . . Though Mr Clymer of the Belknap Investigating Committee says I may be wanted. Still I think this improbable.

I have just been lunching in the House restaurant with Mr Clymer, and am now writing at the table in the famous Committee room where the Belknap exposures were brought to light. . . .

This brings us to the crux of the whole matter: the Belknap case. In a tangled skein one cord leads direct from Washington to the battle of the Little Big Horn. Custer has been using his enforced sojourn in Washington to strengthen his command for the summer campaign, his main preoccupation. But he is advised that he *might* be summoned to testify—to what? To the matter of agencies and traderships on the posts and reservations.

The sutler was a civilian, a licensed merchant on a post. He was the general storekeeper and purveyor from whom officers could supply their households, and enlisted men could obtain such small comforts as they might be able to add to their government-issue rations.

By long-established practice applications for the position of sutler had been passed on by a committee of three senior officers at the post concerned. Their choice was subject to the approval of the commanding officer. This system worked well, in that it fixed responsibility and allowed latitude of choice. On General Stanley's expedition, to take one instance, it was shown that the trader, Mr. Baliran, was well liked by the officers.

In June, 1870, this system was canceled by an enactment that placed all traderships in the hands of the Secretary of War. This tended to create a monopoly, the more so when a further enactment forbade officers to purchase supplies elsewhere, even though they might be near centers where they could have bought in the open market to their advantage.

The inevitable happened. Traderships became not matters of appointment but objects of purchase in Washington. The trader, having paid high for his monopoly, had to get back the purchase price from the customer. One trader complained to Custer he was allowed to retain only one third of his profits, the remaining two thirds going to some one "higher up."

Corruption at the source was bound to affect conditions at the outposts, where conditions were hard enough at best. But to obtain concrete evidence of an outrage of whose existence everyone was aware, and to discover a spokesman with courage to denounce it were no light matters. The Indians were profiting from all this. The War Department was selling the traderships to men who sold weapons—the newest and best—to the hostiles, weapons that would be turned against the servicemen legitimately employed by the War Department.

Custer's letter to Elizabeth of April 10, 1876, had referred to the Belknap case. General Belknap had displayed fine soldierly qualities in the Civil War, and President Grant, who greatly esteemed him, appointed him Secretary of War. A widower, Belknap had married a woman of predatory instincts and with a keen eye for business. It was established that she used her husband's position to sell traderships. She died, and her sister not long after succeeded her as wife to the general and as manager of the tradership business. It was never clearly a matter of record whether Belknap knew of this shabby business and, knowing of it, connived at it to his profit, or whether he was innocently ignorant of it or had shut his eyes to it. In any case it was going on in his department and in his immediate family, and whether he was ignorant or not, the whole affair spoke very poorly of his integrity and competence.

And here was Custer in Washington, ready to testify on the matter of traderships. In his possession was a letter from an Indian agent whom Custer had good reason to believe was honest as well as accurately informed.

John E. Smith to Custer, February, 1874:

Genl. G. A. Custer—I have the honor to enclose statement of number of lodges of Sioux at different agencies north of the Platte and west of the Missouri Rivers, as nearly correct as can be arrived at. It will not correspond with the Agency reports on the subject. I have no way of ascertaining how many Indians draw rations at Ft. Peck, but will say that it is composed of many renegade Minnesota Sioux with Sitting Bull's band. The Agency is a myth, created through Dunfer & Peck's influence for the purpose of supplying hostiles remote from Military Posts.

Ft. Thompson has quite a number of Minnesota Sioux drawing annuities with the Lower Brules at the mouth of the White River. The Yankton Agency, 15 miles from Ft. Randall, generally supplies 150 young men for incursions, though it is claimed they are peaceable. But I know better. They are quiet at home. Fully one-third of the Sioux (Northern) do not visit the White River Agencies at any time, nor those on the Missouri except Ft. Peck where they procure arms and ammunition in great quantities.

Spotted Tail and Red Cloud have no influence over the fighting Sioux, Sitting Bull being acknowledged chief of their nation.

Arapahoes and Cheyennes are cut-off bands and have no connection with those on Arkansas country. Turkey-Leg governs the Cheyennes north.

Fully three-fourths of all the Indians enumerated are Hostiles, the bitter ones being old men.

You can count on each lodge furnishing one and one-half warriors, able-bodied, two-thirds well armed. Fully half the young men have pistols—one or more, exclusive of other arms. About half the warriors remaining at Agencies have repeating rifles, Winchesters & all others have breech-loaders. I have known Indians at White River Agency to have 3,000 rounds of ammunition for a single gun.

Records of traders' "insolence of office" were not lacking. In one case an officer's servant, driving an officer's wagon, had been turned back by a trader with a warning that it was forbidden to procure supplies anywhere but on the reservation and that he would use his "influence" were his monopoly infringed on.

Custer himself had been a victim of this protected insolence. When General Belknap, as Secretary of War, was making a round of inspection of the army posts, he visited Fort Abraham Lincoln. The trader added of his own initiative a case of champagne to the Custer household order. He pointed out this must have been over-looked and would certainly be needed in view of the importance of the expected dinner guest. Custer had no intention of suffering the merchant to dictate what he should serve at his own table and whom he should invite. He promptly sent back the unwanted case, saying it had not been overlooked and was not required. Custer showed Belknap every formal courtesy but did not offer him private hos-pitality, having scant respect for the secretary's character.

The tradership scandal was too flagrant to be hushed up. Belknap had been impeached for "malfeasance in office" before the House of Representatives. But, warned privately beforehand, he cut the ground from under his accusers' feet by resigning before action could be taken against him. Grant accepted his resignation, the sole service he could render his friend. While Grant himself was never accused of profiting illicitly, he believed with dogged soldier loyalty in Belknap, even as he had believed in Babcock, the central figure in the Whiskey Ring exposure, confusing military prowess with moral impeccability.

We return to Custer's letter to his wife written at Mr. Clymer's table in the committee room "where the Belknap exposures were brought to light":

In this room Genl. Belknap was brought to face the Committee and hear the astounding evidences of his guilt. I heard Mr Blackburn (of the Committee) describe the scene, also the interview with Mrs Belknap who besought Mr Blackburn—he has known her from her girlhood—to save her husband.

She tried to convey the impression that Belknap was not only inno-cent but ignorant of the matter and that exposure would destroy her marital relations with him, Belknap being so pure and upright he would discard her. "To think that I have been the means of hurling that man from his high pedestal, and that, when exposure comes, I shall sink so low in the social scale, no one will recognize me." But enough of this painful subject.

Despite Belknap's resignation the case was being briefed for presentation to the Senate.

Meanwhile, General Terry was hampered in his preparations for the Sioux campaign, Custer was chafing at what seemed to him a needless detention at the capital, and the Sioux Indians were organizing.

Custer to Elizabeth, April, 1876, from Washington:
My Darling Sunbeam—I calculate on one week more here. Should I be detained longer I should give up all thought of a summer campaign and send for my Bunkey. Many would rejoice at a summer in the east. . . . But not I.

Tell Bloody Knife I have not forgotten my promise and am bringing him a silver medal with his name engraved on it. [Bloody Knife was a young Arickaree scout in great favor with Custer.]

One reason I desire to leave is that I am called on to do more than I desire. The men in the Army Ring who of late had influence now are glad to hide their heads. I care not to abuse what influence I have.

The Cincinnati "Enquirer" and St. Louis "Republican" and other papers of that stamp commend me in highest degree. The two radical papers, controlled by the Belknap, Babcock, Shepard clique, vie with one another in abusing me. I do not let this disturb me.

I had a long talk on the floor of the House with Ex-Governor Foot of Tennessee who gave me admirable advice. The Belknap clique leave no stone unturned to injure me. Mr Gobright, Agent for the Associated Press, said they had given him a lot of defamatory stuff about me that he had refused to use.

I paid General Belknap every official courtesy on his tour of inspection, of course. It was Tom, not I, who drove him through the precincts.

Tony Forsyth has come out with a letter in favor of Belknap in which he manages to introduce your name. Though intended to contradict, in reality it confirms my testimony.

Yesterday they tried to prove by Seif that I had drawn drafts on James Gordon Bennett (of the N Y "Herald") for several hundred dollars, but I turned the tables on them. I sent for Ralph Meeker and got Mr Clymer to put him on the stand. And he testified that the drafts were drawn for his benefit (by me at Mr Bennett's request) and that I had never received a dollar from them.

I know you are anxious, but I believe I have done nothing rashly. And all honest straightforward men commend my course.

The weather is lovely, spring-like. Lawn-mowers are cutting the long grass, flowers plentiful. I have been luxuriating in lettuce, tomatoes, radishes.

I have dined three times at Senator Bayard's the last time *en famille*.

I have been accused of testifying against Reynolds. I have not said one word against him.

Crook's expedition is generally regarded as a failure.

I telegraphed Tom in regard to papers he is sending me on Government account. Every despatch is overhauled by the Paymaster-General. All unimportant matters will be charged to Tom. My pay has been stopped several times on this account.

Custer to Elizabeth, April 17, 1876, from Washington:

My Darling Sunbeam—If you only knew how truly a sunbeam you are to me! What do you think your Bo did yesterday? Declined all invitations. Shut himself up and wrote, wrote, wrote, finishing a "Galaxy" article which is now in the mail.

To-day I appear before the Military Committee, to-morrow the Board of Managers of the Belknap Impeachment trial, and hope to conclude my errand here. I have urged both Committees to release me. The Belknap Impeachment Committee have not yet decided whether they want me further, but I feel confident they will not, for, as I have informed them, nearly all my evidence is hearsay.

The Radical papers continue to serve me up regularly. Neither has said one word against Belknap.

Last night a reception at Judge Loring's. A number of people sought introduction to your Bo.

Barrett will be here next week with "Julius Caesar," but I shall not be here to see it.

As for ladies' dresses, in the language of the papers, "such sights as I have not seen since I was married," while, as for scandal. . . .

The lines you sent me are lovely. I showed them to a lady at this hotel. She said, "Your sweetheart sent them. Never your wife." I told her "Both are one." "What? How long have you been married?" "Twelve years." "And haven't got over that?" "No. And never shall!"

I have received many compliments on my literary work. General Sherman said, "Custer, you write so well, people think your wife does it, and you don't get the credit." I said, "Well, General, then I ought to get the credit for my selection of a wife."

Your devoted Autie.

His clearance papers, as he thought, in order, Custer started on his return journey. His first stopping place was New York.

Custer to Elizabeth, April 23, 1876, from New York:
Precious Sunbeam—After breakfasting in this beautiful restaurant I started to scribble a few lines to you but was over-run with callers. Mr Sheldon drove in to see me. He is enthusiastic over my "Galaxy" articles, and insists on my sending them in regularly. He will secure an English publication when the book appears here.

Hardly had he gone when I heard Larry Jerome's jolly voice: "General Custer—in there? Writing? Oh. d-mn him. Let him collect his thoughts some other time!"

I saw "Brass" at the Park Theatre, and visited the author George Fawcett who also takes the leading part. I did *not* call on the ladies in the cast.

Afterwards I was invited by a friend to the Argyll Rooms. Saturday night being gala night morals are neither taught there nor encouraged.

Then, a famous oyster restaurant where I saw the demi-monde in profusion. At 1 A.M. went to bed, if a consciousness of virtue establishes a claim to happiness, then—happy.

I have been shopping—a nice shawl for Ann Reed. Left Annie Yates' list of baby-clothes with her mother. Obtained a promise that Annie's brother Dick shall be appointed (by Whitelaw Reid) correspondent with the Expedition.

I get more requests for articles from periodicals and dailies than ten writers could satisfy. I am over-run with invitations. Dined with the Barretts at the Fifth Avenue Hotel. They insist on our spending the fall with them at Cohasset. The New York Hotel where they were staying has been seized by the sheriff. Much sympathy is felt for Mr Risley in his trouble.

Have called on General Horace Porter, have seen hosts of friends. Hope to start in a few days now.

I received a letter from a gentleman at Kirkwall, in the Orkneys, of the name of Custer. He traces our relationship to the family, back to 1647, and gives the several changes the name has undergone,—Cursetter,

Cursider, Cusiter, Custer, all belonging to the same parish. He writes "I have been established in business here for 33 years. I have noted your name, conspicuous as a General, and occasionally as author, and from descriptions of you I am convinced we are of the same stock. . . ."

In Philadelphia, while visiting the Centennial buildings, I discovered another branch of the Custer tree—I enclose their business card—I sent in my name and was most cordially received. The family resemblance is marked. Tell Maggie that when I come into my Orkney inheritance. . . .

Not only build and height and coloring, but they are *nice*, like me. I hope to leave to-morrow night.

Custer to Elizabeth, April 25, 1876, from New York:
My Precious Sunbeam—I cannot express my amazement, disappointment. I am stopped, ordered to return to Washington. I had obtained my formal discharge. . . . I had had several interviews with the Managers of the Belknap Board, representing the urgency of my duties at Fort Lincoln, and had finally received a reluctant consent to my departure.

Yesterday a Deputy Sergeant-at-Arms of the Senate brought me a summons to appear before that body on Wednesday next, as witness in the Impeachment of the Ex-Secretary of War.

I at once telegraphed General Terry who expressed regret. . . . I am in hopes my detention will be but brief. . . . I intend to ask General Sherman to take up the matter with the Board of managers of the Impeachment and represent to them the urgency of my returning to my command. . . .

Custer to Elizabeth, April 28, 1876, from Washington:
My Dear—Arrived yesterday. Reported to the Board . . . had a seat on floor in Senate assigned me. . . . Proceedings most interesting.

I send you a newspaper describing my dress as I sat with Representatives Clymer, Blackburn & Robbins of the Impeachment Board. It states that "Genl. Custer wore black coat and light pants"— Both Tom's— and "white vest." Tell Tom I intend to charge him for having his clothes advertised.

Genl. McDonald is here as a witness. He complimented me very highly on my article on Bull Run.

Weather summer-like. Flowers everywhere.

There is a strong probability—I certainly hope well-founded—that the Senate will decide, Genl. Belknap having resigned, the case lies outside its jurisdiction.

I saw Genl. Sherman to-day at the War Depmt, also had an interview with the Sec'y of War who will write the Impeachment Board, requesting my release to return to my duties.

Do not be anxious. I seek to follow a moderate and prudent course, avoiding prominence. Nevertheless, everything I do, however simple and unimportant, is noticed and commented on. This only makes me more careful.

Custer to Elizabeth, April 29, 1876, from Washington:
I spent last evening at Mrs Christiancy's, playing whist. She had invited several friends to meet me. She is devoted to the Judge, is demonstrative in showing it. She has a beautiful form. I begged for her photograph to show to you. The Judge said "I am not ashamed of her."

Oh, I have so much to tell you. I know that I cannot be excessively vain or my head would be turned, and that it is not likely to be.

I hope before this reaches you to telegraph "I'm a-comin'!"

I hear often by telegraph from General Terry. I believe a mutual good-feeling subsists between us. He is anxious for me to return.

Genl. Ingalls gave the antlers Cook sent him to Holliday, and Prof. Baird pronounces them the largest in existence. The Smithsonian shipped five car-loads of Indian curiosities to the Centennial. Prof. Baird has asked me to procure them a complete lodge.

The decision of the Senate was the expected one: the case lay outside its jurisdiction. Some sentences of Custer's testimony may be quoted here, since they bore unfavorably on his fortunes.

Asked whether he had ever brought abuses of the traders' position to the Secretary of War, he replied, "No, sir. Because I was as suspicious of the Secretary as of the trader."

To the question whether prevailing restrictions achieved their purpose in preventing Indians from obtaining unlimited quantities of rum, he said, "I would hate to testify to the character of any post trader in these times. . . . The profits of the trader left the morals of the Indians far behind."

Why had not he or other officers reported abuses? "An order," he said, "issued by the Secretary of War, March 15, 1873, decrees that 'No officer, active or retired, shall suggest action by Members

of Congress. All petitions must go through the General of the Army
to the War Department. Any officer visiting the National Capital
while Congress is in session, must register with the Adjutant-General and state the duration and purpose of his visit.' "

To the question what effect the alleged corruption had on the
Army, Custer answered, "I think it one of the highest commenda-
tions that could be bestowed on the Service, that it has not been
completely demoralized by the unworthiness at the head."

Once again, believing his clearance papers in order, Custer left
Washington, this time to go direct to his post. He intended stopping at St. Paul for a conference with General Terry respecting the
summer campaign. To his shocked amazement, at Chicago he was
met by an officer with orders from General Sheridan, in accordance with telegraphed instructions from Washington, to detain
him on the grounds he had left the national capital without paying
his obligatory calls on General Sherman and the President.

He set about refuting these charges on the spot. He had called
on Sherman and was informed the general was away but would return shortly. He called again and was told the general's return was
uncertain. Accordingly, as Sherman had been instrumental in obtaining his release from committee duties, Custer supposed that by
leaving his card he was fulfilling his routine duty.

He had called on the President, and General Ingalls, the Quartermaster, in conference with Grant, had mentioned to Grant he had
seen Custer waiting in the anteroom. The President told Ingalls he
did not propose to receive Custer, and he sent out word to that
effect. Custer further had written the President asking the favor of
a personal interview and had received no reply.

Sheridan, as friendly as ever, permitted Custer to set forth this
defense by telegraph and proceed to St. Paul. Here he was greeted
with the worst blow of all. General Terry had received instructions that Custer was not to accompany the forthcoming expedition. It was to be led by Terry in person.

Terry caused this order to be modified. Custer was to be allowed
to lead his own regiment, which would be an adjunct to the expedition under the command of Terry.

Such were the fruits of Custer's visit to Washington. He had freely added to the accumulating evidence against the integrity of President Grant's official family, and Grant had retaliated as one angered soldier against another soldier by depriving Custer of his command. It was a sharp rap at one of Custer's most important assets—prestige. It hampered the expedition by placing it in the hands of Terry, who, though a thorough soldier, had not the practical experience with Indians that was Custer's.

19: The March

IN THE lovely month of May, 1876, the 7th Cavalry Regiment set out from the camp where it had been established a few weeks before, some distance down the valley from Fort Abraham Lincoln. It was about to join General Terry's expedition against the Sioux. Cavalry, artillery, infantry, laden ponies, pack mules, scouts, civilian employees, wagons, an interminable train it seemed. There were seventeen hundred animals and twelve hundred men, and the column stretched two miles. G. A. Custer, Lieutenant Colonel U. S. Army, Brevet Major General Volunteers, commanded. Beside him rode his wife.

In the mists of the early morning the troops beheld a mirage: they saw themselves riding in the sky. The realistic sun, gaining the ascendancy, ended the illusion.

The approach of the cavalry was greeted with a wailing chant in the Indian quarters within the precincts of the garrison, the fatalistic, foreboding note of primitive people when the braves go off to war. Someone at the fort had called out a disparaging remark about the Sioux, and Colonel Tom Custer had called back, with a wave of his hand toward the column, "A single company of that can lick the whole Sioux nation!" and the strains of "Garryowen" filled the air.

It was May 17, and the column made its first night's camp a few miles from the post. This enabled the paymaster to make his disbursements that the men might clear accounts with the sutler. The Government had withheld pay for several months, lest during a winter of inaction it might be spent unwisely. Should the men fall on the battlefield, any change left over in their pockets would, of course, be so much booty for the enemy. Obviously the Government counted on their coming back alive.

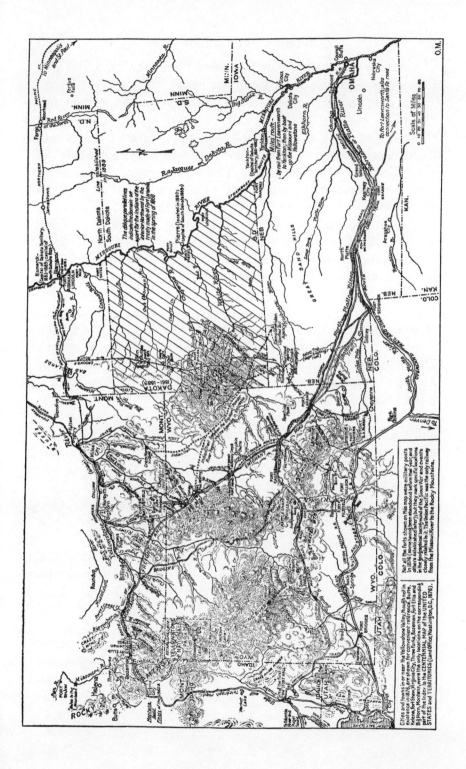

Next morning the paymaster escorted Elizabeth Custer and Mrs. Calhoun back to the post to wait for news.

The column traveled light, for the march would be arduous, nor could they obtain subsistence from the barren country they would traverse. For renewals they relied on a supply steamer that would meet them at designated spots. We have seen how vital a part the *Key West* played in the Stanley Yellowstone expedition of 1873. The river heroines this time were to be the *Far West* and the *Josephine*. Government chartered, ably captained, these river craft formed an important part of the service. J. M. Hanson, in his *Conquest of the Missouri: Being the Story of the Life and Exploits of Captain Grant Marsh*, has described the navigators' struggles with an elemental force as desperate as those which engaged the soldiery on land.

Starting from Yankton when the ice broke up, the *Far West* plowed upstream to Bismarck and Fort Abraham Lincoln. The column having left, supplies were adjusted accordingly. Elizabeth Custer and other women came down to the landing. Captain Grant Marsh, commander of the vessel, invited them to luncheon. Afterward Elizabeth and the wife of Lieutenant A. E. Smith besought him to take them on as passengers to the camp where they would find their husbands. They had received their husbands' permission to join them. But the captain would not assume the responsibility. There were no suitable accommodations, he said, and the boat was not safe from attacks from the river banks. The women would not have minded this threat, but they realized as "camp followers" they might be in the way, and they went back to their quarters to wait and hope and pray.

Rivers were to be an important factor in the expedition. The *Far West* was to steam up the Missouri, the largest tributary in the world, to its own largest tributary, the Yellowstone. At the confluence of the two rivers stood Fort Buford, the steamer's first stopping place. From there it would push up the Yellowstone and stop at the mouths of the rivers that poured into it, and at each place the column would meet it: the Powder, the Tongue, the Rosebud, the Big Horn. The last named is the Yellowstone's largest affluent, and it in turn is fed by the Little Big Horn.

The whole object of the expedition was to meet and vanquish the Sioux. The special provocation was the Sioux attacks on the Crows, a peaceful tribe settled on the Crow reservation, through which the Yellowstone cut its way. The main difficulty expected by the troops was to find the enemy. There was then no means of swift communication, and fleet runners and horsemen were relied upon. The expedition would have to find a way through unexplored regions, always in peril from the race that considered itself sole proprietor of the land and was ready to defend its ownership. The Indians defended and attacked with their own weapons and cunning, as well as with the weapons and cunning of the white man, whose guns they were purchasing freely and using with deadly effect. They were learning also the cerebral processes of the whites.

It was the task of the expedition to find a route that could be traversed by cavalry, infantry, artillery, and wagons from one camp site to another, where they would pause to graze their animals and rest, and so on to a river mouth where they would meet the supply steamer. Rivers were crooked in that region, but at least the waterway was clear, and limited by its banks. It was not so easy for the land forces to find the paths of least resistance from the mouth of one tributary to another.

At the various halting places, letters, borne by scouts across country or by supply craft, would be exchanged with waiting wives. Eager as were the women for news, the husbands were no less desirous, on their weary march, for word from home—chitchat, talk of the daily routine, assurances of a stable domesticity.

Elizabeth to Custer, May, 1876, from Fort Abraham Lincoln, Dakota Territory:

The servants are doing very well . . . we are raising chickens. We have forty-three. So many cats about the garrison keep the rats away. The weather is very hot, but the nights are cool. The lights about hills and valleys are exquisite. The river now is too high for sandbars to be seen.

About a hundred men with John Stevenson in command have gone to the Black Hills. Nearly twenty-five teams have passed by.

Carter has returned and is chief trumpeter. He really sounds the calls beautifully. But his long-drawn notes make me heartsick. I do not wish to be reminded of the Cavalry.

Trumpets for cavalry, bugles for infantry. It is to be remembered that Custer always rode with his trumpeter beside him.

The post was often attacked by hostiles, but the raids were sporadic and not organized. The women became habituated to hearing the long-roll that called out the infantry when the outer pickets were attacked, and after a time they came to feel little anxiety.

Custer to Elizabeth, June 9, 1876: from camp about twenty miles from the mouth of the Powder River, Montana Territory:
We are now in a country hitherto unvisited by white men. Reynolds had been guiding the column, but had lost his way and General Terry did not know what to do about finding a road. . . . I told him I thought I could guide the column. And when, after a hard day's work we arrived here the General was delighted and came to congratulate me.

Boston Custer to his mother, June 8, 1876, from camp about twenty miles from the mouth of the Powder River, Montana Territory:
My Own Darling Mother—The mail will not leave for a day or two, but I concluded I would be in time. We are the first white men to visit the river at this place. We and the command marched here yesterday, travelling thirty-two miles. We found some country you would call rather rough. Armstrong, Tom, Col. Cook, myself, and Lt. Edgerly with his detail, with a few Indian guides, rode ahead of the column, to find a road. We travelled faster than the column, reaching here about half-past three, so far ahead of the train that the General [Custer] sent back word to General Terry that we would not go on, but would remain here all night. So one white man and some Indian scouts went to kill game as we were without anything to eat. But the train managed to get in about half past nine or ten o'clock. I know I did not get my dinner until ten.

It is intended to leave to-morrow on a scouting-tour with six days' rations. The Infantry will escort the wagons from the Yellowstone to where this river empties into it, and the boat that left Fort Lincoln with supplies will be there. Autie Reed is going along I think. He stands the trip remarkably well.

I do hope this campaign will be a success, and if Armstrong could have his way I think it would be, but unfortunately there are men along whose campaign experience is very limited, but, having an exalted opinion of themselves, feel that their advice would be valuable in the field. But I think before this trip is over they will be thoroughly understood by those who should know.

I am feeling first-rate and joke Tom and Mr Cook about their being tired by the ride to camp, for, as soon as a fire was built, they both stretched out for a sleep. I eat much better here than I did at Lincoln. I have only been late at a meal once, when I was not wakened. I don't think we will get back to Lincoln before September, but that will suit me. I would rather be here than in garrison.

Good-bye. I will take good care of myself, and not fail to write to you and Maggie—to you, even if Maggie goes without, for you come first with me in everything, and Maggie next. Sometimes she cuffs my ears, saying that if you did so when I was a child it is perfectly right for her to do so now. And sometimes she starts in on Tom and Jim and I with some good thumps of her fists, and warns us if she repeats it we shall all be sorry.

In print is a careful analysis of Custer's last stand by W. S. Edgerly, Brigadier General, U. S. Army, retired. Here is a letter by that officer, who as a 2nd lieutenant participated in the battle with Benteen's detachment. On this exploratory ride he was in charge of Custer's escort. The letter was not written until over a year after Custer's death, but the facts were jotted down at the time.

Edgerly to Elizabeth, October 10, 1877, from Camp Sulphur Creek, Dakota Territory:
My dear Mrs. Custer—I am sending you some personal recollections of your husband which I wrote at the time after the battle, and which I didn't have the heart to send you until I waited so long I was ashamed to write. . . . I know that to a stranger they will seem unimportant, but I also know that nothing about him will seem unimportant to you.

I mean also to write to Mrs Calhoun and to Mrs Yates—to the former about what I remember of Tom, and Bos, and Autie Reed.

I was in command of General Custer's escort on that ride, several miles ahead of the main command all the time, as the General was guiding the column.

When we first came in sight of the water I exclaimed "There it is." And he answered, "Yes. You and I are probably the first white men to see Powder River at this point of its course."

We still had to travel three or four miles to reach the river—some of the way through the roughest country I have ever known.

When finally we did get to the water the General gave me particular instructions in regard to posting pickets, &c. remarking, "This is just such a place, and the circumstances are almost identically the same as when we had that fight [Washita] in '73." Then he and Tom pointed out similarities in the lay of the land.

We then built some fire, took off boots and neckties, and went to sleep, the General, Tom, Cook, Bos and myself.

About two hours later General Terry came up and exclaimed "Nobody but General Custer could have brought us through such a country."

Next day Col. Weir and I dined with the General. Col. Weir asked him about a "Galaxy" article he had just completed, if he wrote from memory. He said, "No, from notes I brought along."

He ate nothing but bread and syrup for his dinner.

Apparent discrepancies in time may be reconciled by the fact that cavalry in the advance was always ahead of wagons in the rear. General Terry arrived well ahead of the wagons for which Boston had to wait before getting his dinner.

We break off the Edgerly letter to follow the march of the Custer command as it moved from a site on the Powder River to this waterway's point of juncture with the Yellowstone.

Custer to Elizabeth, June 11, 1876, from the mouth of the Powder River, Montana Territory:
. . . . This morning we left camp, I again acting as guide. General Terry had been in great anxiety for the wagons. He had ridden to the mouth of the Powder and he and those with him had expressed a fear that the wagons would not make it in a month, on account of the intervening Bad Lands. He came to my tent early this morning and asked if I would try to find a road. . . . The men had only rations for one day left. One company had been sent out the day before, but had not re-

turned. Sure enough we found them. We have all arrived here safely and the wagons besides.

This letter would go by the *Far West* to Fort Buford, while the *Josephine*, the alternate supply boat, would bring renewals of supplies to the command. Having been denied passage on the one, Elizabeth regrets now that she did not join her husband by the more commodious *Josephine*.

Elizabeth to Custer, June, 1876, from Fort Abraham Lincoln, Dakota Territory:

. . . . I feel so badly I was not on board the boat, but I might have found myself without employment, which, as you know, is my safety valve, and so conspicuous on the steamer, if you had gone off on a scout.

I cannot but feel the greatest apprehensions for you on this dangerous scout. Oh, Autie, if you return without bad news the worst of the summer will be over.

The papers told last night of a small skirmish between General Crook's Cavalry and the Indians. They called it a *fight*. The Indians were very bold. They don't seem afraid of anything.

The Belknap case is again postponed. Of course that worries me. The Prosecution is going to call you as a witness. Politicians will try to make something out of you for their own selfish ends. But I hear you say "Don't cross bridges till you come to them."

I am perfectly delighted with your "Galaxy" War article, but I wish you had not spoken for McClellan so freely. Still, I don't see how you could have consistently given your opinions on the War without giving him his just due. It finishes Mr Chandler as a friend I fear, and for that I am sorry as he can be a very tenacious enemy . . . and of late has been only a passive friend. I honestly think you would be better off with some policy, with such powerful enemies. A cautious wife is a great bore, isn't she Autie?

You improve every time you write. There is nothing like this McClellan article for smoothness of style. I have this month's "Galaxy" with the Yellowstone article. How fortunate you had left it with Mr Sheldon. I am anxious about the one you sent by the Buford mail. The mail was dropped in the Yellowstone and they must have attempted to dry it before the fire, for all our letters are scorched. Maggie's to Jim had been re-enveloped at Buford.

I think to ride as you do and write is wonderful. Nothing daunts you in your wish to improve. I wish your lines had fallen among literary friends. And yet Autie I wouldn't have you anything but a soldier.

It is the hottest day of the season, yet cold chills are running up and down my back at your description of the Yellowstone fight. I am glad you gave Tom his due. Of course you appreciate his valor as a soldier, yet you do not want to be puffing your own family. Mother will be so pleased for "Tommie." Your mention of him would satisfy the most exacting of mothers.

I cannot but commend your commendation of General Stanley. . . . To ignore injury and praise what is praiseworthy is the highest form of nobility. I could not do it. My soul is too small to forgive.

I know you have a gift for finding roads, but how nice of General Terry to acknowledge your skill and perseverance that way.

Maggie and Em are entertaining Dr X and Mr G in the parlor. I went in, for manners, but was too heavy-hearted to stay. Mr. B called. He told me of Buttons' resignation because Grant treated him unfairly, but it was withheld till after the convention.

The wild-flowers are a revelation, almost the first sweet-scented I have ever known. The house is full of boquets. Em gets presents all the time.

With your bright future and the knowledge that you are positive use to your day and generation, do you not see that your life is precious on that account, and not only because an idolizing wife could not live without you?

. . . . I shall go to bed and dream of my dear Bo.

Libbie

After Custer's column had started on that scout, the skipper of the *Far West* put into a mail sack all letters that had accumulated, then dispatched a sergeant and two privates in a small skiff to convey it to Fort Buford. The men were not acquainted with the wild currents of the Yellowstone, and their small craft immediately capsized. All three were drowned in sight of the steamer's crew. The mail sack was recovered with grappling hooks and its contents dried before being sent on with experienced seamen in a stouter boat.

The letter in which Elizabeth Custer tells of receiving this mail never reached her husband. He had gone beyond reach of letters forevermore. It was returned to her unopened and was so kept by her. After many years it has been opened to include it in the Custer story. So, too, another letter to be quoted later.

On June 11, from camp in the Powder River Valley, Major Reno had set out with six troops and ten days' rations on pack mules to reconnoiter for Indian trails. On the fifteenth and sixteenth the entire command was at the mouth of the Tongue River, to which the *Far West* had proceeded. On the nineteenth, word came from Reno. He had sighted Indian trails pointing to the Little Big Horn River and was about to return to the command. General Terry at once sent orders to remain where he was on the Rosebud, there to await Custer.

Custer to Elizabeth, June, 1876, from camp in the Powder River Valley, Montana Territory:

[Reno's] scouting party has returned. I fear their failure to follow up the trails has imperilled our plans by giving the village an intimation of our presence. Think of the valuable time lost.

I am going to send six Ree scouts to Powder River with mail. From there it will go, by other scouts, to Buford.

The entire command now moved to the Rosebud at its junction with the Yellowstone. On the evening of June 21 a conference was held in the cabin of the *Far West*. Generals Terry, Gibbon, and Custer participated. Plans based on Reno's report were mapped out. The Little Big Horn would be the scene of the decisive blow. Custer was to march on the village there and chase the Sioux as they attempted to escape. They then would find themselves cut off by Gibbon and Terry, who, arriving by another route, would be on hand to finish them. The twenty-sixth was established as the probable date. Custer was to set out on the twenty-second.

Reno's estimate of the number of Sioux whose trail he had discovered was eight hundred. To be on the safe side, preparations were made on the assumption there might be up to fifteen hundred, a figure based on official sources and handed to Terry before the expedition had started out. According to the original plans, Terry's command was to have been joined before this time by General Crook's forces. But Crook had been met by unexpected numbers of Sioux warriors at the headwaters of the Rosebud. Under the energetic warrior chief Crazy Horse the Indians had repulsed Crook, who was forced to retire. Since the region between Crook and Terry, spanning a distance of perhaps forty miles, was infested with well-armed Sioux, Crook was not able to communicate to Terry that he had been defeated or that the forces of Crazy Horse were setting out to join the main body of Sioux. Crook had sent this information to Sheridan, however, and Sheridan dispatched at once to Terry the news that hordes of Sioux, hitherto uncounted, were assembling in the area which Terry was preparing to invade. The dispatch was not received until a week after Terry, Gibbon, and Custer had gone into action; the message was twenty days on the way. Knowing he could not count on Crook, unexplainably absent, Terry was not aware on the other hand of the mass reinforcements in the Sioux camp.

Officers of the 7th Cavalry, learning of the dangerous scout ahead of them on the morrow, spent the night playing poker with infantry and navy in the cabin of the *Far West*. Boston Custer sat apart, penciling a letter to his mother.

Boston Custer to his mother, June 21, 1876, from camp at the junction of the Yellowstone and Rosebud rivers:

My Darling Mother—The mail leaves to-morrow. I have no news to write. I am feeling first-rate. Armstrong takes the whole command, and starts up the Sweet Briar on an Indian trail with the full hope and belief of overhauling them—which I think he probably will, with a little hard riding. They will be much entertained.

I hope to catch one or two Indian ponies with a buffalo robe for Nev, but he must not be disappointed if I don't. Judging by the number of lodges counted by scouts who saw the trail there are something like eight hundred Indians and probably more. But, be the number great or small, I hope I can truthfully say when I get back, that one or more were sent to the happy hunting-grounds.

Now don't give yourself any trouble at all as all will be well. I must write Maggie and Libbie, for if the mail should reach Lincoln without a letter from me there will certainly be trouble in the camp.

Autie Reed is going. He will stand the trip first-rate. He has done nicely and is enjoying it. The officers all like him very much. He will sleep with me. I have a small tent. Tell Ann he is standing the trip nicely and has not been sick a day.

Armstrong, Tom and I pulled down an Indian grave the other day. Autie Reed got the bow with six arrows and a nice pair of mocassins which he intends taking home.

Good-bye my darling Mother. This will probably be the last letter you will get till we reach Lincoln. . . . We leave in the morning with sixteen days' rations with pack mules.

Next morning Elizabeth Custer was writing her husband the second of the two letters he was not to receive.

Elizabeth to Custer, June 22, 1876, from Fort Abraham Lincoln, Dakota Territory:

My own darling—I dreamed of you as I knew I should. Col. P. has sent word by scouts that the Post is to be attacked. I don't feel alarmed, because we have so cool and cautious a commanding officer. He is vigilance itself. I am getting this off by to-morrow's mail to Buford. Oh, Autie how I feel about your going away so long without our hearing. . . . Your safety is ever in my mind. My thoughts, my dreams, my prayers, are all for you. God bless and keep my darling.

Ever your own Libbie.

At the same time Custer was writing what was to be his last word to her.

Custer to Elizabeth, June 22, 1876, from camp at the junction of the Yellowstone and Rosebud rivers, Montana Territory:

My Darling—I have but a few moments to write as we start at twelve, and I have my hands full of preparations for the scout. Do not be anxious about me. You would be surprised how closely I obey your instructions about keeping with the column. I hope to have a good report to send you by the next mail. A success will start us all toward Lincoln.

I send you an extract from Genl. Terry's official order, knowing how keenly you appreciate words of commendation and confidence in your dear Bo: "It is of course impossible to give you any definite instructions in regard to this movement, and, were it not impossible to do so, the Department Commander places too much confidence in your zeal, energy and ability to impose on you precise orders which might hamper your action when nearly in contact with the enemy."

Your devoted boy Autie.

To understand in detail the nature of Custer's mission, it is necessary to quote the entire order.

General Terry's order to Custer:

Camp at Mouth of Rosebud River,
Montana Territory, June 22nd, 1876.

Lieut.-Col. Custer, 7th Cavalry.

Colonel:

The Brigadier-General Commanding directs that, as soon as your regiment can be made ready for the march, you will proceed up the Rosebud in pursuit of the Indians whose trail was discovered by Major Reno a few days since. It is, of course, impossible to give you any definite instructions in regard to this movement, and were it not impossible to do so, the Department Commander places too much confidence in your zeal, energy, and ability to wish to impose upon you precise orders which might hamper your action when nearly in contact with the enemy. He will, however, indicate to you his own views of what your action should be, and he desires that you should conform to them unless you shall see sufficient reason for departing from them. He thinks that you should proceed up the Rosebud until you ascertain definitely the direction in which the trail above spoken of leads. Should it be found (as it appears almost certain that it will be found) to turn towards the Little [Big] Horn, he thinks that you should still proceed southward, perhaps as far as the headwaters of the Tongue, and then turn towards the Little [Big] Horn, feeling constantly, however, to your left, so as to preclude the possibility of the escape of the Indians to the south or southeast by passing around your left flank. The column of Colonel Gibbon is now in motion for the mouth of the Big Horn. As soon as it reaches that point it will cross the Yellowstone and move up at least as far as the forks of the Big and Little [Big] Horns. Of course its future movements must be controlled by circumstances as they arise, but it is hoped that the Indians, if upon the Little [Big] Horn, may be so nearly inclosed by the two columns that their escape will be impossible.

The Department Commander desires that on your way up the Rosebud you should thoroughly examine the upper part of Tulloch's Creek,

and that you should endeavor to send a scout through to Colonel Gibbon's column, with information of the result of your examination.
The lower part of this creek will be examined by a detachment from
Colonel Gibbon's command. The supply steamer will be pushed up the
Big Horn as far as the forks if the river is found to be navigable for
that distance, and the Department Commander, who will accompany
the column of Colonel Gibbon, desires you to report to him there not
later than the expiration of the time for which your troops are rationed,
unless in the meantime you receive further orders.

> Very respectfully,
> Your obedient servant,
> E. W. Smith, *Captain*, 18th Infantry,
> Acting Assistant Adjutant-General.

For the state of things the evening of the twenty-first, we return
to the Edgerly account:

I must go back to the evening before we left the Yellowstone to go
up the Rosebud. I went to Regimental Headquarters and sat down with
Col. Cook. Tom joined us, sitting on a log smoking, till Bos and Autie
Reed got him to go to the river for a bath.

Soon the General [Custer] came out of his tent and I said "General,
won't we step high if we do get those fellows!" He replied, "Won't
we!" adding, "It all depends on you young officers. We can't get Indians
without hard riding and plenty of it!"

Letter from William C. Taylor (one of the command):
The first of our three camping-places on the Rosebud was on June
22nd, the only one on the left, or west side of the river. It was here
the General called his officers together and gave his instructions. Troop
"A" to which I belonged was nearest Headquarters, but a few yards
away as the Valley was narrow at that point. So in the early twilight
I could watch the General as he sat in front of his tent which was close
to a high bluff.

It was a scene of great natural beauty. After the conference some of
the young officers joined in song.

The salients of Custer's instructions were that rations must be
husbanded and trumpet calls must not be sounded except in emer-

gency. Marches would begin at 5:00 A. M. sharp. Watches were synchronized.

We conclude the Edgerly account:

He gave us a long talk that night: "We are now starting on a scout which we all hope will be successful, and I intend to do everything I can to make it both as successful and pleasant as I can for everybody. I am certain that if any regiment in the Service can do what is required of us, we can.

"I will be glad to listen to suggestions from any officer of the command, if made in the proper manner. But I want it distinctly understood that I shall allow no grumbling, and shall exact the strictest compliance with orders from everybody—not only with mine, but with any order given by an officer to his subordinate. I don't want it said of this Regiment as a neighboring Department Commander said of another Cavalry Regiment that "It would be a good one if he could get rid of the old Captains and let the Lieutenants command the Companies."

Col. Benteen here asked who he meant by that remark about grumbling to apply to. The General said, "I want the saddle to go just where it fits."

Col. Benteen then asked if the General ever knew of any criticism or grumbling from him? The General replied, "No, I never have, or on any other on which I have been with you."

After a few remarks from Major Reno the General bade us goodnight.

All this I wrote down at the time. I wish to add that nothing of an unpleasant nature occurred on the trip. Everybody was in excellent spirits, and we all felt that the worst that could happen would be the getting away of the Indians.

20: The Last Stand

AT NOON on the twenty-second Custer was ready to set out. He turned back for a final handclasp with Terry, who had said all he had to say officially and now could only add, "God bless you."

Custer's regiment advanced south along the Rosebud, to his left the Tongue River and to his right the Big Horn. Terry's plan, subject to change at the discretion of Custer in the event of imminent contact with the Indians, was that Custer, if he came upon an Indian trail leading west toward the Little Big Horn River, should cross the trail and continue on southward past the headwaters of the Rosebud and on to the source of the Tongue. The latter river is longer than the Rosebud and roughly parallel; toward the south its course converges toward the Rosebud, passes this river's headwaters and finds its own source about due south of the Rosebud. The march to the Tongue source would bring Custer close to the Little Big Horn River, which converges toward the Rosebud from the west. He would swing his column west to the Little Big Horn then turn northwest along its course.

In the meantime Gibbon's command would have set out in a southerly direction from the mouth of the Big Horn. Between him and Custer, and on the banks of the Little Big Horn, would lie the Sioux village. Gibbon and Custer would crush the Indians between them.

One of Custer's troop commanders, Lieutenant Edward S. Godfrey, later a brigadier general, fought through the subsequent battle as a member of Colonel Benteen's detachment. His diary and the notes he made at the time formed the basis of an extended account written for his brother officers at West Point in 1879. His narrative was revised seven years later as the result of interviews he held with

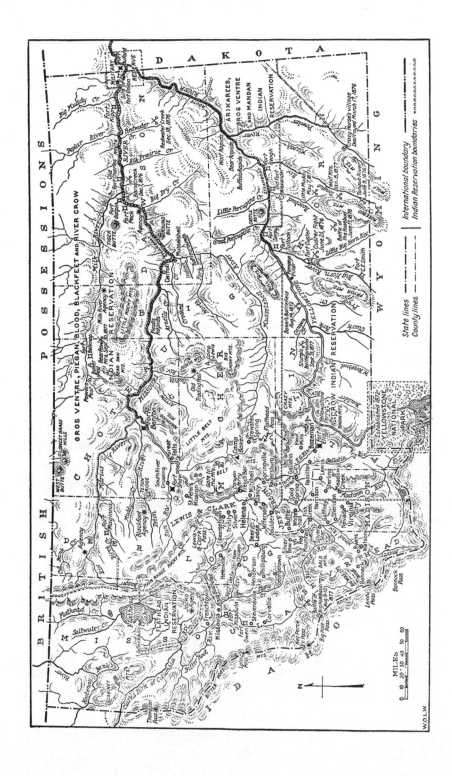

the Sioux chief Gall, who was one of the leaders of the fight against Custer's detachment.

Lieutenant Godfrey's account:

At five o'clock sharp, on the morning of the 23rd, General Custer mounted and started up the Rosebud, followed by two sergeants, one carrying the regimental standard, and the other his personal or head-quarters flag. . . . Eight miles out we came to the first of the Indian camping-places. It certainly indicated a large village and numerous population. There were a great many "wickiups". . . . These we sup-posed at the time were for the dogs, but subsequent events developed the fact that they were temporary shelters of the transients from the agencies. During the day we passed through three of these camping-places and made halts at each one. . . .

June 24th we passed a great many camping-places, all appearing to be of nearly the same strength. One would naturally suppose these were the successive camping-places of the same village, when, in fact, they were the continuous camps of the several bands. . . .

The march during the day was tedious. We made many long halts, so as not to get ahead of the scouts, who seemed to be doing their work thoroughly, giving special attention to the right, toward Tulloch's Creek, the valley of which was in general view from the divide. . . . We had marched about twenty-eight miles. . . .

Lieutenant Hare and myself lay down about 9.30 to take a nap. When comfortably fixed, we heard some one say, "He's over there by that tree." As that described my location pretty well, I called out to know what was wanted, and the reply came: "The General's compliments, and he wants to see all the officers at headquarters immediately". . . . The General said that the trail led over the divide to the Little Big Horn; the march would be taken up at once, as he was anxious to get as near the divide as possible before daylight, where the command would be concealed during the day, and give ample time for the coun-try to be studied, to locate the village, and to make plans for the attack on the 26th. . . . A little after 2 a.m., June 25th, the command was halted to await further tidings from the scouts; we had marched about ten miles. . . .

. . . . General Custer rode bareback to the several troops and gave orders to be ready to march at eight o'clock, and gave information that scouts had discovered the locality of the Indian villages or camps in the valley of the Little Big Horn, about twelve or fifteen miles beyond the divide. . . .

We . . . marched uninterruptedly until 10.30 a.m. when we halted in a ravine and were ordered to preserve quiet, keep concealed, and not do anything that would be likely to reveal our presence to the enemy. We had marched about ten miles. . . .

It was well known to the Indians that the troops were in the field, and a battle was fully expected by them; but the close proximity of our column was not known to them until the morning of the day of the battle. Several young men had left the hostile camp on that morning to go to one of the agencies in Nebraska. They saw the dust made by the column of troops; some of their number returned to the village and gave warning that the troops were coming, so the attack was not a surprise. . . .

The Little Big Horn River . . . is a rapid, tortuous mountain stream from twenty to forty yards wide, with pebbled bottom, but abrupt, soft banks. The water at the ordinary stage is from two to five feet in depth, depending upon the width of the channel. The general direction of its course is northeasterly down to the Little Big Horn battlefields, where it trends northwesterly to its confluence with the Big Horn River. . . . Between the Little Big Horn and the Rosebud are the Little Chetish or Wolf Mountains. . . . It is a rough, broken country of considerable elevation, of high precipitous hills and deep, narrow gulches.

The command had followed the trail up a branch of the Rosebud to within, say, a mile of the summit of these mountains, which form the "divide". . . . The creek that drained the watershed to our right and front is now variously called "Sun-Dance," Benteen's, or Reno's Creek. The trail, very tortuous, and sometimes dangerous, followed down the bed and valley of the south branch of this creek, which at that time was dry for the greater part of its length.

It was from the divide between the Little Big Horn and the Rosebud that the scouts had discovered smoke rising above the village, and the pony herds grazing in the valley of the Little Big Horn, somewhere about twelve or fifteen miles away. It was to their point of view that General Custer had gone while the column was halted in the ravine. It was impossible for him to discover more of the enemy than had already been reported by the scouts. In consequence of the high bluffs which screened the village, it was not possible in following the trail to discover more. Nor was there a point of observation near the trail from which further discoveries could be made until the battle was at hand. . . .

The General . . . had "officers' call" sounded. He . . . said that the scouts had seen several Indians moving along the ridge overlooking the valley through which we had marched, as if observing our movements; he thought the Indians must have seen the dust made by the command. At all events, our presence had been discovered and further concealment was unnecessary; that we would move at once to attack the village; that he had not intended to make the attack until the next morning, the 26th, but our discovery made it imperative to act at once, as delay would allow the village to scatter and escape.

Knowing from experience that Indians were disconcerted by separated attacks, Custer followed the course pursued with success at the battle of the Washita. He split his regiment into three detachments, one each under Colonel Benteen, Major Reno, and himself. Benteen, with three troops totaling about 112 men, was ordered to proceed south and west to a distance of about five miles to intercept any Indians who might try to escape south through the Little Big Horn Valley. Reno, also with three troops, marched on ahead, following the left bank of Reno's Creek to the Little Big Horn. Custer, with 231 officers, men, scouts, and civilians, followed close by, on the right bank of the creek, proposing to make his attack off to the right of Reno.

Captain Francis M. Gibson of the 7th Cavalry and a member of Benteen's detachment penciled his wife a letter a few days later. In it are related the main facts of Colonel Benteen's part in the battle.

Captain Gibson to Mrs. Gibson, July 4, 1876, from camp on the Yellowstone River, Montana Territory:*

. . . Benteen's battalion . . . was sent to the left about five miles to see if the Indians were trying to escape up the valley of the Little Big Horn, after which we were to hurry and rejoin the command as quickly as possible.

We never saw Custer after that. He went on with the balance of the

---

* From *With Custer's Cavalry*, by Katherine Gibson Fougera, Caxton Printers, Ltd., Caldwell, Idaho. Used by special permission of the copyright owners.

command and, when he got in sight of the village, he ordered Reno . . . to cross the Little Big Horn and open the fight, while he kept to the right . . . and would attack the village in another place, and all this time Tom McDougall with B company was about three miles in our rear, bringing up the pack mules. When we got within two miles of the village Benteen got a note from Cooke [of Custer's detachment], which ran thus—"Come on—big village—be quick—bring packs." We didn't wait for the packs as we felt pretty sure no Indians had passed our rear.

When we reached the battleground we found utter confusion. Reno had made a charge and had been repulsed, and driven back, his three troops came riding back to us in disorder, and he at the head, without hat. It was in that charge that McIntosh and Benny Hodgson fell. We then joined our three companies with Reno's, put ourselves in position on a hill, and waited for McDougall to come up with the packs, and just before he reached us the Indians commenced to swarm around us like devils, thousands of them, all with modern rifles, while we were using old carbines, so we were put immediately on the defensive. We heard Custer's command fighting about five miles off in our front, and we tried repeatedly, but in vain, to join him. It was impossible as we could neither abandon our wounded men, nor the packs of the whole command. Reno ordered Weir to take his company and try to make connection with Custer, but he returned saying he could find no sign of Custer's command and that there were enough Indians there to eat up his company a hundred times over. . . .

Along in the afternoon [of the twenty-sixth] our position became so desperate and our force depleted so rapidly . . . that it became absolutely necessary to do something if we hoped to live through the day, so we rallied our men and made three successive dismounted charges on them in all of which the Indians lost heavily, so they thought it wise to give us a little wider berth. The effect produced on the savages encouraged our men greatly, and they commenced to take heart again.

The enemy continued to fight us until about six o'clock that evening, after which we would hear occasional shots, but pretty soon the firing ceased entirely, and about seven o'clock their village and all hands moved out hastily in a southerly direction, going away from us and we began to breathe freely again. In all this time we had heard nothing of Custer so we concluded he had gone with General Terry. . . . Well, that night you may depend upon it we slept well. About eight o'clock on the morning of the twenty seventh we saw clouds of dust arising about five miles in our front. . . . It was Terry with Gibbon's command. That explained the cause of the Indian's sudden departure the night before.

Can you imagine what a relief it was, and how grateful we felt when we saw these troops coming to succor us, absolutely taking us right out of the jaws of death, and such a horrible death. Of course, we inquired immediately for Custer and his five companies, and to our utter surprise and uneasiness we found that they had neither seen nor heard anything of them. H company was sent out over Custer's battle ground for further information and it was not until then that we had any positive knowledge of what had happened to them. There we found them all, over two hundred and fifty souls, every last man of them killed. . . . It was the most horrible sight my eyes ever rested on. A Crow Indian who was with Custer, got a Sioux blanket and made his escape. He is the only living man we know who saw Custer fight. He says the troops fought desperately and killed more Indians than there were soldiers.

The Indians left their village to fight Custer and fought dismounted. . . . In our seven companies they killed and wounded about one hundred and twelve men and two officers.

. . . . On the twenty eighth the command moved to Custer's battle-ground, and buried all the dead. I have been placed in command of C troop and my men buried Custer and Tom and their young schoolboy brother. I had them placed beside each other, and the graves marked.

Custer had parted company with Major Reno a little over half a mile to the east of the Little Big Horn; he turned his detachment north, while Reno continued on and crossed the river at a ford. Reno had been ordered by Custer to "move forward at as rapid a gait as he thought prudent, and charge the village afterward, and the whole outfit would support him." According to Reno's official report, "Lieutenant Cook, adjutant, came to me and said the village was only two miles above, and running away," and then he gave the above order.

Lieutenant Godfrey's account:
Custer had moved off to the right, being separated from Reno by a line of high bluffs and the river. Reno moved forward in column of fours about half a mile, then formed the battalion in line of battle across

the valley with the scouts on the left; after advancing about a mile further he deployed the battalion as skirmishers. . . . The Indians now developed great force, opened a brisk fire, mounted, and made a dash toward the foothills on the left flank where the Ree scouts were. The scouts ignominiously fled. . . . Reno says in his report: "I, however, soon saw that I was being drawn into some trap, as they would certainly fight harder and especially as we were nearing their village which was still standing; besides, I could not see Custer or any other support, and at the same time the very earth seemed to grow Indians. . . . I saw I must defend myself and give up the attack mounted. This I did."

Reno, not seeing the "whole outfit" within supporting distance, did not obey his orders to charge the village, but dismounted his command to fight on foot. The movements of the Indians around the left flank and the flight of the scouts caused the left to fall back until the command was on the defensive in the timber and covered by the bank of the old river bed. . . . While Reno remained there his casualties were few. . . . One man was killed close to where Reno was, and directly afterward Reno gave orders to those near him to "mount and get to the bluffs."

. . . . Reno's command left the bottom by troop organizations in column, but in a straggling formation. . . . The Hostile strength pushed Reno's retreat to the left, so he could not get to the ford where he had entered the valley, but they were fortunate in striking the river at a fordable place; a pony-trail led up a funnel-shaped ravine into the bluffs. Here the command got jammed and lost all semblance of organization.

The command reached the bluffs and soon after were joined by Benteen's detachment, which had hurried up from the south in response to Custer's urgent message dispatched with Trumpeter Martin.

Lieutenant Godfrey's account:
During a long time after the junction of Reno and Benteen we heard firing down the river in the direction of Custer's command. We were satisfied that Custer was fighting the Indians somewhere, and the conviction was expressed that "our command ought to be doing something or Custer would be after Reno with a sharp stick." We heard two distinct volleys which excited some surprise, and, if I mistake not, brought out the remark from some one that "Custer was giving it to them for

all he is worth." I have but little doubt now that these volleys were fired by Custer's orders as *signals of distress* and to indicate where he was. . . .

[According to Chief Gall's later account] when Reno's advance [in his initial contact with the Indians on the west side of the river] was checked, and his left began to fall back, Chief Gall started with some of his warriors to cut off Reno's retreat to the bluffs. On his way he was excitedly hailed by Iron Cedar, one of his warriors, who was on the high point, to hurry to him, that more soldiers were coming. This was the first intimation the Indians had of Custer's column; up to the time of this incident they had supposed that all the troops were in at Reno's attack. . . .

As soon as Gall had personally confirmed Iron Cedar's report he sent word to the warriors battling against Reno, and to the people of the village. The greatest consternation prevailed among the families, and orders were given for them to leave at once. Before they could do so the great body of warriors had left Reno and hastened to attack Custer. This explains why Reno was not pushed when so much confusion at the river crossing gave the Indians every opportunity of annihilating his command.

Not long after the Indians began to show a strong force in Custer's front, Custer turned his column to the left, and advanced in the direction of the village to near a place now marked as a spring, halted at the junction of the ravines just below it, and dismounted two troops, Keogh's and Calhoun's, to fight on foot. These two troops advanced at double-time to a knoll. . . . The other three troops, mounted, followed them a short distance in the rear. . . . When Keogh and Calhoun got to the knoll the other troops marched rapidly to the right; Smith's troops deployed as skirmishers, mounted, and took position on a ridge, which, on Smith's left, ended in Keogh's position . . . and on Smith's right, ended at the hill on which Custer took position with Yates and Tom Custer's troops, now known as Custer's Hill. . . .

The line occupied by Custer's battalion was the first considerable ridge back from the river, the nearest point being about half a mile from it. His front was extended about three-fourths of a mile. The whole village was in full view. A few hundred yards from his line was another but lower ridge, the further slope of which was not commanded by his line. It was here that the Indians under Crazy Horse . . . formed for the charge on Custer's Hill.

All Indians had now left Reno. Gall collected his warriors, and moved up a ravine south of Keogh and Calhoun. As they were turning this flank they discovered the led horses without any other guard than the horse-holders. They opened fire on the horse-holders, and used the usual devices to stampede the horses. . . . Gall's warriors now moved to the foot of the knoll held by Calhoun. A large force dismounted and advanced up the slope far enough to be able to see the soldiers when standing erect, but were protected when squatting or lying down. By jumping up and firing quickly, they exposed themselves only for an instant, but drew the fire of the soldiers, causing a waste of ammunition.

In the meantime Gall was massing his mounted warriors under the protection of the slope. When everything was in readiness, at a signal from Gall, the dismounted warriors rose, fired, and every Indian gave voice to the war whoop; the mounted Indians gave whip to their ponies, and the whole mass rushed upon and crushed Calhoun. The maddened mass of Indians was carried forward by its own momentum over Calhoun and Crittenden down into the depression where Keogh was, with over thirty men, and all was over on that part of the field.

In the meantime the same tactics were being pursued and executed around Custer's Hill. The warriors, under the leadership of Crow King, Crazy Horse, White Bull, Hump, Two Moon, and others, moved up the ravine west of Custer's Hill, and concentrated under the shelter of the ridges on his right flank and back of his position. Gall's bloody work was finished before the annihilation of Custer was accomplished, and his victorious warriors hurried forward to the hot fight then going on, and the frightful massacre was completed.

The *Far West* had pushed up the Big Horn River to the mouth of the Little Big Horn and anchored there. On the twenty-seventh the Crow scout, Curley, who had observed Custer's battle from a safe distance, brought the news of the disaster to Captain Marsh of that vessel. The wounded were carried over the tortuous country on litters. A place in the stern was reserved for Captain Keogh's wounded horse Comanche, the only surviving creature of Custer's detachment. By July 3 the boat was ready to shove off on the perilous 710-mile journey to Bismarck.

The *Far West* nosed downstream, crowding on the steam to the limit of safety. She crashed through amphibious growths, plowed through sand bars, slid along the rapid waters of the Yellowstone between high, precipitous bluffs, veered round the islets of the rushing Missouri. In slightly over two days that truly phenomenal voyage was completed. The *Far West* averaged close to 350 miles a day on uncharted, unfamiliar waters laden with perils, a record not matched on the Missouri to this day.

At Fort Abraham Lincoln the glorious Fourth had just been celebrated. The men had gone in for the usual sports—catching the greased pig, wheelbarrow races, and the rest. In the evening there had been a ball to which the officers' wives were invited. Elizabeth Custer, her worries concerning her husband's dangerous scout leaving her with little relish for gaieties, joined in, having for her partner the young brother of the trader.

As the commanding officer's wife, she was an older sister to her intimates. On the evening of the fifth they gathered in her parlor, distraught for want of news. They tried to sing hymns. One began "Nearer, My God, to Thee" on the piano but was silenced. "Not that one, dear," she was told. They tried other hymns but had no heart for them. They said the "Our Father" and then parted company for the night.

The *Far West* docked an hour or two later, at eleven o'clock, at Bismarck. Three men sprang ashore, followed by others: Captain Smith, representing General Terry; Dr. Porter, surgeon of the command, and Captain Marsh. They hurried to the town, stopping at a camp known as "Bachelors' Quarters" to summon J. M. Carnahan, the telegraph operator, who was staying at the home of Colonel Lounsberry. The colonel was editor of the Bismarck *Tribune* and special correspondent for the New York *Herald*. He would have been with Custer but for his wife's illness.

The group hurried to the station of the Northern Pacific and to a boxcar where the telegraph office was. Dispatch cases were emptied of their contents, and these were sorted in order of precedence.

Early on the morning of the sixth, Fargo heard from Bismarck, "Cut me through to St. Paul."

"What's up?"

"Cut me through and listen. All the Custers are killed."

James Gordon Bennett of the New York *Herald* wired for particulars. He got them. Lounsberry pieced together a coherent narrative from the notes made by Mark Kellogg, who had accompanied the scout in his stead and whose notes up to the onset had been found in a pouch by his side where he fell. Captain Smith, acting for General Terry, prepared a concise statement for the papers.

Carnahan's fingers flew over the keys. "All told, I worked eighty hours, with but six hours' sleep," he wrote.

First tapped out over the wires were the official reports of the disaster to General Sheridan's headquarters in Chicago. Sheridan was in Philadelphia celebrating the Centennial of the Army of the Cumberland, as was Sherman, Army Chief of Staff. The message was relayed to Sheridan there. Before he heard of it officially, however, the news came out in the New York *Herald*. Also the New York *Times* and the Philadelphia papers, scooped by the *Herald*, had reports of the battle.

General Sherman was interviewed in his sweltering hotel room. "General," he was asked, "do you place any reliance in these rumors?"

"Not a great deal."

"But do you believe in them at all?"

"I do not! They come in so roundabout a way."

Sheridan was no less incredulous. Rumors. Roundabout. Nothing official. Before many hours General Sherman had to return to Washington, and Sheridan at last heard from his adjutant general in Chicago that Custer and his command had met their end. He handed the official report to a messenger, bidding him take it to Washington. The messenger was actually a reporter, and it was not long before the confidential document was spread across the front pages of the Philadelphia press. What exasperated Sheridan was that the report put the blame squarely on Custer, and both Sheridan and Terry were hard put to it to lighten the burden of guilt on the departed leader.

In Bismarck, their official duties done, the bearers of bad tidings had personal duties to attend to. At dawn of the sixth the *Far West* slipped moorings, dropped downstream, and crossed the river to the post. The wounded men were placed in the hospital there. Captain Smith, Terry's representative, presented a special report to

Captain McCaskell, who was in command. The captain read the document to his convened staff.

Finally, the news had to be broken to the wives. Dr. Middleton, the post surgeon, and two members of his staff accompanied Captain McCluskey and Lieutenant Gurley. They knocked on the back door of the Custers' quarters to rouse the maid. But Elizabeth Custer, who had only taken her dress off to lie on the bed all night, ran out in her dressing gown . . . the word for which she had been waiting. . . . She met the delegation in the parlor, her "family" about her. And these women stood up gallantly to the authentication of their widowhood.

Captain McCluskey could never forget how Mrs. Calhoun had run after him—her brothers Armstrong, Tom, Boston; her nephew Autie Reed, her husband Jimmie—"Is there no message for me?" she asked.

Message? They had all died fighting.

Elizabeth Custer sent for a wrap. The day was torrid, but she was shivering. There were other wives—wives in officers' quarters and, many with children, in Laundresses' Row—who must be told, and she would stand by at the sad telling.

21: Elizabeth Joins Her Husband

O NLY CUSTER himself could have given a complete report of Custer's last stand. Only those who fought with him could have described it. But all died on the field of battle.

The most reliable source of information is the official report of General Nelson A. Miles, deputed by the War Department immediately after the event to make a thorough investigation of the causes and circumstances of the disaster. For disaster indeed it was, where success had been expected in what was presumably to be a final blow to Indian resistance. As has been shown, the number of hostiles in the field had been grossly underestimated, and the government had been negligent in properly arming and provisioning the soldiery. As Custer had once stated, "It will take another Fort Kearny massacre to bring Congress to a realization of its duties toward the army."

By experience of Indian warfare and deep knowledge of Indian psychology, no one could have been better fitted for the task assigned him than was General Miles. He went over the battleground, watch in hand, tracing the routes of the three detachments of Custer's command and checking on the timing of their movements. The testimony he took, from white man and red, was direct, immediate, not blurred nor pointed up by time. Indian leaders who had been in the field informed him they had left Reno alone, early in the battle, and concentrated on Custer.

General Terry's well-considered plan had been to move three armies in on the hostiles from points widely separated, and at their convergence to make a massed attack. Success would depend largely on surprise, and his awareness of this is evinced by the discretionary powers he accorded Custer in his letter of instructions. Custer's pleasure in the confidence reposed in him appears in a letter to Elizabeth and dispels any suspicion of tension between himself and the commander of the expedition. To all criticisms of Custer can be opposed General Miles's dictum, "It is easy to kick a dead lion."

As to Custer's arriving at the rendezvous ahead of schedule, Miles points out that Custer was a skilled pathfinder, that he neither lost time on the march nor, on the other hand, forced the pace of the march. The approach of the regiment having been discovered by the Indians, concealment was impossible and delay unwise. Custer divided his command into three detachments. Reno, after a brief and bloody encounter, withdrew from the attack; Benteen, summoned by Custer's order to "come quick," paused to rally Reno's troops. Presumably Benteen (whose rank in the 7th Cavalry was that of captain) took orders from Major Reno. The courier who brought Custer's order, General Miles says in his book *Serving the Republic*, was the proper guide to where Custer was fighting; it was Benteen's duty to strike out straight for Custer.

The two volleys of distress that Custer fired were heard by Benteen and Reno, but went unheeded. "Two brave young officers," says Miles, "Weir and Edgerly, after repeated entreaties, were allowed to move out and reconnoitre." Reconnoitring parties may only report their findings to the main command. They saw clouds of dust in the valley where Custer was fighting, they knew his location, but no move was made in his direction by the two detachments.

General Miles's findings conclude with the words, "Custer's flag went down in disaster, but with honor."

Elizabeth Custer was thirty-four. She had been married to George Custer twelve years.

After the first shock of bereavement, with its clarifying vision, all was nebulous. It was said that on the evening of the Sunday following, Elizabeth caused religious services to be held in her parlor and that during them she fainted.

She had sent her carriage to the landing with a note to Captain Marsh of the *Far West*, begging him to come to her. But that intrepid navigator pleaded press of duty. He could not come. Why, what was there for him to tell her that she did not know?

There was the change of status now to be faced, the uprooting. As Custer's wife, a "camp follower," she was entitled to a domicile on the post to which he was assigned. As a widow, she was to exist simply as a name on the pension roll.

She went to Monroe, the town where Libbie Bacon had met and loved the young officer on McClellan's staff "awaiting orders." Monroe—the town she had left to share his fortunes, a proud bride and a happy wife—now saw her return a stricken woman, isolated in grief. Letters of condolence poured in on her. McClellan wrote on August 6:

. . . . As a man I mourn in your noble husband's death the loss of a warm, unselfish and devoted friend. As a soldier and a citizen I lament the death of one of the most brilliant ornaments of the Service and the nation—a most able and gallant soldier, a pure and noble gentleman. At my time of life I can ill afford to lose such a soldier and such a citizen. It is some consolation to me—I cannot doubt it is to you—that he died as he had lived, a gallant gentleman, a true hero, fighting unflinchingly to the last against desperate odds. His death was as he would have had it, with his face to the foe, encouraging his men to the last.

The first time I saw your husband to know him was when he was reported to me as having accomplished an act of desperate gallantry on the banks of the Chickahominy. I sent for him at once, and, after thanking him, asked what I could do for him. He seemed to attach no importance to what he had done, and desired nothing. Whereupon I asked if he would like to come upon my staff as a Captain. He gladly assented, and remained with me until I was relieved of my command.

He has not lived or died in vain, for rest assured that his long record of brilliant service and the manner of his death will long serve as models for those who have the true instincts of a cavalry soldier. I am sure that when the true history of that last battle is known it will plainly appear that Custer did precisely what he ought.

My wife joins me in heartfelt sympathy. . . . May God give you strength to bear up under your burden of sorrow, teach you to look with calm resignation to the day when He will permit you to rejoin him.

Always your sincere friend,
George B. McClellan.

Custer's last resting place was within the precincts of his military home, West Point. Lieutenant Colonel Michael V. Sheridan, representing his brother General Sheridan, escorted the cortège up the Hudson on the *Mary Powell*, banner steamer of the river.

Memorial plans were set afoot. General Sheridan was president of the Custer Monument Committee, August Belmont treasurer. Theatrical stars—Clara Morris, Lawrence Barrett, the Florences—gave fund-raising benefits. The colored waiters of the Grand Union Hotel in New York gave generously.

The choice of a sculptor was unfortunate. His conception of a hero in action was grotesque. Elizabeth Custer could not endure this misrepresentation of "the Service," a cavalryman charging his foe, saber in one hand, in the other a revolver.

"My dear Mrs. Custer," General Sherman, now taking a personal interest in the matter, answered her protest, "I had no idea you were not kept informed." He did not know the design had not been submitted to competent judges.

"I literally cried it off its pedestal," said Mrs. Custer.

The pedestal was retained, with suitable reliefs befitting the man and the place.

For Mrs. Custer, after the first hard readjustments, there was work to do. She would write—not controversially, but descriptively. She would tell how women, gently reared, lived "outside the States." She would describe how they met the perplexities of homemaking, wifehood, housekeeping under harsh conditions. *Boots and Saddles* was her first book, then came *Following the Guidon* and *Tenting on the Plains*.

And she would lecture. Elizabeth Custer was in great demand from women's clubs, and for many of the fifty-seven years yet left to her she spoke from platforms throughout America.

In 1910 the State of Michigan appropriated ten thousand dollars for an equestrian statue of Custer. E. C. Potter was the sculptor, and his work was done into bronze by the Gorham Company of New York.

It will be recalled that Alphonso Taft of the diplomatic service had been for a short space Grant's Secretary of War; Custer, summoned to Washington in the spring of 1876, had been most cordially received by him. Now his son, President of the United States, came to dedicate Custer's statue as it was unveiled in Monroe's public square. Said Taft:

A typical soldier, a great commander whose memory brings out of the past the greatest cavalry commanders of the world—Prince Ruprecht, Murat and others—he stands equal with all. Brigadier General at twenty-three, Major General at twenty-five, he showed in his youth that genius and force that we have at the same age in the great commanders of the world.

The State of Ohio also erected a monument. In 1932 a standing statue of Custer was dedicated at his birthplace at New Rumley. It, too, had cost ten thousand dollars, and was executed by the sculptor Erwin F. Frey.

National recognition was given Custer with the naming of the Custer Highway, a Federal road from Des Moines, Iowa, to Glacier National Park, Montana, a distance of about fifteen hundred miles.

In 1926, fifty years after the battle of the Little Big Horn, a detail of the 7th Cavalry Regiment was ordered from Texas to participate in the anniversary celebration, which was to take place on the battlefield. The path of Custer's expedition was retraced, the detachment meeting a body of Sioux warriors—in friendly reenactment. Half a century had passed, and the Custer story had become a legend.

"It has come down to us this way," said the descendants of the Crows who were Custer's scouts.

"So I have been told," the army sons replied.

The commemoration was primarily a Western project. It was in part commercial and wholly magnificent. It was a dramatic recognition of the fundamental truth that the successes of today are built on the sacrifices of the past. Indeed, Custer's last stand had not been in vain. Its spectacular quality had called attention to serious neglects. Bureaucracy had been jolted from its sloth, complacent and in some instances criminal. There was a housecleaning, insufficient but at least a strong start. Windows had been opened to the light and air.

The West invited Elizabeth Custer to attend the celebration, but she declined. She pleaded frail health and advancing years; subconsciously she must have known her presence would be an anachronism, a forced note in the illusion of historical pageantry.

Her mission was coming slowly to a close. For many years she had dedicated herself to keeping bright the name and honor of her husband. After the centennial celebration hundreds of letters came to her from all over the land. She personally answered over three hundred and dictated replies to the rest, adding to each a personal word of thanks in her own hand. She wanted to live; she did not fear death, but she was afraid that, being dead, she would not be able to answer malignant tongues who would defame her husband. Living, she could confront them with documentary vindication.

Mrs. Custer relied heavily on the published works of General Nelson A. Miles, who had been deputed to investigate the battle of the Little Big Horn. His books, his official report, his personal letters to her strongly defended Custer's course. And General McClellan, soon after Custer's death, wrote that had Custer failed to give battle when he did, he would have been charged with cowardice.

In the course of the years Mrs. Custer's pension had been augmented. Her insurance money and what was salvaged from her patrimony were well invested. To these sources of income were added her own earnings from writing and lecturing, and she was able to live in modest affluence.

An army woman, wife of the commanding officer, Elizabeth had ridden by Custer's side on horseback or in her own carriage. Now, after long years of separation, she rode in a spring wagon for the dead.

To a friend, she had once written: "I was at West Point recently. Autie lies in such a lovely spot, quite alone in that exquisite place. To my relief I found wives with their husbands. . . . For a long time I feared we should be separated."

The strains of "Garryowen," the regimental tune, accompanied the cortège to that "lovely spot." As they neared it, they must have seen, seated at the foot of the shaft that commemorates his name and his proud leadership, a war-worn figure penning a message to his wife . . . the great word of dedication for which every soldier fights . . . Peace.

My Darling—Heart too full for utterance. Peace is at hand. Thank God for PEACE. . . .

On Thursday, April 6, 1933, Elizabeth Custer joined her husband.

Index

Noble, Laura, 38, 49, 113, 114, 163
Noble, Mrs., 78
Nolan, Lieut., 198
Norfolk, 28
North Anna River, 96
North Carolina, 110
North Dakota, 267. *See also* Dakota Territory
Northern Pacific Railroad, 232, 248, 255, 268, 321
Northern Virginia, Army of, 156, 159
North Platte, 246
Nottaway Court House, 165

O'Conor, Charles, 182
Ohio, 241, 285, 328
Onondaga County, 14, 17, 20, 38, 83
Opequon River, 119
Orkney Islands, 3, 291
Osages, 217, 220, 221
Osborn, Mr., 232, 237
Ouachita River. *See* Washita River
Oxford (Mo.), 242

Page, Aaron, 19
Page, Abel, 18-21, 43
Page, Eleanor Sophia, 18-21. *See also* Bacon, Mrs. Daniel Stanton
Page, Harriet, 21, 22, 24, 48
Pamunkey River, 102, 103, 137, 140
Parker, Col., 158
Parsons, Col., 201, 211, 212
Patti, Adelina, 50
Paul (*Times* correspondent), 137, 141, 151
Paulding, Mrs. 47, 51
Pearson, Col., 259
Pendelton, Mr., 118
Pennington, Gen., 67, 104, 133, 138
Pennington, Mrs., 118
Pennsylvania, 9, 11, 54, 58
Peru (Ohio), 15
Petersburg, 110, 114, 146, 148, 160, 164, 165
Petersburg & Lynchburg Railroad, 110. *See also* Lynchburg and Petersburg Railroad
Philadelphia, 124, 186, 292, 322
"Phil Sheridan," 164
Pickett, Gen., 148, 153
Pitts, Mr., 41, 79
Pitts, Rhoda, 39. *See also* **Bacon, Mrs. Daniel Stanton**
Platte River, 204-208, 287
Pleasanton, Gen., 53, 55-59, 61, 66, 67, 69, 72, 73, 75, 86, 87, 90, 91, 114, 180
Plymouth Colony, 14
Poisset, Adm., 247
Pond, Mr., 277
Pontiac, 15, 17
Pope, Col., 133
Pope, Gen., 34
Pope, Maj., 202

Porter, Adm., 163
Porter, Dr., 321
Porter, Horace, 158, 291
Potomac, Army of the, 25, 27, 30, 35, 52, 53, 86, 87, 99, 138, 146, 191
Potomac River, 53, 87, 114
Potter, E. C., 327
Powder River, 298, 300, 302, 305
Price, Dr., 106
Price, Sir Rose, 276
Prospect Station, 162
Prospect Valley, 272, 273

Rain-in-the-Face, 276
Raisin River, 15, 16, 65
Raisinville, 16
Ramseur, Gen., 126, 127
Randolph, Col., 138
Ransom, Col., 115, 206
Ransom, Mrs., 206
Rapidan River, 65, 82, 95
Rappahannock River, 54, 66
Rappahannock Station, 58
Rauch, John, 75, 231, 253
Reams, Vinnie, 178
Recollects, 18
Red Bead, 207
Red Cloud, 287
Redpath Agency, 277
Red River, 167, 168, 219
Reed, Ann. *See* Reed, Mrs. David
Reed, Autie, 300, 301, 306, 307, 309, **323**
Reed, David, 5, 6, 8, 29, 32, 34, 35, 163
Reed, Emma, 53, 78, 251, 265, 304
Reed family, 46
Reed farm, 36
Reed, Mrs. David, 5, 8-10, 25-29, 32, 34, 35, 46, 53, 57, 73, 77, 78, 160, 162, 253, 263, 264, 291, 307. *See also* Kirkpatrick, Lydia-Ann
Ree Indians. *See* Arikarees
Reid, Whitelaw, 239, 271, 291
Reno, Maj., 305, 308, 310, 315-319, 324, 325
Reno's Creek, 314, 315
Republican River, 195, 204
Rexall's Landing, 97
Reynolds, Mr., 272, 290, 300
Richmond, 27, 28, 31, 35, 52, 54, 96, 97, 99, 125, 138, 140, 148, 163-165, 244
Richmond, Loraine, 21, 43, 44
Richmond, Mary, 43, 44, 81, 82, 133, 241. *See also* Kendall, Mrs. Charles
Richmond, Mr., 21, 43, 170
Richmond, Rebecca, 41, 43, 44, 48, 49, 51, 64, 78, 79, 81, 85, 132-134, 136, 144, 145, 147, 170, 210-214
"Rienzi," 166
Rio Grande, 5, 183
Risley, Mr., 291
Riverside Telegraph Station, 207
"Roanoke," 57, 175

Robbins, Rep., 292
Robinson, battery of, 59
Rochester, 15, 83
Rochester, Maj., 92, 112, 123
Rockfish Gap, 138
Romero, Minister, 184
Roosevelt, Robert, 284
Rosebud River, 261, 298, 306-309, 311, 313, 314
Rosencranz, Gen., 69
Rosser, Gen., 122, 123, 125, 128, 132, 134, 249, 251-257, 260, 261, 267, 271
Ruger, Col., 153
Ruliston, Dr., 123
Ruprecht, Prince, 328
Russell, Mr., 126, 181
Rutland, 18

Sabin, Eliza, 41, 42, 44, 84, 182, 183, 191, 240, 241, 268, 269, 284
Sabin, Mr., 84
Sabin farm, 40
Sailor's Creek, 149, 150, 155
St. Louis, 190, 244
St. Paul, 232, 244, 252, 279, 294, 321
Salmon River, 204
San Antonio, 167
Sandusky, 15
Saratoga, 238
Satanta, 225
Savannah, 244
Schofield, Gen., 228
Scott, Winfield, 5, 11, 12, 157
Seif, Mr., 289
Senate, 88, 110, 136, 178, 179, 185, 289, 292, 293
Seventh Cavalry Regiment, 195, 197, 200, 201, 206, 210, 213, 217, 223, 224, 228, 229, 231, 236, 245, 248, 252, 259, 266, 267, 269, 271, 273, 277, 279, 296, 306, 310, 311, 315, 325, 328
Seward, Gen., 128, 131, 136
Seward, William H., 164, 179, 188, 189
Shannon, Gen., 267
Sharpsburg, 35
Sheldon, Mr., 101, 291, 303
Sheldon, Mrs., 101, 106
Shenandoah Valley, 115, 120, 130, 137, 161
Shepard, Mr., 289
Sheridan, Michael V., 156, 229, 327
Sheridan, Philip H., 10, 11, 37, 86, 87, 89, 92-94, 96, 97, 99, 102, 110, 113-115, 119, 120, 122, 125, 130, 131, 133-135, 137-142, 144, 145, 147, 149, 150, 155-160, 162, 164-167, 173, 183-185, 190, 192, 200, 201, 209-211, 214, 216-219, 223-230, 239, 246, 268, 271, 272, 279, 294, 306, 322, 327
Sherman, William T., 120, 146, 160, 162, 185, 206-209, 216, 228, 244, 267, 281, 290-295, 322, 327

Sherrill, Mrs., 177, 178
Shreveport, 167
Sickles, Gen., 89
Sioux Indians, 3, 217, 270, 276, 282, 287, 289, 296, 299, 303, 305-311, 313-320, 324, 325, 328
Sisters of Mercy, 210
Sitting Bull, 280, 287
Skunk's Head, 274
Smith, A. E., 298, 319, 321, 322
Smith, A. J., 29, 95, 198, 201, 202, 209, 232
Smith, Capt., 244, 249, 253, 255, 259, 274
Smith, Col., 128
Smith, E. W., 309
Smith family, 83
Smith, John E., 287
Smith, Kirby, 167
Smoky Hill, 198
Smoky Hill River, 204
Smoky River, 195
Sonora, Duke of, 283
South Anna River, 138
South Carolina, 157, 281
South Dakota, 248, 254, 270. *See also* Dakota Territory
Spotted Tail, 246, 287
Stahl, Gen., 55
Stahl, Mr., 142
Stanley, Gen., 249, 251, 256, 260, 262, 263, 265-267, 285, 298, 304
Stanton, Edwin M., 31, 109, 127, 133, 136, 145, 165, 177-179
Stanton, Mrs., 177
Stark, Pvt., 202
Staunton, 137
Stebbins' Academy, 7, 32
Stedman, Edmund Clarence, 239
Stevens, Annie, 101
Stevens, Miss, 177
Stevens, Mrs., 177
Stevenson, John, 299
Stires, Mr., 89, 92, 121, 123, 128, 146
Stoneman, Gen., 25, 27, 28, 55, 133
Stoughton family, 276
Stranahan, Lieut., 92
Strasburg, 121, 122
Stuart, J. E. B., 55, 66, 68, 96-98
Sturgis, Nina, 246, 247
Sturgis, S. D., 174, 232
Sully, Gen., 216
Sun-Dance Creek. *See* Reno's Creek
Sunracen, Earl, 276
Sutherland, Dr., 177
Sweeny, 126
Sweet Briar River, 306
Syracuse, 232

Taft, Alphonso, 281, 327, 328
Taft, William, 328
Tait, 277
Taylor, Bayard, 239